THE TROUBADOURS
AT HOME

THEIR LIVES AND PERSONALITIES, THEIR SONGS AND THEIR WORLD

BY

JUSTIN H. SMITH

Professor of Modern History in Dartmouth College

178 ILLUSTRATIONS

VOLUME I

G. P. PUTNAM'S SONS
NEW YORK & LONDON
The Knickerbocker Press
1899

The Knickerbocker Press, New York

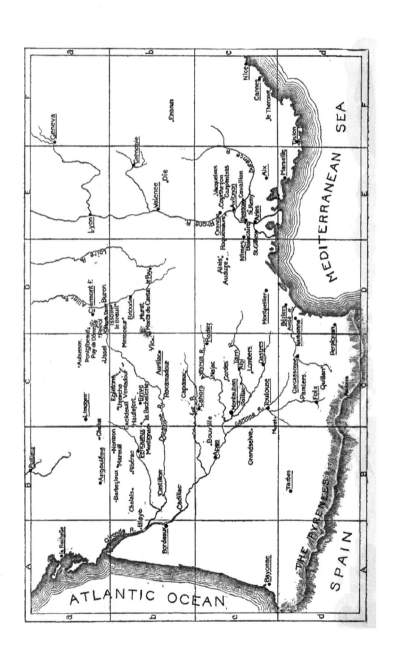

PREFACE

DAUDET tells of a Provençal piper who made delightful music at Montmajour, but at Paris—where the
proper surroundings did not exist—appeared only con-
temptible.

It has seemed to me that the poems of the troubadours
suffer in a similar way. One judges them not only apart
from their music, but—what is even more unfortunate—
apart from the circumstances that reinforced them, without regard to the life, the events, the localities, and the
personalities that formed their setting, and then one
pronounces them feeble and monotonous.

The purpose of my book is to place this literature before
the reader somewhat as it originally appeared, and in a
word I have attempted, within the necessary limitations,
to represent the world of the troubadours, to place them
in it as living persons, and to put into their mouths their
poems as they made them,—only in another language.

The first step was to gain possession of the needed historical facts ; a second was by travelling over the ground,
as I did in 1895 and 1898, to prepare a real stage-setting ,
another was to reconstruct the personalities of the troubadours according to their poems, their environments, and
what we know of their lives,—as indeed one could not
avoid doing when treading the ground they trod, with the
mind full of their sayings and doings ; a fourth was to
translate specimens of their poetry in the original forms,
with some authentic illustrations of their music ; and the

last was to combine this material with pictures, incidents of travel, and descriptions of existing things so as to induce if possible a sense of actuality.

This method savors of historical fiction, only that my object is to state and illustrate facts, not invent romance , and so extremely meagre do almost all of the troubadours appear when presented as historical science leaves them, that it seems to me well worth while to give life and relief to them and their work in this way, even though lack of space compels me to present sketches only and not finished portraits.   For, small as the information about these characters may appear to the reader, I have intended to omit no fact of general interest in the text, and in the notes to supply everything up to the line of the specialist· for him the study of the sources is of course indispensable.

I beg leave to assure the reader, too, that I have used imagination only to combine facts, or, where knowledge ends, to supplement without falsifying it.   Further, I have scrupulously indicated in the text itself or in the notes all that I have invented ; and, by subtracting these things, the reader may easily reduce the book to an account of the present state of our knowledge and opinion according to the highest authorities   This minimum result of my labor will not, I trust, be deemed valueless, particularly in view of the fact that the best book we have in English upon the troubadours was twenty years ago pronounced by the most competent judge " in no respect abreast of our knowledge " (*Romania*, 1878, p. 445).

To secure greater ease, variety, and life, the work has been thrown into the form of a journey, each troubadour is studied as he is met, and the elements of the civilization are grouped as far as they conveniently could be around the persons with whom they associate themselves most naturally; but the whole ground indicated by the title-page will be found as completely covered—within the necessary limits—as if the treatment were more formal, and with the aid of the Synoptical Table of Contents (to be found immediately before the Index) may be studied almost as systematically.

Some of the translations may no doubt be called *tours de force;* indeed, one may perhaps doubt whether sixteen or twenty lines—especially short lines—can be made to rhyme together without producing this impression. Even the originals wear such a look not infrequently, although Provençal was vastly richer in rhymes than English is; and the difficulty is more than doubled for the translator by the necessity of following a prescribed line of thought. But even if the result be sometimes *tours de force,* it has seemed to me well worth while to reproduce the Provençal forms. In the first place, as the troubadours themselves insisted, form and substance belong together. In the second, these forms as a fact of literary history possess a real importance, and no mere explanation or scheme would give a lifelike impression of them. Nor are these the only arguments that could be advanced.

No attempt has been made, of course, to present anything like a complete account of the world of the troubadours,—that alone would have required all the space at my disposal. I trust, however, that enough has been given to constitute an environment and an atmosphere for the poets ; if so, my end is gained.

The illustrations might easily have been made more artistic , but I have not been willing that they, any more than the text, should misrepresent for the sake of effect. Nearly all the views are from photographs taken by myself, and though, on account of cloudy weather, I was compelled to have a considerable number of the photographs copied in order to obtain the relief necessary for engraving, I did not permit the artist to make changes.

As for the manner of the book, I have endeavored to

make it harmonize with the picture which it frames   a
purely and uniformly didactic style would not have
answered this condition, it seems to me   In this quarter
lay, of course, one of the prime difficulties of the under-
taking . to treat a poetical and romantic subject in a suitable literary way without forgetting the requirements of
historical and linguistic science.

The particular attention of the studious reader is invited to the notes, which supplement the text in many
ways.

As will be seen, authorities in proof of the statements
of the book are cited only in special cases, though many
references are given for fuller information.   Had the
method of proving everything been adopted and the necessary explanations added to make the questions and
arguments clear to the general reader, a great deal would
have been added to the size and cost of a book already too
large and too expensive, and this would have tended to
defeat its primary aim, which may be indicated in the
words of Paul Meyer :   " *Nous voudrions qu'il y eût en
France beaucoup plus de tels livres, qui répandraient les ré-
sultats des recherches scientifiques et augmenteraient la somme
de l'instruction générale*" (*Romania*, 1883, p. 627).   My
object is not to prove new facts but to gather and present
the facts already established by investigators.   There has
grown up within a comparatively recent period a body of
scientific Provençal scholarship represented by *Romania*,
the *Zeitschrift für romanische Philologie*, and a few other
periodicals in France, Germany, and Italy, and any one
at all familiar with the subject will see that I have based
my account of the troubadours upon this without regard
to old ideas or the " popular " writers.   When authorities
of equal standing differ on an important point I have
stated the several views, and if it seemed worth while
have discussed the matter briefly   In the few cases where

I have advanced an opinion of my own the point has been noted and argued.

It would have been desirable to print the Provençal originals of the verse, but that also would have added largely to the bulk and price of the work. Neither would the advantage have been great, for nearly all of the pieces are from books not hard to find, a reference is always given, attention is called to liberties of rendering, and specially noteworthy passages are translated literally in the notes.

My standard for the spelling of names has been Chabaneau's text of the biographies ; in case more than a single spelling was given there I have selected the form that seemed preferable, and have adhered to that form throughout.

It gives me great pleasure to acknowledge gratefully the kind assistance of Dr. Antoine Thomas of the Sorbonne, Paris, Professor C. H. Grandgent of Harvard University, Dr. H. R. Lang of Yale University, and Dr. H. A. Todd of Columbia University, who are not responsible, however, in the least degree for any faults the work may possess

I shall be very glad to have my attention called to all oversights that may be discovered.

J. H S.

HANOVER, September, 1899.

CONTENTS

A Synoptical Table of Contents will be found immediately before the Index

xii Contents

ILLUSTRATIONS

Several Numbers indicate as many different pictures

AUTHORITIES

The following list is given not only as an acknowledgment of the author's indebtedness (in many cases extremely slight, in others very large), but also because it may prove useful to those interested in the subject. For the sake of fuller information, and occasionally discussion, a good many references are made to these authorities in the Notes, and for economy of space these references are *by number*.

It should be understood that the books of the list are of all orders of merit from the winnowed results of recent critical scholarship to loose and very misleading productions ; the latter have some value or they would not be mentioned, but must be used with proper caution. A few books and periodicals have been starred ; when the beginner in Provençal is familiar with these he will be prepared to venture upon the rest. I have allowed myself to save space by omitting the place of publication, for whoever wishes to look up the books will do so—first, at least—in the libraries.

PERIODICALS

The dates indicate the issues examined,—not, in all cases, the entire series. Many articles of special value will be referred to in the Notes.

1.—American Journal of Philology. 1880–Mar., 1899.
2.—Annales du Midi, v I-X (April, 1898).
3.—Archiv für das Studium der neueren Sprachen und Literaturen, v. 46–Mar., 1899.
4.—Archiv für Literaturgeschichte. 1870–1887.
5.—Bulletin Monumental. 1874–No. 1, 1898.
6.—Giornale di Filologia Romanza, v. I-IV.
7.—Giornale Storico della Letteratura Italiana 1883–July, 1899
8 —Il Propugnatore. 1868–Apr., 1893.

*9.—Jahrbuch für Rom. und Eng. Literatur. 1859-1876.
10 —Jenaer Literaturzeitung 1874-1879.
11.—Journal des Savants. 1860-July, 1899.
*12.—Literaturblatt für Germ. und Rom. Philologie. 1880-Apr.,
       1899.
12a —Le Moyen Age. 1888-June, 1899.
13 —Literarisches Centralblatt 1880-1889.
14.—Memorie della R Academia di Modena. 1822-1896
15.—Modern Language Notes. 1886-June, 1899
16.—Nuova Antologia 1876-Aug , 1899.
17.—Revue Critique d'Hist. et de Litt. 1873-Apr., 1899.
18.—Revue d'Hist. Litt. de la France. 1894-1895
19.—Revue des Deux Mondes. 1874-Aug , 1899
*20.—Revue des Langues Romanes 1870-1898.
21.—Revue des Questions Historiques. 1866-July, 1899.
22.—Revue Félibrienne, v. I-X.
23 —Revue Historique 1886-Aug , 1899.
24 —Rivista di Filologia Romanza 1872-1876.
25.—Rivista Musicale Italiana, v II and III.
26.—Rivista Storica Italiana. 1884-1895.
*27.—Romania. 1872-July, 1899
28.—Romanische Forschungen. 1882-Jan , 1899.
29.—Romanische Studien 1871-1885.
30.—Studj di Filologia Romanza, v. I-VI.
*31.—Zeitschrift für Romanische Philologie. 1877-July, 1899

BOOKS

ABBESSE (L') HERRADE DE LANDSPERG (A Straub, ed.).—32.
Hortus Deliciarum (1879-1885.)

33. ABHANDLUNGEN Herrn Dr Adolf Tobler .   darge-
bracht. 1895.

ACLAND-TROYTE, C. E —34. From the Pyrenees to the Channel, etc 1887

ADAMS, G B —*35. Civilization during the Middle Ages. 1894.

ALEXANDER, W. J.—36. An Introduction to the Poetry of Robert
Browning 1889.

AMATI, A.—37. Dizionario Corografico dell' Italia 8 v.

AMBROS, A. W.—38. Geschichte der Musik. 4 v. 1862-1878.

ANDRIEU, J.—39. Hist. de l'Agenais. 1893.

40. ANNALES Manuscrites de Limoges (pub. 1873).

APPEL, C.—*41. Provenzalische Chrestomathie. 1895 42. Provenzalische Inedita. 1892. 43. Das Leben und die Lieder des Trobadors Peire Rogier. 1882.

ARMITAGE, FR.—44. Sermons du XII Siècle en Vieux Provençal. 1884.

ARNOLD, M.—45 The Study of Celtic Literature. 1867.

AUBER, L'ABBÉ.—46. Paper read before the Soc Ant. de l'Ouest.

AZAIS, G.—47. Breviari d'Amor de Matfre Ermangau. 2 v. 1862-1881. 48. Archives de la Commission des Mon. Histor. 2 v.

49 AUSG. und Abh. aus dem Gebiete der Rom. Phil. 1882-1896

BABEAU, A.—50. Les Voyageurs en France. 1885.

BAEDEKER, K.—51. Northern Italy. 1895. 52. Southern France. 1891.

BALUZE.—53 Hist. Généal. de la Maison d'Auvergne. Tome II.

BARBIERI, G. M.—54. Dell' Origine della Poesia Rimata. 1790.

BARET, E —55. Les Troubadours, etc. 1867.

BARKER, E. H.—56. Two Summers in Guyenne. 1894 57. Wanderings by Southern Waters. 1893. 58. Wayfaring in France. 1890.

BARRON, L.—59. La Garonne

BARTHÉLEMY, L.—60. Inventaire des Chartes de la Maison des Baux. 1882

BARTHOLOMÆUS DE GLANVILLA.—61. De Proprietat. Rerum

BARTOLI, A.—62. I Primi Due Sec. della Lett. Ital. 1880.

BARTSCH, K.—63. Chrestomathie Provençale. 4th ed. 1880. 64. Denkmäler der Provenz Literatur. 1856. 65 Grundriss zur Gesch. der Prov. Literatur. 1872. 66 Peire Vidal's Lieder 1857.

BASSERMANN, A.—67 Dante's Spuren in Italien. 1897.

BELLEMER, E.—68. Hist. de la Ville de Blaye. 1886.

BENEZET, B.—69. Hist. de l'Art Mérid au M Age, etc. 1885.

BENTHAM-EDWARDS, M —70. France of Today. 2 v. 1892.

BÉRENGER-FÉRAUD, L. J. B.—71. La Race Provençale. 1883. 72. Les Légendes de la Provence 1888. 73. Réminiscences Pop. de Provence. 1885

BERGER, S —74 La Bible Franç. au Moyen Age. 1884.

BERNHARDT, W.—75. Die Werke des Trob N'At de Mons. 1887.

76. BIBLIOTHÈQUE de l'Ecole des Chartes. 1839-1896.

BIRBECK, M.—77. Journey through France. 1814.

BIRCH-HIRSCHFELD, A.—78 Ueber die den. Prov. Troub. bek. Epischen Stoffe. 1878.

BISCHOFF, H —79. Biog. des. Troub. B. von Ventadour 1873

BESCHNIDT, E.—80 Biog. des Trob G. de Capestaing. 1879.

BLONDEL, S —81 Hist. des Eventails 1875.

BOEHME, F. M.—82. Gesch. des Tanzes in Deutschland 1886.

BOHN.—83. Chronicles of the Crusades. 1848.

BONNEMÈRE, E.—84. Hist. des Paysans 1856.

BOUCHE, H.—85. Hist. Chronol. de Provence. 2 v. 1664

BOUCHET.—86. Les Annales d' Aquitaine

BOUDIN, A.—87. Hist de Marseille. 1852.

BOURDON DE ST. AMANS, J. F.—88. Sur l'Antiquité du Dépt de Lot et Garonne

BOURGAIN, L.—89. La Chaire Franç au M. Age 1879

BOURRIÈRES, M.—90. Roc-Amadour 1895

BOUTARIC, E.—91. Vincent de Beauvais, etc. 1875.

BOUVENNE, A.—92. Poitiers Anc. et Mod. 1891

BRAKELMANN, J.—93 Les Plus Anciens Chansonniers Français (1870) 1891.

BRINCKMEIER, E —94. Die Prov. Troub. nach ihrer Sprache, etc 1844 95 Rugelieder der Troub gegen Rom , etc 1846

BROWNING, R.—96. Poetical Works 16 v 1888–1889. (Sordello, v I)

BRUCE-WHYTE, A —97 Hist des Lang. Rom. 3 v 1841

BRUTAILS, J. A.—98. Les Populations Rurales du Roussillon au M. Age. 1891

BURNEY, C.—99. Gen. Hist. of Music. 1782.

CANELLO, U. A.—100. La Vita e le Opere del. Trov. Arnaldo Daniello. 1883. 101. Fiorita di Liriche Prov. 1881.

CANET, V —102 Simon de Montfort, etc.

CAPEFIGUE, R —103 Philippe Auguste. 3d ed 2 v. 1844

CARDUCCI, G —104. Jaufré Rudel 1888 105 Un Poeta d'Amore del Sec XII. 1893 (1881).

CASINI, T —106. Gesch der Ital. Litt (Groeber's Grund.) 1896

CASSELL.—107. The Pictur. Mediterranean 2 v. 1890–1891.

108 CELTIC Ornaments (pub. 1895) from the Book of Kells

CÉNAC-MONCAUT. C.—109. Hist. du Caractère et de l'Esprit Franç. 2 v. 1867

CHABANEAU, C.—*110. Biog. des Troub 1885 111. Orig et Etab de l'Acad des Jeux Flor 112. Poésies Ined des Troub du Périgord 1885. 113. Ste Marie Mad dans la Litt Prov. 1887 *114. Sur la Langue Rom. du Midi de la France. 1885. 115. Varia Provincialia. 1889.

CHERBULLIEZ, V.—116. Le Grand Œuvre. 1867

CLARK, J W.—117. Libraries in the Med and Renaiss. Periods 1894.

CLÉDAT, L —118. Du Rôle Histor. de Bertran de Born 1878. 119. Etude sur le Mystère de Ste. Agnès 1877. 120. Le Nouveau Test, en Langue Prov 1887.

CNYRIM, E —121. Sprichwörter . bei den Prov. Lyrikern. 1888.

COLANGE, L. DE.—122. The Picturesque World. v. I., 1878.

COLOMBIÈRE, M. DE REGIS DE LA.—122a. Les Cris Populaires de Marseille. 1868.

COMPARETTI, D —123. Virgil in the M. Ages. (Tr. by Benecke.) 1895.

COMPAYRÉ, G.—124. Abelard, etc. 1893.

COOPER, F. T.—125. Word-Formation in the Roman Sermo Plebeius 1895.

CRANE, T. F.—126 Med. Sermon Books and Stories (Amer. Philos Soc.) 1883.

CRESCINI, V.—127. Appunti su Jaufré Rudel. 1890 128. Manueletto Provenzale. 1892.

CUTTS, E. L.—129. Scenes and Characters of the M. Ages 1872.

COUSSEMAKER, E. DE.—130. Hist. de l'Harmonie au M Age. 1852 131. L'Art Harmon. aux XII et XIII Siècles. 1865.

DANTE ALIGHIERI.—132. The Divine Comedy. (Tr. by C E. Norton) 3 v 1891-1892. 133. The New Life. (Tr. by C. E. Norton.) 1867

DAUDET, A.—134. All books touching on Southern France.

DELPECH, H.—135. La Tactique au XIII Siècle 2 v. 1886

DEMAY, G.—*136. Le Costume au M A d'après les Sceaux 1880. 137. Le Cost. de Guerre et d'Apparat, etc. 1875.

DESTANDEAU, A —138. Promenade dans la Ville des Baux. 1890.

DEVIC ET VAISSETTE.—*139. Hist. Gén. de Languedoc. New ed. 15 v 1872-1892.

DICKENS, C.—140 Pictures from Italy. 1845

DIEZ, F.—141. Etymolog. Wörterbuch der Rom. Sprache. 5th ed. 1887. *142. Leben und Werke der Troub. (Rev. by Bartsch.) 1882. *143 Poesie der Troubadours (Rev. by Bartsch.) 1883.

DOUTREPONT, A.—144. La Clef d'Amors. 1890

DU CANGE, C DU FRESNE.—145 Glossarium Med et Infim. Latinitatis. Ed. Favre. 10 v 1883-1887.

DUMAS, A —146. Le Midi de la France. New ed. 2 v 1887.

DURUY, V —*147. Hist of the M. Ages (Notes by G B. Adams.) 1891

EBERT, A.—148. Hist. Gén. de la Litt. du M A., etc Trad par Ayméric et Condamin. 3 v. 1883–1889

EICHELKRAUT, F.—149. Der Troub. Folquet de Lunel. 1872.

EMÉRIC-DAVID, F. B.—150. Hist. de la Peinture au M Age. 1863 (1811–12)

EMERTON, E —*151. Mediæval Europe. 1894

ENGEL, C.—152 Musical Instruments. 1876.

ENGEL (A.) ET SERRURE (R).—153. Traité de Numismatique du M. A 1891–1894

ERDMANNSDORFER, E.—154. Die Reime der Troub.

EYTON, R.—155. Court, Household, and Itin. of King Henry II, etc 1878.

FAGNIEZ, G.—156. Etudes sur l'Industrie   . à Paris. 1877.

FARCY, L. DE.—157. La Broderie du XI Siècle, etc. 1890

FARNELL, I.—158. Lives of the Troub. 1896

FAURIEL, C C.—159. Dante et les Orig. de la Langue et de la Litt Ital. 2 v. 1854. 160. Hist. de la Poésie Prov. 3 v. 1846

FLACH, J.—161 Les Orig. de l'Anc. France v. II. 1893.

FOURNIER, P.—162. Le Royaume d'Arles et de Vienne. 1891.

FRANCKE, K.—163. Social Forces in German Lit. 1896.

FRANKLIN, A.—164 La Vie Privée d'Autrefois. 21 v. 1887–1897.

FRAYMOND, E.—165 Jongleurs und Menestrels. 1883.

GALIUS, T.—166. Musique et Versif. Franç. au M Age. 1891.

GAUTIER, [E T.] L.—167. La Chevalerie. 1890

GAUTIER, T.—168. Loin de Paris. New ed 1881 169 Voyage en Espagne. 1873.

GAY, V,—*170. Gloss. Archéol. du M. Age, etc. 5 fasc. 1882–1887.

GÉLIS-DIDOT ET LAFFILÉE —171 La Peinture Décor. en France du XI au XVI Siècle

GERMAIN, A.—172. L'Ecole de Droit de Montpellier. 1877.

GIDE, P.—173. La Condition Privée des Femmes. 1867.

GILLY, W. S.—174. The Romaunt Version of   . St. John. 1848.

GIOVANNI, V. DI.—175. Filol. e Lett. Sicil. 2 v. 1871

GIRALDUS CAMBRENSIS.—176. Hist Works trans. by T. Wright. 1881.

GISI, M.—177. Der Troub G Anelier von Toulouse. 1877

GITTERMAN, J. M.—178. Ezzelin von Romano. 1890.

GOBIN, L —179 La Géog. d'Auvergne. 1896.

GORRA, E.—180. Delle Orig. della Poesia Lirica del Medio Evo 1895.

GORSE, M. M.—180a. Au Bas Pays de Limousin. 1896.

GREEN, MRS. J. R.—181. Henry II. 1892.

GOULD, S. BARING.—181a. In Troubadour-Land 1891. 182. The Deserts of So. France. 1894

GRAF, A.—182a. Roma nella Mem e n Immagin. del Med. Evo. 2 v. 1882-1883.

GRAS, F.—183. Li Papaliuo 1891

GROEBER, G.—*183a. Grund. der Rom. Philol. 2 v. 1890-1896.

GUARNERIO, P. E.—184 Pietro Guglielmo di Luserna. 1896.

GUÉRIN, P.—184a. Dictionnaire des Dict.

GUESSARD, F.—185 Grammaires Prov de H. Faidit et de R Vidal de B. 2d ed 1858.

GUIFFREY, J.—185a. Hist. de la Tapisserie. 1886.

GUILBERT, A.—186. Hist. des Villes de France. 5 v. 1844-1848.

HALLAM, H.—186a. Introd. to the Lit. of Europe. Am. ed. 1880 187. View of . . Europe during the M. Ages Am. ed. 1880.

HAMLIN, A. D. F.—188. Hist. of Arch. 1896.

HARDWICKE, C.—189. Hist. of the Christian Church. 4th ed. rev. by Stubbs 1874.

HARE, A. J. C.—190. Cities of North and Central Italy. 3 v. 1876. 191. South-eastern France. 1890. 192. South-western France. 1890

HAVARD, H.—193. Dict. de l'Ameubl. et de la Décor. 4 v. 194 La France Artist. et Monument. 6 v 1892-1895.

HAWTHORNE, N.—195. French and Italian Note Books. 2 v 1871.

196 HIST LITTÉRAIRE de la France v X, XX, XXVIII, XXX

HOLLAND and KELLER.—197 Die Lieder Guillems IX. 1850.

HOPF, K.—198. Bonifaz von Montferrat, etc. 1877

HOUDOY, J.—199. La Beauté des Femmes, etc. 1876

HOVEDEN, R. DE.—200. Anuals, trans. by H T. Riley. 2 v.

HOWELLS, W. D.—201. Italian Journeys. 1867.

HUEFFER, F.—202. Der Trob. Guilhem de Cabestanh 1869. 203. The Troub. 1878.

HUGO, V.—204. Alpes et Pyrénées. 1890 (1839 and 1843). 205. En Voyage. 1892 (1839).

HUNNEWELL, J. F.—**206** The Hist. Monum of France   1884.

IMBERDIS, A.—**207**. Hist Gén. de l'Auvergne.   2 v   1868

JACQUEMART, A.—**208**. Hist. de la Céramique   1873   **209**. Hist. du Mobilier.   1876.

JAMES, H —**210** A Little Tour in France   1885

JANVIER, T. A.—**211** An Embassy to Provence.   1893.

JEANROY, A.—*****212**. De Nostratibus Medii Ævi Poetis.   1889. *****213**. Les Orig. de la Poésie Lyr. en France au M A   1889

JORET, C.—**214**. La Rose dans l'Antiquité et au M A   1892

KAWCZYNSKI, M.—**215**. Essai Compar. sur l'Orig. et l'Hist des Rhythmes   1889.

KIRCHHOFF, A.—**216**. Die Handschriftenhandler des Mittelalters.   2d ed   1853.

KITCHIN, D. B.—**217**. The Study of Prov.   1887.

KITCHIN, G. W.—**218**. Hist. of France.   3d ed   3 v.   1892-1894.

KLEIN, O —**219** Die Dichtungen des Monchs von Montaudon.   1885.

KOLSEN, A.—**220**. Guiraut von Bornelh   1894

KRETSCHMER, K —**221**. Die Physische Erdkunde im Christl. Mittelalter.   1889.

KUTTNER, M —**222** Das Naturgefuhl der Altfranzosen, etc. 1889

LACROIX, P.—**223**. Costumes Histor. de la France.   **224**. Manners, Customs, and Dress during the M. A.   **225**. Military and Religious Life in the M A.   **226**. Science and Literature in the M A. **227** The Arts in the M. A.

LA CURNE DE STE PALAYE.—**228** Hist Litt. des Troub   (Millot)   3 v.   1774   **229**. Mém. sur l'Anc Chevalerie   2 v   1826

LAFUENTE, M —**230**. Hist. Gen de España   30 v.   1869.

231 LA GRANDE ENCYCLOPÉDIE (as far as published)

LAINCEL, L. DE.—**232**. La Provence   **233** Voyage Humour. dans le Midi   1869.

LANG, A.—**234**. Aucassin and Nicollette.   1887

LANG, H R —**235**. Das Liederbuch des Königs Denis von Portugal   1894.

LAROUSSE, P.—**235a**. Grand Dict. Univ.

LASTEYRIE, F DE.—**236**. Hist de l'Orfévrerie.   1875

LAURIE, S. S —**237**. The Rise and Early Const of Univ.   1891.

LECOY DE LA MARCHE.—**238**. L'Esprit de Nos Aïeux   1888 **239**. Le Treiz Siècle Art.   1889.   **240**. Le Treizième Siècle Litt. et Scient.   1895.

LEDAIN, B.—**241**. Savary de Mauléon, etc. (Mém. de la Soc. des Antiq de l'Ouest) 1880

LEFLOCQ, J.—**242**. Etudes de Mythol. Celt. 1869

LE GRAND D'AUSSY, P. J. B —**244**. Fabliaux ou Contes, etc 3d ed. 5 v. (v. II.) 1829. **245** Hist. de la Vie Privée des Français. New ed. 1815.

LENIENT, C.—**246**. La Poésie Patriot en France. 2 v. 1891

LENTHÉRIC, C.—**247**. La Grèce et l'Orient en Provence. 1878. **248**. Le Rhône. 2 v. 1892. **249**. Les Villes Mortes du Golfe de Lyon 5th ed. 1889.

LEROUX, A —**250**. Géog. et Hist. du Limousin. 1890

LESPINASSE et BOURNADOT.—**251**. Le Livre de Métiers (Hist. Gén. de Paris). 1879.

LEVY, E.—**252**. Der Troub Bertolome Zorzi. 1883. **253**. Guilhem Figueira. 1880. *****254**. Prov. Supplement-Wörterbuch. 6 parts.

LÉVY, E.—**255**. Hist. de la Peinture sur Verre. 2 v. 1860.

LÉVY, E —**256** Le Troubadour P. de Marseille. 1882.

LEYMAIRIE, A.—**257**. Hist. du Limousin. 1846.

LOLLIS, C. DE.—**258**. Vita e Poesie di Sordello di Goito. 1896

LONGFELLOW, H. W.—**262**. Outre Mer. 1866.

LONGNON, A.—**259** Atlas Histor de la France 1889

LUCHAIRE, A.—**260**. Orig. Linguist. de l'Aquitaine 1877. *****261**. Manuel des Instit. Franç 1892

MACGIBBON, D.—**263**. The Architect. of Prov. and the Riviera 1888.

MACKEL, E.—**264**. Die German. Elemente in der Franz. und Prov. Sprache 1887.

MAHN, C A. F.—**265**. Die Biog. der Troub 1853. **266** Die Werke der Troub. 4 v. 1846-1855. **267**. Gedichte der Troub. 4 v. 1856-1873.

MAISSIAT, J.—**268**. Annibal en Gaule. 1874.

MANDET, F.—**269**. Hist. du Velay. v. III. 1861.

MARCH, F. A.—**270**. Latin Hymns. 1875

MARIÉTON, P —**271**. La Terre Prov. 1889.

MARSH, A R.—*****273**. Prov. Lit. (in Johnson's Cyclopæd.).

MARTIN, H —**274**. Hist. de France. 16 v 1855-1860

MARVAUD, F.—**275**. Etudes Histor. sur l'Angoumois. 1835

MAS-LATRIE, COMTE DE.—**276**. Trésor de Chronol., d'Hist , et de Géog. 1889

MASSON, G.—**277**. Mediæval France. 1888.

MAUS, F. W.—**278** Peire Cardenals Strophenbau. 1884.

MÉRAY, A.—**279.** La Vie au Temps des Trouvères 1873

MÉRIL, E. DU.—**280.** Poésies Populaires Latines Ant. au XII Siècle 1843.

MÉRIMÉE, P.—**281.** Les Arts au M. Age 1875 **282.** Un Voyage dans le Midi de la France. 1835. **283** Un Voyage dans l'Ouest de la France. 1836. **284.** Un Voyage en Auvergne. 1838.

MÉRY, J.—**285.** Marseille et les Marseillais. 1860?.

MEYER, P —**286.** Alex. le Grand dans la Litt. Franç. du M. A. 2 v. 1886 **2 8.** Daurel et Beton 1880. **288.** Frag. Inéd. d'un Lapidaire Prov 1862 ***289.** Girart de Roussillon. 1884 ***290.** La Chanson de la Crois. contre les Albig. 2 v. 1875–1879 ***291.** Le Roman de Flamenca. 1865. **292.** Le Salut d'Amour, etc. 1867. **293.** Les Dern. Troub. de Provence. 1871. ***294.** Prov. Lang. and Lit. (in Encycl Brit.). **295.** Recherches sur l'Epopée Franç. 1867.

MEYER, R —**296** Das Leben des Trob. G Faidit 1876.

MEYER-LÜBCKE, W —**297.** Gram der Rom Sprachen. 2 v. 1890–1894.

MICHEL, F.—**298.** Recherches sur les Etoffes de Soie, etc 2 v. 1852–1854

MICHELET, J.—**299.** Hist. de France. 6 v. 1833–1844.

MILÁ Y FONTANALS, M.—**300.** De los Trovadores en España. 1861.

MILLIN, A L.—**301** Voyage dans les Dép du Midi de la France. 5 v. 1805–1810.

MILLOT —See La Curne de Ste Palaye.

MILMAN, H H.—**302.** Hist. of Latin Christianity. 2d ed 6 v. 1857

MINTO, W.—**303.** Daniel Defoe. 1879.

MISTRAL, F —**304.** Les Iles d'Or 1889 **305** Mirèio. (Trans by H. W. Preston.) 1891.

MOLINIER, A —***306.** Administ. Féodale dans le Languedoc. (Hist. Gén.) 1879 **307.** Les MSS. et les Miniatures. 1892

MOLINIER, G.—**308** Las Leys Damors (Ed. by G Arnoult.) 3 v. 1841–1843.

MONACI, E.—**309.** Crestom. Ital dei Primi Secoli 2 v 1889–1897. **310** Facsimili di Antichi Manoscritti. 1881.

MONE, F. J —**311.** Latein. Hymnen des Mittelalters 3 v. 1853–1855.

MORANDI, L.—312 Origine della Lingua Ital 1894.

MORGUES, J.—313. Les Statuts et Cout du Pays de Provence. 1658.

MOORE, C. H.—314. Develop. and Char. of Gothic Archit. 1890.

MORLEY, HENRY.—314a English Writers. v III 1889

MOTT, L. F.—315. The System of Courtly Love. 1896.

MÜNTZ, E.—316. Tapisseries, Broderies et Dentelles. 1890.

MUSGRAVE, G —317 Nooks and Corners in Old France. 2 v. 1867

MYERS, P V N —318 Outlines of Med. and Mod. Hist. 1886.

NAPOLSKI, M VON.—319. Leben und Werke des Trob. Ponz de Capduoill. 1880.

NAUMANN, E R. W.—320 Hist. of Music. (Trans. by F. Praeger) 1876

NEALE, J. M.—321. Mediæval Hymns. 3d ed. 1867.

NEANDER, A —322. The Life and Times of St. Bernard. 1843.

NORGATE, K.—323. England under the Angevin Kings. 2 v. 1887

NOSTRADAMUS, J. DE.—324. Les Vies des Plus Célèbres et Anciens Poètes Prov. 1775.

OMAN, C W. C.—325. A Hist of the Art of War. v. II. 1898.

PALAZZI, P. G.—326. Le Poesie Ined. di Sordello 1887.

PALUSTRE, L.—327. Hist de Guillem IX, etc. 1882

PANNIER, L.—328. Les Lapidaires Franç. du M. Age. 1883.

PAPON, J. P.—329. Hist. Gén. de Provence. 4 v. 1777-1786.

PARIS, G —330 Hist. Poét de Charlemagne. 1865. *331. La Litt Franç au M. Age. 1890. *332. La Poésie du M. Age. 1887. 333. Les Contes Orient. dans la Litt. Franç. du M. Age. 1875. *334. Orig. de la Poésie Lyr. en France au M. A 1892 335. Penseurs et Poètes. 2d ed 1896 336. Tristan et Iseult 1894.

PATZOLD, A.—337. Die Individ. Eigenthum. einiger Hervor. Trob. 1896

PELAEZ, M —338. Vita e Poesie di Bonifazio Calvo. 1897

PENNELL, J. and E.—339. Play in Provence 1892.

PETIT DE JULLEVILLE, L.—*340 Hist. de la Langue et de la Litt. Franç. v. I. 1896.

PETRARCA, F.—341. Rime. v IV (Trionfo d'Amore.) 1827.

PHILIPSON, E.—342. Der Mönch von Montaudon

PLEINES, A.—343. Hiat und Elision im Provenz. 1886.

POLYBIUS —344. Hampton's Trans. 5th ed. 2 v. 1823.

POWNALL, GOVERNOR —345. Antiquities of the Provincia Romana of Gaul. 1788

PRATSCH, H.—346. Biog. des Troub. F. von Marseille   1878

PRESTON, H. W —347. Troub. and Trouvères   1876.

PROPERT, J L —348. Hist of Miniature Art   1887

PROU, M —349 Facsimilés d'Ecritures, du XII au XVII Sièc. 1892   350 Manuel de Paléogr. 2d ed. 1892

PUTNAM, G. H.—351. Books and their Makers 2 v. 1896–1897.

QUICHERAT, J.—*352. Hist. du Costume en France. 1875   353. Mélanges d'Archéol. et d'Hist. (1886.)

RACINET, A.—354. Le Costume Histor   6 v   1888.

RAJNA, P.—355. Le Corti d'Amore. 1890

RAMBAUD, A.—*356. Hist. de la Civiliz Franç   2 v   1885–1887

RASHDALL, H.—357. The Univ of Europe in the M. Ages. 2 v. 1895

RAYNOUARD, F. J. M —*358. Choix des Poésies Orig. des Troub 6 v. 1817. *359 Lexique Roman   6 v. 1836–1843

REACH, A. B.—360. Claret and Olives. 1852.

RÉNAN, E.—361. L'Art du M Age. 1862   362. La Poésie des Races Celt. (in Essais) 1860

RESTORI, A.—*363. Lett Provenzale (French ed , 1891).

REVOIL, H —364 Architect Rom. du Midi de la France   3 v. 1873.

RIEUNNIER, A.—365. La Médicine au M. Age. 1892.

ROBERT, L.—366. Catalogue du Musée d'Artillerie   1890.

ROBERT, U.—367. Les Signes d'Infamie au M. Age.   1888

ROBIDA, A.—368. La Vieille France : Provence

ROBUCHON, J.—369 Paysages et Monum de Poitou. 1890.

ROCHEGUDE, DE.—370. Le Parnasse Occitanien. 1819.

ROEMER, L.—371. Die Volksthüm Dichtungsarten der Altprov. Lyrik   1884.

ROGER-MILÈS, L —372. Comment Discerner les Styles   1896.

ROQUEFORT, J B B DE.—373. Gloss. de la Langue Rom   3 v. 1808–1820

ROUARD, E —374. La Bibliothèque d'Aix, etc   1831

ROUMANILLE, J.—375. Contes Prov

ROWBOTHAM, J. E.—376. The Troub and Courts of Love. 1895.

RUTHERFORD, J.—377 The Troub. 1873.

SABATIER, B —378 Vie de St François d'Assise   1893

SACHS, K E. A.—379. Le Trésor de Pierre de Corbiac. 1859.

SACHSE, M —380 Ueber das Leben und die Lieder des Tr. Wilhelm IX, etc. 1882.

ST. HILAIRE, R —381. Hist d'Espagne. New ed. 14 v. 1844-1879.

ST. MARTIN, J.—382. La Fontaine de Vaucluse 1891

ST. MARTIN, V. DE.—383. Nouv Dict de Géog. Univ. 7 v. 1879-1895.

ST. YON, M DE —384. Hist des Comtes de Toulouse. 4 v. 1859

SALA, G A.—385. A Journey Due South. 1885

SANTY, S —386. La Comtesse de Die. 1893

SCHACK, A. F. VON —387. Kunst und Poesie der Araber, etc. 2 v 1865.

SCHERILLO, M.—388 Alcune Fonte Provenz. della Vita Nuova di Dante 1889

SCHINDLER, H —389 Die Kreutzzüge in der Altprov . . . Lyrik 1889.

SCHLEGEL, A. W. VON.—390 Observ. sur la Langue et la Litt. Prov 1818.

SCHMELLER, J. A.—391. Carmina Burana. 1883.

SCHMIDT, C —392. Hist. et Doct. . . . des Cathares et des Albig. 2 v 1849

SCHOPF, S.—393. Beiträge zur Biog. des Troub Peire Vidal 1887.

SCHULTZ, A.—*394. Das Höfische Leben zur Zeit der Minnesinger. 2d ed. 2 v. 1889

SCHULTZ, O.—395. Die Briefe des Trob. R. de Vaqueiras an Bon. I. 1893 *396 Die Provenz. Dichterinnen. 1888.

SELBACH, L.—397. Das Streitgedicht in der Altprov. Lyrik. 1886.

SETTEGAST, F.—398 Die Ehre in den Liedern der Troub. 1887

SHAW, H.—399 The Art of Illumination. 1870.

SISMONDI, J. C. L. S. DE.—400. De la Litt. du Midi de l'Europe. 4 v 1829.

SMOLLETT, T.—401. Travels through France and Italy. 2 v. 1766.

SOC. DE L'ECOLE DES CHARTES.—402. Album Paléogr. 1887.

SOC. DE L'HIST. DE FRANCE.—403. Annuaire-Bulletin. 1879

SPRINGER, H —404. Das Altprovenz Klagelied, etc. 1895

STEELE, R.—405. Mediæval Lore   1893.

STENDHAL, DE (H. Beyle).—406.   Mémoires d'un Touriste. 1854.

STENGEL, E —407.   Die Beiden Aeltesten Prov Grammatiken. 1878   *408. Rom. Verslehre (Groebers Grund).   1893.

STEPHENS, W. R. W.—409.   Hildebrand and his Times.   1888.

STERNBECK, H.—410. Unrichtige Wortaufstellungen, etc.   1887.

STICKNEY, A —411. The Romance of Daude de Pradas.   1879

STIMMING, A.—412 Bertran von Born. 2d ed   1892.   413. Der Troub. Jaufre Rudel   1886   *414   Die Prov. Lit. (Groebers Grund)   1893

STORRS, R. S —415. Bernard of Clairvaux   1892

STOTHARD, C A —416 Monum Effigies of Great Britain. 1876.

STRUTT, J.—417. The Sports and Pastimes of the People of England   1801.

STUBBS, W.—418. The Early Plantagenets   1876

SUCHIER, H.—419 Denkmäler Provenz Lit und Sprache. 1883. *420 Le Français et le Prov   (Tr. by Monet.) 1891   421. Prov. Diätetik   1894.

SYMONDS, J A.—422. Sketches and Studies in Southern Europe 1880   423. Wine, Women, and Song (Med Student Songs). 1884.

TAINE, H.—424. Carnets de Voyage (1863-1865)   1897

TANON, L.—425. Hist. . . . de l'Inquisition en France. 1893

TARDIF, A.—426. Coutumes de Toulouse.   1884

TAYLOR, B (Editor) —427. Picturesque Europe. v. II.   1878.

TAYLOR and Others.—428 Voyages Pittor et Romant dans l'Ancienne France   Languedoc.   1834

THOMAS, A —429. Les Poés Comp. de B de Born   1888   430 Francesco da Barberino et la Litt Prov , etc   1883

TIERSOT, J.—431. La Chanson Populaire en France   1889

TOUR-KEYRIÉ, A. M. DE LA.—432. Proverbes Prov., etc   1882.

TOURTOULON et BRINGUIER. — 433 La Limite Géog. de la Langue d'Oc, etc   1876.

TRICHAUD, J. M.—434 Les Principaux Monuments d'Arles, etc. 24th ed   1885

VERNEILH, F DE —435 L'Architect Byzant. en France   1851.

VIDAL, P —436 Les Pyrénées Orientales   1879

VILLEHARDOUIN, G. DE.—437 Hist. de la Conquête de Constantinople.

VILLEMAIN, M —438. Cours de la Litt. Franç. (1840).   1890.

VILLERMONT, M DE.—439 Hist. de la Coiffure Féminine. 1892.

VINCENT DE BEAUVAIS.—440. Speculum Naturale.

VINCENT, M. R —441. In the Shadow of the Pyrenees. 1883.

VINSAUF (GALFRIDUS DE VINOSALVO).—442. See *Bohn*.

VIOLLET-LE-DUC, E. E —443 Dict. Raisonné de l'Archit. 10 v. 1858-1868   444 Dict Raisonné du Mobilier Franç. 6 v. 1871-1875.   445. Hist. de l'Habitation Humaine   1875.   446 La Cité de Carcassonne.   1888.   447. Milit. Archit. of the M. Ages.   1860.

VOLLMÖLLER und OTTO.—448. Krit Jahresbericht . . . der Rom. Philol.   2 v.   1890-1894.

VUILLIER, G.—449. En Limousin (Tour du Monde, v. 65).   1893. 450. La Danse.   1898.

WERDT, E —451. Hist. du Livre en France   5 v   1861-1862

WEISS, H.—452. Kostümkunde.   3 (5) v.   1860-1872

WEST, A. F —453. Alcuin and the Rise of the Christian Schools 1892.

YOUNG, ARTHUR.—454. Travels in France.   3 v.   1793.

ZELLER, B.—455. L'Hist. de France racontée par les Contemp. v. X-XII.   1882-1884.

ZENKER, R —456. Die Gedichte des Folquet von Romans.   1896. 457. Die Prov. Tenzone   1888

ZINGARELLI, N.—458 La Personalità Storica di F. di Marsiglia. 1897

The above list omits a number of books on local history and geography which I consulted while travelling, but of which I did not take a complete bibliographical note. Such are M. C. Compayré's work on the region about Albi, Monteil's history of Aveyron, Tardieu's history of Clermont-Ferrand, etc.

The following were not accessible, but were known through extracts or reviews :

ALBUM des Monum de l'Art Anc. du Midi de la France.

AZAIS, G.—Les Troub. de Béziers.

BARTH —Ueber den Troub. Wilhelm IX.

BEKKER, I.—Prov. Geistl Lieder des XIII Jahrh.

BIADENE, L.—Cortezie da Tavola in Latino e Prov.

BOROTTI, G S.—Trov Prov. alla Corte dei March. di Este. 1889.

CAMUZZONI, G —Soave e il suo Castello.   1893.

COULET, JULES.—Guilhem de Montanhagol.   1898

CRESCINI, V —Sordello (Conferenza).   1897.

ETHÉ, H.—Ueber Persiche Tenzonen   1881.

FISCH, J. G.—Briefe uber die Sud. Provinz von Frankreich. 1790

GAUCHAT, L.—Les Poésies Prov. conservées par des Chansonniers Franc

GROEBER, G —Die Liedersammlungen der Troub. 1877.

JORIAUD, P DE.—Richard Cœur-de-Lion. 1887.

KELLER, A —Guillem de Berguedan. 1849 Lieder Guillems IX 1848

KLEIN.—Blacasset. 1887

KNOBLOCH, H.—Die Streitgedichte im Prov und Altfranz 1886

LA LAUZIÈRE —Hist d'Arles.

LEROUX, A.—La Civilis en Limousin pendant le M A

LÉVY, E —Gui d'Uisel

MERKEL, C.—Sordello e la sua Dimora presso di Carlo d'Angiò 1890.

MISCEL. di Filol e Ling in Mem N Caix e U. A Canello 1886

NAPOLSKI, S. VON —Beit zur Char. Mittelalt Lebens an den Höfen Sudfrank

RAMORINO, F —La Pronunz Pop. dei Versi Quant. Latini. 1893?

ST. LAGER.—Recherches sur les Anciens Herbaria. 1886

SARTORI.—Trov. Prov alla Carte dei March. in Este. 1889.

STIMMING, A.—Ueber den Prov. Girart de Roussillon 1888.

VIT, A. DE.—Cunizza da Romano. 1892.

WOLFFLIN, E.—Ueber die Allitt Verbind. der Latein Sprache. 1881

ZANICHELLI —Fiorita di Liriche Prov. Tradotte 1881.

PRONUNCIATION

The pronunciation of mediæval Provençal is, for a number of reasons, an extremely intricate subject. The following indications are intended only to help the reader pronounce the proper names in this book with something like correctness. To attempt more than this would only cause the reader confusion. VOWELS are to be sounded as in modern French *De* is pronounced *day*. DIPHTHONGS: *au = ou* in *out; ai = i* in *fight; ei = ey* in *they, oi = oi* in *oil*. CONSONANTS All the consonants are to be sounded, and there are no nasals like those in French. In general they are to be given the same sounds as in English *Ch = Ch* in *Charles; g* is soft before *e, i,* and *y* (*i. e.,* as in French) ; *gn = gn* in *mignon-ette, ll* or *lh = lli* in *million, gu =* hard *g* as in *get; qu = k, z* at the end of a word *= ts*. ACCENT : The last syllable has the accent if it ends with a consonant ; otherwise the last but one

THE TROUBADOURS AT HOME

I

AIX

Savaric de Mauleon

THE place to read the poems of the troubadours is the south of France,—Provence, in the broad meaning of the name.

In this poetic region one is in the midst of hills and valleys that gave pleasure to their eyes, and among a people that have inherited something from their hearts. Reminders of their age greet one at every turn. Love—not pictured on the vase, but in life—" still pants and still enjoys" here. The delight in existence flashes out gaily in the merriment of the dance, as when the world was many generations younger. Castles in ruins, mantled with whispering ivy and vocal in the wind, appear to be giving out echoes of the music that once enlivened them ; and the very skies, filled with warm splendor, seem the reflection of Golden Isles[1] of romance, barely veiled by the purple horizon.

It is a land overflowing with tears and laughter, classic but not severe, glad but not thoughtless. The bees are still a-wing in its meadows ; and in this Provence, under the olive and the vine, in the midst of roses and haw-

thorns, bygone days of chivalry and song grow present
and seem to live again.

Aix, however, is a shadow in the picture. A hundred
years ago Charles de Brosses called it the prettiest city in
France after Paris , but Victor Hugo, for all his genius,
could find only this to say . " It has two *clochers ;* one is
merely a square tower, the other a fifteenth-century spire of
quite good style."   France has moved, but Aix has not

It is a city of country nobility, landed proprietors living
on the rents of to-day and the traditions of a century ago,
epicurean but sad   Behind the solemn façades are great
staircases made for the robes of Presidents of the Parliament, and salons with enormous antechambers once peo-
pled with lackeys.   Perhaps in the corners there are
lingering echoes of the " finesse and caustic wit" that
Thiers thought characteristic of the people , but to the
stranger it seems half dead, and the greedy light of Provence, devouring all the color, has left everything grayish

The only live people seem to be the small tradesmen,
and they live only once a week.   Every one has a *bastide,*
a garden in the suburbs, and he may always be found there
on Sunday   In the shade of his arbor he drains a flagon
of good wine, expands his chest, bandies mocking pleasantries, sings out the old songs of Provence, and with a
turn of the eye repeats its old proverbs   " A man's
shadow is worth a hundred women " ; " To lie well is a
talent, to lie ill a vice " , " One half of the world laughs at
the other half"; " Praise the sea, but stay on dry land ";
" Water spoils wine, carts spoil roads, women spoil men."

We look in vain for the monuments of a long, historic
past   As Governor Pownall observed in his calm fashion,
" Aix, although the first settlement and town the Romans
had in Gaul, although it was for some time the principal
and always a considerable place, exhibits in these latter

days the fewest remains of antiquity of any place once so possessed and occupied.'' The same basin of low hills is here, but what else remains?

From the walls of Aix the plucky Consul Marius and his impatient legionaries gazed upon the vast masses of Cimbri and Teutones who had tasted grapes and wine and were off for Italy. Day after day they marched past, jeering the Romans on the wall and offering to take messages

THE ANCIENT PALACE OF THE COUNTS, AIX.

for their wives and sweethearts, and then a hundred thousand of them laid their gashed bodies on the ground a few miles from here at Pourrières.² The children at play still keep alive a memento of Marius and his iron discipline, but their fathers have pulled down the walls.

Where is the ancient palace of the counts of Provence, with its Roman foundations and the great hall of the parliament upholstered in blue velvet *à cartisannes d'or?* Like the walls it has vanished. Plain enough the old palace looked, no doubt, but many a troubadour went in by that portal. There was Raimon Berenguier the Fourth, count of Provence, who wrote a poem to his horse—no, better than that, wrote a dialogue *with* his horse, calling him, " Flesh-and-fingernail," to show how close the attachment between them was.[2] There, too, were Bertran de Lamanon,[4] one of his nobles, the famous Blacatz, the still more famous Sordel, and many another troubadour whom we are soon to know. But this precious monument was needlessly torn down. Not a palace, not a church, not a rampart, not a tower, can be found that the troubadours ever saw.

Yet a happy chance, kinder than the intentions of Aix, has preserved a fragment of the age we came to study.

THE OLD DOORWAY.

In destroying an ancient church the architects found that one of its doorways must be spared, for it had somehow got built into the new cathedral ; and the doorway is open still. From the youth (1080) of the earliest of the troubadours this bit of Romanesque masonry has witnessed the coming and going of the generations, and a procession of troubadours was passing under its lintel during the entire life of their poetry. It is not a wonderful monument, this portal ;

but it helps lend an air of reality to remote and shadowy events.

There is another memento of the past in Aix which some would think of, perhaps, as a much more personal relic of the troubadours. René, that "Mark Tapley of Kings," resided here as well as in Tarascon, and the public library contains a *livre d'heures* illuminated by his own hand.

But the troubadour age was long past when René came upon the stage, and his mummeries were only a burlesque of the true Provençal poets. The troubadour was the companion of noblemen, and though not always of aristocratic birth, always felt himself a gentleman at least. He was a chevalier with a nightingale in his casque.

RENÉ'S CASTLE, TARASCON.

Allied with him, but distinctly of lower station, was the joglar— an ancestor of our juggler — who assumed the various rôles of a vaudeville performer, and besides his less dignified accomplishments played and sang the music and poems of the troubadours.' In the period of decadence the joglars assumed the title of their betters, and so brought a distinguished name to very common uses. In fact, they and René and their successors have given the word *troubadour* a color so different from its real meaning that one is tempted to discard it altogether, and call the Provençal poets—as they called themselves—*trobadors*.

But the leanness of Aix is an advantage in one way, for it leaves us time to look abroad and think of the journey we are to make

It is to be a journey, in fact,—a voyage of discovery in the fair Midi, amid the plains and valleys, the hills and mountains, the castles and picturesque towns of southern France, from the Alps to the sea, from the Loire to the Pyrenees ; and not in France only, but in delightful corners of Italy and of Spain   .

It is to be a journey in time   we shall go back just seven hundred years from to-day, and then with a liberal tether of one century shall browse on either hand.

It is to be a journey in degree, for we shall find ourselves no longer among commoners and plebeians, but in the society of gentle folk—nobles, princes, and kings, the finest aristocracy of the age. We shall meet intimately the spirit of brave and open-handed chivalry in its most brilliant estate, and many of the persons within our circle will be figures of rare charm or great historical importance.

It is to be a journey to another and a fascinating civilization, amid which we shall discover the beginnings of our own. Better than any other period this one represented certain phases of human nature and achievement that are too precious to forget   It shows us, for example, the three great faiths—religion, poetry, and love—in life and in action.

But this does not mean sentimentality. It was an age of strength and growth. Everything had the keen zest of what chemists call the nascent state   The troubadours were full of a young-heartedness that made life joyous even amid the discomforts and perils of a rude and warring age, and when we read their songs we almost feel that the dead of their time are more alive than the quick of ours. The manners, the learning, the wars, the adventures, the daily doings of the age were full of interest. Life was a drama. The crusades were launched in a troubadour city and their war-songs were composed by troubadour poets. Nothing was " sicklied o'er." Not even the shadows of Cervantes, Rabelais, and Voltaire had come in sight. Nobody doubted, everybody looked forward. The modern world was forming. Woman became something more than a link between two generations. Universities arose. Free thought began. Industries were organized and the arts took shape. The pope and the emperor began to hew at each other, the people lifted its head, and civil liberty appeared. Of all these things we shall have glimpses as we go

More than anything else, it is to be a literary journey, and we shall even reach the springs of our modern intellectual life. As it has been said of Washington that he was given no children in order that a nation might call him father, we may say of troubadour poetry that it has no lineal descendant in order that all our modern literature may look to it as a parent This may sound extravagant, perhaps, for our literature has a thousand ancestors, not a single one. But so the Amazon has a thousand sources ; yet we select the spring that deserves the title best and call it " The Amazon," and if we do the same with modern literature we must say " The Troubadours." Their literature was the first which took form ; it modified every other, and it was long entirely independent.[6]

No doubt in some ways we shall suffer disappointment. It is true that Provençal literature shows no grand figure like Dante, Homer, or Shakespeare. But that is a fact which enhances its interest. It was not the work of a great man, but the spontaneous outgrowth of influences that underlie all our modern development. It was the product of an age, not of an individual ; the voice, not of a genius greater than his time, but of the time itself ; the general beauty of spring, not the grace of one prize tulip.

It is true that we shall think the poetry formal, for it was the expression of courtly life, and had, also, a finished etiquette of its own.   But no beauty of form was approved by the leading troubadours, unless genuine feeling lay behind it, and their ability to sing tunefully through an exacting technique impresses upon us the vitality of their inspiration.

It is true that we shall find signs of immaturity in their culture.   But this was inevitable.   We must consider what they had to build upon, and a glance at the tenth and the early part of the eleventh centuries will moderate our criticisms.   The butcheries of Goths and Saracens, Northmen, Slavs, and Huns had brought men down almost to the level of brutes.   Nobody expected to live out his days.   To die in a bed was luxury, and men were quite satisfied to be killed like Christians.   Traditions and the constant experience of fire and slaughter made passions terrible and violence natural.   To fight was the one business of the strong ; to suffer, the one resource of the weak. Murder was so common that robbery scarcely seemed a crime at all.   Hardship, bred in-and-in, resulted in stolid brutality   The heaviest, roughest, and coarsest were best off ; refinement would have been torture   Physical appetites, as fierce as wild boars, trampled beauty and rent the beautiful.   Too often the popes were politicians, the monks drunkards, and the priests worse.   Terrible famines carried off millions, and fearful pestilences millions more. The sky was filled with awful signs by day, and when the sun had set the earth seemed given over to the fiends.

As the year 1000 approached, all became satisfied that the world was to be destroyed   Despair paralyzed what remained of intellectual life   Even the churches were allowed to fall in ruins   When the fateful year passed it

was concluded that destruction was reserved until the
millennium from our Lord's death—not his birth—should
be filled out, and another whole generation shuddered
under the black shadow of doom and damnation. As the
time drew near a famine more terrible than any that had
gone before it laid Europe waste. For three years (1030–
1032) there was neither seed-time nor harvest. Starvation
ravened from Greece to England. Roots, grass, and white
clay were eaten. Men devoured each other Even the
dead were dug up and gnawed Wolves appeared in
troops and herded with people almost on terms of equality.
And this was less than fifty years before the line of the
troubadours began.

But we may do more than excuse. Immaturity—full
of life, hope, and promise—has a charm of its own. We
delight in the youth of others and would gladly re-live
our own. Here we may study and live over again the
youth of our civilization

It is true, also, that the literature of the troubadours
was narrow, and possibly may seem rather frivolous. Love
was by no means their only theme, as we shall find. Besides weaving sentiment into the *canson*, they discussed in
the *tenso* every sort of debatable question, and the *sirvente*
expressed their views on politics, religious and moral
topics, and personal issues. But love was the principal,
the ever-recurring note, and such devotion to this one
idea surprises us until we understand it.

Let us take as an illustration one of the famous tales of
the period, and a poem that grew out of it.

Away up near Angers and Nantes is a little place called
Châtillon-sur-Sèvre, and a rich lord named Savaric de
Mauleon ' had his castle there. Savaric was a great soldier, a leader in the wars of King John's time, and a partisan of his nephew, the unlucky Prince Arthur, and he
was in love with a countess who lived at Benauges in the

Sauterne region to the south of Bordeaux.   But she was very coy, this Madame Guillerma.   Every now and then she would send for Lord Savaric, and no matter where he was or how pressing his affairs, he would hurry off by land or by sea down to Benauges—a serious journey in those days, and not without peril.   When he arrived, afire with ardor, she would be as distant and unapproachable as ever, giving him fair words and perhaps a present of a girdle, a banner, or a jewel, but not her love.

One day he made her a visit with two other young noblemen, Elias Rudel and Jaufre Rudel.[8]   The situation was difficult, for all her guests were suitors and each had been given encouragement.   But the countess was no ordinary coquette   Jaufre Rudel, who sat facing her, was favored with loving glances.   Elias, placed beside her, was delighted with a lingering pressure of the hand   As for Savaric, on the other side, it happened that her foot pressed upon his, and a smile and a sigh interpreted the accident   The three departed happy, but on the way Jaufre told Savaric of the glances he received, and Elias told him of the hand that met his.   Savaric said nothing, but he felt very much distressed, and sending for two other troubadours (for he was a poet as well as a baron and a soldier) he asked them to discuss with him in a tenso which of the three suitors had really been preferred.[9]

Gaucelm Faidit, a celebrity whom we shall meet before long, declared that the fairest gift is received by the one on whom beautiful eyes rest their faithful glance   Only from the heart can such sweetness proceed, and therefore it is a hundredfold the greatest honor.   As for giving the hand, it is a favor bestowed by ladies on all they meet ; and pressing the foot is nothing.

The other friend was Ugo of La Bacalairia [10]—Labachellerie, they call it now—not far from Périgueux   Ugo was no less positive, but his opinion was different.   He maintained warmly that a glance could signify but little, for the eyes look upon this one and that one and have no other power; but when a white hand, ungloved, softly presses yours, then heart and feeling are assuredly full of love.

Savaric found himself compelled to fight his own battle, but declared boldly they had left him the best part, for pressing the foot was a token of true love hidden from tale-bearers, and the smile that accompanied it proved the love sincere.

"No," cried Gaucelm, "glances are messengers of the

NEAR LABACHELLERIE.

heart, for the eyes reveal to lovers that which fear keeps back in the bosom, and so are the bringers of all love's joys. But often a lady presses many a person's foot in laughing and chatting, with no special intent whatever, and taking the hand is positively without significance."

"Ah," replied Ugo, "the eyes have betrayed many a lover, and if a false lady should press my foot for a year, still it would not make me glad. Truly, you cannot deny that if the heart were not filled with love it would never have sent forth the hand."

Neither would yield; and so it was agreed to lay the matter before three judges, one of them the famous Maria

de Ventadorn, the second, Guillerma herself, and the
third, another flame of Savaric's.[11]

Now it may well amaze us to see a great baron like
Savaric, deeply engaged in war and politics, devoting
himself so earnestly to a question of gallantry, but something very different from frivolity actuated him, and a
broader issue than one might think was really involved
Love, as we shall find, signified vastly more than it does
now, and other things vastly less The intellectual life
just opening its eyes needed something to interest and
employ it, and there was little else A quiet home life
meant hardly more than hunting, tilting, and fighting,
eating, drinking, and sleeping—almost pure animalism,
worthy of the stigma it bore. There were no journals,
no magazines, no books in comparison with ours, and in
fact, the ability to read was an accomplishment. The
universities were barely forming Religion could not be
discussed. Philosophy hardly existed. There were no
science, no drama, very little painting or sculpture, little
architecture, no inventions, and no discoveries.[12] Music
was only a tinkle. For all but a very few the whole world
of ancient culture was buried as deep as Pompeii ever was.
Almost the only poetry was the singing of the troubadours
themselves, and that was merely the blossoming of love.

Love was everything, and we cannot wonder that much
was made of it. Its hopes and fears were the drama of
that day. Sweet and passionate thoughts were the con-
cert and the opera. Tales of successful and unsuccessful
wooing were the novels Recalling the beauty of loved
faces and describing them to others was the painting.
Love was at once the diversion and the fine art of the age
beyond everything else. It was even more The warm
hearts of the troubadours were the hotbed of a new civilization. Love, as we are to learn, was the shoot of modern
culture, and the tree that now overspreads us with its

boughs bloomed, even in their time, into a poetry as un-
surpassed and as unsurpassable after its kind as the epics
of Homer.

In Arizona there is said to be a chalcedony forest. A
miner lost his bearings and stumbled upon it by chance ;
and when he found his way home he cried out, " I 've
seen a petrified forest of petrified trees, with their petrified
branches full of petrified birds singing petrified songs."
That is the feeling of one who becomes acquainted with
the mediæval literature of Provence. These old poems
represent a complete civilization, dead but still erect.
The boughs do not move, but they seem about to move
in a breeze that almost blows. Birds are there—nightingales at that—and their music, far from being lifeless, is
graceful, rich, and surprising.

Our present mission is to explore the forest of chalcedony.

The Notes, to which the " superior figures " refer, may be found
at the end of the volume, divided into chapters corresponding to
those of the text.

CARPENTRAS, VACQUEIRAS, ORANGE, AND VAUCLUSE

Gui de Cavaillon. Raimbaut de Vaqueiras

NOT far from Aix a typical troubadour—Raimbaut de Vaqueiras—was born, and we resolved upon visiting his early home at once.

But first, Cavaillon—bowery Cavaillon—famous for its melons. Dumas presented the town with a set of his works on the condition that it should pay him an annual tribute of its fruit ; but no such material attraction drew us to the place, nor even the archæological interest of the triumphal arch and the cathedral. Gui, the lord of Cavaillon in the days of Magna Charta (1215), was not only a diplomat and soldier but a troubadour. His poems thrill yet with the keen passions of the time, and the scorn of cowardice and treason They sound the trumpet call to battle, and the cry for help against overwhelming odds , and, aided by their living colors, we can picture the bold knight riding all day in harness, giving blows and taking them from the French invaders, snatching a hasty supper while the attack waned, and then pacing to and fro till morning between the wall and the moat of his castle to guard against the chance of a night assault. A worthy figure, we must agree, to introduce a greater one.[1]

At our next halt we were again forwarded on our journey toward the past Carpentras, one of the most poetic cities " roasting in the sun of Midi," is full of life but has also the dignity of great age Pliny knew of it. Once it bore the name of a Roman emperor, *Forum Neronis*. Conspicuous beside the winding Auzon it attracted the fatal admiration of Goths, Vandals, Lombards, and Saracens, and was ravaged by each in turn. A year before Bruce routed the English at Bannockburn (1314) a pope, the fifth Clement, found the place worthy to be his residence. A Phœnician inscription has been discovered here, and one in Greek praising Thebe the daughter of Thelhui because she never scolded her husband. Centuries ago it was a place of refuge for the Jews, and a colony of schools ; and while the inscription on a bench : " Seat to sit upon," may seem to justify the modern epithet " Bœotian," it once boasted its coterie of wits , and when the rector had three unpopular men appointed consuls, a local poet celebrated him in some verses as greater than a Roman emperor , for Caligula only made his horse a consul, but the rector had made consuls of three asses at one time.

If history failed us we could get a strong flavor of the past from the sculptured portals, the massive tower of the Orange gate or the Campagna-like aqueduct spanning the wide meadows with its countless arches ; and even the life of the town seems olden.

In the square behind the great gate, shadowed by an iron belfry typical of Provence, is a market that carries us back to the mediæval fairs. Everybody who cares to buy or to sell is there, jostling his neighbors and driving his bargain. The merchandise is at hand. Would you eat ? Here are fresh radishes with the smell of earth upon them yet, looking so much cooler than they will taste,—leeks, oranges, dried peas and beans, onions, corn, and a dozen grains. Are you thirsty ? Here are the wines of the country, some of them no dearer than three sous a litre.

Does your kitchen lack ? Pots and pans are before you, kettles lined with porcelain, chopping-knives, mortars not for war, pestles not for sickness, ladles, wooden bowls, gridirons. Pocket-knives flank a pile of combs, hinges suggest pliability to stacks of boots and shoes that seem to need the hint, handkerchiefs insinuate them-selves toward trousers pockets, corkscrews alliterate with calicoes. On one side green plants and blossoming flowers offer themselves. On another, hens and chickens fettered with cords are piled on the straw in panniers,— too curious about others to be alarmed for them-selves. Kids lie in bonds on the ground, and in little pens are rabbits, every one struggling to hide under every other one.

THE BELFRY, CARPENTRAS.

Amidst all these and a thousand other things a town-ful of men and women—principally women—crowd and wriggle, with a hearty salutation to right and left, a sharp retort for some old enemy, endless chaffering and bargaining and infinite satisfaction. Most are bareheaded, some have white caps, and a very few wear bonnets. Knives and forks are studied and discussed, radishes are sternly scrutinized, clothing is railed at, eggs are nicely weighed in the hand, pullets are shrewdly pinched and poked.

Amidst the throng rises the quaint old Romanesque fountain, crumbling without a doubt, but defiantly spouting its four bright streams from the puckered mouths of bodiless cherubs, and stoutly asserting to every passer-by that it never felt younger in its life. And over the whole scene towers the huge gateway—its flights of stairs broken, grass and shrubbery triumphant upon its arch, but still bold and martial, telling a story that is ancient but written to endure.

Our horses and barouche and the smart driver cracking his whip to right and left impress the people. They open before us and salute so respectfully that we fancy ourselves lords of the land visiting our faithful town. In such state, pushing on when we have inspected the market, we survey the rest of a fascinating picture. The carriage-builder is hammering at the wheel of a cart. The blacksmith is manœuvring to slip a hood over the eyes of a refractory horse. The harness-maker has just hung out the specimens of his art on a peg outside the door, and lingers a moment on the threshold smoothing his leather apron softly with both hands. The painter is absorbed in striping a cart with red that will warm the countryside as it rolls along next winter.

THE ORANGE GATE.

Outside the Orange gate five hundred carts, little two-wheeled affairs, are tilted up on end, like so many idlers resting on the small of their backs, while the horses and donkeys are discussing the quality of hay in stalls near by, and the proprietors are trafficking in the market.

Stages are coming and going, spinning threads between Carpentras and every town of the region Some, the grandees of the tribe, push for distant Avignon,—what tales they must confide to their humbler brethren!   Others are hastening to bury themselves in the blue mountains. Some look staid and sombre ; others—the greater number —have bright lemon-colored wheels, a yellow body slightly toned with green, window sashes of pink, and the brightest of red curtains.   Who could be melancholy in such a vehicle ?

The country toward Vacqueiras we found interesting though not remarkably beautiful Gardens bordered the road and the skilful cultivation was always to be admired. Streams of clear water flowed beside the highway, and here and there entered the fields by sluices.   Cherry trees and' plum trees were in full bloom We discovered where the pansies and the mignonettes that we had seen in town came from.   Singly or in groups the peasants were hastening to market, or at a more leisurely pace return-ing, well ballasted with silver and copper coins.   Many a cart was filled with women sitting on boards or in chairs, and buxom lasses not a few rode with dangling feet at the end of some neighborly vehicle.   Here and there a man breakfasted as he went, munching a loaf and walking smartly.

Many brown houses beside the way ; Aubignan, with bric-à-brac ramparts and picturesque roofs ; Beaumes a little way off, extending a pleasant invitation that we could not accept ; the ruins of Barroux on its rock and other crumbling castles in the distance,—these were the accents of the drive.   On the right, the torn side of a hill showed the grey limestone of Provence almost from top to bottom, decked with a few wild olives, patches of grass, bushes, and scattered cypresses.   And above that and us and all, rose the great lord Ventoux,[2] the windy mountain,

calmly watching our progress from the midst of his hilly
court. What land would not be proud of such a peak,
the " maker of thunder," the " great compeer of the
mistral," the holy mount of the region ? As firm as Atlas
it stands,—one foot in the north, the other in the south,
firs on the northern slope and olives on the southern. In
its frown or smile the peasants read the purposes of Jove ;
and once when it loosed all its winds 6000 olive trees,
uprooted between Aubagne and Roquevaire, attested its
power

At another brown village two women are washing
clothes in a stone tank by a fountain. Our driver pulls
up, and turning with a look of bewilderment on his face
announces, " Vacqueiras ! " Why should any one drive
so far to find so little ? he is thinking. All the eye can
see is a dull, sadly decayed village of stone, so brown and
so old and so weather-worn that it seems less the work of
man than a part of the soil. There are first some modern
houses, but passing these we come to a mediæval town on
the top of the low hill. The original wall is there still,
yet not a wall exactly but a continuous line of solid houses
heavily built on the outside, with their doors and most of
their windows opening within. Two gateways rear their
arches on the two sides of the diminutive burg, and give
access to the wriggling knot of alleys inside. If the decay
of years was evident before, we now see the decay of centuries. Many of the houses are tenantless, many are
guiltless of roof, or door, or window. But the paving
testifies that once there was a population here, for the flint
cobblestones are deeply marked by the wear of mediæval
wheels.

At the summit of the hill stands a church, built into the
wall like the houses below, so that its belfry could serve
also as a watch-tower ; and next the church, fronting on
the open space before the gate is the one large building of

Vacqueiras, a château-like edifice with a round bastion, a sort of tower, at the corner. It was formerly the man-

A STREET IN VACQUEIRAS.

sion-house, but some time ago was given to the Sisters for their school. Of course it does not go back to the day of the troubadour, but the site itself must, I think. A narrow street winds around the high wall, and the masonry shows the marks of centuries. Evidently here was always the residence of the village grandee. Here, I feel sure, Raimbaut de Vaqueiras was born ; and in the open space within and without the gateway, when nearly two thirds of the twelfth century had joined the past, while the walls of Notre Dame were rising fast at Paris and the Rhone was beginning to foam at Avignon against its first bridge, there was playing here a certain bright and sturdy boy, destined to be famous as a musician, a poet, a soldier, and a lord.[3]

This, then, was the centre of his early life ; what was the circumference ? Here the lad grew ; what was the compass of his world ?

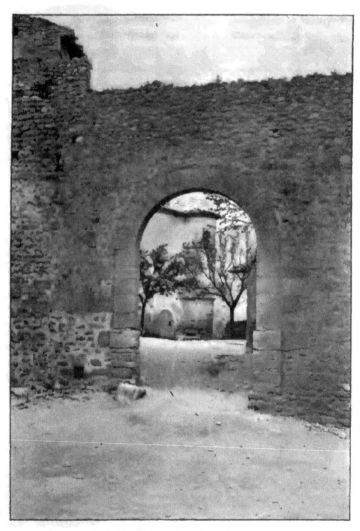

THE OLD GATEWAY OF VACQUEIRAS.

Ventoux was close at hand, no easy climb if we believe
Mistral :

> To tufts of lavender and roots of box
> I needs must cling ; and as my feet I ground
> In the thin soil, the little stones would bound
> With ringing cry from off the precipice,
> And plunge in horror down the long abyss.[4]

Petrarch, during his four years of schooling at Carpentras, made the ascent with his brother despite a shepherd's
warning, and found himself so overwhelmed by the grandeur of the view and the panorama of thought inspired by
it, that after reading aloud a passage from the *Confessions*
of St. Augustine he closed his lips and kept silence until
the sun went down.   But I cannot believe with Mariéton
that Petrarch was the first who reached the summit.
Would not Raimbaut venture as much as Petrarch, and
was not his experience equally profound ?

AVIGNON.

Earthward as well as skyward there was enough to
rouse and instruct him.   Arles, rich now in fragments of
its Roman splendor, was richer then.   Tarascon was happy
in its dragon [5] and untroubled by Daudet.   Beaucaire
offered a sightly castle and a fair-ground celebrated even
beyond the Syrian deserts.   Avignon, the "ever drowsy,"

not yet City of the Popes, was already city of the sun ;
not yet, as Victor Hugo described it, " a little town of
colossal aspect," for its palace had not risen ; but already
superb, for it had the noble view from the Rupes Domi-
norum (*Rocher des Doms*).   All these left their impress on
the boy's mind, but everybody knows them and this bare
mention will suffice ; Orange and Vaucluse require a word
or two.

Orange is one of the most remarkable places in existence.
Simply a pleasant sizable town, we first thought it, sur-

THE ARCH OF ORANGE.

rounded with sweet grassy
meadows, lightly drifted
with sheets of snowy nar-
cissus and streaked with
trails of golden buttercups,
wordless idyls from pagan
Greece, offering heaven the
incense of sheer joy in the
delight of a sunny exist-
ence.   But looking farther
we found that it consisted
chiefly not of meadows,
houses, and people but of a
History, a Hill, and a Title.

The History is very concrete.   Besides traces of an
amphitheatre, a triumphal arch tells of the Roman occupation.   Dumas made merry over the five distinct systems
that he declared had undertaken to explain the arch, for
each had fallen upon another like Joab upon Abner, and
the last one made away with itself because it felt unworthy to live.[8]   Still more to the point for us is a Roman
theatre seating seven thousand people, with its proscenium
wall still erect and solid, a precipice of cut stone three
hundred and forty feet long and seven feet thick, that
could have buried the entire audience and then have made

A RELIC OF THE CASTLE, ORANGE.

amends by giving every victim a monument.' Raimbaut saw the theatre often but he never thought of that, for in his youth the lord of Orange appropriated the wall, and built it into his castle as a sort of bastion.'

The Hill, too, is very visible. Thrust sharply in among the houses we found the end of a narrow table-land five times as high as any of the buildings, I should say, and far steeper than any of the roofs. On the brow of it stood the castle,—which had become one of the strongest fort. resses in France at the time of Louis XIV.; but it stands there no more, for it belonged then to the "asthmatic skeleton" William of Orange, king of England, and the Grand Monarque had it so completely demolished that the fragment of a buttress is the sole remnant of any size.

But while the History and the Hill are concrete the Title is wonderfully abstract. Migrations of races are impressive, migrations of plants are curious, but here is a migration that outdoes every other—the migration of a title ; for the town gave its name to a princeling, and afterward the dignity journeyed and manœuvred till it fixed itself in the crowns of England, Holland, and Prussia. Now this wonderful title was created when Raimbaut was a lad, and the second man who bore it was his patron and friend, as we shall see.

Dearer to him than any of the places we have named, if we may let imagination answer for it, was Vaucluse, *Vallis Clausa*, at the distance of a sturdy walk from Vaqueiras

And what is Vaucluse ? It is a gorge ; it is a gorge leading up to a rock three times as high (650 feet) as the monument on Bunker's Hill, a huge forehead of bare stone, a vast sad cliff, still and solid for eternity , it is a cliff with a fathomless mystery beneath it, a spring, a fountain, a river issuing from the heart of the earth,' *chiare, fresche, e dolci acque.* Quaking with astonish-

ment and white with excitement, the water—so still a
moment since—pours over the side of its crater, foams
through the gorge, and then settling down to the realities
of prose calls itself the Sorgue, and flows peacefully on
through the stone braids and through the delicious idle-
ness of L'Isle, catching what glimpses of the sky it can despite the trees, and eddying dutifully against the huge
water-wheels that start so fitfully and stop so mysteriously
day and night, splashing and dripping and in their soft,
moist way creaking.

> Here are no palace courts, no stage to tread,
> But pines and oaks the shadowy valley fill,
> Between the green fields and the neighboring hill,
> Where musing oft I climb, by fancy led

So Petrarch described Vaucluse in a sonnet, and it is of
him that the spot reminds us first.[10]

Mounet Sully once declaimed here those lines of Sou-
lary : " The happiness that is not within reach of the
hand is but a dream." How true of Petrarch, but in how
different a sense ! Laura, seen for a moment in the convent church of Ste Claire at Avignon and instantly the
mistress of his heart, could never be his,—happiness was
" but a dream " for him ; but it was a dream filled with
music and the march of numbers. For while he sat pon-
dering by the soft green ripple of the Sorgue in shepherd's
garb, he planned or at least conceived all of his great
works. The first of the men of letters he may also be called
the last of the troubadours, and his life was an epitome
of their literary influence All his poems were in honor
of his lady, the thought of whom was never absent from
his heart for forty-eight years, whether he sojourned in
France or in Spain or in Italy or in Germany, whether he
was musing or writing, receiving the laurel crown in the
capitol, discovering the world of lost classics, or unravel-

VAUCLUSE.

ling the skein of diplomacy; until the glimmer of morning from the Adriatic dimmed his lamp in the little study at Arqua on the Euganean mountain, his head bowed softly upon his book, and the silver cord was loosed forever." Through love to the intellectual life, this was the meaning of Petrarch's career, and it was also the meaning of the troubadour dispensation.

It was a poem by Raimbaut de Vaqueiras that suggested Petrarch's *Trionfo d'Amore*," and if this Vallis Clausa meant so much to the one it must have been dear to the other. Raimbaut was a dreamer, too, and his boyhood was full of visions, for he once declared that from the day of his birth it had been his study how to protect his lady.

Indeed, visions of the future and dreams of great deeds must have been the boy's chief solace and encouragement , for Peirol his father was only a poor crazy knight, and the actual world looked far from pleasant. Wherever Raimbaut went he proved the brightest, quickest, and first among those of his age, but I fancy he was seldom allowed to find much pleasure in his victories Nobody would forget his village, his family, his meagre purse, his unpromising future. He was entitled to enter the castles of the neighborhood, and mingle with the sons of nobles in their games of strength, skill, and wit ; but he paid for the privilege by submitting to many a slight and sometimes a taunt. They were hard to bear, but his visions gave him strength to endure and profit by his trials. Trained to self-reliance, he studied whatever he saw, and made the most of every opportunity. His father, for all his queerness, let fall now and then a precious idea about the great world where he had once moved, and the boy pondered till he found out all it meant. Strolling joglars were happy to teach their songs to so quick an ear, and imparted something also of the poet's art. In spite of suffering pride he obtained the schooling of castle hall and tilting ground.   At Carpentras and Avignon and Orange, while his companions jested and laughed, he jested and observed.   And when some chance which we cannot explain invited him about his twentieth year to Italy, to the court of Monferrat among the hills of Piedmont, he was prepared to go [13]

III

LES BAUX AND TORTONA

Raimbaut de Vaqueiras (*Continued*). **Guilhem del Bauz.**
Albert de Malaspina

RAIMBAUT seems to have remained in Italy several years (1179–1182), though not all of the time in Monferrat perhaps, but for one reason or another his visit came to an end, and he was again in Provence. Vaqueiras lay in the principality of Orange, and very naturally he looked for a home at the capital. Guilhem del Bauz, called the Fourth, a prince of about his own age, had just begun (1181) to reign there, and at his little court the troubadour continued his novitiate in life and in art.[1]

Del Bauz in Provençal is Des Baux in French, and we are fortunate in meeting the name ; for no spot could summon before us the warlike spirit of that day and illustrate its tragic realities better than Les Baux. It is the shattered stronghold of an iron family, and this crater of a feudal volcano is the perfect emblem of its age,—grand, fascinating, terrible, and extinct.

But the Midi loves antithesis, and we approach the epic in riven stone through blooming idyls called St. Remy and Maillane.

Maillane hides beneath plane trees and cypresses,—the true oriental cypresses, tall, sombre, and magnificent ; but none the less it is a very proud village, Maillane. For there, in his modest farmhouse, lives the poet Mistral, the

king of all this region, not to say the god ; and the plain-
est peasant may offer him a greeting and a jest in the
patois made classical by his poems and his *Trésor.*[2]

But St. Remy is the real idyl   Once a country-seat of
the counts of Provence, and frequented by many a baron
and troubadour,[1] it is now a town of gardens—flower gardens—worthy to be cared for by Roumanille, the father of
the Félibrige. Streams of sparkling water glide through
borders of bloom ; hedges of flowering hawthorn bind
rather than divide the fields ; century-old plane trees,
gnarled and hollow, look benignly down upon the verdure like age upon childhood ; over walls and hedges,
up and down the avenues of plane trees, filling the " Green
City " as the dream-like haze fills the valleys of Sardinia,
come the perfumes of the flowers, that symphony of odors
which Baudelaire dreamed of, while above us crouches the
guardian lion of Arles—Mt. Gaussier—" cousin to the
lion of St. Mark," his nostrils of rock opening wide to
inhale the incense of the valley.

Pressing on toward Les Baux we have a foretaste of the
summer sun.   From heavens of azure to an earth of green,
a vast illumination blazes through the firmament.   The
heavens quiver with excess of light, and the earth seems
mantled with a veil of gauzy flame.   The radiance dazzles,
burns, excites.   It buries us in the waves of a torrid sea,
not to drown but to inundate us with life.   We feel within
us the Provençal expansiveness   Something of the spirit
of Tartarin mounts to the brain.   We long to be gay,
to jest, to laugh   We talk, and grow intoxicated with
talking—" *on se grise en parlant.*"   And why not ?   Is
it not a fête of the sun, " Lord Sun," " Saint Sun," " the
great sun of Provence," to whom Mistral intoned a
hymn ? Apollo, god of the sun, was the god of poets ;
and it was not by chance that the muse of modern
poetry sang first in the sunny Midi.

Beautiful to think of and fair to behold is the chain of the Alpines, perfumed with thyme and lavender, which make purple clouds on the horizons of Provence ; but with all the aid of French engineering, it is a long and weary climb to the city of Les Baux.   There are terrors also—

A DISTANT VIEW OF LES BAUX.

at least for the imagination.   Not only do we encounter gorges and cliffs, but the ridge over against us appears to watch, to follow, to pursue.   We fancy ourselves making the ascent in the old days, winding through chasms, creeping beneath precipices, turning huge crags, climbing always by a rough and slippery bridle-path in the face of a stubborn enemy, as few were bold enough to attempt. We pass the city gate, still—to our own fancy—invaders, and a single narrow, winding street opens grimly before us, enclosing us in a gauntlet of houses—almost forts— of hewn stone, which threaten like the fabled cliffs of the Dardanelles to close up the handbreadth of passage.   It is a relief to emerge.   An instant more and a magnificent panorama is before us.

La Crau !

Yes, it is the Crau.   Once the waves of the Mediterranean broke at the foot of the rock, but now there is a sea without billows, thirty thousand acres as level as a threshing-floor, a mass of round stones thirty to fifty feet deep.⁴ A threshing-floor it is, in fact ; and the mistral,⁵ the *masterful* wind, rushing from the slopes of the frozen Alps, is the thresher. Strabo knew of the mistral—the Black Boreas, as he called it—and has told us how it threw men from their steeds, carried away their arms, and

THE MAIN STREET OF LES BAUX.

even stripped them of their clothes. Not a tree stands erect in all this region. Ordinary winds blow, but the mistral groans, hisses, roars, explodes. Sometimes it rushes across the plain as a whirlwind, and the stones waltz like autumn leaves. Sometimes it charges straight forward, driving the stones before it in clattering blasts. Sometimes it sweeps the ground with a besom of destruction ; and sheep, shepherd, and cabin, taken at a vantage, find themselves carried away, beaten, crushed, ground, and annihilated Jupiter made La Crau , for when two giants attacked Hercules here on his return from Iberia, the god of the air overwhelmed them with a shower of stones ; and then, it would seem, he turned it over to his mistral

But Adam de Craponne has conquered Jupiter. The Durance, the swiftest and most joyous of rivers, has been made to work , and, covering the stones more and more with the richness of its vernal floods, is redeeming the waste. More than a million sheep journey to and from its pastures every year. Many green oases vary the brown Wide reaches of meadow land fill the eye,—here patched with olive orchards, there lined off with rows of mulberry trees ; here lustrous with bowing wheat, there dotted with clumps of dark cypresses. Close below us are Fontvielle and the windmill of Daudet, could we but make it out; and yonder, scarcely visible, stands the church of Les Saintes Maries where Mirèio found consolation for her sweet grief. Still farther away a whitish spot on the scorched horizon represents Arles ; while to the left, in the extreme distance, a bright streak of silver marks the edge of the Mediterranean, the *étang* of Berre.

Les Baux was once a capital, and some eight thousand people jostled where now perhaps a dozen exist. The wind of ruin has passed this way. Undermined by the policy of Richelieu and overwhelmed by his wrath, the castle and the town perished. The population is lizards by day and bats by night Doors are open but not in welcome, windows unshuttered but not for faces. Here is a carving that Revoil admired, but the portal it adorns is used only by strangers. Everywhere we see great masses apparently ready to fall ; vast breaches, crumbled halls, stairways lacking steps, ramparts broken off, sentry walks ending in mid-air The wind whistles in the crevices, and roars

through the chambers   It is all a picture of desolation.
Men determined to build habitations that should never
pass away ; the habitations remain but the men are gone,
and we realize that an empty city is more melancholy
than a buried one, sadder than one dissolved in the earth.

The frame accentuates the picture

We stand hundreds of feet above the plain.   At our feet
descends a precipice almost sheer, graced a little with
dwarfish almond trees that shimmer in the sunlight.   To
the left runs the long crest of the Alpines, bent forward
like an immense billow ready to break   Twenty gorges
zigzag down between the crags.   We look around upon an
amphitheatre of rocks, a panorama of concentric abysses, a
cataclysm of gigantic blocks, colorless and shapeless, and
hung at random to bedeck frightful chasms   We see
the footprints of the earthquake, and the handiwork of
the lightnings.   Here lived the witches.   Here opens the
Valley of Hell, piercing far into the mountain, the home
of the bats.   Here came Mirèio to the fearful grotto of
the elves

Les Baux forced Dumas to pray, and it was Les Baux
that set Mistral dreaming.[6]   Dante came here brooding
over the Inferno, and this has been thought his pattern
for the scenery of hell.[7]

In such an eyrie dwelt the lords Del Bauz, and the
eagles did not discredit their nest.   About sixteen years
before Hugh Capet shut up the last of Charlemagne's race
in the tower of Orléans and founded the monarchy of
France, Pons and Profecta built a home on this rock.[8]
The strong hot blood of Ligurian chiefs, their fathers,
beat hard in their veins, and for centuries it kept the
pulses of their children bounding.

We feel ourselves in the presence of those intrepid lords.
Among these rocks they lived and plotted and threatened
and sometimes fought   This is the precipice down which

they hurled their enemies.   Yonder stands a bit of their
castle, no ordinary fortress built of stone, but hewn out
of the living rock, a limb of the mountain.   Here bloomed
many a fair lady, too, like a gleam of sunshine amid the
tempest ; and in a later time the lovely Passe Rose, the
fairest of them all.   Here Vaqueiras was welcomed and a

THE CASTLE OF LES BAUX.

host of other troubadours, for after the tilting came the
feast, and after the battle came " dance and Provençal
song."

But Les Baux was a state as well as a city; and, though
the fortune of war was sometimes harsh, its lords were
supposed to own seventy-nine burgs scattered up and
down from the Rhone to the Alps, and from the sea to
the northern side of Vienne.   Far wider still was the
scope of their activity.   As counts, princes, kings, po-
destas, generals, and admirals they kept the world in commotion all the way around from Spain to Sicily.   Their

titular possessions reached even to Achaia, and they
finally called themselves Emperors of Constantinople.
Every turn of fortune, every twist of policy, every brilliant scheme, every bold deed, every virtue, every vice,
and every tragedy of the mediæval noble were illustrated
in their house. On their blood-red banner blazed a mystical star of white, the star that guided their ancestor—
so they asserted—to the infant Christ.⁹ "As it may,
Balthasar," rang out their strange battle-cry.¹⁰ It sounded
like a challenge to fate, and as a challenge fate accepted it.

Prince Guilhem, Raimbaut's patron, was typical of the
family. Talented, brilliant, bold, and ambitious, he was
also scheming, unscrupulous, grasping, violent, and rash.
His life was a checkerboard, and the squares were luck
and misfortune. Falling out one time with a neighbor,
Aimar the Second, count of Die and Valence, he ravaged
a part of his estates, but as he came down the Rhone in a
boat some fishermen of Aimar's captured him. Doubtless his ransom was vexation enough, but it was even
worse to have Gui of Cavaillon ridicule him in verses that
everybody sang

Once he seized a French merchant on the highway and
plundered him of no little wealth. "And the merchant,"
says the Provençal account, "went and made complaint
before the king of France, and the king told him that he
could not right the wrong   it was too far away   'But I
give you my word' [he said] 'that you may get satisfaction in whatever way you can'   And the burgher went
and had the king's ring counterfeited, and had letters
written [as] from the king to Lord Guilhem del Bauz, that
he should come to the king, promising him great benefits
and great honors and great gifts. And when Guilhem
del Bauz had the letters, he rejoiced greatly therefor and
prepared grandly to go to the king   And he set out and
came to the city of which was the merchant he had robbed,

for he knew not whence the merchant was. And the
burgher when he knew that Lord Guilhem was within the
city, caused him to be seized and all his companions.
And he agreed to restore all that he had taken and repair
all the harm ; and he went away poor, despoiled." Not
a smile ripples the demureness of the narrator, but we
may be sure there was laughter inextinguishable in the
merchant's town that night."

With such a lord Raimbaut's existence could not fail to
be a lively one. His duty was to act in all things as the
comrade, partisan, and *alter ego* of his chief. Guilhem
was himself a poet, and of course Raimbaut made verses
with him. Guilhem found himself at odds with Raimon
the Fifth, the count of powerful Toulouse ; and Raimbaut
not only rode to battle at his side, but composed martial
sirventes to encourage their allies and reproach the friends
that abandoned them " " While one is young," he sang,
" one should follow war and chivalry ; repose is fitting
only for the agèd." And when real strife subsided into
the mimic warfare of the tourney Raimbaut helped in the
tilting as an esquire, and at the feasting as a minstrel.

We have a poem that he composed for such an occasion ;
and while the splendor of tournaments is painted for us
by Scott and Ariosto, Raimbaut gives us a precious touch
of their every-day-ness Here we find ourselves not upon
the stage before the bright eyes of an audience, but in the
wings laughing in our sleeves. Dragonet's charger gets
frisky, pitches his master heels over head upon the ground,
and gallops off delighted The count of Beaucaire's fine
grey is relieved of *his* burden by the lord of Monlaur.
Barral of Marseille (mark the name) comes on in fine
array, but soon is thrown whirling into a vine-arbor and
falls head first, as limp as a drowned man. Presently he
revives, gives chase to his steed, and catches him by an
ear. Another baron goes down before an esquire riding

a nag so lean that one can see the large vein in her neck. Another has his helmet crushed on his head, and the bits fall to the ground , everybody laughs and then he laughs, too, crying out that he minds it not a whit. So goes the fun.[13]

Trouble was pretty sure to arise between two such men. Raimbaut was bent on growing. No trifler was he, content with careless joys. The uncertainties of life impressed him and he saw the need of prudence. " When a man is unfortunate," he sang once, " people say it was from lack of sense " ; " Wise and considerate would he be who would give as good counsel before one is in trouble as afterward " , " No man can be well-informed who does not often observe that one goes up and another down, and does not take pains both to make friends while he can, and once made to retain them " He was always thinking and studying, and forever conning romantic and martial tales, of which apparently he had a collection. In one way or another he acquired at least four idioms besides his vernacular · French, Gascon, Genoese, and Portuguese [14] In music and poetry, in arms and in the graces of courtly life, he was constantly striving to perfect himself. Prudent, studious, and always gaining ground he appeared, no doubt, rather shrewd and even calculating ; for it is among the misfortunes of the talented poor, that in reaching the place designed for them by nature they must pass others on the way, and must seem to love advantages which they only wish to set their feet upon.

Evidently the prince observed that Raimbaut was getting on. It struck him that he was making the most of his opportunities. He thought of the lowly youth of Vaqueiras, compared him with the courtly troubadour, reflected on the horses, arms, and clothing he had given him, forgot half the services rendered in exchange, and finally concluded that he had been too generous and the other man too grasping Raimbaut reflected no less, and recalled many a brusque word and many a haughty fashion of his lord. A tenso ended it.[15] Raimbaut reminded the prince of that mishap on the Rhone, and likened him to a pike on the fisher's hook ; and the prince retorted that Raimbaut cared only for what he could get, and would some day be pronounced as crazy as Peirol, his father. Friendship outlived this quarrel—at least on the part of Raimbaut ; but none the less he felt that the time to separate had come, and so transferred his residence to the court of Aimar, himself a lover and maker of rhymes.

Here perhaps he might have settled for the rest of his life, but a lady made his fortune. Unable to win her love the poet threatened he would leave her and home, and go to try his fortune at Tortona. This, too, was in vain. True to his word Raimbaut replenished his purse as he could, looked well to his horse and harness, donned his best apparel, said his adieus, and viol in hand mounted and rode away for Italy.[16]

This period of wandering minstrelsy, beginning we do not know exactly when and lasting we cannot say just how long, was precisely in keeping with his profession. All the troubadours that made a livelihood of their art roamed more or less after this manner, true knights-errant of song. There were no music halls, no opera houses, no reading public then ; to make their talents bear interest they must find a patron who would borrow them, and to find they must seek. The travel itself, too, was of the greatest value. Their wits were sharpened, their feelings deepened, their versatility broadened, their skill practised, their store of songs and anecdotes replenished, their knowledge of things and of people enriched. Gifts often repaid their efforts ; honors and praise were still more plentiful. Bright eyes flashed for them, and many a time the wicket gate of a gentle heart opened softly at their knock.

There was another side Even in New England, musicians playing at a rich country house are sometimes invited to dine with the servants. Even in London the chief use of a drawing-room singer is often to furnish the accompaniment for a chorus of talk Raimbaut probably concluded that the Lombards deserved their reputation for stinginess. He sometimes found a baron rude, no doubt ; he had chased a stag all day in vain. The next lord was a boor and preferred wine to song. At another time a jealous lover forced a quarrel upon him. Not long afterward it was a brace of robbers that put his life in jeopardy More than once the castle gate refused to open Darkness was upon him, and the storm. Inn there was none. How the cold wind sifted and the shower drenched him ! Famished besides, he urged his horse along the rough and broken road till he found an abandoned hut, open to the wind, the roof half gone. In the dry corner he bestowed his viol, the horse had the next best—for viol and horse were essentials ; and so he passed the night as he could. What a sorry spectacle he was in the morning, his fine clothes pressed in wrinkles, and not a denier in his purse ! But he only muttered to himself as we find him saying once in a poem, " A man forges cold iron who thinks he can make a gain without a loss "

Love affairs were a part of his vocation, and these too sometimes went awry. Once—whether at this time or earlier we cannot be sure—he made love to a lady of Genoa, and we know from a waggish poem of his own how he fared." Bowing low, the troubadour began ·

" Earnestly have I besought, lady, that you would be pleased to love me, for I am your slave For you are noble and accomplished, and endowed with all good qualities, and therefore your friendship gives me delight. [And] since you possess every courtly grace, my heart is fixed upon you as upon no other lady of Genoa. There-

fore it will be an act of mercy, if you love me ; and then
shall I be more amply repaid than if the city of the
Genoese were mine, with all the riches gathered therein.''

" Mountebank," she answered, " you are a boor to tease
me for what I will not think of doing. Your friend I will
not be, were it only to spite you. I 'll be the death of
you now, [you] cursèd Provençal . .   Never will I
love you, for I have a husband handsomer than you are,
—*that* I know. Off with you, friar , ill take you ! ''

This was harsh enough, but the troubadour was the
priest of a new cult,—that grace of manner, that courtliness of bearing which it was the great achievement of the
upper classes in the twelfth century to create. Without a
wince he began again :

" Fair and prudent lady, sprightly, excellent and discerning, let your own penetration be my helper, for you
are controlled by noble spirit (*joi*) and young-heartedness,
by courtliness and love of distinction and wisdom, and by
good ideas of every sort ; wherefore I am your faithful
lover without reservation,—sincere, humble, and beseech-
ful ; so strongly am I beset and overpowered by that love
for you, which is my delight. And so it will be sagacity
to make me your lover and friend.''

" Mountebank, you seem out of your head, to talk to
me in that fashion. Ill to you coming, ill to you going
(*mal vignai, e mal andei*) ! You have n't sense enough
for a cat. Why do you hate me so ? What a bad thing
you seem to be ! . . . Do you take me for a stupid ?
Faith, you 'll have me not ! If you can't get on without
my love you 'll freeze to death this year. The Provençals
are outrageous rascals ! ''

So went the journey ; but finally after many such ups
and downs the troubadour arrived at Tortona.[18]

How his brave heart was beating, as with a new mantle
and a fresh mount he pricked gaily down the broad valley

that the Po sends up toward the Ligurian Alps, and came
in sight of the same ruined castle that dominates the town
to-day,—then with the moss of less than fifty years upon
it. As he drew yet nearer he plucked softly at the strings
of his viol to see if they were still unbroken, and now at
the gate he began to plume and poise himself, conning
fair phrases and counting his chances of a favorable reception.

A favorable reception he was given, indeed, and not then
only but every time he came, with many smiles, glances,
compliments, and cordial pressures of the hand, but at the
end of a laborious year he could not discover so much as
an inch of progress. He was completely mystified, and
words that he has used explain quite clearly why. The
lady would not let him go. She vowed she loved him.
She praised him and fêted him and even petted him; but—
whenever he tried to come nearer, she suddenly found that
she had a grievance against him. How could he have
been so forgetful, so cruel ? How could he have slighted
her so ? For a whole week he had not been to see her.
He was false ; he loved another. Then came a debate,
protestations, and tears, and a general misunderstanding
followed, only to be cancelled by a new song or two and
redoubled attentions,—at least, so it would appear.

The first time that sort of thing occurred the troubadour
doubtless felt that he was a brute, the second time he was
very penitent, the third time he was deeply sorry, the
fourth time he realized that he did not understand it, the
fifth time he thought nothing at all, and the sixth time he
became suspicious. At last he resolved to clear up the
mystery, and so composed a song to this effect " :

" Well I know that when I despair of love, I sacrifice the
fairest fame, for love makes the worthiest more noble and
betters even the worst. It makes the cowardly brave, the
awkward lovable, and the poor as rich as kings. Truly I

TORTONA.

find so much in her to praise that I would gladly be her lover were my love returned.   But she must not set too high a value upon her beauty, her cleverness, her cordial smiles, and her sweet words.   She must not fancy that she can have me for a servant, because the noblest praise her, and she sees in her mirror the brilliancy of the crystal and the ruby.   She must not imagine that I have lost all control over my heart   If she will listen to my prayer, I am hers to command ; but if she wish someone to pick quarrels with, let her find another suitor.   And yet, dear one, Floris when he took leave of Blancheflor was not so wretched as I shall be if we must part.''

It was well that the troubadour fell back on common sense, for the lady was only making sport of him all the time.   It was a fine thing to have a talented poet composing songs about her.   Such a man was valuable, and worth a few smiles.   But as for love, the marquis of Malaspina— he was the man , and so, when the issue was forced, she threw Raimbaut over with a biting sarcasm.

The Marquis Albert of Malaspina had been behind the mystery all the while.[20]   A younger son of a great house, clever, fearless, and dashing, and a poet besides, he was an important figure in Piedmont though in truth only a reckless adventurer.   His castle stood not far away, and he was allied with Tortona in her war against Genoa.   All the advantages in the rivalry were his ; and, to make it still worse for Raimbaut, Albert had seen him in dire straits at Pavia,—in fact had given him aid.   We can easily imagine how the picture of the poor '' fiddler '' was drawn for the lady's eye,—his drooping nag, his dingy clothes, his dismal air, and how the two laughed together over his aspirations, his tenderness, and his devotion , for their pleasures had exactly the needed contrast as they exchanged witticisms over the poor devil Raimbaut, galloping gloomily into the hills that very moment.

Not content with this, Albert attacked him publicly
with a tenso .²¹ " Tell me, Raimbaut, if it please you : is
it a fact that the lady you have been singing so much
about has jilted you, as people say ? "   I think Raimbaut
must have felt a grim joy when his enemy came out into
the open, and thus challenged him to a duel of wits   His
brand was out in a twinkling.   Four times they closed.
The marquis taunted him with poverty and ill success in
love , Raimbaut paid him back with reminders of folly,
of perjury and broken faith, of robberies on the highway,
of battles lost and of distrust won.

Our hero felt keenly the lady's treatment , but he bore it
manfully, reflecting, perhaps, that the true heart is least
ready to suspect and guard against the false.   There was
much remaining to live for, and he was able to sing : " It
is not so difficult to win honor and happiness even without
love, if one strive aright.   Though love deserts me I will
achieve all the good I can.   Though I lose my lady, I
will not lose my fame and my talent.   I can still exist
with honor, and there is no need of doubling my hurt."

His thoughts went naturally to the field of war, and
his battle-cry revealed his true quality .

> In heat and cold to come and go,
>   To trot and gallop, run and leap,
>   To toil and suffer, scarce to sleep,—
>   This is the life I 'm now to know ,
> My inn the roadside or the grove at best,
> With iron and steel and ashen spear oppressed,
>   With stern sirvente instead of love and song,
>   The weak will I defend against the strong.²²

Time and suffering had not been lost.

Neither had the poet failed of all success, for though a
lady had not been found a patron had been.   The young
lord with whom he had sung, campaigned, and gone a-
wooing during his former visit in Italy, had begun to

reign (1187) as Bonifaz I., Marquis of Monferrat, and he welcomed the troubadour as both a guest and a friend." The novitiate in poetry, arms, and love was over ; and Raimbaut, a mature man of about thirty years, now began the real work of his life."

But what became of his earlier patron, Guilhem del Bauz ?

No one of his extraordinary family gained so high a title, and no one met so terrible an end as he did   By siding with the French invaders against the count of Toulouse and the Albigensians he realized the ambition of his family, and was able to call himself the " King of Arles and Vienne " " Exulting in success and pride he rode haughtily and happily down the hill of Orange one day (1218), crossed the meadows full of buttercups and narcissus, and went his royal way, joyous with memories of love and song.   Before night the men of Avignon caught him, flayed him alive, cut him in pieces, and hung up his dripping members over the gates of their town.

MONFERRAT

Raimbaut de Vaqueiras (*Concluded*)

MONFERRAT—in Italian *Monferrato*—lies in the rugged and untravelled region between Milan, Genoa, and Turin. Charlemagne planted an outpost of his empire there, and the Frankish earl appointed to govern it became the founder of a brilliant line of marquises.

None of them was nobler, however, than Guilhem the Third, the father of Bonifaz, and we find a charming portrait of him in a Lombard chronicle : " Of medium height, well made and strongly knit, with a full and rosy face and hair almost white, eloquent, virtuous and wise, blithe and jovial, magnificent yet not prodigal.'' Courage and the spirit of enterprise never forsook him ; and assuming the cross late in life, he spent his last years battling for his grandson, Baldwin the Fifth, in Palestine

The sons proved worthy of their sire. William Longaspada, as we know him in English histories of the crusades, became the count of Joppa and Ascalon and finally the king of Jerusalem Conrat, whom Scott in his uncritical fashion misrepresented in *The Talisman*, was the king of Tyre. Bonifaz, too, won a crown , and in the next generation a daughter of Bonifaz, Agnes, became the empress of the East.[1]

The region about Casale still abounds in reminders of

this noble family.[2] To the west is Chivasso, where the
marquises had their court sometimes ; and one may see
there, hard by the parish church, a rectangular tower
once belonging to their residence. To the south of west
rises *bellissimo* Moncalvo a thousand feet above the
Gulf of Genoa, spreading its wide promenade grandly to
the sun, and exhibiting, in the church of San Francesco,
a pair of standards taken by them from the infidels. Only
five miles from Casale, to the east of south, lies Occimiano
with a hill for a pillow and a torrent at its feet, and in
this town—their usual residence—meagre traces of fortifications are still to be seen.

Casale itself, though not so closely associated with our
history, is by no means a place to be overlooked. Picturesque hills encompass it, and only a little way distant
flows the Po, here a shifting, shiftless affair, roaming
about within low banks of sand and gravel, but still a
river, gleaming brightly through a screen of poplars.
Flanking three large cities as it does, the position is one
to catch the eye of a strategist, and from the time of the
Lombards there has always been a fortress here. The
walls are still formidable, though the children race up and
down their approaches unterrified , and the castle and the
citadel still re-echo to the clash of arms, as they have done
for more than a thousand years.

Within the ramparts there is many a quaint mediæval
corner, as I soon discovered in exploring the crooked place
with neither guide nor map There is also a certain professor in bronze in one of the squares, where I always
arrived sooner or later when I lost my way ; and I shall
never forget how his domical forehead rose higher each
time, his preposterous foretop of hair peaked itself more
sharply, the twist of his features grew still more cate-
chetical, and with more and more severity he seemed just
removing his eye-glasses and demanding. '' Tell me now,

how did you get here, and what do you come here *for?*"
Palaces, too, may be found, if one care to look for them,

A CORNER IN CASALE.

and — best of all — broad shady walks by the ancient bastions. Here the imagination feels quite at home. When the moon comes out of her cloud even the tall chimneys of the furnaces outside the town, craning their necks for a peep within, look picturesque and romantic; and Monte Rosa, dominating the keen line of Alps in the northwest, seems in very truth a "dread ambassador from earth to heaven," returning like the great lawgiver with a face too holy to be looked upon.

But for us the chief attraction of Casale is the central market-place, where the booths have been set up for the morning traffic, and a sharp-faced woman on a stool is glibly telling fortunes by the cards. At the time we have reached (1198), the people of the town rebelled against their master-city, Vercelli, and Bonifaz' aided them. Here, though with no positive certainty, we feel that we are upon the track of Raimbaut the soldier. Knighted by Bonifaz and made his brother-in-arms as the most signal mark of confidence and regard, he fought side by side with his lord; and we can fancy them riding to-

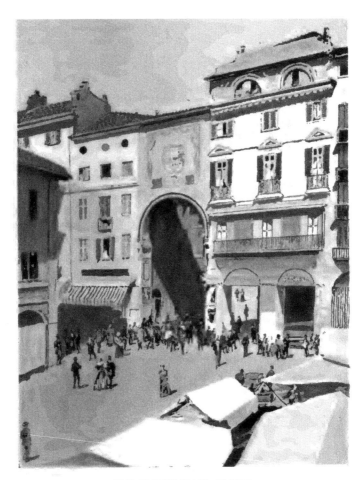

THE MARKET-PLACE, CASALE.

gether into this market-square followed by a goodly plump
of spears,—the brave air of the marquis weighted with
cares of state, and the troubadour's no less martial face
lightened with poetic thoughts.

For though he forswore love Raimbaut had enough to
do We have a long poem of reminiscences that he addressed to Bonifaz, and from that we can picture his manner of life.' Even when he was in Italy as a youth of
eighteen or twenty years, the two distinguished themselves by deeds worthy of a riper age. " The first thing
a young man of rank has to do," says the poet in this
piece, " is to decide whether he will gain renown or let it
go." Bonifaz resolved upon the path of honor and with
him went Raimbaut. Thenceforth when duty called or
glory beckoned, no danger was feared Just after supper
one evening news was brought that Lady Jacobina was to
be carried off to Sardinia, and married against her will.
Bonifaz and Raimbaut with a few others mounted instantly and rode all night. In the morning Raimbaut
snatched the lady from her captors, and back they turned
pursued by foot and horse. Suddenly they were confronted by a body of hostile Pisans : and hiding as best
they could they heard trumpets and bugles on all sides,
and saw the flashing lights of their pursuers. For two
days there was nothing to eat or drink. When at last it
appeared safe to venture forth, twelve bandits fell upon
them. Leaping to the ground Raimbaut led the attack,
and though wounded in the neck succeeded with the aid
of two others in routing them. For dinner one loaf supplied the company, and after eating they pushed on to
Nice. The lady was married the next day to her true
love, and then for dowry Bonifaz compelled a usurping
uncle to restore her patrimony.

At the assault on Quarto, Raimbaut flew to rescue
Bonifaz when the marquis, with scarcely ten companions,

was fighting against four hundred. There, too, he had the satisfaction of helping save Albert de Malaspina's life At Messina he found Bonifaz surrounded,—darts, arrows and splintered lances at his breast and throat ; and unmindful of himself covered him with his shield. At Palermo and at numberless other places he was among the first that mounted the wall, and he was able to remind his lord : " No man can say against me that I ever wished to be away from you in war or feared to die for your glory."

But Raimbaut was not the man to give up love for ever because Tortona was false , and indeed he could not, for the world required him as a knight and a troubadour to pay homage to some fair lady. The marquis had a daughter, Biatritz (Beatrice), worthy to be the ideal of any poet and soldier, and Raimbaut came to love her. One day when she thought herself unobserved she caught up her brother's sword, and went through the manual of blows and thrusts as she had seen them practised.' Raimbaut saw her, and after that celebrated her in his poems as the Fair Knight , for it was a custom with troubadours to conceal the identity of their ladies under fictitious names. Biatritz understood very well that he was dying for love of her, and of course others knew the same ; yet the poet dared not avow his passion, though he kept on singing of her beauty, and gained for her many admirers and friends, as we read

This brings us face to face with courtly, chivalric love, the gospel of the troubadours ; and we must pause a little to make sure of understanding the matter.

It was love for married women,'—not in every case (probably Biatritz was unmarried), but certainly as a rule, and the fact staggers us. At first we are inclined to say as Mistral once thought at a ball in St. Remy, and as Daudet felt in writing *Numa Roumestan* " The Midi is

polygamous ! " And yet, directly opposed to Christianity
as this love appears in some of its principles and results,
it could have existed only in the bosom of a Christian
civilization. That is not all. " Ask and ye shall receive " , to this distinctly Christian doctrine has been
traced the courtly principle that love could not be resisted. One more step must be taken ; the central truth
of the gospel is the saying of St. John, " God is love,"
and by simply reversing this we obtain the central principle of the chivalric poets, " Love is God." More or less
consciously, more or less honestly, somewhat Christianly,
somewhat paganly, this principle was undoubtedly held
and followed. And so, as Jeanroy says, " If one place
before his mind what a Christian thinks of God and of his
greatness and power, of the duties owed him, and the joys
awaiting the pious, he will obtain an accurate idea of the
troubadour's feeling toward love."

A glance at history, too, will help us understand this
matter. In the dark and brutal ages the Latin *uxor*,
legitimate wife, had vanished, and all over Roman Europe
the names *femina* and *muher* came to be used, suggesting,
as Carducci has remarked, something similar to concubin-
age This degraded matrimony . and the looseness of its
bonds became so great that the maternal relationship
superseded the paternal in importance,—fatherhood was
recognized as uncertain. Men married simply because
women could inherit and transmit wealth, and because
they wished legal children to succeed them. The heiress
and the mother were valued ; wives were only " married
women." Naturally matrimony came to be servitude for
the women, a bond forced upon them by the ambition and
interest of their guardians [6] , and since love is by the nature of things free and spontaneous, people came soberly
to the conclusion that love and matrimony were essentially incompatible [7] As Martin has declared, " The

feudal marriage deserved this anathema"; and while women had more privileges in the Midi than in many other regions, the sentence applied even there.

Rebellion and revolution were inevitable, unless womankind were to become something else than human. "Resistance to tyrants is obedience to God."

Wives could not be expected to remain contentedly at home in a state of semi-imprisonment under the guard of a menial, the *guirbaudo*, while their husbands cantered freely about on quests of gallantry. As a troubadour sang of them, "Anybody would drink even water rather than die of thirst," and ladies wedded by compulsion to lords who cared absolutely nothing about their wishes or feelings took such love as came within reach. In time society found it best to allow them a safety-valve, and they were permitted to receive the homage and praise of knights and poets and listen to their passionate avowals, with the understanding that nothing beyond the line of decorum should be done We shall see Bonifaz endorsing Raimbaut's love for his daughter, and the proud Richard Plantagenet urging another troubadour to woo his married sister

Indeed the ideal must compel our own admiration : a man and a woman drawn together solely through congeniality, and wedded in spirit wholly above the plane of ordinary relations ; he, serving with boundless affection of the heart and boundless devotion of the will, living only to win distinction through courtly words and chivalric deeds, and laying his trophies at her feet in utter forgetfulness of self : she, ever mindful both of love and of duty, rewarding every act of service with appreciation and praise, and crowning every achievement with the shining diadem of her approval In this beautiful way the might of love was employed to conquer the other passions and purify itself at the same time.'

Was this the reality of courtly love ? Sometimes. The kiss received by a lover as his pledge of acceptance was often the only one he ever gained. It was common to be suspected of faults that did not exist, and to boast of favors not received. There was certainly less immorality than a suspicious reader of the literature would imagine. But whatever is higher than the ground risks a fall. " Hot blood o'erleaps a cold decree," and formal became too often passionate love. It was a great thing for humanity that the ideal existed, but humanity could not fully attain unto it. Men did not live in their heads then, but in their whole bodies : not in the spirit, but in the flesh. An insult meant a blow, a feeling meant an act. Life was bold, energetic, physical. In a world still half barbaric, occasional coarseness and even outbursts of startling brutality were inevitable. War was the business of life, and tremendous passions were a necessity. Married women were as a rule the only ones met in society. It was difficult for a man to have the word love on his tongue very long without having its fire in his heart, and the fire was liable to involve the other heart

Then, too, there was much besides the contagion of love to tempt the fair sex. While a woman married was a chattel, a woman really loved was a queen. As Gaston Paris has pointed out, the danger she incurred earned her the utmost devotion of her lover and seemed a justification of every caprice ; while he, conscious that she could withdraw her favor at any moment, was compelled to stand on a plane of inferiority, humility, and timidity that exalted her immeasurably. She could require deeds of surpassing courage and greatness as the proofs of his devotion, and the honor of them was accounted more hers than his. And no doubt, as the perils of illicit love attracted the adventurous knight, its intrigues had an equal charm for women of leisure. So let us admit that not seldom courtly love became real passion, and yet firmly deny that the troubadour world can fairly be termed " corrupt " [10]

What shall we say of this system as it actually worked ? We must call it wrong, right, and necessary. Neither is this a paradox. Treason is odious yet we revere Washington, and the case must always be judged according to the circumstances   It is impossible to see how, as the world was, anything but love could have raised humanity from its almost bestial state   As we saw at Aix there was little else to quicken men's intellects ; and the love needed to be insecure and uncertain, hard to win, scantily enjoyed, fruitful of mental strains, and retained only through incessant efforts after fresh distinction.   William, afterwards known as the Conqueror, when he first met Emma, his wife-to-be, seized her and threw her to the ground as an evidence of his love.   In England a future queen had to take refuge in a convent from the lust and violence of the nobles.   But in the land of the troubadours, a lover knelt before his lady, and pledged himself to strive for excellence and for distinction.   Blacatz, a great baron and troubadour, even sang to his lady that should a worthier than he appear, it would be her duty to transfer her affections

" By their fruits ye shall know them." This love concentrated men's faculties and fixed their wills   It gave them both a noble purpose and the power to achieve it nobly.   It made life poetical ; and, in the language of the troubadours, love and poetry were expressed by the same word.   Few may have reached the ideal, but it is more important to remember that many strove.   Out of the crude fighting-man was thus forged the gentleman, and barbarism was started on the road to culture   In this way, besides having the beauty of poetry and something of the sacredness of religion, love became, as Carducci defines it, " the formal expression of the highest civil ideal, the supreme principle of all virtue, of all moral worth and of all glory," and the troubadour Miraval informs us that when a man made a failure of life, all said, " It is evident that he did not care for the ladies "

In short, just then and just there loving another man's wife was in truth a means of grace and a hope of glory; it saved woman from despair and ruin , and, as men prize what they see prized by others, it had a tendency, besides its other good effects, to make them appreciate and love their own wives "

These ideas well settled in our minds, let us return to Monferrat and Raimbaut de Vaqueiras.

There is one spot more interesting than any of those I have named, if we may trust the historian of Casale, the " studious and erudite " Berardi, as Carducci calls him. Not far distant from Occimiano eastward lies Pomaro, and above the village on a rugged and woody hill stands the Castle of the Vale, *Castello della Valle*. It is comparatively a modern edifice, but happily not the whole of it. On the northern side rise three battlemented towers dating from an earlier time, and with these we may associate with reasonable confidence the chief event of Raimbaut's personal and poetic history.

A summer day was drawing to its close, and silence reigned in the hall of the castle. Near a window stood the table that was usually fixed in one corner of such a room, in this case a handsome piece of work made of oak from the slope of Monte Rosa and ornamented with a running vine cut in the edge. Beside the table was a chair of the same rich wood, its arms carved as lion's paws and its high back rising into the shape of a coronet. The chair was occupied by a lady, the only person in the hall, and from a poem by Peire Vidal we are able to sketch her portrait,—black hair, thick and long, eyebrows rather heavy, a nose as much of the falcon type as beauty would permit, eyes that shot " arrows of delight wrought in the fire of love and tempered with sweetness," and in all her bearing an air befitting her princely, royal, and imperial family, for the lady was Biatritz de Monferrat.

THE CASTLE OF THE VALE.

Looking up from her work—she was embroidering with gold a little banner of crimson silk—she rested her arm upon the edge of the table and looked out through the casement, where sprays of ivy wrought their dancing patterns on the glass. Below the castle the torrential Grana hurried on to bury its restless waters in a calmer stream. Not far away the strands of the Po itself, ruffled by the breeze, gleamed through their light veil of willows and poplars. Beyond lay the wide rich valley of Piedmont, curving like a shell toward the north into distant hills toned by the light haze of a summer afternoon, beyond which, canopied by a sapphire sky, sate the royal conclave of the Alps, robed in the white samite of eternal snows.

In the doorway behind the lady appeared the figure of a man, and as it paused there a long moment we may sketch this portrait also. It was a form somewhat above medium height, shapely but spare and muscular, graceful but suggestive of the tilt-yard rather than the boudoir. The face, martial and bronzed, had features that were both striking and agreeable,—a long nose, keen and straight and bent slightly to the left, the ears of a king, as Mistral would say, and large, deep, and luminous blue eyes The ample forehead was ploughed with two strong furrows from side to side, and a short one cleaving the eyebrows The blonde hair seemed thin and greyish on the temples, and worn a little all around by the helmet ; and two curving wrinkles at the corners of the mouth, in the edge of a crisp and closely cut beard, suggested that bitter draughts had passed that way

With the air of one who understands that he is risking everything, Raimbaut came forward slowly to the corner, sat down upon a stool that was there, and bent forward over the table till he could look across the lady's face.

" Gracious lady," he began, " may I dare to ask your counsel ? I love one who is far above me, so beautiful, so noble that . . . I have no right . . . What shall I do ? Shall I hide my love still and die, or shall I open my heart to her ? Counsel me,—in the name of God ! "

With splendid composure Biatritz replied, as the Provençal narrative tells us :

" Raimbaut, it is very right that every true lover, if he love a high-born lady, should fear to declare his love. But I counsel him that rather than die he tell it to her, and beseech her to accept him as servitor and friend. And I do firmly assure you that if she be wise and courtly, she will not take it amiss nor [count it] as dishonor, but

will esteem him the more and regard him as the better
man for it   And you I counsel that you declare your
heart and wish to the lady whom you love, and pray her to
take you for her knight, since you are such as no lady in
the world should scorn for knight and servitor.   .   "

Then Raimbaut rose, and coming before Lady Biatritz
fell upon his knee, and confessed that it was herself whom
he loved.   That she knew right well and she loved him in
return, but she knew also that her family was great and
that Raimbaut was of no estate   She knew that her
brother had given him all that he possessed.   She knew
that she could banish him from Monferrat for what he had
just said.   For an instant her pride flashed, and she looked
at him as if she meant, " You dare all ?   Then lose all ! "
The troubadour's glance replied, " Then naught is worth
saving."   Another flash ; and, her black eyes opening wide
their violet depths, she melted from Brunhilde into Francesca da Rimini   Still another, and she was herself again.

" You are welcome, Raimbaut," she said with noble
simplicity.   And then she bade him strive " to excel in
word and in deed and in worth," and told him, with plain
reminders of her duty and her honor, that she accepted
him as her knight and servitor

Other words passed then which need not be repeated;
and the same proud, grand spirit filled them all.   Looks
told more than speech ; but even the messages of the
lovers' eyes were knightly and controlled.   Intensity of
feeling shunned instead of seeking the endearments of a
shallow passion.   Everything was high and measured.
But none the less—nay, all the more—it was also true,
beautiful, profoundly significant, and when, finally, the
troubadour begged for a lock of hair as the pledge of
love, it was given him,—frankly, superbly, like the love
itself.[12]

Raimbaut's candles burned that night until the east was

gray, but his heart was happy, and over and over he said to himself, as he sang once, " How bright is joy to the true lovers ! " Yet there were many cooling flavors in his draught of bliss It was no primrose path that he was entering, but the arduous ascent to distinction. Effort, self-denial, and many unsatisfied longings awaited him there, to be repaid by the approval of a noble woman, the satisfaction of his own heart, and the praise of the world ; and so the new poem that he sang on the morrow uttered the feelings not of a sentimentalist, but of a courtly soldier, thoroughly bent upon distinguishing himself, and rejoicing gravely as well as profoundly in the acceptance of his love.

> Now tears and sighs are mine and sleepless care,—
> The wonted pains required by Love's decree,
> Because a peerless lady counselled me
> To love the one whose graces are most fair,
> And so win praise and honor, never fearing
> Deceit or harm, for she would scorn to feign ;
> And since none equals her from main to main,
> I bring to her a love unfeigned, unveering.
>
> To one so peerless no man ever sware
> A love so high ; and matchless—as is she—
> The love I bear her as she counselled me
> Is more than Pyramus himself could bear ;
> The first in worth yet light of heart appearing,
> With dignity and bounty in her train,
> She greets the base with looks of high disdain,
> While brave and good men welcoming and cheering.
>
> E'en Percival had not a joy so rare
> When on the knight in red he set his knee,

NOTE —One of the peculiarities of Provençal verse was the carrying of rhymes from stanza to stanza The translations reproduce this peculiarity, and the effect can best be gained by reading them aloud.

As I was given when she counsellèd me;
Yet Tantalus was punished with such fare,—
    She gives her love but checks my persevering
    To taste her gift, yet I will not complain
    Young-hearted, noble, she was born to reign,
    Charming with grace and wit both sight and hearing.

Emenidus at Tyre did not compare
    With me in daring, when I urged my plea
    That you would hear my tale and counsel me,
And grant that favor of the lock of hair,
    But still, methinks, the bolder be my steering,
    The greater praise and honor I obtain,
    And one must dare so much for such a gain,
    That bliss or death is swiftly, surely nearing.

Let not my prince his love and grace forbear
    Though, to be with her, fair Orange I flee,
    For—as I'd speed in that she counselled me—
If nobler woman live, I know not where;
    And all my pride would be in volunteering
    To follow her, were mine a king's domain,
    For true to her my heart will e'er remain—
    To her alone in love and trust adhering.

    On this, Fair Knight, my tower of hope I'm rearing:
        That since no others on this earth attain
        To truth like yours, my faith cannot be vain,
    For you have counselled, and my sky is clearing.

    And while, my Queen, you find the world revering
        Your virtues which my valiancy explain,
        In praising you my songs will grow less plain,
    And borrow grace from beauty so endearing [13]

That Raimbaut felt nerved after this with still higher
purpose to win distinction both in arms and in poetry the
closing lines of his poem show, and in his heart he realized
all that glad impulse to great deeds which the troubadours
called "joy." But alas, his bliss was soon over. Busy

bodies, we read, gathered around the Lady Biatritz and said, "Who is this Raimbaut after all, even though the marquis *has* made a knight of him? And he dares fix his affections on a lady of your rank! Know well, it is an honor neither to you nor to the marquis" So after a time Biatritz grew angry with Raimbaut, and told him to get another love, one befitting a person of his station, and no longer dare think of her.

At that time two French joglars (jongleurs) came to the court of Monferrat, and one day they played an *estampida* that delighted their audience. Raimbaut, however, sat unmoved, revolving in his mind no doubt some of the caustic thoughts we find in his poems "Everybody gives himself trouble and labor to make slippery the happiness of true lovers"; or this, "Be handsome, graceful, and generous, but not rich. all your good qualities are naught; be he wealthy, the worst of men, the meanest rascal, is welcomed by the fair" Finally the marquis demanded of the troubadour why he was downcast, especially when so beautiful a lady as his daughter had accepted him for her knight. Raimbaut answered shortly that he could not be merry. And then the marquis, who knew the whole story, bade the Lady Biatritz intercede with Raimbaut, and beg him for the sake of her love to be joyous again. That she did; and thereupon the poet, recalling the French air they had been listening to, composed upon it a song that was a marvel of skill, as delicate as the lacework of the Genoa silversmiths." Well could he feel, as once he said, "In my experience I have found that sweetness may grow out of bitterness."

Many other songs he wrote in honor of Biatritz, and among them was the famous *Carros* (war-car), which suggested the *Trionfo d'Amore* to Petrarch, and was imitated by Pulci, by Boccaccio, and, it is thought, by Dante also in a poem now lost.

An ugly war, my friend,
  The ladies hereabouts,
Like hostile towns, intend
  To wage, and all the scouts
Report they recommend
  To build immense redoubts
    With towers;
      For Biatritz o'erpowers
Her sex, and must offend
  Self-love with bitter doubts;
    Bright flowers
      Adorning verdant bowers
Resemble her, and she so far surpasses
All others, that against her come their masses,
With banners, fire, and dust through plains and passes.

The citizens attend
  To build the moat and wall,
And thither ladies wend
  Ere yet the trumpet call,
Their youth and charms to spend,
  From dignity to fall,
    I fear
      'T will cost my cavalier
Hard work to fence and fend,
  For she is graced with all
    That 's dear,
      Good, courtly, and sincere;
And just because her virtues have no measure,
She has no quiet; as, to guard his treasure,
Her father has to make stern war his pleasure.

The townfolk now descend,—
  Their war-car urge along;
Decrepit, they depend
  On buckler, strap, and thong,
And o'er their bones suspend
  Their pigskin armor strong;
    They bear
      Great bows, and quivers wear;
Their doublets well they mend

Lest rain should soak the throng ;
    Prepare
    To see what deeds they dare !
On every side they now begin to batter;
The worth of Biatritz they hope to shatter,
But were they four to one it would not matter.

    Her walls they strive to rend,
      Siege engines they complete,
    And mangonels they send ;
      Great stones against them beat ;
    Greek fire begins to ascend,
      The arrows fly like sleet ;
        They play
        Huge rams where'er they may ,
But she 'll ne'er condescend
    To yield her person,—sweet,
        And gay,
        And fair in every way.
" On, on ! Help, help ! " I hear the ladies crying;
Some cheer the others, some their slings are plying,
And some drag engines up, on them relying.

    Now Biatritz will end
      The strife,—she mounts her steed ;
    Defence her virtues lend,
      No other mail she 'll need ,
    Sure deaths o'er all impend
      That would arrest her speed ;
        With blows
        She routs where'er she goes
All that in tilt contend,
    And, spurring fast indeed,
        O'erthrows
        The war-car of her foes ;
So many she 's unhorsed and killed and taken,
The courage of those agèd folks is shaken,
And in their Troy she pens them up forsaken.

Fair Knight, no cheer, no joy have I partaken,—
No bliss, like that your love and charms awaken,
While other ladies feel dismayed, forsaken.[15]

We hear no more of inconstancy., the busybodies had
done their worst and failed.'" None the less a separation
came. The fourth crusade was proclaimed. Bonifaz, invited to become the leader of Europe (1201), met the
chiefs at Soissons in France, " and they fall at his feet,"
says Villehardouin, " with many tears, and he in turn
falls at their feet and says that he will gladly do it."
Raimbaut had at first no dream of leaving the Fair
Knight ; but his lord, his brother-in-arms, called, and the
contagion of the crusade enveloped him   Then his viol
forgot its Lydian airs and thrilled with the music of a
crusading song.

> The Maker of air and heaven, earth and sea,
> And heat and cold, and wind and rain and sky,
> Bids all the pious raise their sails and fly,
>   And he will guide us as the magian Three
>   Were led to Bethlehem ; the Turks, elated,
>   Seize plain and mountain ; God checks not the loss,
>   For we are bound, as He endured our cross,
>   To fight for Him , to live despised and hated
>   And die in shame choose they who do not go ;
>   For we are slaves to sin, as all should know,
>   But he that Jordan bathes is liberated
>
> Yet so corrupted by our sins are we
> That life is death,—a truth that all deny,
> And there is none so merry or so high
>   That cares do not offset his pride or glee,
>   Affronts and slurs the fame so dearly rated,
>   A thousand pains one pleasure light as floss ;
>   But God is bliss—for Him we take the cross,
>   And gaining Him we gain all things created ;
>   And I would rather, if God will it so,
>   Go there and die, than risk eternal woe
>   By lingering here, though crowns my brow awaited.
>
> For us God let them nail Him to the tree,
> The passion suffered, even stooped to die,

From rascally Jews bore many a taunt and lie,
  Was buffeted and bound for all to see,
    Was scourged with knots till hate itself was sated,
      Was laid on slimy timbers from a fosse,
      And wore a crown of thorns upon the cross,
  The heart is hard that is not desolated
        At all the wars and toils we undergo
        Because the land where God walked to and fro
  And lay in death, is foully desecrated.

      Shall I, Fair Knight, account my soul as dross
      For your sake whom I sing, or take the cross?
    To go, to stay—in vain have I debated;
        Your beauty, while I see you, lays me low,
        And, lonely though the company o'erflow,
    I seem to die when we are separated.[17]

The call of duty and of honor prevailed, and the troubadour went with Bonifaz. Who does not know the glory
of their achievements? Guided by the wily Venetians
the crusaders' host became an army of conquest. The
great capital that had triumphed over more than twenty
besieging armies fell before them, and the empire of the
East was theirs. Not without truth did Raimbaut sing:

      Louis' great glory scarce begins
      To equal ours, nor Charlemagne's
      Nor Alexander's; and the pains
      Of Roland and his paladins
        Ne'er won so fairly and so well
        An empire such as this we quell,
          And under our dominion bring;
          For many an emperor, duke, and king
          Have we created, and thrown down
          The walls of many a captured town.[18]

Bonifaz, narrowly missing the imperial crown, became
the king of Thessalonica and the lord of Crete, and the
troubadour was recompensed with lands and honors. His
largest hopes were far more than realized   Rich, famous,

and powerful he could recall the old watch-tower of
his little village, and reflect that he now possessed more
than all his wistful eyes had looked upon there as far
beyond him.

THE WATCH-TOWER OF VACQUEIRAS.

But the shadows did not fail to appear. His religious
fervor had received a shock. Once he had seen seven
thousand of the pious crusaders desert their standard in a
body. He knew what they were, and in bitterness of
heart he sang :

> These pilgrims, exiled and forsworn,
> Who leave us on the field, I scorn ;
>   To plead their cause is love misled,—
>   They 're all worth less alive than dead. [18]

Far worse, his Biatritz was near him no longer , and
out of his oriental splendor came this lament :

Nor spring nor winter makes me gay,
Nor leafy oaks, nor skies of blue ;
From triumphs only frets accrue,
  And heart-aches from the merriest day ;
    Ennui turns leisure into woe,
    And hopes to desperation grow ;
      It is like water to the fin
      To give my love and love to win,
        And now, cut off from this delight
        Like one in sorrow or in flight,
          To live is dying o'er and o'er,
          And pleasure weariness the more.

Fine arms, good soldiers in array,
Picks, engines, sieges, I review,
See broken ramparts old and new,
  See castles won and many a fray,
    But still the world has naught to show
    That merits love, where'er I go ;
      As errant knight I then begin
      'Mid tilts and battles, dust and din,
        To enjoy the praise, the spoil, the fight ;
        But love is wanting,—day is night,
          The world as tedious as before,
          My tuneful art but weary lore.

Then what are conquest, wealth, display?
The joy of riches once I knew—
Affection met affection true,
  And toils had gracious love for pay ;
    For one such rapture I 'd forego
    My lauds, and all I have bestow ;
      For as my gain in power has been,
      The heavier load I 've had within,
        And happiness avoids my sight,
        For I have lost my loved Fair Knight ;
          Nothing can cheer and heart restore—
          'T is *that* makes pain so deep and sore.[18]

But at last the pain ceased, for the heart no longer beat. In the year 1207 Bonifaz perished on an expedition against the Bulgarians "Alas," cries Villehardouin, "alas, how grievous a blow it was to the Emperor Henry and to all the Latins in the land to lose such a man, one of the best and most generous lords and one of the best knights of the whole world ! " and upon that he ends his chronicle as if he could no longer bear to write.

Faithful to the last, Raimbaut de Vaqueiras fell doubt-less with his brother-in-arms.[19] What a loss was that also ! Sweeter tones than his and warmer tints we shall find among his fellow poets, but no talent more broad or true, no art more excellent and personal.

As a man he commands our admiration,—sagacious, true, and brave; as a troubadour he embodied perfectly the ideas and feelings of the élite of his age, equally approved by men and by women Lord-service, lady-service, and God-service were the three great offices of the troubadour, and he was pre-eminent in each.[20] Above all, his mind, character, and life were a symmetrical whole ; his thoughts became deeds, his acts were poems.

COURTHÉZON

Raimbaut d'Aurenga

A VERY quaint little town is Courthézon, a grey cap
on a low round hill. Its mediæval walls are still
pretty solid, and the battlemented gates frown porten-
tously. But they intend no harm. They frown only to
keep in character ; and in reality, knowing right well the
fine appearance they make in their strong old age, they
think only of enjoying their distinction and enhancing
their pictorial effect with every accessory they can summon. Would you have the proof? Study a little spot
by the eastern gate.

For the space of some ten rods between the tower of the
gate and the corner turret of the wall, the rampart has
been entirely removed. The ancient moat is there still,
and the brown water slips drowsily along out of one low
arch and beneath another. Just here its inner edge is lined
with reeds, and beyond the quivering stalks and waving
blades you find a little tree-garden. At either end are
the two great towers with ivy mantled thickly upon them.
Patches of fresh grass decorate the ground   A few cac-
tuses are there, some fir trees, plane trees wreathed with
vines, and towering above them some great pines, not in
the prim and complacent mood that pines often affect, but
leaning far out over the moat—quite beyond it, four of
them—as if longing to get away to the forest   Benches

and seats of mossy stone tempt you to discover the entrance, and if you succeed you will sit for an hour or two
in the swaying glances of the sun, and watch in peace and
happiness the goings to and fro and up and down of the
dusty thoroughfare outside

Scarcely less delightful is the western gate, the Porte
du Prince, almost hidden in a bower of foliage.   Here begins the wide smooth street of the faubourg—proudly
termed the "boulevard"—encircling the wall, shaded
with handsome plane trees and lined with those essentials
of even the smallest burg, the cafés ; and here, too, in
the shadow of the tower is the *auberge* where I stay.   It
is an odd little inn, conducted not for tourists but for the
natives, and therefore it smacks richly of the country.
Everybody is at home in the public room—even the dogs,
and when a table is spread for me in a corner, they come
and rest their muzzles on my knee as I dine, gazing up
into my face with eyes half-closed, feasting in luxurious
dreams upon the savory contents of my plate, hungry
but contented and happy, like a poet musing on a fair
landscape

But their languor and my activity are broken into.
Monsieur the Mayor descends the hill with his portly
presence, issues from the gate and comes to extend a
greeting to the visitor from beyond the sea   This is delightful , so is his lecture upon the history of the town—
all delightful and much of it correct.   Then I must become acquainted with the local antiquarian, and view the
unpublished records of the principality of Orange for its
last hundred years or so.   Then I am whirled through
the town within the walls, and fresh volumes of information are spread before me with all the ardor, the rush, the
downpour of southern hospitality.   The son of the antiquarian, a young fellow just home from the *lycée*, appears.

"Monsieur is interested in ancient castles?   Assuredly

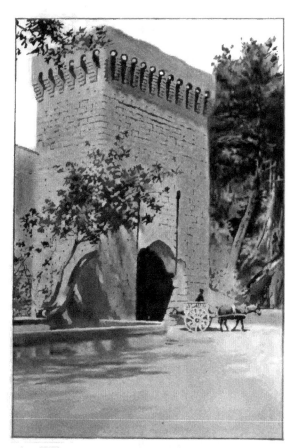

THE EASTERN GATEWAY, COURTHÉZON.

he wishes to see Châteauneuf-des-Papes and the Tour de
L'Hers, *n'est-ce pas ?* ''

Without a doubt, for will they not bring him nearer to
the Past, the troubadours ?

'' Quick, a carriage, a carriage for monsieur ! '' and
we are off,—Henri, his sister with her hair in a pigtail,
and myself

The popes loved Avignon but they loved also a full
breath of the country when spring came in, and where
could they get it so well as here ?   Beside the roads were
hedges of thick hawthorn—at any rate they are here now
—topped with sprays of bloom and bestarred with delicate
blossoms not their own   Ranks of tall cypresses, shoulder
to shoulder, were on guard against the wind.   Almond
trees began where the hedges rested.   Apricots decked
themselves early in their thick yellow-green, and the
slopes were dotted with olives and cherry trees.   No less
pleasant was the summer ; for the wind was sure to be
moving either up or down the Rhone, and could not fail
to visit the hill of Châteauneuf.   And best of all, I doubt
not, was the autumn   For on these fair slopes ripened
the grapes of Mathieu, the wine-grower and poet who was
third in the order of the Félibres ; and if he and Roumanille and Mistral, drinking of the golden juice in his
arbor out of cups brimmed with youth, dreams, and hopes,
called themselves '' pillars and chiefs of the new-born
race,'' could not popès enjoy good wine, too, and quaff
the bliss of Olympus while they quaffed its nectar ? [1]

But a pope would have been rich prey for a count or
baron to plump into his game-bag, and so the summer
house must needs be a fortress.   Yonder it stands,—at
least a corner tower of it and a good bit of wall besides.
There the Apostle of Peace could sojourn in security.
There he could keep the palace and the city of Avignon
in his eye, and if need be could exchange news by his code

of beacon lights.   And so the place is known still as
Châteauneuf-des-Papes, "the popes' new castle."

But why talk of the popes?   All that is of yesterday.
Hasten across the fields to the Tour de L'Hers.[2]   St.
Louis is said to have tarried here on the way to embark
for his crusade (1248), and tradition has it that he slept
in the castle.   He certainly must have been tempted to

THE CASTLE OF L'HERS.

rest there, for a sightlier, more picturesque tower it would
be difficult to find.   Indeed it would even make a romantic poet happy if romantic poets were capable of happiness,
—so Théophile Gautier wrote as he sailed by in a fit of
despondency.   But the castle is really much older than
St. Louis, dating farther back than even the oldest of the
troubadours.   And it is easy to see why.   Just beside it
flows that swift and abounding river—still a divinity in
the heart of many a peasant—of which the Provençal
boasts, "He that has drunk up the sea may drink up the
Rhone"; and the Rhone, violent though it be, the im-

petuous offspring of one hundred and sixty glaciers, coming down from the Alps like a wild bull rushing to the sea, has never been able to drive back the fleets. In spite of itself, in spite of the fury that so impressed the Latin poets, it was for centuries the highway of nations ; and the people on its banks, fearless and shameless robbers, could not overlook this bold crag washed by its eddies.

" Oh, there they are!" cries Henri " There they are ; they are coming ! "

Three specks are crawling along the edge of the shrubbery, a quarter of a mile away.

" It is my sister and her *cousine* from the farm ; and oh ! *la petite fillette ! Venez donc, venez donc !* " Then, realizing that they cannot hear a word and will be long in arriving, he dashes down the hill like a chamois.

After a while they all come tugging up together. *La cousine* is a buxom country girl of sixteen almond harvests, and *La Petite* a demoiselle of six, with short hair tied in a humorous queue The *bise* whisks off a hat—never mind, it is recovered. The *cousine's* skirt blows into her face ; the purple ribbon comes off the *fillette's* queue and the hair flies blustering over her face,—never mind, so much the more fun. *La Petite* trips on a big stone and is righted up with a pull and a shout. So up they come, laughing and chattering, putting themselves to rights and getting put wrong again by the pranky wind, holding each other fast, and Henri holding most of all the rosy *cousine.* The next moment we are down again for another point of view, *monsieur l'américain* with the rest. We all get into the mud. We all have wet shoes. We all get mixed up. We all laugh.

Suddenly I feel a shock—in thought. Just where I am skipping little Jeanne across the mud-puddles and laughing at the chatter of two school-girls, the fierce Punic eyes of great Hannibal were once gleaming out from under that

tangle of heavy hair.[3] Here galloped his Numidian cavalry. Here marched those thirty-seven elephants that
were counted upon to tread down the picked legions of
Rome as grapes were trodden in the winepress. On this
bit of stony plain, now lined off with shrubbery along the
brooks and here and there dotted with olive trees, was
fought the first skirmish in the terrific struggle of the
Second Punic War ; and here the great captain, that idea
made man, poised himself like an eagle for his daring
flight over the Alps.

La Petite, all curls and laughter—Mathieu and the
Félibres—Châteauneuf and the popes—Hannibal . such
overtones as these accompany the melodies of the troubadours in their native land.

At Courthézon we have the melody itself.

Within the walls it is another of those old cities laid out
with no thought of system, unless to make it as perplexing
as possible to an enemy. Tourists fall under this head
apparently ; but there is the perpetual charm of unexpectedness in such a place, and this—to a Bostonian—is at
least homelike Happily the old pavement has been rooted
out and a cousin of Mr. McAdam put in its place,—a great
advantage where one has to try four streets to find one.

Still the maze appears to have a centre, for wherever
you go you sooner or later find you have travelled up the
side of the conical town, and there above you is the same
mysterious old wall Hither tend all the winding streets.
Hither lead all the stairways of rugged stone. A mystery
it is, and a mystery it bids fair to remain.

But if you are fortunate enough to know the good
Abbé Lévézou the mystery opens. First he shows you
the kitchen fireplace of the ancient counts ; and you see
the very spot, if tradition and appearances may be trusted,
where a chicken was often broiled for Raimbaut de Vaqueiras and Prince Guilhem when they came home from

a day's hunting ; for while Aurenga (Orange) was the
official residence of the lord, Corteson (Courthézon) was
his home abode.

But fie on broiled chickens !

Mount these few stairs and you will issue upon the
mystery behind the wall. It is a level piece of ground,
perhaps a fourth part of an acre, a cross between a
trapezoid and an irregular polygon, bounded all around
with a parapet. This was the palace garden, the *cour
d'amour* of the princes and counts. In the wider part
some young olive trees rustle in the wind ; toward the
polygonal end lurks a well ; and on the western side,
where the two parts come together, their junction is
accented with a belvedere, to which we mount by a tall
flight of steps. The stairs are new, and so are the odd
pottery ornaments—to speak euphemistically—at the top ;
but the tower itself, loaded with vines and screened with
cypresses, dates from the olden time. It was in fact, as
we are told, a watch-tower, where the sentry kept guard in
the eye of his lord, and where the lord himself could go
in times of danger to observe the enemy or communicate
by signals with his capital, four or five miles distant.

This was the pleasure-garden, and in fancy we lay it
out after the rule of Albertus Magnus [1] : first a smooth
greensward, carefully weeded, a genuine tapestry of verdure, perfectly uniform ; at the southern end some trees,
—pears, apples, laurels, cypresses, olives, and others—with
vines interlacing in such a way as to shield the grass from
the sun and afford a pleasant shade ; in the rear of the
lawn, aromatic herbs to please and refresh the sense of
smell ; and beyond these, around an elevated space where
people could sit or lie at ease, flowers of many colors,—
violets, lilies, gladioli, and above all roses, both the red
and the white, both the single and the double, for the
double were cultivated even then. Amid such surround-

ings did Raimbaut de Vaqueiras and Prince Guilhem sing many a time, just here, for the fair ladies of the court and neighborhood

But the spot is especially associated with another troubadour, an uncle of Prince Guilhem's, known in history as Raimbaut III., count of Aurenga

He was not really count of Orange, for he and his brother divided the earldom between them, and Courthézon was his chief town ' But considering the man, this diminishment of estate was a piece of rare good luck. Important enough to be respected but not loaded with cares, rich enough to be courted but not inviting attack, he found himself in the best possible fix to enjoy life. In short he was free to live a jolly old dog, and a jolly old dog lived he   Hunting, hawking, jousting, singing, making verses, hearing and telling good stories, feasting often, and making love always,—these were the merry employments of his years

As a poet we must at once pronounce him clever but shallow.   Raimbaut de Vaqueiras lived in the golden age of the troubadours, and Raimbaut d'Aurenga, a generation before him, belongs among the later pioneers ; but even at that early stage he reached the theory of art for art's sake, the predestined goal of those who really have nothing to say but would fain be admired for saying it. Many of his verses were difficult and skilful performances , many wear a courtly, well-bred air ; a few have a touch of real sentiment , but most of them seem nothing more than exercises in dexterity, and as they do not come from the heart they do not reach the heart.   We are tempted to say as of some poetry not so ancient, and of some painting and music, '' Very well done, only not worth doing.''   No doubt he set an example of technical ingenuity, introduced an abundance of new expressions—often forced but frequently of real value—and in such ways made himself an

THE COUR D' AMOUR, COURTHÉZON.

important link in the development of poetic art ; but he pointed the way toward a fatal artificiality, and the word *trobador*,[6] used first by him, is perhaps his most valuable contribution to literature

As a personality, however, I find him vastly entertaining. " Young-hearted, fresh, and in perfect health," he describes himself ; and nobody can resist the contagion of his animal spirits when he bids the joglar strike up a lively air and begins his latest song :

> With wits refreshed and fresh desire,
> With knowledge fresh and freshened fire,
> In fine fresh style that ne'er will tire,
>   A good fresh poem I 'll begin ;
> My fresh new verses will inspire
> Fresh life in every knight and 'squire,
> And freshen pulses old and thin ![7]

His full round throat delivers the words fondly, as he would release a lady's hand. His well-filled body gives a sounding resonance to every tone. The bright pink of his plump cheeks deepens to an actual red, glowing warmly down into a soft brown beard. The hair, thick and short and set with rotary cow-licks all over his big head, seems waltzing electrically. And when each stanza is concluded he reinforces the interlude with amorous looks or jocund laugh, his bright eyes roving from side to side meanwhile to gather in the largess of smiles and applause.[8]

To be sure all this is the purest egotism, but its very purity saves it. As a loud voice can dispense with argument and a lively fancy get on without knowledge, his convincing self-confidence is its own sufficient plea. Were he a half-way egotist, his assertion of himself would be offensive. If he demanded only an even share and that diffidently, he would be called mean and grasping by those who expected to get the whole. But as he assumes

from the start that everything and everybody are his, and
that whatever he does n't approve " is not worth a rad-
ish," * those of his own sort depart for easier prey, and
those who remain are the kind that yield.   Of course he
should have whatever he wishes, because—because—why,
because he always has had it.   And so his claims and his
egotism—frank, spontaneous, and complete, not only pass
unchallenged but in the end even excite admiration.   In
peace he makes himself a sun of gladness by assuming
that because he is enjoying himself everything is for the
best ; and in difficulties he is comfort and cheer, because
he feels sure that the enemy will get frightened and make
a blunder.

You and I come under the spell.   He is really a capital
good fellow, this mediæval Jean Aicard.   With one of us
on each arm he promenades about the parapet.   How
affably he displays before us the noble view   On the east
and northeast lie Carpentras and Vaqueiras if we could
only discern them, and a little to the south Vaucluse with
its gorge and its river.   Farther still to the south he
points out where, if the mistral had cleared the air a bit
more, we could see distinctly the range of Les Alpines
and possibly a corner of the rock-hewn castle at Les Baux
To the west, beyond the low hills, the swift Rhone veils
its turbid whirlpools with an azure stolen from the sky.
There to the northwest, looking across the tiled roofs and
past the signal-turret on the corner of the wall, we find
the lordly hill of Orange.   Only Mt. Ventoux and the
sun divide with us the sovereignty of the landscape , and
with them we look down in the nearer distance upon wide
and smiling plains, rich in harvests and fertile in tribute

With a broad wave of the arm, Lord Raimbaut sweeps
the view of his possessions ; then, satisfied with his back-
ground of wealth, brilliancy, and fame, he begins gravely
to moralize · " Talking too much is the worst of crimes,"

"Baseness rusts, wears out, and seals up young-heartedness," "'The crime is born before it appears", then he
piously—or patronizingly—thanks God for the pleasant
day, the congenial company, and the smiles of his lady;
next he brings out a few allusions to the Bible and the
story of Tristan—about all the learning he possesses; and
finally, when he has thus established a character for seri-
ousness, too, he comes boldly home to himself and declares
with all gravity, "Since Adam ate of the apple there never
has been a poet, no matter how loud he screamed, whose
art was worth a turnip compared with mine", and then,
"Whoever gives me the lie, by my father's soul let him
quickly take hauberk, lance, and shield, and I will make
him bite the dust." [10]

But we cannot have the famous troubadour to ourselves.
The rest of the company begin to clamor, the joglar tunes
his viol, a fresh cup is passed, and then he gives us another
song :

> I 'll sing; pray, gentlemen, attend,
>   Though what you 'll hear I can't foretell ;
> I scarcely know what I intend,—
>   No name would come within an ell ;
> Nor is there any way to mend
>   What I attempt, if not done well,
>> For nobody ever knew anything in this style to
>> be undertaken by man or by woman, either in
>> the present age or in time past
>
> May naught, I beg, delay my friend
>   If love to loving acts impel ;
> Postponements on and on extend,
>   If 'gainst one's impulse one rebel ;
> No other dame—on this depend—
>   Shall e'er so deftly catch and quell
>> The man whom you are listening to; and all
>> this I am saying for the benefit of a lady who
>> makes me languish with fine words and long
>> delays, I know not why; can it be pleasant for
>> me, gentlemen?

Four months of waiting I expend
  That seem a thousand years ; *ma belle*
Cares not, and will but condescend
  . To promise that she 'll quench my hell ,
Oh, lady, since I can't defend
  My heart, bid joy my griefs dispel !
        Help me, O God, in the name of the Father
        and the Son and the Holy Ghost ! What will
        be the end of it ?

You make joy bless me, anguish rend,
  Gay songs and sad ones you compel,
Until in me three beings blend
  That all the world save you excel ;
In courtly singing I unbend
  And turn joglar, the slanderers tell ;
        Lady, you can't do exactly the way you please, as
        Lady Aima did with her shoulder [and the rest
        of her lovely person], bestowing it just where
        she liked.

Now my *I-know-not-what* shall end,—
  I meant the thing as it befell ;
And 't is so new, I recommend
  That all adopt this way to spell
Its name ; whoe'er the time will spend
  To learn it, may the lay retell ,
        And if anybody ask him who made it, he can say
        it was made by one who knows well how to do
        every sort of thing that he takes a mind to.[11]

The jolly old dog ! Well, well ; it does one good to
know him   But let us not be envious. Even egotism
has its trials, and Raimbaut's heavens were not always
clear   One day he sang, " Neither squirrel nor buck is
as light as I," " My heart laughs even while I sleep";
the next he cried out, " A thousand wretches would be
sated with the misery I feel," and vowed that he bore the
very " flower of misfortune "   " Poor relations " were
partly responsible for his troubles, but of course it was

chiefly the fortune of love that played pranks with his
mightiness. We must fear he was not always contented
with his ring, as he asserted he was, nor even satisfied
long with any Dulcinea—so indeed his biography declares [12]; and this gave excellent opportunities for the
prying tale-bearers,—those "hard, cruel, tormenting busybodies, envious, low-bred, evil-tongued," as, with a touch
of feeling unmistakably sincere, he described them.

Even love itself had inconveniences. It was only
touch-and-go with him—"a cup of glass breaks not more
easily than love," he sang—and he felt no call to take
things in earnest, as the ladies occasionally did. Even
his biggest compliments had a suspicious ring :

> So sweet the smile her lips bestow
>   I feel that God Himself hath smiled ;
> Four hundred angels all aglow
> With smiles could not entrance me so,
>   Though high their heavenly gifts were piled ;
> My bliss could make delight o'erflow
> A thousand hearts now filled with woe,
> And all my relatives forego
>   To eat, with happiness beguiled. [13]

He did not wish to be hampered with serious affection.
"She can scarce feel joyous without breaking out into
Greek fire," he once complained. Sometimes he was
persecuted by a very undesirable acquaintance—at least
so he felt when the new love was safely on :

> Of all bad women ever found
>   I 've parted from the very worst ;
> And now, of all the country round,
>   I love the fairest and the first. [13]

But let us not misjudge him What if his affections did
seem light ? It was not levity, he tells us himself, but
only that he felt it a duty " to wear a look of gayety in

the midst of his griefs " ; and besides, when a lady jilted
him, was he not serious enough to denounce her treason
as greater than Cain's against Abel ?

At any rate he was in earnest when he wished his
wishes gratified, for he did not care to " fish without
water ", he was brilliant, witty, clever, and famous ;
good-looking, we assume, and a jolly old dog, we know ;
he made skilful use, no doubt, of the usual tokens of
affection,—girdles, diadems, ribbons, bracelets, clasps,
rings, and sachets of musk : above all he was not a particle deceived about the ladies or a particle afraid of them :
and so there were always a plenty to love him and some
to love him devotedly.

Whereby there hangs another song, to a very different
air.[14]

VI

DIE AND VALENCE

The Countess of Dia

IN the firmament of the twelfth century shines one
bright star that bears a woman's name The woman
was a poet, and she has been called by later ages the
countess of Dia.

Where was that unfamiliar spot?

Northward from Courthézon and Orange we find the
valley of the Rhone at its best.   Miles and miles of rich
meadow lands marked off into gardens, grass fields, vineyards, and olive orchards; hedgerows of hawthorn ; lines
—long and short—of tall maidenly *peupliers* attired in fresh
green poplins; trenches of water skilfully decoyed through
fields and gardens ; clumps of green-black cypresses holding aloof from the general cheer of the spring landscape,
and reaching up to warm their cold verdure in the sunlight , hydrocephalous willows darting long shoots from
their dark brown heads ; buff-colored cottages here and
there amid the green,—their overhanging roofs crisp with
round tiles ; cherry trees and apricots like groups of young
girls in a fluff and flurry of pink and white ; mulberry
trees just putting out their first yellow leaves on the
queer, scraggly branches , a patch of lilac once in a while;
sunlight and blue shadows everywhere,—this is the swift
panorama as we fly along.

It is all very interesting and beautiful ; and yet the

Rhone valley gives one a sense of depression and almost of melancholy. Hawthorne called the region bleak, barren, brown, and bare. To be sure he saw it in winter, but even in early spring we have a little of the same feeling. Beyond the verdure stand the great rounded bluffs,—scorched and calcined. What look like patches of black furze cap their tops, and reach scantily down their sides ; while roads climb up in dusty zigzags, cramped or sweeping as the ravines dictate. " Old as the rocks of Provence," the proverb says. Not merely old, they seem, but dead, the bleached skeleton of a land once young, a fit guardian of ruined forums and amphitheatres and the fallen temples of perished gods. Even the valley seems withering in their ashen grasp. The straight white roads burn. The watercourses are already drying.

THE WALL OF DIE.

Stronger yet is the tinge of sadness as we turn abruptly from the Rhone, and for thirty miles climb the valley of the Drôme. Little that is verdure cares to follow us. Close by, instead of far away, are the rocky walls now, and now they bristle and threaten. Beside us runs the grey river, vexed and restless, gnawing the stony slopes. We are among the outposts of the Alps, and here at their feet is Die (Dia).[1]

Once an important Roman post between Turin and Vienne, the Mother of Emperors, Die is now only a poor little town quite out of the world. There is one good street, leading down from the heavy Roman gateway past lines of dingy shops, and upon this thoroughfare the whole place balances, one side rising to the fragments of ramparts, the other sinking toward the channel of the Drôme. A valley winds from the west around the city on the south, turning then into pleasant meadows toward the east and north ; but stern Mt. Glandaz walls it in, and a bastion of the Alps blocks it. Elsewhere the fields have been

LOOKING FROM DIE.

found richest in broken sculptures, crumbling pillars, medals, and inscriptions. The hills, brown as dust, are almost hidden with clouds of powder set awhirl by chilly blasts from the northeast ; and the effect of the pleasant meadows is offset by a vertical, bristling wall of rock, as black as iron, where drifts of snow tell of winter lurking still behind the crest in the abysses of Mt. Aiguille, and eager to return.

VOL. I.—7

Over this dark town ruled Aimar II., the count of the region about Valence and Die. We know him already, for he was a patron of Raimbaut de Vaqueiras, and a troubadour himself, though not a famous one ; and we now meet Philippa, his wife, who derived from this town her title in literature, for she, too, made verses.

Francesco da Barberino tells a number of interesting stories that no doubt concern this countess of Dia. She insisted, as many other ladies did in that age, that hers was the superior sex. Look at the hands of man and of woman, she said ; his are strong and rough, like those of a being created to serve ; hers delicate and shapely, fit only for agreeable employments. Besides, man was formed of the foul mud, but woman of a human rib, earth already purified and ennobled by divine working.

In her older years the countess was very devout, and coming one day upon a profligate knight making his fastidious toilet she exclaimed : "You who bathe your body so scrupulously to keep it clean, how can you remain covered with the filth of sin ? Even though God should pardon and mankind not despise you, why should you not keep your soul equally clear and pure, simply for love of a blameless life ?" Her exhortation struck home, we are told, and the knight reformed from that time.[2]

But the stories disappoint as much as they edify ; is this all that can be said of the famous countess of Dia ?

Down at the lower edge of the city, hidden from the bustle of trade and the eyes of careless visitors, is a little garden, and within it a terrace overlooking the Drôme. There, on a column of granite beneath a weeping willow, is the bust of a woman,—the head poised, the face in reverie, the eyes cast down. This is the portrait—the imagined portrait—of a poet ; and she, not Philippa, is meant when we say "the countess of Dia."

But this only deepens our perplexity.

The fixed stars, the infinitely great masking itself in infinite littleness, have a surprising peculiarity : the telescope instead of enlarging seems to diminish them. Sirius is a great splendor in the sky but in the lens he appears minute, and no instrument is powerful enough to reveal any actual body. Such our star of poetry would seem to be   The Sappho of Provence never set foot in Dia so far as we know, and certainly was not its countess. Investigation made it appear that she gained her title from being confounded with Philippa. She had never possessed a name, apparently; and now she lost even that substitute for one   Who she was and whence she came, appeared an insoluble mystery. Only an unsubstantial beam of light remained. The Sappho of Lesbos herself was better known.

Happily within the past few years we have become able to believe if not able to know. It now seems reasonable to suppose that she was the mother of Aimar II., the daughter of the lord of Vienne, the wife of the count of Valence ; and that she bore in her own right the name of Biatritz (Beatrice). It was this quite real person who composed the five poems of " the countess of Dia," and from her biography of just thirty words we learn further that she loved the gay Raimbaut d'Aurenga.'

It is a singular compensation that while we know so little of the lives and acts of the troubadours, their poetry is of the lyric and subjective kind, and portrays vividly their personalities   We know our neighbors by their goings and comings, by their dress and by their features, yet can only guess at the pains and joys, the desires and motives of their hearts ; but these mediæval characters, though seven centuries divide us, reveal to us their inmost thoughts, their most personal emotions   We know them better than we do our intimates, better than we do ourselves. The superficial is gone, the essential remains. So in the work of reconstruction we have set us the easier half of the task , for, as old Spenser knew, " soul is form and doth the body make "; and if Cuvier delighted to rebuild an animal from one of its bones, what fascination there is in trying to restore from his poems, from his mind, from his heart, a poet—more yet a poetess —of the age of chivalry !

Somewhere the Lady Biatritz met the famous trouba- dour of Courthézon. Raimbaut had been told of her wit and her love of the new culture. Probably he had lis- tened to a song of hers, and better yet had known of her listening to one of his. He found her interesting as well as beautiful, made himself entirely agreeable, and with no difficulty obtained an invitation to visit her quiet court

For the first time in her life the countess felt the de. light of companionship. Each read verses to the other, and when the quivers were empty they tried their strength in the mimic warfare of the tenso Once a tournament was given; and the dashing visitor, handsomely equipped, bore himself in arms like a knight of high degree. In the castle hall he was always the centre of the group A proved gallant, he showed himself no less masterful in the subtler competition of my lady's chamber, and it was not long before there existed a feeling of more than com- radeship between the countess and him.

It was indeed predestined,—one would know that only to see her Let us not be sentimental or extravagant in describing even a Sappho, but let us try to be truthful. Slender and petite, she added much of the light grace of a girl to the fuller beauty of a woman Her face had no color save a slight olive tint, and her features were deli- cate though drawn with firm lines. While almost all about her were of fair complexion, she like her mother was very dark, with eyes as black as the thick wavy hair that shadowed her rather small forehead. Her voice had

the color of Alban wine, with overtones like the gleams
of light in the still, velvety depths of the goblet ; and
when she smiled, it seemed as if she drew from a harp a
slow deep chord in the mode of Æolia. Though not
at all diffident and not at all prudish, she wore usually an
air of shyness, the shyness of one whose thoughts dread
intrusion ; and her look, always much in advance of her
words, appeared to judge the person it rested upon,—not
to condemn or approve, but to decide.'

She was just the woman to fall in love with the handsome, dashing, clever, popular count of Orange, for people
of that sort are always taking it for granted that others
have the same hidden virtues as themselves. Sincerity,
depth, and constancy were so thoroughly natural, so in-
stinctive with her, that only sad experience could teach
her to suspect the want of such commonplace merits in
others; and besides, her poise of judgment was quite upset
by Raimbaut's dash and impetuosity. So she lost herself
in admiration of the cheap but showy qualities that she
lacked, and before she knew it had given a true diamond
for one of paste.

For a time she was happy. Such companionship was
not only delightful in itself, but it brought out her hidden
qualities, made her shine, and won her a new meed of
praise and admiration ; for naturally she was reserved,
and, though not sombre, pensive. " On gladness and
young-heartedness I feast,—may they [ever] be my meat,"
she sang, " for my friend is the gayest of all, and so I too
am gay and attractive " Companionship and friendship
grew into intimacy, intimacy into love, and before long
the count was pressing her close with all the varying arts
of the gallant. But a commonplace intrigue was not in
her thoughts, and she maintained a fitting reserve. Then
he withdrew. Reluctantly she understood that with him,
at least, love could not pause midway, and she sang, " Now

I see that I am abandoned because I have not given [all] my love." With exultation she cried, " My heart have I made his, and my love, my [every] sense, my eyes, and my life." Raimbaut came back, and happier days than ever were the recompense of her sacrifice °

But after a time the visits grew less frequent again. We who understand her lover from the beginning are not surprised, but she could not believe him faithless.

> Since I love my love so deeply,
> It *must* be that his love is deep,
> For never will his love seem cheap—
> Never could I prize it cheaply.[6]

He could always give excellent reasons why he did not come, and she found reasons for him ; yet after a time she began to be anxious, and on his next visit they had a tenso in earnest.

Biatritz. Dear friend, you do not begin to realize what it means to me when I do not see you. How can you pretend that you love me, when you compel me to bear all the ill ? We are not sharing evenly.

Raimbaut. My lady, love is so contrived that whatever pain one of two lovers endures the other suffers the same. Truly, I thought I was bearing all the unhappiness myself.

Biatritz No, you do not feel a quarter part of what I feel If you did, you would understand my burden. But it is all one to you whether I am happy or miserable

Raimbaut. It is the spies and gossips that are your enemies. That is why I have not visited you oftener of late. People are beginning to talk, and already they have done you such a mischief that our joy is at an end.

Biatritz. Do not give yourself the pains to be more careful of my reputation than I am myself. I do not thank you for staying away out of regard for my welfare when I wish you here

Raimbaut. But I fear exceedingly that if the gossip continue, in the end it will utterly wreck our happiness. If you lose sand thereby, I lose gold. You are the thing I value most.

Biatritz The simple fact is this . you are a flatterer and gallant. You have abandoned chivalry and gone into trade : your only thought is now of 'change. Yes, your mind is full of some one else, for you care not for my trouble.

Raimbaut. May I never bear falcon again, may I never have another fair day's hunting, if I have wooed another since you gave yourself to me. They are envious traitors that would make me out untrue.

Biatritz. I will believe you, dear, if I find you ever loyal after this.

Raimbaut. I shall think of no one in the world but you '

Harmony was restored, but the fickle gallant wearied more and more of a serious affection. Fresh neglect received sharper censure. Reproaches grew more bitter. Then of course he assumed an air of injured innocence and righteous indignation, drew himself up haughtily, and coldly renounced the bond.

Valence has always been a tedious place, it would seem, and its associations are all depressing. In its earliest historic days it was the dull refuge of disabled Roman soldiers. Henry II gave it away to his mistress. Cæsar Borgia ruled it. Pius VI. died there. Constantine was there made a prisoner. There Napoleon wooed Grégoire de Colombier and was rejected, and there he buried himself in the volumes of a compassionate bookseller. The town itself is low and flat The boom of artillery practice is its music. ¡Streets and houses conspire together for gloom ; and just across the Rhone there scowls a line of high cliffs, naked, arid, and stained, that rob the morning sun of his gladness and the evening sun of his glory.

Sadly the countess looked across the river from the castle at this dark and bristling scarp.[8] Storms and frosts had carved it into savage forms that seemed to her fancy like ruins piled on desolations. Here and there were twisting lines of snow in the chasms. Above were masses of heavy clouds driving over the crest: " Whither ? " she asked herself. Below ran the swift Rhone pouring its

LOOKING ACROSS THE RHONE, VALENCE.

troubled eddies on and on, and again she asked herself, " Whither ? " Nearer at hand was the old Roman pavement, and that she did not need to question : she knew where Cæsar, the lictors, and the legions had gone.

Then she thought of Corteson and the garden of love. The sun shone brightly there, she fancied, and the open west was piled with splendor instead of gloom. In the garden laughed a brilliant and witty throng, gay with songs and pleasantries., and gayest of all was the count himself, the centre of the group,—lively, sparkling, gracious, and gallant, and, if he thought of her at all, thinking only with haughty indifference. Her heart, conscious of its worth, was full of bitterness. The long musing at the window broke out in a fury of resentment that set her pacing the room . . "I, no common, dull, plain woman—then it would be natural—but a poet like himself, his equal in rank, true when God knows how many are false. . . . Who is the woman that—?" Her tongue felt like a quiver of arrows, and she longed to let them fly. But she had tried all that before, and she knew it could not help her.'

At last she resolved to make one more attempt "I will go to him now as a suppliant, for a suppliant I am." There would be relief in that ; and so, calling upon her muse for aid, she put her heart with all its tumult of feeling into words in which, after seven centuries, her personality strill throbs.

> I now must sing of that I fain would not,—
> So dark and sad my friend hath made my lot ;
> Compared with him I love naught else one jot,
> Yet all my grace, my favor, he 's forgot,
>   And worth and wit and beauty are in vain ;
> Betrayed am I, the victim of his plot,
>   As well I might be were I dull and plain.
>
> In this is comfort : I have never failed
> In aught that could have with your heart availed,—
> Less warmth than mine Valensa's love exhaled ,
> And I am proud because my love prevailed
>   O'er you, dear friend, the best in Love's domain ;
> But now the rest with gracious looks are hailed,
>   And me alone with haughty airs you pain.
>
> I can but wonder that you seem so proud,
> And there is reason that my grief be loud ;

It is not right your love be elsewhere vowed
For bitter words I should not have allowed ;
  Remember, too, our bliss when first we twain
Began to love! To God my heart is bowed
  That fault of mine cause not our love to wane.

The strength and valor, in your soul that dwell,
Your fame, your worth, my constancy compel ;
For near or far there 's none that would repel
Your love, unless 'gainst all love she rebel ;
  But you, dear friend, to whom such things are plain,
Which heart is truest, surely you can tell !
  And then our pledges,—do not them disdain !

My worth, my rank, my beauty, too, must weigh,
And, more than all, my faithful heart should sway ;
And so I send you, to your home, to-day
A song to tell you what my voice would say ;
  And, fair, sweet friend, I pray you to explain
Why 't is you treat me in this barbarous way,—
  I cannot see,—doth pride or malice reign ?

And one word more, my messenger, convey ·
Oft haughtiness brings ruin in its train.[10]

"Love swells like the Solway but ebbs like its tide."
Unlike the Solway tide it never flows back. The ships
do not wait With whatever they bear they sail for another anchorage, and the port they visited is empty. So
far as we know or conjecture the messenger of Lady
Biatritz carried no loving answer home to Valence.

We have one grain of satisfaction. The sins of the
fathers are visited upon the children, and, as Raimbaut
had no son, his nephew paid ; for it was Aimar's fishermen that caught Guilhem del Bauz and made him the
laughing-stock of Provence.

The poor countess of Dia may not have lived to see
even this trifling bit of retribution, but her fidelity did
not fail of a reward Her star is fixed in the heaven of
immortal fame, and will shine there for ever.

ANDUZE

Ugo de Sain Circ. Clara d'Anduza

I NEVER expected to feel so much like Stephen the martyr as I did at Anduze.

Not figuratively, like poor little Alphonse Daudet, who taught school at Alais, less than ten miles distant, and after the training in wretchedness that he obtained there was able to enjoy the Paris garret, the three sous' worth of cabbage-soup, and all the other miseries of his literary novitiate. No, literally. Anduze like Alais lies in the fringe of the Cevennes, and the mountain floods have brought it millions and millions of cobblestones. The town is built with them ; the streets are paved with them ; the walls are laid with them ; and as I picked my way along the glum alleys, they seemed actually bulging from the mortar in their eagerness to get at me.

Yet rough Anduze (Anduza) was a place of no slight importance in the age of the troubadours. Bernart, one of its lords, was among the barons whom Raimbaut de Vaqueiras assailed for giving up the cause of Guilhem del Bauz, and this is only one out of many proofs that he was a leading character of the time. What is more surprising, we find here literary figures also, that will at least entertain us

Ugo de Sain Circ, born (about 1170) some ten or fifteen years later than Raimbaut de Vaqueiras, was of Quercy,

the youngest son of a small nobleman whose castle was
destroyed in the wars.[1] His elder brothers—and they
were numerous—resolved upon lightening the ship by
casting overboard little Ugo,—in other words, making
a churchman of him ; so they packed him off to school at
Montpellier. "And when they thought he was devoting
himself to letters," wrote his biographer, probably his
autobiographer, "he *was* devoting himself to love-songs,
and verses and sirventes, and tensos and stanzas, and the

LOOKING TOWARD ANDUZE.

doings and sayings of the notable men and the notable
ladies of those or of former times." It was a poor prepa-
ration for orders ; and before long—a young man of some
twenty years, as Casini figures—he gave up canonicals,
and set forth to earn a living with his music, his poetry,
and whatever other arts of entertainment he possessed.

Ugo seems to have been something of an exquisite. To
borrow yesterday's argot of the Paris drawing-rooms, he

was cut out for a " zebra," the ornamental fetch-and-carry
of an elegant *mondaine*. He delighted to vow, protest,
and implore. He would talk of kissing his inamorata's
feet , declare the little purse that she made him worth a
star or two ; and beg a million pardons when he cared
not a straw for one. He always wore a compliment in his
right eye and an impertinence in his left, and could say
either in such a way as to make it seem the other. An
interesting cough, an elegant headache, a charming languor, and a seductive melancholy were also in his baggage
For him life had countless annoyances and required incessant consolation. Wine had no flavor unless a white hand
passed him the cup. Breath had to be scented a little or
his nostrils were liable to stop it. Or at all events, if the
age was too early for precisely these refinements, the spirit
of the thing was in him.

He was not a bad fellow, though. His mind was busy
and he was always trying to learn. We must call him
good-hearted—that is, if we call it a heart at all—for we
read that " he willingly taught others " what he knew.

As a lady's man he was aptly contrived : lively, com-
panionable, sentimental, never in love but always able to
appear so, as the biography states, always ready with a
song, fully stocked with gossip, glad to be petted, and
mightily happy to be ordered about on dainty errands.
With men however it was different. His patrons—bold,
vigorous barons—quickly discovered two vices in his mak-
ing-up : he was expensive and he was lazy ; and from
these vices grew, I take it, his two unfortunate broils.

The story of each is expounded in a tenso. First it was
the count of Rodes (Rodez).²

" Count," sang Ugo, " there is no need of your being
frightened and anxious on account of me, for I have n't
come to ask or obtain anything, since I have all I require ;
and I see that pence are so scarce with you that I have n't

the heart to ask anything, but [feel that] I should be doing a deed of great charity if I gave to you."

And in the same rhymes and metre the count replied :
" Sir Ugo de Sain Circ, it galls me greatly to send away
rich you who came to me less than a year ago poor, naked,
and wretched; for you have cost me more than two archers
would, or [even] two horsemen.   And yet I am right sure
that if I were to offer you [now] a fine horse (God keep
me from doing it !) you would take him, and that quickly."

With the viscount of Torena (Turenne), a name famous
in troubadour history, the difficulty was on the other line.

" Lord viscount," sang the poet, " how can I endure
the hardships that you compel me to suffer ?   Night and
day you keep me galloping about so that I am left no time
for repose or [even] sleep.   Indeed I could not be worse
off even with Martin d'Algai [the famous brigand]; [and]
my very food seems scrimped."

The hardy baron was disgusted with such flaccidity,
and he, too, answered in verse : " Well enough you know,
if you will tell the truth [about it], Sir Ugo de Sain Circ,
that I did not have you hunted up in Quercy [and brought
here] to show you my estates.   On the contrary it an-
noyed me greatly to see you come.   God chastise me if I
did not wish in my heart that you had gone to Spain ! "

It is easy to suspect that our exquisite was not one to
find a congenial home easily ; and so it proved.   After
quitting Torena he visited the dalfin (dauphin) of Auvergne, a very important figure in the troubadour world
as we shall find, but for one reason or another did not remain with him long.   To Spain he then went, indeed, and
slowly traversed about all the Christian parts—Catalonia,
Aragon, Castile, and Leon.   Next he appeared in Gascony, and wandered about there for a long time in desti-
tution, " sometimes afoot, sometimes on a horse."

A poet's life was not play even then, we see.   Sain Circ

was able to make verses, even good ones,—that was easy
enough ; but to get a living so was quite another matter.
Long ago though it was, poetry had already been over-
done. The seed was in many gardens and the crop in every
mart. A new song met comparison instantly with one by
Raimbaut de Vaqueiras and a host of others. Already,
too, there were ghosts in competition, for there had been
troubadours fifty—even a hundred—years; and besides
the high merit of some of these pioneers, many people
were disposed to think the older necessarily the better :
even then the " good old times " were often set above the
present.

It looked unpromising for Ugo, but at last he succeeded.
In Gascony was Benauges ; and at Benauges, as perhaps
you remember, lived that arch-coquette Guillerma. The
poet won her good graces and she made his fortune. In
short, his vocation was found, and he became a zebra. In
a thousand ways he amused and served her. It was he
for example that carried her message to Savaric de Mauleon
when she wished him to cancel his appointment with another lady. And after he had attended her a long while,
the brave Savaric—apparently to do his lady a favor—
took him up, befriended and supported him, and gave
him a position in the world.

After perhaps ten or fifteen years of this roving existence Ugo drifted to Provence, a well seasoned man between thirty and thirty-five years old. There he moved
about from castle to castle, and meanwhile became acquainted somehow with a brilliant woman of Anduza.

The countess of Dia and her daughter-in-law Philippa
were by no means the only ladies to wear Provençal bays.
As a class, troubadours of the fair sex were, to quote
Fauriel, " feebler and less painstaking " than the men
They were moons rather than suns, imitating instead of
originating artistic effects ; and for that reason were

necessarily less bold and less masterly. On the other hand they were not always wanting in frankness of speech or intensity of feeling   In all we know the names of some twenty—two of them ladies of Italy—and from most of them we have lines,—though Biatritz of Dia with her scanty five pieces is the most voluminous

Next after her in poetical value ranks Lady Castelloza of Auvergne, "very gay, very accomplished, and very beautiful," as the biography says, who reminds her wild and heedless friend that if he allow her to die of love, he will be guilty of a great sin " before God and men " [3] Notable too is a countess of Provence who urges a nameless lover, meaning probably Gui de Cavaillon, not to be diffident,—" for a lady dare not make advances." [4] Still more interesting is Clara d'Anduza who sings in graceful numbers ·

> Fair friend, I pray you give yourself no fear,
>   Untrue to you that I shall ever be ;
>   Though fifty knights left other loves for me,
> No voice but yours would ever gain my ear.[5]

Lady Clara, says the manuscript, " was very clever and accomplished and agreeable and beautiful : and she had a strong desire to be famous, and to be heard of both far and near, and to be on terms of friendship and intimacy with the good ladies and the men of note." But how could she bring it about ? There were no magazines to print her verses, no society journals to describe her frocks and her mantles, no reporters, no opera-boxes with door plates and a directory, no Horse Show, no Patriarchs, no Newport. Worse yet, Anduza was away off in the border of the mountains. To her fancy it seemed forever struggling to crawl yet farther back into the Cevennes, and though just then stuck fast in the gorge of the river, who knew but it might finally get through ?

And then, too, it was such a dark and stuffy place,—
who would care to come there? The mountains brought
their grey heads so near together that the torrent and the
narrow road were closely pinched. There was no modest
plain, there was not even a ledge for the little town to
stretch itself half-comfortably upon. The houses clung
helter-skelter as best they could to the rocky skirt of Mt.
Julien, fearful of slipping
any moment into the
Gardon, and were always
looking timidly up at Mt.
Pierremain on the other
side, beseeching it not to
fall upon them. The town
had nothing to boast of
but a Roman tower ; and
that, while perhaps it
already displayed the
sun-dial that still marks
the hours on its wall,
had not yet evolved the
brown rooster with red-
dish feathers around his
neck that makes it now
an artistic triumph. The
outlook down the river
toward the great world
was grimly barred by a
spur of the mountains,
where I doubt not some

AT ANDUZE.

castle or watch-tower was cameoed against the twilight
sky as Tornac is now ; and the days were so short in this
pit of a town and the evenings were so long, that her
complexion might be ruined by the candle-light ere people
should learn of her charms.⁶ It was indeed a dark prob-

lem,—how to shine before the world in such a place as that.

But fortune, though feminine, loves to help a clever and beautiful woman. In the nick of time, as it would appear, she met the now famous troubadour of Sáin Circ; "and

Sir Ugo," says the manuscript, "perceived her wish [to become celebrated] and well knew how to serve her in that she most desired. For in all those regions there was no good lady with whom he did not place her on terms of love and familiarity, and from whom he did not obtain for her letters and notes of greeting and jewels, as tokens of accord and honor. And Sir Ugo, indeed, made the letters that were proper, in reply to the ladies, as returns for the compliments they sent."

TORNAC, EVENING.

Needless to say a love affair grew out of this. Before long the poet was singing :

> I dare not show you how my heart 's afire,
> Nor how I die from longing and desire.[1]

He could make verse, however—precisely what his lady wished—and utter his despair in musical and complimentary phrases :

> What shall I do, my lady ?   I can find,
>   Apart from you, no earthly thing to treasure ;
> What shall I do?   Unless by you they 're twined
>   Bright wreaths of joy bring me no touch of pleasure ;
>   What shall I do?   A love that hath no measure

> Directs and guides me, follows, flees, o'ertakes ;
> What shall I do? My heart all else forsakes ;
> What shall I do, and how shall I get free,
> If you, my lady, will not harbor me ?[1]

There was a singular propriety in the words, " follows, flees, o'ertakes." Clara proposed to keep the serviceable Ugo as a zebra,—neither less nor more, and would neither loose him nor grant his prayer for love. When his pursuit became too warm she found an excuse to quarrel with him, "and they made many wars and many peaces between them," says the manuscript. When he had been hovering about her long enough to be fired with enthusiasm, she would perceive that gossip was beginning to wag its tongue,—for, as Raimbaut d'Aurenga made clear, tale-bearers and busybodies were as convenient for the pretending lover as they were vexatious for the genuine ; and she would pack him off instantly to chant her praises and execute her commissions in the neighboring castles. Then to " o'ertake " him, she composed a pretty song, and one fine morning he received it :

> By sore distress and sore perplexity
>   My heart is troubled, and by sharp debate ;
>   For slanderers, guessing falsely, lie in wait
> To murder gladness and felicity ,
>   Since you, dear friend, for whom alone I languish,
>   Are forced to leave me and afar to roam,
>   While I, who cannot see you, here at home
> Am perishing of sorrow, grief, and anguish.[8]

So the pretty game went on, Clara winning whichever lost, until in the course of time a neighbor of hers interfered, and attempted to capture the troubadour for her own use.

How shall we enable ourselves to realize the passion of a twelfth-century woman to be celebrated in the songs of a poet ? Partly no doubt we can imagine her feelings, but would it not be interesting to read them as in a book ? Fortunately we can do exactly that   It was not Abelard the philosopher, not Abelard the brilliant lecturer, not Abelard the winning talker that captivated Eloïse, but chiefly Abelard the poet ; and in one of her letters her feelings about it and those of other women are vividly portrayed   " You composed many verses in amorous measure," she wrote, " so sweet both in their language and their melody that your name was incessantly in the mouths of all, and even the most illiterate could not be forgetful of you. This it was chiefly that made women admire you ; and as most of these songs were on me and my love, they made me known in many countries and caused many women to envy me. Every tongue spoke of your Eloïse. Every street, every house resounded with my name." And if such was the effect on great-hearted Eloïse what must it have been on weaker minds ?

Madame Ponsa, at any rate, was not able to overcome her longings for a poet. She, too, was " very beautiful," " very courtly and very accomplished." She felt no doubt entirely satisfied of her equality with her fortunate neighbor, " and she had great envy of my Lady Clara because of the fame and honor that Sir Ugo had caused her to obtain." So she gave the troubadour to understand that Lady Clara had other lovers to whom she was kinder than to him, while if he cared to love *her*, she would say and do the things that would please him. Ugo had been quarrelling with Clara just then, it appears, and so, yielding to the fair looks and fair words of his admirer, he put on the new love and said many hard things of the old.

But he only found himself deceived as before, and by a shallow mind instead of a brilliant one   " The man that loves a silly woman spends his days in folly," he once declared, and after persisting for a long time he decided

to make his peace with Clara. He was not one to stickle
on terms when resolved upon surrender. "Lady, if you
are offended with me I make no defence," we find among
his other sentiments. An admiring friend of Clara's,
herself a poetess, came to the rescue ; Ugo explained what
led him to be unfaithful, and in a little while the zebra
found himself once more in his agreeable stall.'

Well, it is a very moderate climax, this, but it is all
there was. The life with Clara went on as before, luke-
warm affection and quarrellings about nothing—Mérimée
and the dark-eyed *inconnue*, and eventually the poet
wearied of it. When about fifty years of age he left
Anduze, Clara, and his native land for good. For several
years he moved about in Lombardy , and then, as if determined to outdo all the other poets—as he did—by completely circumnavigating the troubadour world, he passed
on to the " joyous march of Treviso," near Venice. Still
irrepressible he plunged there into another showery love
affair,'' quarrelling and making up " as happens in love."
But as time passed it occurred to him perhaps that he was
getting on in years. He concluded it was time to settle
down, and at about fifty-five, marrying a " fair and noble "
lady, he devoted himself to gathering olive branches.
Love-songs he forsook as became a family man ; but he
still composed political sirventes, and finally toward the
end of life achieved his most important work

Many questions were asked him in that far-away corner
of Italy about the famous troubadours whom he knew.
Still ready to impart, he talked freely of them, and so
after a while bethought him to set down in writing what
he could tell of their lives. It was an easy thing to do,
but it has meant a deal to the later world. Certain
biographies of the troubadours we undoubtedly owe to
him, and it is conjectured that several, perhaps most, of
the others come from the same pen.

Thus we picture him at the last: an old man—no, an
old gentleman—white-haired, with a long white beard,[11]
good-natured and gossipy still, surrounded by his children, and writing down priceless annals for his own day
and ours.[12]   In this pleasant fashion he rounded out at
least his threescore years and ten ; and we may feel sure
that as he went over in thought, after the roaming manner
of younger days, the varied scenes of a long career, there
came frequent recollections of stony Anduze, and of the
bright, ambitious Clara.

VIII

MONTPELLIER

Peire de Corbiac

NO doubt many troubadours besides Raimbaut de Vaqueiras made visits to Arles, for the city of straight noses and crooked streets had many things to interest them

There were the famous women of Arles, large and supple, full of sudden and vehement feeling tempered with a grain of Attic dignity, happy in the joy of abounding physical life and the pride of Greek descent, thinking themselves all queens, and walking like queens, too—as well as the cobblestone pavement would permit There stood the Roman Amphitheatre, not as it is now, a Cyclopean ruin that might be taken in the moonlight for Vulcan's forge, but a town of itself, densely packed with houses. And there, too, was the Aliscamps, the most famous graveyard of Christendom, the mausoleum of the Rhone valley, where there hangs now the grand melancholy of buried centuries like a mist of drifting souls.[1]

At Nismes one at least of the troubadours paid court and sang ; and at Lunel, when the market-place drowsing before us in the heavy shadow of the church tower was crowded with merchants, not only troubadours came and went, but one of them made his home [2]

Montpellier, however—or Monpeslier, as it was called then—is of far greater interest to us than any of these

places, and that for several reasons. 'To begin with, it was
a city of schools, and we are curious to learn how much
the world of the troubadours knew, and how it was in
the habit of looking at things.'

THE AMPHITHEATRE OF ARLES AS IT WAS.

If, as Rousseau said, the land of illusions is the only
one in this world fit for men to dwell in, what rare good-
fortune fell to the people of that day ! As Gaston Paris
has reminded us, the age was essentially poetical, religious, and imaginative. Men lived like children, spontaneous and naïve. Life was not sure even for a day,
and the reflectiveness developed by generations of quiet
culture had no chance to grow up. Pure reason was
utterly unknown. Existence consisted for the most part
of monotony brusquely alternating with excitement.
The new culture had not yet struck root very deeply, and
individual passions were given practically a free rein.
There were almost no restraints, little compromising,

little blending.   Appalling crimes could ride side by side
with amazing virtues, and complete self-renunciation follow close on the heels of unmeasured self-indulgence.
The watch-night for the dead was given up to laughter
and orgies.   Wild songs and pious hymns were sung at
Christmas to the same airs,—the
hymns so heavenly that it seemed
as if the sky must open, the songs
often so indecent that according
to Gascoigne a certain worthy
man died of mortification, simply
because he could not forget them.
Even the institutions of society
were based less upon reason than
upon feeling.

Religion corresponded, — one
part dogma and three parts legend, as Graf has analyzed it.
The universe was conceived of as
thoroughly penetrated with life,
with love and hate, with joy and
pain.   Creation was a vast stage
on which men, devils, and angels
enacted together a drama full of
passion.   God in a way controlled
it all, but He too was emotional ;
and rich, complex, and infinitely
varied entanglements were the

THE TOWER, LUNEL.

accepted rule.   The real world was constantly invaded
by emissaries from above and from below ; and men
and women—admonished by some and tempted by the
others — tore on through the hazardous and thrilling
experiences of this terrestrial probation, theoretically masters of their destiny, but—no matter what their intentions at the start—never sure of the outcome.   Love,

wonder, dread, and joy abounded ‸The groves of paradise and the fiery abysses of hell seemed scarcely veiled from the eyes of the flesh, and both were looked upon as actual, substantial, and material.   No wonder that, as Bourgain declares, the pulpit was never grander than during the twelfth century.

Science was dominated by the poetic and religious feelings   Precise thought was no more in existence than instruments of precision.   The diamond was gravely pronounced less pure and true than other gems, because, if the first syllable were taken from its name, *diaman*, the rest signified *lover*.   Creation was looked upon as a vast symbolism.   Natural history was made a sort of Christian mythology   The world existed to glorify God and allow mankind a chance to win heaven.   An obscure phrase of the Bible was often thought decisive against ascertained or demonstrable facts   To meditate was more useful than to observe, and allegory more edifying than explanation   The stars were considered the shining book of human destinies.   History, it was agreed, must occur in periods corresponding to the days of creation   Men felt sure that universal knowledge might be grasped, and believed that in some discoverable word all wisdom and all power were summed up   " The profoundest questions were asked without a suspicion of their significance, and the most confident answers given without a suspicion of their worthlessness."   In fact the mystery of the universe and the inmost secrets of heaven and hell seemed to lie just before the trembling student ; after that, the transmutation of metals was a commonplace, and all ordinary facts of nature trivial

There were certain special features of social life that intensified these tendencies away from calm observation and reasoning toward fancy and emotion.

One was the comparative seclusion of women.   As a

A WOMAN OF ARLES.

rule they hardly saw men except at church and at fêtes.
In the rest of their hours, occupied perhaps with some
great work of embroidery, they cherished the memory of
glances and words until in their amorous reveries everything assumed the tone of mystery and passion.   Such a
temper could not fail to affect profoundly all the relations
of men and women,—that is to say, the whole social
fabric ; and while there were more freedom and less intensity in the south than in the north of France, as there
were less imagination and more pleasures, these influences
played no slight part in the world of the troubadours.

The monastic system tended in the same direction.   It
was unnatural, and it accentuated morbid and fantastic
moods.   In the cell, demons and angels made themselves
visible both to monks and to nuns   Amid the darkness
and silence, terrific battles were fought with all the intensity born of long-sustained concentration.   Frightful
vices and celestial graces were evolved.   The peace of
God that passeth understanding poured the benediction
of ineffable joy upon fortunate souls, and beside them others fell a prey to that strange melancholy, the mysterious *acedia*, bitter and hopeless, that ate away the heart as
leprosy eats the body.'   And as the churchmen were the
only lettered class and monasteries almost the only abodes
of thought, we can see how great the effect of all this
must have been upon intellectual conditions.

A cool, still more a scientific habit of mind was truly
impossible.

Yet we must not infer that people did not wish to know .
a greater blunder it would not be easy to make.   The law
school of Montpellier, the oldest in France,' goes back to
about 1180, and the medical school was in existence forty-
three years before.   About 1180 a certain Roger de Parma,
who was perhaps a chancellor of this institution, wrote a
treatise on surgery, which was translated into Italian,

French, and Provençal, and finally (1209) into Provençal verse. A universal history appeared in French (1223–1230) about the time Ugo de Sain Circ married, and a second followed some twenty or twenty-five years later.

Still more striking are the encyclopædias. Vincent de Beauvais, born in the last years of the twelfth century, covered natural science in his *Speculum Naturale;* and one reading of his table of contents will forever dissipate the notion that all the men of his age preferred to be ignorant. Not long after Dante was born (1265), Bartholomew of Glanvilla, an English Franciscan, prepared a Latin encyclopædia based on Vincent's work that had an enormous currency all over Europe. A little later Matfre Ermengaud [6] began to write a similar work in Provençal verse, called the *Breviary of Love;* and his thirty-five thousand lines cover in an orderly way about every subject of thought, from God and the angels to stones, plants, and animals, and the duties and faults of everyday living.

Unfortunately the desire to know was poorly fed. Ideas intended for the masses were put into the vulgar tongue, and usually cramped into verse to aid the memory ; and each of these processes resulted in distortion. Even the knowledge of the learned was little more than a repetition of Latin science imperfectly understood, or of Greek science badly transmitted by the Arabs, both of them strangely mixed with the products of untrained imaginations. Vincent de Beauvais held that the earth was a globe suspended at the centre of the universe ; the venerable Bede represented it as an egg floating in a liquid ; and indeed after the eighth century all serious cosmogonists, following the lead of Aristotle, taught the sphericity of our planet. But the Church considered a belief in the antipodes proof positive of heresy ; and Vincent, though sound on this point, counted the transmutation of metals almost as definite an art as agriculture, and said of the marvellous tales in his book that God is able to do anything and they might safely be accepted   Hugues de St. Victor, who prepared a Latin treatise *On Beasts and Other Things* and died about the same time as Raimbaut d'Aurenga (1173), attributed to the stag a life of nine hundred years, and wrote of the dove that with her right eye she contemplates herself, and with her left eye God.

Bartholomew is no less worth while : oysters open their shells at night in the springtime, and the dew, falling within and uniting with the inner parts of the fish, breeds the pearl , lightning is caused by hot and cold vapors smiting together like flint and steel, and when the winds arouse too great a commotion inside the bladder-like cloud it bursts, and makes a frightful noise called thunder ; the planets appear to move because they are " ravished " every day from east to west by " the violence of the firmament "; the cockatrice kills animals by breathing upon them ; the phenix, fauns, mermaids, griffins, and satyrs are as real as dogs ; the beavers when they build a dam lay one of their number on his back, pile sticks between his legs, and then drag him and his burden home ; while the elephants if they fall sick gather good herbs and make use of them after heaving up the head and praying God for help.

Herrat, the talented abbess of a convent in Alsace, wrote in the last quarter of the twelfth century a work entitled *The Garden of Delights*. Much of it was devoted to piety and theology, and a portion to verses against usury and simony ; but science was not wholly overlooked Falling stars were explained as bright sparks struck out by the wind in disturbing the ether, which occupies the space between the moon and the firmament of heaven as air fills that between the earth and the moon.

Geography, merely a nameless division of geometry, was of the same piece. To the average man there were only two main facts : Jerusalem and his own estate, just

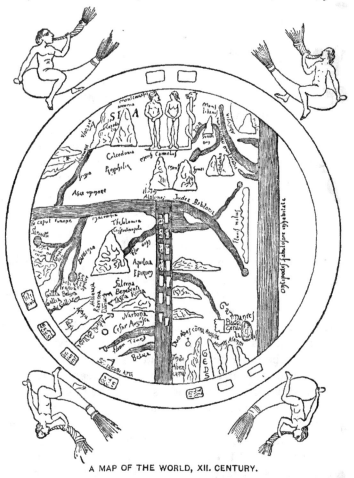

A MAP OF THE WORLD, XII. CENTURY.

as ancient history was epitomized for him in the three names: Troy, Alexander, and Cæsar. But inquiring

minds roved much farther afield.   Rome dwelt powerfully still in the memories and the imaginations of men,
impressing them by the monuments it contained, the
ideas for which it stood, and the events with which it was
associated.   Paris had already begun to be recognized as
the centre of culture, a model city shining brilliantly
though afar.   Equally real, however, were countries
where there was neither sun nor moon; races of men with
skins harder than iron, so that they went into battle without armor ; men whose teeth and shins grew out of their
breasts ; men with lions' claws on their hands and feet ;
the land of Bucion where people wore horns like sheep ;
and the region of Buridane where they bayed like mastiffs.

A Bestiary had this to say . " The nature of the wolf is
such that when he sees a man before the man sees him,
he deprives the man of speech, but if the man see him
first, the man deprives him of strength.   .   .   .   When
a viper sees a man naked it dare not look at him, it is in
such fear ; but when it sees a man clothed, it has no fear
and springs upon him.   .   .   .   The aspic is the serpent
that guards the balsam   When a man wishes to gather
balsam, he puts the aspic to sleep with the music of instruments and thus secures the balsam ; and when the aspic
sees how it has been tricked, it stops one ear with its tail
and rubs the other on the ground until it also is stopped :
then it cannot hear the music, and so it keeps watch "

For some reason pagan ideas about the precious stones
and their virtues had an extraordinary vitality , and all
through the middle ages there were poems in full currency
stuffed with notions too unscientific for Pliny.   A Lapi-
dary asserted · " If you bring the calcofons near the fire
and then bear it reverently on a chaste person, it gives a
voice of double strength that never becomes hoarse."
The beryl was thought useful to preserve affection between husband and wife   Marbodus ' in his comments on

the twelve foundation stones of the Apocalypse remarked :
" The emerald is found only in a dry and uninhabitable
country, so bitterly cold that nothing can dwell there but
griffins and the one-eyed arimasps that fight with them."

In medicine the state of things was considerably better.
One great step in advance was made, for while Aristotle
attributed a portion of the mental qualities to the body,
the mediæval doctors placed them all in the head.   Some
of the medical knowledge of Vincent de Beauvais surprises
us, and some of his remedies possess a genuine value.

There were mistaken opinions enough, however. "The
lung is there for respiration," says the *Breviary of Love*,
" to draw cold air to the heart."   In six hundred words
Bartholomew was able to expound the whole mystery of
body, and brain, veins, nerves, psychology, and life, proceeding after this manner : " By heat working in the
blood, there is caused in the liver a strong boiling and
seething, and thereof cometh a smoke, the which is pured
and made subtle by the veins of the liver, and turneth
into a subtle spiritual substance and airly kind that is
called the Natural Spirit. . . .   And this same Spirit
turneth heartward by certain veins ; and there, by moving and smiting together of the parts of the heart, the
Spirit is more pured and turned into a more subtle kind,
and then it is called of physicians the Vital Spirit. . . .
The same Spirit, piercing and passing forth to the dens
of the brain, is there more directed and made subtle, and
is changed into the Animal Spirit.   And so this Animal
Spirit is gendered in the foremost den of the brain, and
is somewhat spread into the limbs of feeling.   But yet
nevertheless some part thereof abideth in the aforesaid
den, that common sense, the common wit, and the virtue
imaginative may be made perfect.   Then he passeth forth
into the middle den that is called Logistic, to make the
intellect and understanding perfect.   And when he hath

informed the intellect, then he passeth forth into the den of memory ; and, bearing with him the prints of likeness which are made in the other dens, he layeth them up in the chamber of memory."

If such was the theory, the practice was naturally uncertain   Arnaud de Villeneuve [*] wrote a pupil to tell his patient, if he were unable to diagnose the malady, that he suffered from an obstruction of the liver.   " If the sick man replies, ' No, master, the pain is in my head,' make haste and answer, ' That comes from the liver.'   Use the word ' obstruction ' for they don't know what it means."

It was perhaps natural that common people chose to rely upon old wives' remedies, upon downright incantations, and upon herbs gathered with auspicious prayers like this   " Now do I beseech all potent herbs and pray to your majesty, since mother earth hath brought you forth and given you to all peoples, imparting to you the medicine of health and majesty, that you may be to all humankind a most useful aid." [*]

Surgery was given over to the barbers, and the sale of drugs to the spice-merchants.   Dentistry was almost a lost art ; for while Martial could laugh at an old lady for laying aside her robe and her teeth at the same time, the twelfth and thirteenth centuries were at the mercy of nature ; and St. Louis, though king of France, had to get on in his last days with but a single tooth in his lower jaw.

Hygiene flourished, however, and we have a manual in Provençal verse, which in the course of its four hundred and forty-eight lines gives much interesting advice. [10]   For spring it recommends to take physic and be bled, to court the ladies and to eat hearty meals,—fat quails and partridges, fresh eggs and stuffed chickens, roast goat at dinner, and at supper lettuce.   For summer it prescribes veal with sour wine, young kid, pomegranates, tart apples, cu-

cumbers and squashes, an acid grape sauce with the fish
and meat,—no bleeding and no love-making. Autumn
was regarded as the melancholy season : people were advised to eat more heartily than in summer,—warm, sweet,
and savory dishes, ripe grapes, sweet figs with wine, fat
sheep two years old, chickens and wild birds, with a good
sauce flavored with ginger or saffron,—no cabbages, no
légumes of any kind, and love sparingly. Then came
winter : one should eat still more, and exercise and warm
himself and stay near the kitchen ; water-fowl should be
eaten, and hens, cocks, and capons broiled over the coals,
roast meat, puddings, broiled pork, and pork from the
spit—all well spiced and peppered. Good wine and
piment should be drunk, and no medicine taken save as
much love as possible. The conclusion of the piece is
better yet :

> In gladness let a man arise,
> In gladness pray with heavenward eyes ;
> In gladness let his form be dressed
> In clothes the goodliest and best ;
> In gladness let him tell his tale,
> Or hear what others would unveil,
> With joy and gladness don and wear
> A comely mantle new and fair,
> With gladness mount and ride all day
> To meet and drive the foe away,
> With gladness go for lawful gain,
> With gladness turn toward home again ;
> For joy and cheer from morn till night
> Prolong one's life and make it light.

Still closer to our interest is the *Treasury* (*Tesaur*) of
Peire de Corbiac.[1] " Master " Peire, as he proudly
termed himself, was a Gascon troubadour of Sain Circ's
time, and merited fame for a compliment he once paid :
" Lady, you are the bush that Moses found green amid

TOUR DE LA BABOTTE, MONTPELLIER.

flames of fire", but his great work was a poem of eight
hundred and forty Alexandrines, on a single rhyme, in
which he tells us exactly what he knows. This, mind
you, is a head, not a book ; and I, at least, find it peculiarly fascinating to walk about this troubadour brain,
drawing drawers and lifting lids.

The ten arts and the ten orders of angels were alike
familiar to him.   He knew all Biblical history : how
Joshua conquered thirty-one kings ; how David sank
three stones into Goliath's forehead, and then cut out his
tongue and put it in his game-bag, as the angel advised ;
and how when Herodias obtained the head of John the
Baptist she was very glad, for, as it would appear, she
loved him and her love had been scorned, and so she
kissed the dead lips and then vanished away.

In Grammar he could speak and construe Latin.   In
Logic he could argue and if need be entangle his adversary
in a web of sophistry.   In Rhetoric he could accuse or defend with varied and many considerations, and color his
words to please the ear.   In Law, though not so strong,
he could manage a case well and reasonably, and please
the audience.   In Music he knew the four principal and
the four secondary sounds, the solfeggio, the seven modu-
lations, and the five strings of the viol,—the lowest one
rather gruff but sounding sweetly with the string an octave
higher.   In Arithmetic he could add, multiply, and sub-
tract, and keep accounts,—even a king's.   In Geometry he
was an adept, and lying on the ground he could with the
aid of a stick find the height of walls and towers.   Astronomy was among his chief accomplishments, and he takes
manifest delight in telling us of Saturn,—proud, wise, and
ambitious to rule—,of Mars,—malevolent and bad, pro-
voking strife and battles—,and of the sun hung in the
midst of the planets, three above and three below him,
born and renewing his youth each day, harmonizing the

cold and damp with his own heat and dryness, and so
tempering the world for all living creatures

Of Medicine he knew a good deal, but surgery was
despicable—he was " never apprenticed to cutting and
sewing." Black art, " all the incantations," the auguries
by birds, and more tales of mythology than Ovid or lying
Thales knew, hundreds and thousands in fact, were his ;
and in History he knew of Troy and Thebes ; how Æneas
came to Lombardy; of Cæsar and Pompey; of Vespasian
and Titus , of the twelve Emperors, and Constantine the
twelfth , of Greece, and how Alexander, after conquering
twelve kingdoms in twelve years, divided them at his
death into twelve parts , of France from Clovis down , of
England, and how Brutus came from Troy to Brittany,
and then crossing the Channel conquered the giant Cor-
nilieu; and finally of wild Merlin and his dim prophecies.
In songs and poems of every style he was perfectly at
home , and besides everything else he was a finished man
of the world, agreeable to all, skilful to avoid bores and
annoyances, getting on as well as possible with fools,
esteemed wise among the wise, and ever praying God to
save him at the last day.

Just how much of all this varied lore, just how many of
those extraordinary fables, just what scraps of geography,
of astronomy, of history, of medical knowledge, each of
the troubadours and each of his patrons possessed, it is
of course impossible to say ; but we need to know that
such was the knowledge of their time, and we should
remember in what kind of an atmosphere the poems we
are studying grew.

But this was not the only reason for our interest in
Montpellier

Its people are fond of calling it " *coquette*," and the
term fits. For it is no ancient dame of sombre dignity,
but a gay modern-looking town, perched jauntily on its

turtle-back hill, and long the Mecca of English valetudi-
narians Smollett found the streets full on the Sunday
of his arrival here, and the people sitting at their doorways and gaily chatting well on into the night. Fisch
saw the working folk dance in the public square on holidays, and the onlookers—caught up by the rhythm of
drum and pipe—joining the dancers. Even now there is
a musical tone in the speech of the city, and one feels the
spirit not of revery but of life in the senses, physical
vitality, youth.

But, though still youthful, Montpellier goes back to a
village already growing up in the midst of a great forest
at the close of the tenth century, and it was a very busy
and picturesque city in the time of the troubadours. Ben-
jamin of Navarre tells us what he found · " Merchants
are there from the country of the Algarbes [Africa], from
Lombardy, from the kingdom of great Rome, from all
parts of Egypt, from the land of Israel, from Greece, from
Gaul, from Spain, and from England ; so that one sees
people of every tongue, not to mention the Genoese and
Pisans." The rhythm of the gold-beaters' hammers
resounded through the alleys, the perfumes of spices—
especially at Christmas time when they were pounded—
overflowed the streets, and the products of the dyers in
scarlet—a special industry of Monpeslier—filled the open
spaces with flaunting color like the banners of a triumphant
host.

There are still reminders of that age. Here is the fine
promenade of the Peyrou with its gorgeous magnolias and
its Claude Lorraine outlook : the castle stood here, and
in its hall Count Guilhem VIII., as we shall find from
time to time, showed hospitality to the troubadours for
almost a generation (1172–1202), during the palmiest day
of Provençal song." Below are broad meadows watered
by a stream that Ste Beuve likened to the rivers of

Greece [13] ; where, instead of the groves, vineyards, and gardens, and the long arcade of the aqueduct, the mediæval traveller saw that luxuriant crop of aromatic flowers, drugged by the rich, unhealthy soil, which set Arnaud de Villeneuve about the manufacture of perfumes. Yonder is the *Tour des Pins*, [14] begun probably while Sain Circ was quarrelling with Clara, and now — the city archives within, ivy without, and two evergreens flourishing on the top—reminding us of a green old age, cherishing the past and hailing the future, a Nestor, a Goethe, a Gladstone. Farther away is the *Tour de la Babotte*, a tremendous tower, said to date from a

TOUR DES PINS.

period as remote. And in the distance, just as they were in the days of the troubadours, we see to the north the rugged Cevennes, to the south—only seven miles away—the gleaming Mediterranean, to the southwest the blue Pyrenees—like clouds fettered to the horizon,—and in the far northeast a pale outline of the snowy Alps. [15]

IX

NONTRON AND MAREUIL

Arnaut de Maruelh

AS the evening of a certain July day drew on in the year King John of England was excommunicated (1209), the hilltop of Béziers was the spectacle of the universe. The people of the earth—far, far beyond the range of vision—were gazing up to it, the Pit emptied itself to look, and all the inhabitants of heaven, dumb with consternation, stood watching it from the battlements.

But we shall come to that soon enough. Just now we stand with very different thoughts on the terrace before the church of St. Nazaire.[1] The Cevennes and the snowy Pyrenees have come nearer since we left Montpellier, and the waves of the Mediterranean are brighter. At our feet is the river Orb, winding down through fertile plains from the mountains of Lodève, and lingering under its bridges a little as if dreading the sandy dunes and the salt sea beyond To east and to west extends a work of man scarcely less great, the famous Canal du Midi, along which pass rich cargoes from Toulouse and Bordeaux to Italy and the Levant, like beads of gold slipping on a thread of silver. Above the river and the canal ancient houses, wondrously disordered and picturesque, straggle upward to the rocky height on which we stand. And here, between a beautiful sky and a beautiful earth, we reflect that Béziers was the central point of the sweetest, the tenderest idyl of Provençal romance, blooming amid wars and tragedies like a green and shadowed valley cradled in the iron cliffs of the Pyrenees.

But the beginning of the tale is far away to the north-west among the hills between Périgueux and Angoulême, and we approach it by the way of pretty Nontron.

A place to put us in a better humor we could scarcely find. Nontron is hidden in its valley almost out of sight; and the valley, or I should say gorge, is so bent and sinuous that we can never see it all at once   Here is a viaduct and there a bridge, here an archway and there a terraced esplanade, here a sightly modern edifice and there some ruins of an ancient castle.' Where none of these presents itself we meet a long flight of stairs escaped from an etching, dividing half way up,—not evenly like the grand stairway of the architects,—but capriciously as the brooks fork, one branch wide and the other narrow, one straight and the other winding, one long and steep, the other short and easy   The streets are like seals at play, diving one under another, coming up just where you are not looking, and taking another plunge as you are puzzling over the first one; while the foot-paths, like the nimble young chaps, go under and around them all When they tire a little of one another, the coquetry of the dark-eyed river sets them off again; and at last—river and roads and paths—they all sober down and go off together for a midday nap under the trees.

Some ten or twelve miles to the west of Nontron is Old Mareuil on the river Beautiful, *Mareuil-sur-Belle;* and there, about the time Raimbaut d'Aurenga began to rule in Corteson (1150), a child known afterward from his home as Arnaut de Maruelh was ushered into the world.

His father and mother, servants in the castle, perhaps, were of no position, and their life was narrow and scant;

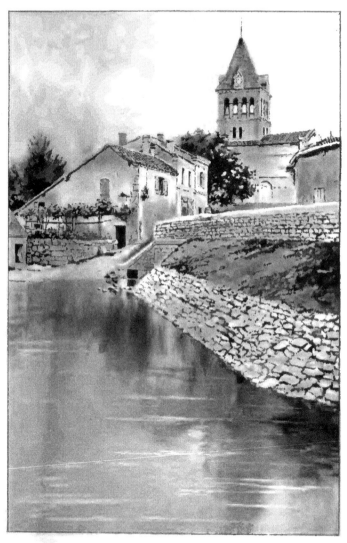

OLD MAREUIL.

but the boy found something outside the walls of his poor
home, for nature was there and nature is always rich and
wide. The tidy village—its houses of cream-colored stone
looking very winsome under the pale red of their tiles—
curled up contentedly in the lap of a wide and open valley. Beside the river and about the village lay rich and
lustrous meadows, through which the windings of the
stream were accented by lines of poplars along the banks.
Here spring came early with its birds and its flowers. In
opening summer the thick grass was generously sprinkled
with clover and with bees. As the season advanced, the
bent heads of the tall wheat in the grain-fields gave all
who looked that way the sense of coming wealth. And
when autumn arrived and the harvests had been gathered,
even the stubble seemed of a deeper brown than elsewhere,
as if the earth would show that it still was fat.

Beyond the meadows an easy slope began on either
side, fields changing into pastures. Like the uplands of
green Vermont, the land was decked here and there with
clumps of bushes and with patches of brake. Here and
there a great oak or a group of larches gave relief. Sheep
roamed over the fields, watched by sun-browned women
in wooden shoes, distaff in hand. Close mats of purple
heather, and golden spots of wild *trèfle*, with a score of
other flowers, bloomed until St. John's day had passed,
and hot July came upon them with scorching winds.

There was little to suggest the ambitions and rivalries
of courts, nothing to teach the arts of a cunning world.
It was the place for long and simple thoughts, for deep
and quiet sentiment.'

Many a time the boy witnessed a sunset like the one
that I saw there A tremendous mountain of cloud, mass
upon mass, crest beyond crest, head above head, gathered
—vast and black—in the western sky, seemingly more
solid than the earth it menaced. Presently the escaping

sun appeared between its massive floor and the low hills,
quite unclouded but of a crimson deep enough to be
looked steadily upon, and floated there like an anchored
galley in a sea of yellow flame. Then the sea cooled
through all the tones of light and was blue again   Little
clouds, dressed in burning purple, gathered about the sun
Finally the mountain took fire, and blazing upward from
its foundations drifted to the zenith, burning and melting
away as it rose ; and so in the end, when the sun had set,
there hung in the place of the vast black cloud only Venus
the evening star, undimmed and serene   And the boy
Arnaut stood and looked on, absorbed and still, gazing
with all his large soft blue eyes at that sublime demonstration of hope, thinking nothing, feeling everything,
drinking in without knowing it a great thought, a boundless faith, that sometime his dream would come true, that
a full and clear and splendid satisfaction like the closing
of that day would sometime and somehow come to him,
that it was in the order of the world, and sooner or later
it would surely come.

Religion did something to fulfil this hope, this faith,
but more to deepen it and lead it on.   The dark Romanesque church at the centre of his village had few worshippers more constant than he.   He loved to steal in by
himself when only two or three old crones were dozing on
the pavement.   Kneeling in a corner, praying perhaps
but surely dreaming, he would keep his eyes fixed on a
beam of light that fell from the tower across the shadows
of the transept, until his mind almost lost itself in a
trance   At vespers especially he was quite sure to be
found, still dreaming more than listening, more than
praying.   The service was not elaborate, but his imagination was the freer because the mind was not overpowered
by the senses   He felt rather than heard the music and
the chanting of the priest   He felt rather than saw the

ministrations about the altar. His nature, good but more sensuous than devout, recognized in all this not piety, not worship, but the same teaching as in the evening sky, the same gospel of hope, the same faith in a coming satisfaction, only more definite, more precise, more sure. So, quite unconscious of himself, his feeling growing constantly stronger but wholly undirected and undrawn, he waited long on his knees ; while the music filled him with a delightful unrest, and the incense enveloped him with suggestions of exquisite sweetness, until the light suspended in the midst of the chancel became like another Venus in the evening sky, and the dark walls and the massive tower dissolved like the cloud, leaving him free beneath an open heaven, wide as the earth, infinitely deep, inexpressibly tender, and lighted still by the fair bright star of hope.

As a man Arnaut fulfilled the promise of his boyhood and kept its faith in his heart. His large white hands, dimpled over every joint, betrayed his affectionate and simple disposition. His rather small, close beard and its glossy softness, showing that no razor had cut it, suggested the naturalness of his development. His forehead, low and shapely rather than capacious, and the backward turn of his full head showed that his strength was in feeling rather than in intellect. His eyes rested upon others in a waiting manner, as if instead of perusing them he expected them to give him an impression of themselves. He was not a bold man, quick to think and quick to act like Vaqueiras, not a popular dashing fellow like Count Raimbaut, not a clever lady's man like Sain Circ. The centre of his life hung between thought and passion in the dim and languorous region of revery, dreams, and sentiment

No one had thought him beautiful as a boy—his eyes were too large, and his face too thin—but suddenly all

saw that he was a handsome young man, and he was the
last one to discover it. Manners came to him in the same
way. He never studied grace or dignity, but for him it
was easiest to be dignified and graceful. His first few
visits at the unpretending castle of Maruelh added the
needed touch of courtliness, and his bearing became such
that aristocrats envied 'it, wondering not a little because
it showed no trace of the artificiality that courts betrayed
as yet.

Character and education kept pace with sentiment and
manners. "No one can be excellent," he once declared,
"who does not flee baseness, and one cannot flee baseness
unless he knows how to distinguish it,"—a saying that
shows not only good intentions but moral thoughtfulness.
Again he sang : "One can leave estates behind him and
cause a son to inherit them, but worth he will never have
unless it is in his heart." And again "I know that it
is harm and dishonor not to cheer up those who are disheartened." It is easy to believe that a boy so excellent
and amiable enlisted the aid of his lord. At all events,
in one way or another he gained a clerkly education,
learned how to read stories agreeably—doubtless the
French romantic poems—and acquired the arts of singing
and of making verses

The calling of scribe and notary was the one he undertook as a livelihood ; but we can easily see how little he
was qualified for work of that nature. Close-fisted prudence, petty shrewdness, and hard-grained business judgment were not his gifts. To write letters, deeds, and wills
for horny-witted peasants, to dun unlucky debtors, to
evict insolvents,—his bullet-headed rival across the way
was ten times as good a man for that. Arnaut failed as a
notary ; but he discovered meanwhile that his voice was
liked, his presence enjoyed, his reading listened to, and
his verses praised in the retired circle where he was

THE CASTLE OF MAREUIL.

known. The great world lay beyond the hills, the old
hope was in his heart ; and thus it came to pass that with
many doubts but more faith he bade farewell to Maruelh,
and struck out resolutely for a wider life beyond the
horizon.'

Where was destiny preparing him a place meanwhile ?

Stephen, the good-hearted but feeble king of England,
had a son, Eustace. The son almost came to be king
during his father's reign, for the barons were made to
swear allegiance to him. But he died before Stephen ,
and Constance his wife, queen as she was called and sister
to the king of France as she was in fact, came down to
Languedoc the very year Henry of Anjou became Henry
II. of England (1154), and there married the fifth Raimon,
the count of powerful Toulouse. A castle was built for
her at Burlatz in the lovely valley of the Agout, and in
this castle there was born a daughter, Alazais (Adelaide),
called from her birthplace the countess of Burlatz. There
she was born and there she grew up ; until, when she had
barely passed out of girlhood, her father made peace with
the viscount of Béziers (Bezers), and as a seal and pledge
of the treaty gave him Alazais to wife. So she rode with
her maidens down to the city by the Orb and became the
mistress of castle and court (1171), two years before Raimbaut d'Aurenga was gathered to his fathers, and three, it
may be interesting to note, before the leaning tower of
Pisa was begun.'

It must have seemed a rude change. Viscount Rogier,
her husband, was a strong lord but not a gentle one. His
father had been assassinated by the citizens of Béziers in
the church of Mary Magdalen, and Rogier determined
that the punishment should be no less notable than the
crime. The king of Aragon aided him with foreign
troops ; they were introduced into the city, and on a
signal fell upon the people. With steel or cord the

men were so completely exterminated, that in order to
give the city a population the Spanish soldiers married
the widows and daughters of their victims.   With such
memories fresh and bleeding about her, Béziers could not
have been altogether a safe or pleasant residence for the
young countess.   Murmurs were loud and alarms rife.
But she soon grew accustomed to danger, though we
may believe she never forgot it, and set herself to have a
court as brilliant and enjoyable as could be made.

Taine remarked of civilization at the beginning of the
twelfth century that it was a mixture of precocity, black-
guardism (*polissonnerie*), and extravagance ; and the
great work of the élite nobility during the next hundred
years was to construct from such materials a refined and
elegant social life.   Naturally their success was not complete ; there were too many harsh influences all about, like
the cold winds of early spring , and more centuries were
demanded also by the mere hardness of men's fibre.   But
the present age, familiar with polite usages to-day and in
the past, is in danger of forgetting how much was accomplished and what pains were taken.

It was precisely in the land of the troubadours and
keeping time by the music of their songs, that a gay,
brilliant, and polished society was first developed in the
modern world.   Partly by instinct, partly by feeling, and
partly by taking thought, a code of ideas and a system of
conduct were elaborated, to break and put in training the
rude ways and ungoverned passions of the feudal world
The starting-point was love for woman as we have already
discovered.   As the result of love came that *joi* of which
we already know, a gladness and lightness of heart that
illuminated and vivified the inner world like another sun,
and prompted to all noble, beautiful, and self-denying
acts.   Joi led especially to the boundless generosity that
frequently almost ruined wealthy nobles, and even made

robbers of them sometimes.   Along with such qualities
went naturally a passionate fondness for social pleasure,
witty conversation, and gallantry.   All these together were
summed up in the word *joven*, that youngness or young-
heartedness which has already been mentioned more than
once ; while feebleness of spirit and meanness of life were
signified by the contrary word, oldness.   Over all this were
thrown the bonds of self-control and moderation, expressed
by another word always on the lips,—*mesura*, measure,
which endeavored to bring even the virtues into æsthetic
form.   The precious fruit of so much striving and study
was known as *cortesia*, courtliness, the perfect bearing and
conduct of a finished gentleman according to the code of
chivalry and poetry ; and the rewards a man gained from
this were the excellence or worth that he felt within himself, and—far more important, as a rule,—the repute or
credit with others that all were passionately bent upon
winning.[6]

These were the principles that guided the court of
Béziers.   But we must not go to the other extreme and
take the people too seriously.   In a very real sense they
were by Anglo-Saxon standards only grown-up children.
Indeed they were almost literally such   As we learn from
the poem of *Flamenca*, love began to claim a girl at thirteen, at fifteen she was marriageable, at sixteen she was
aging, and if she had not given her heart at twenty-one
she was believed incapable of perfect love.[7]   Girls were
actually wedded at the earliest of these ages, for example
the daughter of Count Guilhem VIII. of Montpellier
Through generations of such marriages the whole race
acquired or preserved the charm and likewise the immaturity of youth   Such a people could show no likeness to
our own great hero Beowulf, born under a sullen sky,
nurtured on the pride of will, inflexible, unswerving, and
able to gaze unmoved into the jaws of horrible death.

The difference was like that which Pericles, or at least Thucydides, portrayed between the Spartans and the Athenians.

The countess of Burlatz and her friends enjoyed existence and existed to enjoy Their ambition was to please and to be pleased ` Self-denial and disappointment they hated.   Life was a luscious grape to be taken gently upon the tongue, pressed softly against the palate, and lingeringly tasted as it surrendered its bouquet.   Graceful manners passed current for gold.   '' The sweetest of good things is a fair address and a courtly answer,'' they were fond of saying.   '' A good refusal is worth more than a rude gift,'' sang Arnaut.   Culture had not yet been able to penetrate far below the surface, but for that very reason its colors were the more brilliant.   '' Hidden wisdom bears no fruit,'' the proverb ran, and everybody intended to display all the graces he possessed.

The feelings, too, were on the surface, and for that reason they were swayed by external causes.   Unswerving heroism was perfectly possible, but only under the influence of an overpowering emotion.   The bravest of soldiers could tremble without shame in sight of a hostile army, and the strongest could swoon before the woman he loved.   Brilliancy was offset by shadow; nadir answered to zenith.   Society was in short a kaleidoscope, a medley, a shifting dream, compounded of all the human motives, qualities, and emotions   Wit, gayety, color, motion, and sparkle, poetry and song, April tears and April laughter, burning desires, romantic exploits, intense pleasures, and bitter griefs, intrigue, suspicion, jealousy, and falsehood , sharp and sudden quarrels ; astonishing weaknesses and marvellous daring , utter devotion, shocking betrayals, and ideal faithfulness ; matchless generosity, beauty, and glory,—all these were there and more, not without a prophecy of Tartarin, ceaselessly acting and reacting, and

all endeavoring to arrange themselves, as not infrequently
they did, into forms of mobile grace and stately dignity.

We must remember also that the court of Béziers was
not a mere coterie. Aristocratic life in the Midi was much
freer than in the north. Not only the lords of neighboring fiefs and of subordinate estates were entertained there,
but a descending scale of nobility down to simple knights.
Below these were a class of semi-aristocrats, men of noble
descent—Gallic or Visigothic—merged among the towns-
folk, and they, too, were invited to the castle. Nay, even
the burghers themselves might come, would they but make
themselves agreeable ; and a poem by Arnaut intimates
that many such were found at court handsomely attired
and correctly mannered, bearing themselves acceptably in
the dance, the tourney, and the service of ladies.' With
all the rest an endless procession of interesting and picturesque travellers came and went. There were no hotels
then, only taverns ; and hospitality was not only a courtesy
but a duty All decent people were made welcome ; and
at many gates, according to the precept of boundless generosity, no comer was rejected Béziers like Montpellier
was on a great through-line, and the castle hall was almost
a caravansary. Princes, nobles, captains, and ambassadors were always passing and repassing. Wealthy merchants, lordly but suave, made their visits Bishops and
legates of the pope came and went. Troubadours flashed
their wit and verse for a day or a week, and many a joglar
tarried a night or two for the humbler display of skill in
music and sleight of hand.

Among the poets came Arnaut de Maruelh, and Lady
Alazais greeted him courteously as a hostess always took
pride in doing. Of more than courtesy she had no thought,
but she was one of those whom a consciousness of beauty
and high degree makes unaffected, simple, and winsome.
Without stepping an inch from her pedestal she caused

the stranger to feel at home, and impressed him with a
sense of herself that he could not forget.   Learning that
he was practised in reading the romances, she listened to
him with her friends   Then he was invited to sing, and
all were charmed with his agreeable person, his elegant
manners, and his artistic skill   The countess bade him
stay on at her court, and said politely that she wished to
hear him again and often.   " Chance and the stars " had
led him, as the biographer says, to his destined place , and
the troubadour, pleased with his reception and more than
pleased with his hostess, cut short his journeyings at
Béziers.'

X

BÉZIERS AND BURLATZ

Arnaut de Maruelh (*Continued*)

IT required but little time for Arnaut de Maruelh to become a favorite in the court of Béziers, and he needed
hardly more to fall in love with Lady Alazais.

> Fair days and sweet and rich in love
> Are these when verdure springs anew,
> And light of step and blithe I view
> With gladness every opening flower,
> And sing of love with hopefulness and cheer ;
> For morn or eve no care or thought comes near
> Save thoughts of love, my joyous bosom thronging.
>
> For I adore one far above
> The fairest that I ever knew,—
> So noble, too, so good, so true,
> Her virtues e'en her charms o'ertower ;
> And this is why I tremble and I fear ;
> I cannot win her ; yet, the more 't is clear,
> The more I love, the keener is my longing.[1]

It was no base and selfish passion that he felt. The
gathered energy of a loving and aspiring heart had simply
found the directing it had long awaited. To love so beautiful a lady, one so exalted in station, so charming in manner, so graced with all the accomplishments of courtly
life,—to his mind this was the only natural, the only
reasonable course. For while the Greeks and Romans

viewed love as a fatality that overwhelmed a man like a
sudden catastrophe, Arnaut and his age regarded it as to
be sure a fatality but a blessed one, a necessity created by
the man himself rather than forced upon him, a necessity
that won his consent through free deliberation quite as
much as by emotion and enthusiasm, a necessity that
might indeed bring with it griefs, yet even in its pangs
was ennobling and sweet   So love justified itself to
Arnaut's reason and sense of "measure," and not only,
like every natural and reasonable action, was a delight in
itself but brought with it other delights to his musing
heart.

> As live the fish in waters clear and spacious,
>   Live I in gladness nothing can destroy ;
>   For Love hath set me on so fair a quest
>   That my affection fills my life with joy ;
>   Yet when I think how she excels the rest,
>   I both am proud and fain would hide my face ;
>   Aspiring zeal so shares with love my soul,
>   That reason guides and measure hath control.
>
> And, lady fair,—glad, excellent, and gracious,
>   This love, though vain, shall e'er be my employ ;
>   So Love decrees,—can I his will contest ?
>   And since he knows my love hath no alloy,
>   He shows a way my heart may still be blest :
>   In thought I kiss, caress you, and embrace,—
>   Dear wooing, sweet, and potent to console,
>   And mine in spite of Jealousy's patrol.[2]

As the days went by, the love that began with simple
admiration struck its roots more deeply into his life.
When the duties and the pleasures of his vocation took
him now and then from Béziers, absence threw his mind
back upon itself. Long, delightful reveries deepened his
impressions then, and fixed them. His thoughts occupied
themselves constantly with the one most pleasant theme ,

and, released in the hours of slumber, found their sweetest
repose in still pursuing it.

> Whatever call me and whate'er be keeping,
>   My love, kind lady, is so true and leal,
>   My heart goes not as I am forced to do,
>   And in my dreams I oft return to you ;
> We talk and laugh, and I have joy while sleeping,
>   But when I wake, I see and know and feel
> 'T is all but naught, and laughter ends in weeping.[3]

It may appear strange that a musing lover, a dreamy
poet, like Arnaut ventured to express himself so boldly in
songs publicly rendered   But it seems that he contrived a
stratagem.   Some of his pieces he avowed as his own, for
he was a poet by profession and must prove his mastery
of the art ; but those which uttered his feelings clearly,
and might have told the story of his aspirations, he sang
as the work of another.[4]   Though burning with desire he
remembered the proverb, " By hurrying you lose, by waiting you overtake."   Besides, as he himself sang, " He
that beseeches timidly loves better than he that beseeches
boldly," and he felt sure that his lady would understand
in time the sincere affection hidden in his poems.   But
after a while he could bear disguise no longer.   " Love
constrained him," says the meagre history, and in simple
words he laid bare his heart.

> Your manner noble and gracious—
>   A memory ne'er to die,
>   Your smile, your glancing eye,
>   The grace your looks imply,
>   My noble lady, so
> Constrain my heart to sigh
>   In love no words can tell,
>   That if you will not show
>   Some pity for my woe,
>   Death soon may come and well.[5]

" And the countess did not put him off, but gave ear to his plea, and accepted it, and granted it, and she provided for him, and made him bold to compose songs of her and to sing them. And he was in great honor at her court " So runs the biography.

Once more we must clear our minds of the idea that such a relation of lover and mistress represented a low intrigue or a transient amour   Acceptance was somewhat like a betrothal, somewhat like the entry into knighthood. If no others witnessed the compact, Love himself was called upon as a divinity to sanction and solemnize its mutual pledges. Service on the one side and gracious recognition on the other were the essential elements as we have seen.   To Arnaut acceptance meant that the countess of Burlatz became his patroness in a very near and special sense.   It signified confidence, esteem, admiration, and at least a possibility of tenderer emotions   His heart overflowed with happiness and cheer, and it mattered little that as a concession to his lady's pride of rank the compact was to be kept secret.

> We three, my lady,—you and I and Love,
>   We only know the covenant that raises
> My hope so high, but come, no telltale phrases !
>   For I am yours ; I gave myself to you,
>   So fixed my heart, so firm the bonds I wear
>   Of love sincere and of affection deep,
>   For aught besides, I have but little care.
>
> And I am thankful that with vaunts above
>   All truth, each troubadour his lady praises
>   As best of all on whom the sun e'er gazes ;
>   For while their vaunts are foolish through and through,
>   Amid these boasts my song will safely fare,
>   Suspicion, malice, and the rest will sleep,
>   For all will think my glowing praise they share [6]

It was not without good reason that out of numberless

beautiful spots Burlatz was chosen as the country home of Queen Constance. The heart of Alazais must have turned often to it from the bustle, the intrigues, and the restless pageants of Béziers, and we know that she often held her court there. When the sun of April rose high, we can imagine her with a little cavalcade of chosen friends, well guided and well guarded, ambling comfortably along to Castres, and thence after a halt some five miles farther to the home of her girlhood.

The route from Castres to Burlatz, as I shall try to believe, was exactly as it is today, for nothing could have been more suitable.'

It ascended so gradually as to seem almost level, winding right and left as every road should,—not by the art of a roadmaster, however, but by the planning of nature, for it followed the turnings of the river Agout among the hills. Plane trees threw mild shadows across the path. On the water side ran an ancient wall, low, broken here and there, and covered with ferns and mosses. Sometimes the river lay straight down below the coping, sometimes there was a strip of meadow. Boats lay moored under the trees at intervals, with the most *dolce-far-niente* carelessness. Here the travellers found a dam already old, and beside it a ruined mill ; there in a thick grove stood an ancient water-wheel, resting now, but preparing to toil in its lazy fashion day and night through the hot summer, lifting water from the stream and pouring it into conduits of mossy stone for the refreshment of distant fields. Hills and valley alike were clothed in the softest of greens ; and, enriching all nature with celestial intimations, there hung over the view a stilly, Corot-like atmosphere just a-thrill with simple but haunting bird-notes.

The castle of Burlatz did not perch like most of its cousins upon a steep and bristling crag, but nestled at the river's brink, surrounded with fair and smiling mountains.

The space was not great but it was ample. First the cavalcade passed the church, a fine Romanesque building constructed for the countess of Burlatz or her mother, and paused a little to admire the free and skilful workmanship of capitals that please even the connoisseur of today. Then it moved on through outworks of which one is reminded now by a heavy square tower, and paused again at a triangular space between the river Agout and the castle front,—a shady corner where plane trees caught every fresh breeze voyaging up or down the valley as the barons laid tribute on merchants travelling by the Rhine.

The castle itself—built as a residence, not a fortress—was of a graceful Romanesque style, satisfying to those who saw it often and surprising to those who came for their first visit. The water side, looking directly down upon the river, had been designed with special elegance. The windows, as we may judge from the little now to be seen, were sheltered under heavy round arches, low and broad, which rested on clustered columns. The rich capitals were adorned here with doves and other animals, and there with human figures. Stars decorated the face of the arches, mouldings the face of the wall; and between the windows ran a fillet in the pattern of a vine, cut with Byzantine feeling, that would be admired even in Venice or Siena.[8]

The party from Béziers arrived some hours ago and the early dusk begins to be felt in the valley. From the bridge across the narrow stream we already see a light, and catch glimpses of moving figures in the castle hall. Then the countess herself comes to a window, throws it open, and stands with a hand upon the casement, inhaling the freshness of the evening. It is easy to recognize her, for she wears the form of a queen's daughter and the face of a poet's love. We recognize her, too, by the particular features her lover has described : " the fair blonde locks,

BURLATZ AND THE REMAINS OF THE CASTLE

the forehead whiter than lilies, the laughing eyes changing color with her mood,' the straight firm nose, the fresh
face outvying the white and vermilion of the flowers, the
small mouth and white teeth, the chin and throat like
snow or the wild rose, the fair white hands, and the
fingers both smooth and slender.'' '' By more spiritual
traits as well, we recognize the woman whose praise is the
entire body of Arnaut's poetry. For more than beauty
of person belongs to her. She has the charms of the north
added to the charms of the south With fineness from
Paris she has inherited warmth from Languedoc. Her mo-
tions have that slow and caressing grace which overpowers
a man's self-possession Every look—deliberate and long
—seems like a procession of piquant thoughts and impulses. Her words, as few as they are choice, fall enveloped with the mysterious fascination of both revery and
passion. To be with her is to risk the triple intoxication
of wine, music, and poetry.

Behind the countess—we cannot be mistaken—is the
troubadour, our poet of Maruelh, his pale face and
thoughtful eyes aglow with just this intoxication. We
cannot hear what they say—indeed we would not, but
from scattered words of his, and the '' sweet laughter ''
that we know is hers, it is easy to fancy the gay banter,
the compliments, the meaning pleasantries, and the skilful repartee that we cannot follow. A long while they
stand there, now looking down upon the river that flows
untroubled out of the past and into the future before their
eyes, and now looking up at the verdant mountain called
the Rock of Paradise, which rises high above them on
the other side of the stream. Then they withdraw, the
window closes, and the lights multiply.

But stay, here comes a figure in a mantle,—it is Arnaut.
Crossing the rude bridge he makes his way to a little beach
on the opposite bank just below the castle. He is think-

ing of the morrow, for a *fête champêtre* has been decreed by the countess, and he knows that a new song will be called for.   Never was it easier for him to compose.

THE LITTLE BEACH, BURLATZ.

Plainly there is a bevy of Ariels in his brain.   Pacing dreamily to and fro he finishes the poem that has been some days upon his anvil.   The lines fit his turnings back and forth.   He points his verses with long looks at his lady's window. And before his task is done the moon has risen above the hills, throwing over castle and river the enchantments of interlacing radiance and shadow.

In due time the morrow arrives, bringing with it a sun and a breeze no way disappointing.   When the hour is fairly past noon a party of four gentlemen and four ladies issues from the castle, followed at some distance by a retinue of laden servants.   The ladies have taken off the trailing robes fashionable for the house, though frowned upon by the church, and soon to be condemned—but vainly —by the council of Montpellier (1195), and wear garments that are elegant and rich but suitable for a walk.   As no prying eyes need be feared, veils and wimples " have been dispensed with, and their heads like the gentlemen's are

covered with pointed hoods. At a distance, indeed, it is
not easy to distinguish the women from the men, as the
countess, for example, wears garments of precisely the
same name as Arnaut.

Still there are differences.   Her *bliaut* or frock of purple
samite, enriched with gold embroidery at the neck, wrists,
and hem, and revealing the ermine edge of her robe at the
neck and wrists, has sleeves that grow wide instead of
narrow from the shoulder down ; it is fastened at the neck
with a button of gold and laced at one side to fit her person closely ; and it reaches to her feet instead of stopping
half-way between the knees and the ankles as Arnaut's
does.   Under the fur at her neck and wrists can just be
seen a silk-embroidered edge of fine white linen, the hem
of a chemise.   Instead of a belt she wears a heavy girdle
of crimson silk, braided, and its pendant ends are adorned
with agates and sapphires alternating.   Her snow-white
mantle, made of silk mixed with the finest wool and
trimmed with the fur of the black squirrel, is fastened
under the chin instead of over the right shoulder.   A
pretty alms-purse hangs by a long chain from the girdle
of each lady, while in the place of such purses two of the
men carry daggers in their belts.   All the ladies are gloved
with chamois-skin, too, while the men are not."   Thus
attired they turn slowly down the valley two by two, but
all in merry conversation together

Every fine river invites one to companionship, but the
Agout crowns invitation with enticement.   The banks
are unceasingly changing their aspect.   Sinuous lines of
poplars lead the eye on from one surprise to another.
The waters are so swift and sparkling as to seem partners
in the gayety, and so vocal as to share in the conversation.   But they do not babble ; and their silver music—
silver in the double sense of mellow tones and foamy
waves—is made golden by intervals of silence ; for now

and then the current steals over to the other side beneath
the trees, and catches at sprays of ivy and boughs of locust,
as if it would linger and learn a new song from the birds
chaunting rounds in the depths of the shade.   Next the

ON THE AGOUT BELOW BURLATZ.

river gathers itself and
sweeps masterfully
around the abutment
of a hill.   And then,
parting into a hundred
white streams, it hur-
ries down the rapids,
where countless is-
lands and islets,
though no more than
a single small rock,
have each its offering
of verdure,—a clump
of trees, one willow, a
few bushes, a handful
of reeds, or a bunch
of grass, as the chil-
dren of Israel brought
before the altar a lamb
or a kid of the goats,
two turtle doves or
two young pigeons, or
at the least the tenth
part of an ephah of
fine flour.

Through such a scene the party stroll and chat, and
meanwhile the servants arrange in the loveliest spot some
frames—" horses," we should call them—and upon them
boards, as they would to make dinner-tables in the castle
hall.   Cushioned benches are placed on either side, and
over the boards is thrown a cloth of heavy linen dyed in

the precious and watchfully guarded scarlet of Montpellier.

As this is the usual hour for dining and appetites are made keen by the active life of the time, a hearty lunch is spread. At either end of the table stands a venison pasty, and a gilded platter in the centre contains robust slices of boar meat. Between and around these dishes are stationed plates of silver filled with choice bits of duck and breast of peacock. Here and there trays of glass offer green shoots of precisely what kind I do not know, and radishes of which I am certain, balanced with jars of lettuce. Bread both dark and white occupies the corners. Preserved ginger waits to sharpen the flagging taste, while dishes of pepper and salt—some of silver, some of gold, but all more or less ornamental—hover about like esquires at a tourney, and fresh violets bloom at intervals in vases of crystal.

For dessert there are apples—the " hard, white fruit of Auvergne " cried so lustily by venders in the streets of Paris—fresh oranges from Spain, dried figs, and raisins. A large dish of wrought brass is piled high with walnuts, and beside it lie implements of carved oak to break them with. Pure wine, both red and white, wine mixed with honey, spicy piment," and sweet cakes await the end of eating ; and for each of the gentlemen there is a drinking-cup of silver weighing five marks—and the work upon it is worth as much more—while each lady has a smaller cup, gilded and inlaid with enamel.

In due time the party arrive and seat themselves on the benches As they lunch they still chat and laugh, not without eyes for the river and the occasional boats, loaded to the brim, that are forced slowly against the current with poles,—a labor as delightful to observe as it must be wearisome to perform. And all the time, while a gilt censer is swung at a little distance by a handsome page so that the light air brings them its perfume, the nightin-

gales in the grove rehearse their spring songs to each
other and to them, and far overhead a lark, singing at
heaven's gate, distils upon them through a dreamy air
the bodiless music of his joy.

Finally the lunch is over, and the servants bring again
the ewers and basins of figured brass for the washing of
hands.¹⁴ Tapestries that have come from Damascus by
the way of Venice and from Persia by the way of Alexan-
dria are now spread upon a bank near by, where ivies
choose their own loves among elms, locusts, and oaks ;
and, led by Alazais, the ladies seat themselves there, carefully assisted by the gentlemen, for their close garments
make assistance not only polite but necessary.   More conversation follows, for the flow of southern wit has always
been exhaustless ; and finally the countess orders the instruments of music brought.   One after another both
gentlemen and ladies try their skill and win due applause,
while Arnaut is reserved by common consent for the last.
Finally all eyes turn to him, and Lady Alazais interprets
their demand :

" Come, Sir Troubadour, the nightingales have not yet
been shamed into silence, it appears.   Take your viol and
show them what music is like when sweet sounds are interpreted with sweeter words." ¹⁷

Quite prepared for the summons Arnaut rises and throws
back his hood, leaving on his head a close visorless cap of
the white linen of Reims, woven with small spots and sewn
with dark blue silk.   As he tunes the viol we have time
to note the rest of his costume.   From the little cap down
to the red shoes brought from Douai, which are fastened
with a button of mother-of-pearl, his attire, though not as
rich as would have been donned for a more formal occasion, is fresh and of close, elegant fit   His stockings and
breeches—which might have been silk—are of Bruges
linen, the former a dark brown, the latter saffron, though

perhaps it is hardly worth while to mention them at all since but a few inches of the stockings are in view, and the breeches can be seen only when the bliaut and robe, parted at the sides below the hips, are accidentally opened.

The robe, a dark blue garment of close woollen cloth trimmed with a fur called *gris*, from the back of the Siberian squirrel, is a garment made for warmth ; but, as usage demands, the bliaut is almost solely for ornament. It is a beautifully moulded cendal ¹ᵇ—a sort of taffeta—of a deep crimson color, fastened under the chin with an agate button, and trimmed at the hem, neck, and wrists with broad bands of gold embroidery. Around it is a rather wide belt of buff leather with an elaborate silver buckle of Paris make weighing a full mark, but the bliaut is drawn up through the belt and falling back hides it completely with a statuesque fold. The mantle, a very dark green brocade cut in the semicircular pattern, bears the singular but fashionable squares of heavy cloth, two at each corner, embroidered richly and encrusted with small emeralds, sardonyxes, and pieces of enamel, and is brought together at the right shoulder with a frog of golden hair wrought by the countess herself. It is indeed a very charming picture, Arnaut's graceful figure, as he stands with his right foot advanced and his mantle falling back on his left arm, smiling at the conversation, and making his own pleasantries in a half-absent way meanwhile ; but now the strings are perfectly in accord, the company become silent, and with all the fervor of his love he sings the verses finished the night before.

> Fair to me is April, bearing
>   Winds that o'er me softly blow,—
> Nightingales their music airing
>   While the stars serenely glow ;
>   All the birds, as they have power,
>   While the dews of morning wait,

Sing of joy in sky or bower,
　　Each consorting with his mate.

And as all the world is wearing
　　New delight while new leaves grow,
'T would be vain to try forswearing
　　Love which makes my joys o'erflow;
　　　　Both by habit and by dower
　　　　　　Gladness is my rightful state,
　　　　And when clouds no longer lower
　　　　　　Quick my heart throws off its weight.

Helen were not worth comparing,
　　Gardens no such beauty show:
Teeth of pearl,—the truth declaring,
　　Blooming cheeks, a neck of snow,
　　　　Tresses like a golden shower,
　　　　　　Courtly charms, for baseness hate,—
　　　　God who bade her thus o'ertower
　　　　　　All the rest, her way make straight!

Kindness may she do me, sparing
　　Courtship long and favor slow,
Give a kiss to cheer my daring—
　　More, if more I earn, bestow;
　　　　Then the path where pleasures flower
　　　　　　We shall tread nor slow nor late,—
　　　　Ah, such hopes my heart o'erpower
　　　　　　When her charms I contemplate.[16]

The abrupt introduction of the lady at the third stanza causes a little flutter in the group, especially as the quickness of the turn betrays how thoughts of her fill the poet's mind. All know who is meant, but they would be uncourtly to show it. Alazais herself, trusting the troubadour's address, will defy suspicion, and assuming a critical and somewhat quizzical air she observes .

" It is a pretty song—though shorter than the rule, is it not?—and we all thank you. Only it is a pity you will not reveal the name of this peerless beauty who seems to excel so greatly all of us.''

'' My lady,'' answers the troubadour, '' when match-less beauty veils itself in modesty it were wrong to pluck away this loveliest of the graces.'' ''

Then he assists her to rise ; and if there is a pressure of the hands, who can see it ?

BÉZIERS

Arnaut de Maruelh (*Concluded*)

WOULD you like to read a love-letter of the time of
Richard Cœur-de-Lion,—a love-letter written before there were looking-glasses,[1]—a troubadour's love-
letter ?

Béziers was Arnaut's home, but he could not remain
there all the time. Every troubadour was a rover, and
roving was a part of the profession as we have seen.
Arnaut seems to have gone as far as Monferrat. Our
Bonifaz was perhaps his friend, and in his castle he perhaps met Raimbaut de Vaqueiras, and bowed low before
the Fair Knight , or possibly Guilhem III., whose portrait we had from the Lombard chronicle, was reigning
still at the time of his visit. And he may have been at
the Castle of the Vale when he sat down to write the
Salutz d'Amor, the Greeting of Love, that has come down
to us.[2]

The letter was of course in verse, and it was written on
sheets of parchment in a single column that left wide
margins on both sides At the head of the first sheet
there were two portraits, drawn so skilfully that, as people
who saw them declared, they seemed actually to breathe,
yet so very subtly that only those in the secret could tell
whom they represented. The figure at the left was
Arnaut kneeling and supplicating. From his lips issued

a flower that bent downward and touched the beginnings
of the lines below ; while another flower, embracing the
ends of the lines, brought them to the ear of the figure on
the right, Alazais, near whom stood Love in the form of
an angel inviting her to listen to the words presented by
the flower.

Though parchment was dear the letter was not brief,—
and indeed how could it be ? For lovers know there is
only a single thing worth talking about, but that is one
which includes everything.

Lady,
Whose charms my words defy,
For whom I ever yearn and sigh,
This friend of yours, sincere and leal,—
His name you can divine, I feel,—
His faithful greeting would present,
And crave that answering word be sent,—
For naught he wishes but from you.   . .
O courtly lady, skilled to do
What pleases all,—discerning, taught
All grace of action, word, and thought,
Your beauty and your graciousness,
Your pleasant words and sweet address,
Accomplishments and sterling worth,
Fresh cheeks and form surpassing earth,
Your lovely smile, your glance that arms
With amorous might your other charms,
Your grace, your wit,—they all unite
To keep me pensive day and night.
  Because your face I cannot see,
All cheer and joy are gone for me ;
For me are gone all cheer and joy,—
To lose you quite would life destroy ;
For lingering hope and lingering care,
Too many a vigil, sleep too rare,
And longings for a glimpse of you,
So break my peace whate'er I do,
That countless times each night and day

For death or else your love I pray.
　Your love should God bestow ou me,
Far less my own than yours I 'll be ;
For, lady, all I say or do
That 's good, has come to me from you.
The very day I saw you first,
Love flamed with such an instant burst
That I have burned with hot desire
Unquenched, uucooled since roused to fire ;
Since roused to fire it hath not ceased,
But day by day hath e'er increased.
When far from you my journey lies,
My love still grows and multiplies ;
And when kind fortune gives me grace
To see and gaze upon your face,
I lose in dreams all sense of things ;
And so I 'm sure from error springs
The proverb we so often find,
That " Out of sight is out of mind."
Not out of mind are you to-night
Although, dear lady, out of sight.
　When I shall see you, who can say ?
But my true heart, which chose to stay
With you the very day I learned
Your loveliness, hath u'er returned ;
Hath ne'er returned to me again,
But e'er hath dwelt with you since then.
Where'er you be 't is there with you
Both day and night your love to woo. . . .
　O lovely lady, would I might
For all my truth see day or night
Ere life departs, when—free and bold
Or even in secret—I could fold
Within my arms your fair, sweet form,
And gaze and lavish kisses warm
On lips, on eyes, until in one
We melt a hundred,—still not done,
And faints for joy my blissful soul !
I 've said too much, but self-control
Cannot forbid me once to say
The wish I 've thought this many a day. . . .

My lady, I could not declare
A hundredth part of all the care
And pain I feel, and anguish, too,—
Yes, martyrdom—for love of you.
For love of you I burn alive,—
In pity's name I pray you strive
To pardon, if too much I dare.
    Oh hear and listen to this prayer,
My lady, who the loveliest far
That nature ever fashioned, are,
Beyond all I can know or say ;
Fairer than fairest days of May,
The sun of March, the summer shade,
The rose of June,[3] the rain that made
Fair April green, beauty in flower,
Mirror of Love's delight and power,
Casket of honor, key of worth,
The queen of spirit, grace, and mirth,[4]
The home of bounty rich and free,
The root and branch of culture's[5] tree,
The chamber of joy, the lover's nook,—
To you I pray, to you I look.
    Accept of service on my part,
And tell me I shall have your heart.
I ask no more, no more were right ;
Let mercy, as it will, requite.
Leal homage of myself I do,—
Grant in return a hope of you.
A hope of you will comfort give,
And cheer and bless me while I live.
In hope so good I 'd rather die
Than live for aye, and vainly sigh,—
No more will I presume to crave.
    God bless you, lady, guard and save.
Reply, so be 't your pleasure to.
Since Love hath vanquished me for you,
For me may Love, who conquers all,
In like degree your heart enthrall,
My lady.

The passion of this letter reminds us that love is not all

joy, and so the poet realized more and more. "He made many good songs of her which show that she caused him many joys and many woes," says the biographer; and Arnaut sang, " Never have I had a joy that cost me not a tear "

Knowing as we do the troubadour and the world he lived in, we should expect nothing else. There were many aspirants to the favor of Alazais ; there were many aspirants to the favor of Arnaut   There were born med- dlers, born blunderers, born mischief-makers   There were countless intrigues liable to compromise the most innocent man.   Rivalries, jealousies, envies, and mis- understandings dozed for blissful days, but were sure to awake. And his lady herself, the daughter of a great noble and a titular queen, the niece of an actual king, and the wife of a powerful baron, was liable to feel her pride keenly touched when she was reminded or bethought herself that her lover was a mere poet living on her bounty.

Arnaut was no hard and subtle strategist, able to work through difficulties like those to his personal end.   Often indeed he quoted to himself the familiar saying, " Only the fool runs after that he cannot catch," but he always fell back upon the conviction, " I cannot gainsay nor fore- fend what Love commands me." When the countess reminded him that he presumed to love beyond his rank, he only sang, " All the complaints you bring against me come to this   that you charm and delight me." If she swept by him in disdain he only thought as his eyes fol- lowed her, " It would take you but a little while to show me such love and fair looks, that I could live upon them forever " In his desperation he once exclaimed, " A woman is by nature a fickle creature "; and at another time, " A feeling lasts not long in a woman's heart "; but affection and loyalty always brought him back to this,

" Whatever you do to me, whether good or ill, I love you and shall love you always."

Under no circumstances must we think of him as gloomy. He was not permitted to settle into that comfortable melancholy, which mitigates pain by deadening the faculties. The gay world had no tolerance for such a mood, and he voiced its opinion when he declared, " A sad man is worse than dead " No matter how he suffered, he knew he must be entertaining ; and no better picture could be drawn of the court and of himself, than a stanza of his own.

> From worth repute must start,
> Worth from a warm, glad heart,
> Now this must love impart,
>   And love, a sprightly lady ;
>   Gay talk gives sprightliness,
>   And comes of courtly breeding ;
>   So while the days are speeding
>   I 'll triumph o'er distress,
>   And complaisance possess
>   To sing and laugh no less
>   Because my heart is bleeding.[6]

One drop of cheer always remained in the bottom of his goblet,—hope.

> 'T were hard indeed if bliss came not at last !
> The pains of love consume and wear and shatter ;
> Yet love's delight, with misery bound fast,
>   Both makes woe felt and makes it seem as naught ;
>   Undone were I did not a blissful hope
>   Enrich my life and comfort me and bless :
>   I wait for joy, and so can bear distress [7]

After this manner the troubadour lived on in gladness and in pain, not for weeks and months but for years ; but at last hope brightened and light appeared in the east.

One day the countess was standing at a window in the hall alone. Her husband the viscount was no longer alive,[8] and she felt very lonely. Arnaut crossed the hall. She called him.

"Arnaut," she said with a new tenderness, "I fear I have seemed unmindful of your fidelity and devotion all these years, but I have not been. Do you remember the kiss that you asked for in your song at Burlatz,—long ago?"

And before he could reply, she threw her arms about his neck, and gave him the pledge of love with all her heart. The surprise of it and the sweetness of it ravished away his breath, and before he could speak a step was heard.

"Go now,—but soon," she whispered, with lifted finger.

Overjoyed, the troubadour set himself at once to compose a new song for his lady ; and in gratitude made an allusion, though very covertly, to the pledge of love that she had given him.[9] Then he awaited blissfully her further good pleasure.

Events delayed the countess. Amfos (Alfonso II.), the king of Aragon and count of Barcelona, passed that way

and made her a visit. Closely associated with the late viscount, and obliged not infrequently to go through Béziers on his way to Provence beyond the Rhone, another of his possessions, he long had known and admired Lady Alazais but knew that he

IN OLD BÉZIERS.

could not permit himself to make love to her. Now however she was free to care for him if she would, and he appeared upon the scene intent on conquest. No gallant had better grounds for expecting a triumph. A rich king, a brilliant man, a poet, a famous " lady-killer," he possessed every quality and every art that pleased and conquered. Delighted and flattered, the countess omitted no effort for the entertainment of her illustrious guest. But the king's face grew dark instead of bright as the days went by, for he observed the loving glances that passed now and then between Lady Alazais and her troubadour. With all his address he set this one and that one at work, as we learn from the biography, to undermine his rival ; and after a while, seeking an audience with his hostess, he delivered his own blow.

" Madam," said he with the air and the accent of a courtier and a king, " Madam, I crave permission to take leave of your court and yourself, with heartfelt thanks for entertainment far beyond my worth. My troop await me I bid you a reluctant farewell."

" But, my lord King, is not this leave-taking—sudden ? Is my castle so poor ? Are the ladies of my court so dull ? "

" As for the ladies I know not,—I have seen but one. The castle is like what we hear of in eastern fables."

" Has aught—perchance—crossed you, my lord ? "

" Madam, I have no will to speak of such a thing, but since you ask I will reply. You have here a certain troubadour, who has made free to pass between my poor self and the beauty that is more to me than the sun in heaven. I love poetry, you know well ; but poets have their place Were he in my court   .   .   . But the castle is yours and I am already too much honored in sharing your hospitality. Only mine is the fault if I place my crown where the first adventurer   .   .   ."

He paused and the countess reflected.

" Madam, farewell."

" Till evening," she answered, offering her hand with
a smile

Conscious of triumph the king assumed an air of profound humility, kissed her fair hand with the utmost
deference, and withdrew.

Still the lady reflected.

At length she said to herself, " What must be done had
best be done quickly " ; and to her attendant, " Call
Arnaut "

The happy lover was in the fervor of composing.   As
he paused in the labor his mind went back to the fête at
Burlatz of which Alazais had reminded him so sweetly,—
the happiest day of his life until then.   Still farther back
it went, as when we gain the summit we trace our path to
the starting-point.   His boyish dreams, his great faith,
his vast hope,—how they flooded his mind again   He recalled the church, and realized for what he had unconsciously been praying there.   He remembered the sunset,
and understood what happiness it prophesied.   He saw
again the star, and recognized whose beauty it fore-
tokened.   His bliss——

Receiving the summons he left his pen in the ink and
hastened gayly with a smile on his lips to answer it.

" Arnaut, you know the covenant between us, and you
know what you dared to say in your last song "

Dumbfounded by the manner and the words of Alazais
the troubadour fell upon his knees

" Pardon, my lady ' I was wrong.   I——"

" You were wrong, but I cannot pardon   The covenant
is broken.   You must leave my castle at once—to-day.
Never enter my presence and never sing of me again."
Then she swept from the room.

It was indeed quickly done.   In an instant it was all
over.   Arnaut still existed, but he lived no longer.
Gathering his faculties as best he could he left Béziers

forever, and found a refuge at the court of Guilhem of Montpellier. From there he craved forgiveness, pity, hope. All his entreaties were in vain. His viol broke like his heart. No love-song was ever heard from him again. He soon disappears, and it is believed that he did not long survive.

Happily he possessed the consolations of honesty. Having nothing within to condemn and reproach him, he seems to have reached serenity after a while, and from this time appears to come a didactic and moral poem intended for young men, perhaps the last work of his pen.

Serenity was not the only reward of his true love. As a man he won the admiration of the centuries ; for troubadour though he was he committed no lyric infidelities, he sang of love to but one woman in all his life.[10] As a poet he stood among the first of his age. His fellow troubadours enjoyed quoting him. Dante admired and Petrarch studied him Some have called him the Tibullus of the middle ages. An anonymous Italian poem of the fourteenth century on Hero and Leander placed him at the head of the Provençal poets. Sismondi did the same. His delicacy and sincerity of feeling, his clear and easy language, the style of notable elegance and sweetness that he was master of, combine to make him far dearer to us than many poets of greater breadth, originality, and power.[11]

And what of Alazais ? She did not escape retribution. Her Spanish lover died within two years,[12] but he does not seem to have been faithful even so short a while. Indeed a contemporary declares that he robbed her during this time of two cities and a hundred castles.[13] And aside from that he was imperious, blasé, and fickle.

If the feelings demand a sense of greater punishment they have not far to seek. The black thunder-cloud of the Albigensian crusade was gathering on the horizon

before she closed her eyes, and it was not slow to burst.
The utmost example of distress and harassment was con-
tributed by her father's family ; the most hapless victim
of savage fury was chosen from her own , the most frightful instance of massacre and ruin was the city of her
abode.   The crusaders deluged her fair land with fire and
blood.   Her Béziers was consumed   They destroyed her
court, killed her friends, exiled her brother, and murdered
her son.

*Glory to God in the highest ; and on earth peace, good will
to men !*

On the 22d of July in the memorable year 1209, the
followers of Jesus and sons of the true Church had a field
day near Béziers.   The clergy of the region were present.
Many chief bishops had come from far.   The abbé of
Citeaux, the special legate of the pope, was in supreme
authority.   White vestments, the garments of purity,
abounded.   The lamb, emblem of meekness, was conspicuous.   The cross, badge of piety and self-sacrifice,
was everywhere.   The laymen, however, outnumbered
the churchmen   There was a vast throng of them, an
army in fact, with banners, trumpets, swords and shields,
armor and battle-steeds "   But all were there in the name
of the Prince of Peace.

Had they come to visit and admire the city on the hill ?
That would have been worth their while   Cæsar was delighted with it and showed his regard by the new name
he gave it, Julia Biterra.   Vandals, Goths, and Saracens
followed Gauls and Romans, and all were glad to be there.
It was thought an abode fit for kings, and a Latin proverb even said that if God should choose a dwelling-place
on earth it would be at Béziers.

And it had never been more beautiful than it was that
summer morning.   Rich, populous, and cultured, it shone

THE CHURCH OF ST. NAZAIRE, BÉZIERS.

afar. And above it in magnificent guardianship, issuing
as a dark and powerful shape from a mass of ramparts,
rearing its tremendous bulk in grandeur on the brow of
the hill, the church of St. Nazaire lifted its crosses, battlements, turrets, and mighty tower against the silvery blue,
dominating earth in the name of heaven."

But no, these godly people had come—not to admire
beauty and strength—but to do the work of their compassionate Master. It had been told them how certain of
Béziers, scandalized by the rapacity and corruptions of
the churchmen, believed as Albigensian preachers taught
that God would hear them even if they prayed without
the help of priests ; and all this assembly, full of pity and
affection, reverent in the fear of a common God, tender in
love to a common Redeemer, meek as men who could err
themselves, humble as men who needed forgiveness for
their own sins, had come to set abuses right, and lead
home these wandering sheep to the fold and the shepherd.

But the men of Béziers appeared to discover another
temper and a different purpose in their visitors. The
gates were shut. The walls were manned. Presently
there was a clash of arms between the city and the
camp. The legate, the bishops, and the knights bestirred
themselves   Simon de Montfort and other chief captains
ranged the followers of the Lamb as armies are ranged.
A signal was given, the priests chanted the *Veni Creator*,
and the host rushed on toward the city,—to redeem, to
save ? No , to ravage and to kill.

The wall was attacked. All the implements of slaughter
were drawn. The moat was filled. · The foundations
were battered. Picks dug at the stones. Long poles
armed with powerful hooks tore at the battlements.
Great stones were hurled by engines at the men on the
wall   Arrows and light spears flew like rain.

Meanwhile the defenders were not idle. They fought

with arrows, spears, swords, and axes. They threw timbers and rocks upon their assailants. They poured down scalding water, melted pitch, and boiling oil. The scaling-ladders, crowded with soldiers, they threw back upon the struggling mass below They hurled from the wall those who gained a footing upon it. Yells, curses, groans, defiances, taunts, cheers, orders, rallies, drowned the singing of the priests. The clash of weapons became a terrible roar.

After a time the defense grew feeble, and it was evident that the wall and the gates would soon yield. The men of war, touched in the midst of rage and slaughter with a feeling of humanity, came to the pope's legate.

" In yonder town," they said, " there are surely some true sons of the Church ; how shall we know and spare them ? "

" Kill all," replied the abbé. " Kill all, for God will know His own." [16]

The town fell, and the troops that still resisted were crushed Battle ceased ; but massacre began. Everywhere bands of furious crusaders—a cross on every left shoulder—went about the city hewing down the people they met, and seven thousand persons, as we know, were killed in the church of Mary Magdalen.

A similar slaughter took place in St. Nazaire. A multitude of helpless folk crowded into the church. Surely, they whispered one to another, surely they who wear the cross will respect the house of their Saviour. Not a stone of the pavement could be seen. Not a cornice, not a window-ledge but had its pallid tenant The mass was suffocating, and still throngs pressed at the doors.

Suddenly there were loud shouts and cries, and the pressure instantly ceased. What did it mean ?

The red butchers had come, and those outside the church had fled.

There was a breathing space.   The butchers had come ;
but they hesitated.   The clergy of the church robed in
their sacred vestments were standing before their flock; the
consecrated bells tolled ; the holy names were invoked.

The butchers hesitated,—but not long.   Another band
rushed up.

" Kill all, kill all ! " they shouted.

" Kill, kill ! " answered the first, and united they
rushed upon the church.   .   .   .

.In time the massacre was achieved, but the work was not
yet done.   The priests and captains took counsel together,
and the soldiers of the cross—butchers and ravishers,
drunk, frenzied—were set in motion again.   The bodies of
the wounded and the slain were dragged together in heaps,
timbers from dismantled houses were piled on the heaps,
and then more bodies were thrown upon the timbers.

Then the piles were lighted.

The flames mounted and spread ; they invaded the
dwellings and tracked down all who had found holes to
hide in.   Soon the hilltop was ablaze, and a tempest of
fire swept the sky.

Down below, thirty thousand " Christian people—many
dead, many alive — men, women, and children — white
locks and golden tresses—were burning.   Wounded men
gathered strength from despair, staggered on a little, fell,
and were licked up.   The stunned and swooned were
awakened by the touch of fire,—for the heaps of corpses had
charred down to them.   Penned in the timbers fair women
saw the red flames advance, inch by inch, until   .   .   .

Yesterday Béziers was an abode for the gods ; today it
is a heap of embers and its people are ashes.   *Glory to the
Devil and the pope !*

And the prelude to all this was the tender poetry of
Arnaut de Maruelh.   Just so amazing were the contrasts
of that age !

RIBÉRAC, AGEN, AND BEAUVILLE

Arnaut Daniel

IN his journey through purgatory Dante met Guido
Guinicelli and began to extol the " sweet ditties "
that he composed. But Guinicelli disclaimed the honor,
pointed out another as the master who excelled all, and
humbly effacing himself before this greatest of the poets,
disappeared " through the fire, even as through the water
a fish going to the bottom." [1] It would seem hardly possible for Dante to introduce this poet with more signal
distinction ; but he found a way,—allowing him to speak,
not in Tuscan, but in his own language : " I am Arnaut
who weep and go singing."

Who was this poet ?

His full name was Arnaut Daniel. He was a troubadour. And as it was he that Petrarch had in mind when
he called the singer of Maruelh " the less famous Arnaut,"
we cannot refrain from placing the two side by side at
once.

Curiously enough they came from the same diocese.
Ribérac is but a few miles to the south of Mareuil, and
there on the hill overlooking the village and the river
one may still see the traditional site of the castle where
Daniel was born ; while hard by, as a witness to the local
history, stands a venerable Romanesque church, the core
of which was originally the baron's chapel

AT RIBÉRAC.

But the careers of the two had little similarity ; for, to
begin with, Daniel was a notable wanderer. It is pretty
certain that he visited not only Spain but Italy. We
know that he was present at the coronation of Philippe
Auguste, king of France : and he certainly visited the
court of Richard Cœur-de-Lion, king of England.

A very amusing story is told of this visit ; for though
Daniel's tears flowed in purgatory, he seems to have
laughed and made others laugh in the upper world.
" Who gladness sows shall reap delight," he sang ; and
next after a good song he loved a good joke.

Another craftsman, it appears, challenged him to a test
of skill ; the challenge was accepted and the two staked
their horses on the result. Each was then confined in a
room and allowed ten days to compose, and five more to
learn and practise his piece. When the day of trial came,
Daniel asked leave to sing first and started forth right
manfully But scarce had he begun when the other
cried, " For God's sake stop ; this is my song "

" Your song ? " said Richard, " how can it be ? "

" That I know not, lord King ; but it is. Ask him "

So the king demanded of our poet what it all meant ;
and after a great laugh Daniel told him the story.

It seems that somehow, like Byron in the storm at sea,
he could not compose. His mind was not in the mood to
create One day his rival called to him (for their rooms
were not far apart) and inquired how he was getting on.
" I 've been ready for three days," Daniel answered
promptly, though really he was in utter despair. The
next evening he overheard the other man rehearsing, and
in like manner the following days, until in the end he
knew the song quite as well as its author. Then since he
could do no better he resolved to amuse the court, and so
delivered his rival's piece The king was delighted, for
a clever turn like that suited his witty soul He returned

each horse to its owner and loaded both the poets with gifts,—only he insisted that Daniel still owed him a song.[2]

But the troubadour's favorite resort was nearer home, for according to his biographer he paid court more than anywhere else at Beauville (Bouvila) some fifteen miles from Agen.[3]

This is a region not unloved of the muse. In Agen itself one still may see the little shop where Jasmin was trimming locks and shaving chins less than thirty years ago ; and where, if pressed a little, he would admit that God had made only four Frenchmen poets . Corneille, Lafontaine, Béranger, and Jasmin.[4] In the time of Daniel, Elias de Barjols[5] went out from these parts, and by dint of good fiddling and good singing gained himself an estate and a name beyond the Rhone,—by dint also of shrewdness, we should add perhaps, for he was keen enough to discover that " A man is a fool if he gives himself too much trouble about what does not concern him." In Agen Daniel himself stopped more than once, I am sure, on his journey to Beauville, and we can do no better for a few moments than follow his example.

The district about us is far from level ; but instead of being plain and hill, it is plain and valley. This may sound ungeographical but is only the better if it does ; for " geography treats of the surface of the earth," and here there is no surface. In other words the original crust has nearly all been worn away, occasional spots resisting erosion, and standing up now as islands and peninsulas of rocky plateau. Along the northern side of the town rises one of these bits of crust, with a line of summer villas just below the edge; and here, in the shade of plane trees and firs,. we gaze luxuriously over a balustrade of carved stone upon a landscape of sumptuous charms.

Far, far away are the Pyrenees, a jaggèd line of blue upon blue. To the right flows the wide brown current of the Garonne, spanned by the famous viaduct of the canal. Close at our feet is the city of Jupiter, Diana, and Bacchus,' which has outlived its gods and thriven in spite of Goths, Franks, Normans, Saracens, and a more terrible enemy than all, the river. Beyond it extends a green champaign fertile in every good thing. Fields of wheat and rye are already waving. Apples and pears and peaches and almonds we can almost see in the distant orchards Strawberries and cherries we know are ripening. Melons are setting, plum trees are loading themselves with the fruit that enriches Agen, and the cattle that beautify its fairs are combing their glossy backs with sunshine The breeze comes to us perfumed with the fragrance of the locust blossom. Chestnuts are blooming behind us. Roses hang over the walls. The hawthorn softens the outlines of the stone-work. Cypresses have brought dignity and the ivy grace The rustle of palms accentuates the gentle stir of air. And all the while, to the low accompaniment of the fountain, a score of nightingales vie together in the sweetness and variety of their songs,—maidenly birds, trim, little, demure, and shy ; who could refuse to love them ? '

It is a spot like this and the company of roving bees that best help one understand the troubadours.

Provençal poetry is called monotonous, and more than one writer has declared that all of it might have been written by a single author. It has often been termed conventional. It has been likened to soap-bubbles, beautiful but unsubstantial.

Much of this criticism is due to a lack of knowledge ; and the reader has already begun to suspect, I hope, that perhaps the troubadours were not all alike, nor their songs all of a piece. Many another body of literature wears an appearance of uniformity until it is carefully read ; and, as Paul Meyer observes, " While many of the ideas of the troubadours are now commonplaces there was a time when they were not.''

Still there is much to excuse the criticism. The troubadours were obliged to work under many restrictions.⁸ The conventional reference to spring, found at the beginning of many poems that do not seem to require it, was a relic of the past which tradition had made almost as obligatory as a preacher's text. Again, the troubadour's affection for his lady, however genuine, was of necessity expressed in elaborate and finished forms, else it had not seemed courtly or artistic. Neither could it have passed unchallenged, for while society permitted such a love, few husbands were able to approve the system when it endangered their particular selves. Besides, the richness of modern development did not yet exist, and the fulness of modern thought had not dawned. As Gaston Paris remarks, the material, the moral, and the spiritual worlds appeared fixed and unchanging. Questionings about the future life, ponderings on profound moral problems, doubts concerning the basis of happiness and even of virtue, tragical conflicts between individual aspirations and social rule,—these were ideas of which they had no conception. In particular, the natural world had not yet opened its unending vistas of significance ; and while the troubadours were not without a keen sense of the beauties of nature, they were too much a part of nature themselves to study and enjoy her deeply, and their eyes like their minds lacked the generations of experience and culture absolutely needed to make them see the natural world artistically.⁹

Finally we must remember that many distinct centres of poetical activity existed, and there were several generations of poets. Songs that come to us in a bunch were perhaps never side by side in their own day. Similar feelings and circumstances gave rise to similar expressions. One poet sang at Orange, another at Béziers, an-

other at Barcelona, with no thought of imitating one
another ; successive generations of ladies were loved and
praised ; and when we collect the pieces and study them
all together we observe a sameness.

For impossibilities we cannot ask,—the spring wild-
flower of the Alpine slope and the New England vale cannot equal the rose of summer or the chrysanthemum of
autumn. Yet if we have the Maying spirit they are no
less beautiful. A hundred knots of arbutus are not
wearisome, nor a hundred shady glens carpeted with
violets. And here in the garden above Agen, in the very
home of the troubadours, with the same breeze on our
cheeks that they felt, looking at the hedgerows of hawthorn as they saw them, and listening as they listened to
the melodies of the rossignol, we come to understand their
songs ; we know why the lyric was enough to content
them ; we know why they loved variety of form rather
than solidity of thought : we feel that their poetry was
evanescent, only as the flowers are ; and we realize how
love and spring, the garden, the rose, and the nightingale
were to them themes ever fresh and ever delightful.

It was on a day like this, presided over by

Smiling May
In a more rich and sweet array,

that Arnaut Daniel continued his journey from Agen to
Beauville,—a trim, small man with a clerkly beard and
careful attire, his manner quiet but his eyes alert. Spring,
which he called " the season that colors and paints," was
displaying her finished canvas. Recent storms had replenished the fulness of the soil, and every leaf was in
full *tenue*. If the road was not paved with diamonds, at
least the fields were strewn with silver and gold,—buttercups and marguerites. The wheat was pushing fast, and
among it blossomed those corn-flowers which the poet ex-

horts young girls to pluck; while the owner of the field
exhorts them to refrain from plucking.   The first wild
roses were scenting the breeze ; and in the woods—far
thicker and far nearer than today—the nightingales made
the stillness rich with amorous melodies.

THE APPROACH TO BEAUVILLE.

Beauville is a long peninsula of rock, another survival
of the original surface like the bit of plateau at Agen; and
at the very tip of the tongue, where the gendarmerie is
now, the castle of the baron stood then, looking straight
into the eye of the setting sun, as high in the heavens as

itself. Miles away, Daniel could begin to study the long line of houses on the ridge. For more than an hour, as he pricked along the bridle-path, he could see a welcome before him, and anticipate the roaring fire, the hearty greetings, and the savory good cheer that awaited him in the shining castle.

Very different was the town as he found it from the Beauville of today. Swallows clamoring noisily under the eaves were not the majority of the population at that day. The walls towered instead of crumbling Instead of a hôtel-de-ville bearing on a weather-stained board the legend "Apartments to let," he found the lord's bailiff exercising a busy authority and the steward collecting rents. Instead of a rambling old public square where even the boys feel subdued, and the dogs roam lonesomely about as if they had no masters, he crossed a lively market-place through a jostling press of the baron's retainers drinking wine and clanking swords Instead of the grey landlady of the greyer inn, insisting upon the traveller's tasting her chartreuse without a sou of recompense, there awaited him the fair lady of the castle, more graceful though not more hospitable, ready to greet him before the wide hearth with all the dignity of courtly breeding.

After the long climb it was very delightful to glance back. Eastward from the castle ran the narrow ridge occupied by the houses of the common folk ; but through the rest of the circle, 340 out of the 360 degrees, he looked down upon long slopes that swept away like skirts from the craggy foundations of the castle, and beheld a rich, smiling valley some four hundred feet below—rougher no doubt than now, and more wooded, but still much the same—filled with grain-fields and grass-fields, and shaded with poplars, elms, and oaks

Better still was the cozy gossip after dinner. All the news was canvassed ; all the friends were inquired after ;

all the neighbors were discussed ; all the jokes were told ; and then—music. Of course Daniel had brought a new song and he thus began :

The branching boughs,
Once hid with leaves,
This wind
With bitter blasts reveals ;
The tree
Bears,
Stammering or dumb,
The once gay birds,—
Mates
Or not mates ;
So minstrelsy
That joy unseals
I 'll try,
For love of her
Who causes all the woe
My heart conceals,—
My life 't will yet destroy.

Though she avows
That she receives
With mind
Unmoved all my appeals,
My plea
Dares
As a wish to come :
And, shunning words,
Waits
At her gates ;
Death sweet would be,
But hope, which heals,
Is nigh ;
And to prefer
Petitions cheers me so
My heart e'en feels
There is no other joy.[10]

Is the song disappointing ? Do we prefer the " lesser

Arnaut '' with his melodious and flowing simplicity?
We are not alone if we do.

Dante himself bears witness that Daniel was not popular   Even his fellow craftsmen could not understand
him.   He was forced to defend his poetry with the plea
that while easy verse would answer for the happy lover,
an unsuccessful suitor like himself required enigmatical
expressions, hard constructions, and unusual rhymes;
but when he sang, '' I am Arnaut who chase the wind,
hunt the hare on an ox, and swim against the stream,''
the wicked monk of Montaudon only retorted, '' Since he
began hunting rabbits with an ox and swimming up-
stream, his songs are n't worth a hip.''

Fauriel said that he was one of those who did the
most injury to Provençal poetry; that he robbed it of
imagination and sentiment, reduced verse to pure mechanism, and astonished rather than charmed the ear.   Indeed
we have reason to complain of him.   Like the Symbolists
of today or yesterday, he prided himself on the difficulty
of his verse and the obscurity of his meaning.   The artificiality of Raimbaut d'Aurenga he multiplied.   Of the
eighteen songs that he has left us, only four can clearly
be made out.   It astonishes us to hear Petrarch call him
'' First among all, . . . great master of love, who still
does honor to his country with his novel and beautiful
diction.''   We wonder still more at Dante's admiration,
and the tradition of reverence that continued down even
to Tasso's day.   We think of Cowley, looked upon by the
great of his time as greater than themselves, and greater
than all who had gone before; and of Malherbe and
Boileau who so '' improved '' the language of Ronsard as
nearly to extinguish French lyric poetry.   So keen has
been the disappointment that critics have tried to believe
that Daniel's best work has been lost.   Witte held that
the romance of Launcelot, which precipitated the passion

of Paolo and Francesca, came from him; but Gaston Paris
has pointed out that Dante and Petrarch appear to have
had no more of Daniel than we have, and Paget Toynbee

IN BEAUVILLE.

thinks he has found in old French the very romance that
Paolo and Francesca read together that fatal day.

But, as Canello has proved, this is only one side of the
matter.   Daniel's passion for " rich rhymes " and the
obscure style was not mere affectation, mere striving for

novelty. His mind was naturally reserved and self-contained, not easy and effusive. "He that would earn praise must govern himself," he sang ; and again, "Love bridles my mouth." His subtlety is shown for example by the fact that he never alluded to the existence of such a thing as a jealous husband,—the shrewdest way of saying that nobody needed to be jealous of him. Such a man was not likely to be satisfied with a ready, flowing style. Besides, he was nobly born and well educated, and naïve poetry was too simple for him. He knew and felt the power of words Not content with the purest form of the troubadour tongue—his mother-speech—he winnowed and elaborated it. He used many words that we find in no other troubadour, dressed Latin words in Provençal forms, employed familiar terms in a new sense or in an original sense already lost, and still further enriched his diction with racy idioms."

All these are the marks of an artistic poet rather than a poet of sentiment or ideas, and from that point of view we must regard him. Restricted in thought, feeling, and imagination, he distinguished himself by carrying such thoughts, feelings, and imaginations as were his to their ultimate development, and expressing them with a unique force Others personified love, but he made love speak and even act as a living person While others declared that love enabled them to be joyous even when the earth was dark and gloomy, he seemed intent upon detaching himself altogether from nature and dominating it. While others used the antithesis of word and phrase, he made it a fundamental element of his verse and of his thought.

Others had been rich in the variety of their rhymes, but he surpassed them all. To secure striking effects he ran the whole vocal gamut of vowels and consonants, and even studied to obtain haunting chords by employing almost-rhymes. Others, as the translations have shown, carried rhymes from stanza on to stanza , but he, to avoid commonplaces and secure more delicate results, made the rhyme within the stanza entirely subordinate. Look for a moment at the piece just presented. Out of seventeen lines only seven are capped in the same stanza ; for answers to the rest the ear must wait and listen, until the corresponding line is reached in each of the six stanzas that follow.

This principle was carried to its ultimate in his sestine —that proof-piece of his wonderful skill in form—which was imitated by Dante, Petrarch, and many others. In this he completely discarded the rhyme of the stanza, and relied upon the assonances of his terminal words—which a translation cannot reproduce—and the subtle musical effect of their recurrence in a surprising but regular order.

> The fervent wish that often comes
> When wrath is hot, will ne'er strip beak and nails
> From my defamer, bound to lose his soul ,
> I dare not punish him with club or withe ;
> So, privily, where I shall find no uncle,
> I 'll taste delight in garden or boudoir.
>
> Whene'er I think of that boudoir
> To which, alas for me, no man e'er comes,
> There 's none less dear than nephew and than uncle ;
> I 'm all a-tremble to the very nails,
> As children are when threatened by the withe,
> So much I fear I have not reached her soul.
>
> I would be more to her than soul,
> Would she but slip me into her boudoir ;
> It hurts me more than smart of rod or withe,
> That where she goes her servant never comes ;
> I cling to her as fingers cling to nails,
> And ne'er will heed advice of friends or uncle.
>
> Not e'en the sister of my uncle
> Is dearer, nor so dear, upon my soul ;

As close to her as fingers are to nails
I'd be, did she permit, in her boudoir;
And love for her, which storms and overcomes
My heart, can bend me as one bends the withe.

Since Aaron's rod grew like a withe,
And from Lord Adam nephew sprang and uncle,
Desire so true as this of mine which comes
From thoughts of her, ne'er pained a loving soul;
Go she abroad or stay in her boudoir,
My heart cleaves to her like her very nails.

For my affection grips and nails
Itself to her like bark upon the withe;
My tower of joy, my palace, and boudoir,
I love her more than cousin, brother, uncle;
And heaven's joy she'll double to my soul,
If there, for loving truly, one e'er comes.["]

Looking at Daniel then not as a poet in the usual sense, but as a word-artist, as the " smith of . . . speech" that Guinicelli called him, we inquire, Was his labor worth while?

In view of its evil influence on Provençal poetry we answer at once, No. But then we reconsider our verdict. As Gaston Paris has remarked, " By giving each word an exaggerated value he prepared for the expressive, concise, personal, and individual style that was to shine out with incomparable lustre in the *Divine Comedy*."

But what shall we say of it in itself as an artistic result?

His refinements in metre and rhyme must have had real effect or he would not have employed them. Today one might imitate him to please the eye with ingenuities of form, but his poems were made to be heard, not seen. It seems to me that while his art is too subtle for us, and was no doubt beyond the general then, it must have been directly appreciable in the finer ears of his cultivated audience. The Greeks, we are told, could see but very few shades of color   In our own *Beowulf* horses and the ocean are yellow, and scarcely any other colors are mentioned, but only degrees of light,—bright, white, grey, murky, swart, dark, and black.   The sense of sight has been enormously developed during the past centuries , has not the sense of hearing, in some respects at least, retrograded ?

It seems to me clear that Daniel addressed ears more delicate and a sense more tenacious than ours.   His verse was like the " music of calculation "   It was like those exquisite vases which ravish our cultured vision precisely because their curves are so refined, so slight.   It was like a violin air of Bach's compared with a thumping rhythm for the banjo.   It was like the harmony of Chopin's scattered chords, contrasted with the obvious chiming of a choral   And this tension of refinement was attained in Provençal verse, remember, while our own poetry was only a stammer :

> And heo scal mine wunden
> Makien alle isunde,
> Al hal me makien
> Mid haleweige drenchen [13]

Perhaps you consider these niceties of technique wearisome , at all events the lady of Beauville appears to have found them so.   And though Daniel seems to have earned his title " great master of love " by preaching and practising endless hope, discretion, patience, persistence, and fidelity, she never loved him in return

As time went on Beauville and all the other castles closed their portals, and like so many other gay troubadours, Daniel realized that he had no settled position. His strength failed.   His clerkly beard grew long and white   Poverty was upon him ; and, worse than all, he felt that his pleasant sins had separated him forever from the number of those who may see God.

At last he found himself a messenger, and sent him with a noble poem, his swan-song, to the kings of France and England and the many princes to whom he once gave pleasure, praying for their assistance ; and the messenger returned laden with gold.

" Now do I see," cried the agèd poet, " that God will not abandon me " ; and, assuming the monastic dress at once, he lived blamelessly the rest of his days "

So it was not his destiny to pass the door where hope is left behind, and he could say to Dante : '' Contrite I see my past folly, and joyful I see before me the day I hope for.''

'' Then he hid himself in the fire that refines them.'' "

XIII

NARBONNE

Peire Rogier

BY all means leave the train at Coursan : the guard will see to your hand baggage, and the trunks will take care of themselves.

A heavy bridge spanning the tawny Aude, trees in pose for landscape artists, quaint houses, a fortified Gothic church with bells hung in the familiar framework on the top of the tower,—these compose the town. But the real Coursan is the little square in front of the taverns

Old men and maidens, young men and women, they are all out, particularly the young men and maidens The teamsters, hearty and handsome fellows, make a stop here in their long trips, the first halt after leaving Narbonne or the last before arriving. Whichever it be there is excuse enough for jollity. Some lounge on stools inside the taverns, glass in hand Some lounge outside, whip under arm. Jesting with each other, flirting with the girls, telling and hearing news among the old folks, comparing horses, discussing the prospects of the wine crop, looking after the hostlers, kissing a baby here and there, laughing very often and occasionally scolding, they make a picture such as we have at home only in the *festa* scenes of the opera.

From Coursan to Narbonne one goes by the Little Omnibuses, as they are called. We inquire of a driver how soon his vehicle will set out, and shortly after become aware that half a dozen people are keeping us under surveillance. If we show a disposition to move away, some one reminds us that the omnibus is about to go, though it evidently has no thought of such a thing, or we are detained by an inquiry, "You are going to Narbonne, is it not, Messieurs?" It is a bit mystifying at first, but ere long we learn the secret. There is competition. Each of the rivals has allies and scouts. Our first inquiry pledged us to go by that line, and now we shall be guarded till we enter the car.

COURSAN.

But we had no intention of backsliding. Our choice had been made with deliberation and was wholly satisfactory. Perhaps our 'bus was not painted quite so smartly as the other, but the personnel was beyond comparison. First, there was a handsome young fellow at the front with a blue blouse, an artist's cap—big and loppy—and a cigarette. Beside him stood another handsome young fellow, with a blue blouse, an artist's cap— big and loppy—and a cigarette. The first one was our charioteer and guided the three steeds, harnessed abreast.

What the other would do, we found ourselves quite unable to guess, but in the end it appeared that his cherubic
face, angelic smile, and lively manners were counted upon
to keep the young women all along the line in cordial
alliance with his 'bus   Finally, at the opposite end was
another handsome young fellow in a fresh blue uniform,
with a stiff blue cap trimmed with gold, and marked with
the title of his imposing office, " *Contrôleur.*"

So guided and guarded we bowl along a magnificent
road, built high above the meadows, wide, smooth, and
hard, and shaded without intermission for the distance of
four miles with a double row of handsome trees   Every
now and then we meet or pass one of the jolly teamsters.
His cart, little more than a couple of substantial timbers
some twenty-five feet in length mounted on a pair of
wheels, is laden with wine-butts.   Under the cart swings
a basket six feet long for the teamster's bed, and in one
such nest we see the bird himself sleeping soundly while
the march proceeds   Four horses, one behind another,
draw the cart,—great, well-fed animals, their heads all up
and their noses all in.   Each team is a cavalcade in itself,
stretching out its length some fifty feet, and as the horses
pace proudly along with the tops of the great hames and
the huge point of the collar, covered with bright-colored
stuff, swaying from side to side as they step, they seem
like yachts rolling on the billows of the deep blue sea.

Then we pass throngs of women going home from their
work in the fields, and enter Narbonne.

It was by the same route, no doubt,—the straight line
of the Roman road, that the countess of Burlatz, with
Arnaut de Maruelh at her side and a retinue behind,
cantered often down from Béziers on a day like this.
But how different a city they found ! It was a close,
walled town then, full of reminiscences of Roman glories,
rich and busy.   The ships of Genoa and Pisa crowded its

harbor. The merchants of the Levant thronged its bazaars. And in a castle that still echoed the songs of a famous troubadour, they found a second Zenobia as the head of the fief and theme of the songs. But stay,—before entering upon that we must rid ourselves of modernity.

Come then to the heart of the town—Place de l'Hôtel-de-Ville, they call it now—and view the three towers of the ancient palace of the archbishop.[1] Look at the powerful

NARBONNE.

square donjon at the corner—a hundred feet high, and the curious fountain at its base. Pass in review the long façade. Turn then to the left, and through a heavy archway enter the twilight Passage of the Anchor. Mysterious courtyards open to right and to left. Here is a loggia with a promenade on its roof, there a lofty balcony ; now towers rise high above us, now we have a glimpse of the great cathedral ; next archway follows close on archway, and meanwhile queer windows of all sizes seem to be keep-

ing dark secrets behind their screens of knotted bars.
Then up an odd flight of deep-worn steps, through a door,
under a groined arch, and we reach at last the heart of the
mystery,—a mouldering cloister between the cathedral
and the palace.

I hardly think I could ever be afraid of a gargoyle or
even of gargoyles, but if I could I should tremble here
Some have crumbled, some have broken,—and it is fortunate ; for those which survive are fierce with such an intensity and fixedness of gaze that all seem starting at us
from their brackets,—they must have caught that expression from memories of Moor and Christian who struggled
here once in fury and hate.   Even the trees are twisting
and writhing as if in mortal passion, and seem to nourish
the same tradition of defiance and rage, despite the sacred
stillness of the cloister.   But above the wall at the left rise
trees of another kind,—tall, easy, and neighborly ; and
straight ahead, out of a tremendous Gothic arch, springs
the mighty tower of the church oblivious of discord, mount-
ing heavenward past the trees, past the moss-grown wall,
past the grated windows of the clerestory, past the flying
buttresses, the double ranges of battlements, the turreted
pinnacles—all beautiful and strong, and what a maze of
them !—until it becomes a turreted pinnacle itself, defying
the clouds.

Here we enter the Basilique of St. Just, the church for
which Raphael's Transfiguration was ordered.[2]

Imagination is a more cunning builder than the masons,
and an edifice that aspires to be impressive should either
have the discretion to remain unfinished or the wisdom
to begin crumbling.   St Just has both   The pattern was
too grand for our modern age to complete, and eager time
began long since to gnaw the stones.

St Mark's is the embodiment of a Venetian piety,—rich,
commercial, warm, lavish, and intense ; St. Just brings

before us the bold and virile Goth, soaring in aspiration, fearless in originality, scornful in freedom, massive in purpose, disdainful of finish. The "glorious choir" springs into the air more than one hundred and thirty feet, a flawless piece of engineering; the pillars are remarkable for lightness; the vaulting, says Viollet-le-Duc, is no way inferior to any in the north; the singular arrangement (for the whole church is only a choir) adds an effect of mystery; and the rudeness of the carving, compared with the loftiness and beauty of the form, gives us the feeling that we stand in one of God's own temples, a house not made with hands.

Returning to the cloister, we descend the steps, and in fancy make an exit through the passage that once ran directly under the mass of stone. Now we are in a little garden, among the neighborly trees that we had a glimpse of just now, looking up still at the palace and the church, this wonderful memorial of priests that were dukes and soldiers that were archbishops, a fit emblem of church and state united. And here, under the trees and overshadowed by such a monument of the past, we can talk of the troubadours and their times.

Ermengarda, the viscountess of Narbonne, was really what we called her just now, a Zenobia. Forty-nine years she held her own among the warlike nobles who came and went meanwhile. Virtuous, wise, and brave, she both inspired admiration and commanded respect. She presided in the court of justice, her voice was heard in the council of princes, and on more than one occasion she led her troops to war. Like all the progressive rulers of the region, too, she favored the new culture, fostered poetry, and patronized the troubadours. Many a poet shared her hospitality and repaid it with a song; and for one of them her court became a home.

There were special reasons why Peire Rogier was accorded so high a place in Ermengarda's favor. She was a serious woman at heart. Her little realm, its honors, its duties, and its cares were her main interest in life. She desired to indulge her taste for poetry ; she enjoyed polite sentiment ; she liked a compliment ; she was ambitious to be in fashion ; but practical gallantry was not in her thoughts

In Rogier she found a serious man, as well as a talented poet. To the cooler nature of the north and the reserve of a mountain home he added the culture of a clerical training and the dignity of a churchman's office. Auvergne was the scene of his early life,[1] and while still a young man he reached the place of canon at Clermont. But poetry occupied his thoughts, and as the world showed all its brightness just then to those of poetic turn, he resigned his canonry, and after gaining experience in other courts made Narbonne his residence. Sedate, sensible, and for the times proper, he bore himself decorously in the society of the castle. Usually he appeared thoughtful, for as he once expressed it, " One that would maintain himself in high repute is weighed with heavy cares"; and, as he said at another time, " The higher a man is, the lower he descends if he permit himself to fall." But on occasion he unbent, remembering that, as he often remarked, " There are places where folly will help you more than sense." Whether grave or gay, however, he made an agreeable figure, discreet and polite, enjoying the wine of high life without intoxication, and always at hand with a well-bred song when a song was in order. In reality he was Ermengarda's poet laureate, bound by a pretty definite understanding to celebrate the charms and virtues of his noble patroness in exchange for her bounty; and he said his compliment with a full round emphasis that could not fail to satisfy.

No man who sees her e'er will say
A fairer lady has been known :
Her eyes are mirrors to his own,
And so resplendent is her face
That night becomes like shining day
If one but look upon it full.[4]

Doubtless Lady Ermengarda knew as well as anybody
that she was not the most beautiful woman in the world—
particularly after her second marriage ; and she had not
the remotest thought of damaging her reputation by an
intrigue.   But she kept her face as straight as the poet's ;
and she listened with her best semblance of a blush while
he sang with his best counterfeit of a passion :

Of singing ill I 'm ne'er afraid
When praising her whom I adore :
How could I brilliancy evade ?
A boorish man I 've never seen
That did one moment's converse hold
With her, and still to rudeness clave.
So understand, I pray, she gave
The wit I show in praising her.

Good lady, many a sigh I 've paid
And grief and pain in ample store
For love of you,—love ne'er to fade ;
To see you helps me not , and e'en
When I no longer can behold
Your face, my heart I cannot save ;
To you it flies,—a truant knave ,
And all I value comes from her.

Ah me ! " What, sighing ? " I 'm dismayed.
" Your trouble ? " Love. " Sincere ? " So sore
I 'm dying. " Dying ? " Yes. " Seek aid ! "
There is none. " Why ? " My grief 's too keen.
" Who caused it ? " She, as I have told
" Bear up ! " No use ! " Then pity crave."
I do. " You win it ? " No. " Be brave,
And though you suffer blame not her."

I 'll leave her. "What?"   My plan is made.
"Do not!"   I will.   "'T will hurt the more."
What can I do?   "Would you persuade
    Her heart?" Ah, yes. "Then hear." You mean—?
      "Be humble, generous, true, and bold."
        She 's harsh. "Endure."   I 'll be her slave.
        "You will?"   I promise. "Thus behave,
        And fear not, you will vanquish her." [5]

This dialogue between the poet's heart and his mind, or between himself and Love, recalls the central incident in a famous Provençal romance.[6] Flamenca, so the poem runs, was confined by her husband in a close tower, for no reason at all but groundless jealousy. He kept the key himself, visited her in the tower, and let her out only for church. After a time Lord Guilhem of Nivers (Nevers) —young, rich, and distinguished, of course—heard of the sad case, and resolved upon doing something for the captive. The situation seemed rather difficult, but Love himself became his counsellor. By his advice, Guilhem generously sent the clerk of the curé to study in Paris ; and then, discovering that he had sinned in turning aside from the sacred career he once began, Guilhem persuaded the curé to tonsure his fair locks and give him the place of clerk. Naturally it became his duty at every mass to offer Flamenca the pax, and the very first Sunday he whispered, "Alas !" Touched with pity and curiosity the lady replied a week later, "What pains?" Then at successive services they conversed as follows, two syllables at each mass, while the husband sat by, wholly unsuspicious :

" I die."—" The cause ? "
" 'T is love."—" For whom ? "
" For you."—" Can help ? "
" Yes, cure."—" But how ? "
" By ruse."—" Arrange."

" 'T is done."—" Tell how."
" You 'll go ? "—" But where ? "
" The baths."—" Yes, when ? "
" Right soon."—" I will."

The merciful intervention of holy days reduced the
duration of this dialogue to three months ; but that was
time enough for sleepless nights, for prayers to Love, for
taking counsel of him, for fasts, and for swoons. Meanwhile Guilhem had excavated a passage underground
from his dwelling to the baths—the famous Bains de
Bourbon ; and when the lady entered them, a square of
the pavement was cautiously raised and the lovers fell
into each other's arms. So jealousy earned once more its
due reward, as those who listened to the story doubtless
agreed.

Beside these questions and answers and their very
practical result, Rogier's dialogue seems rather pale, but
none the less it was very significant.

We already know something of the social and sentimental checks upon the practice of chivalric love, and one
must admit that the difficulties, the dangers, and the requirements were in the total somewhat appalling. Still
the serious people desired yet more strictness, for they
realized how vitally important it was to prevent love from
becoming license. Their expedient was to make it a
science and an art. Rules and regulations were devised,
and passion was to be bound with a rigid etiquette like
that of chivalry or that of social intercourse. It was to
be mainly an affair of sentiment and honor, not wholly
Platonic to be sure, but thoroughly desensualized. Four
distinct stages were marked off in the lover's progress :
first, he adored for a season without venturing to confess
it ; secondly, he adored as a mere suppliant ; thirdly, he
adored as one who knew that his lady was not indifferent ;
and finally he became the accepted lover,—that is to say,

the chosen servitor and vassal of his lady, her special knight. The means of reaching this happy state came to be no less formally defined. Guiraut de Calanson represented the palace of Love as approached by four steps; and these, according to Guiraut Riquier, were honor, discretion, gentle service, and good sufferance.

Quite in line with such ideas were the troubadour Courts of Love, of which every one has read,—or, more precisely, *might have been*, for no such Courts existed.

It is not a little singular that admirers of Provençal poetry have clung so affectionately to this fanciful institution, for it would prove the love and the songs of the troubadours artificial to the last degree; and it is even more singular to find writers descanting upon the fancy still, after scientific study has placed it among the curiosities of literature.[1]

There is an absolutely fatal argument against these Courts : they were never so much as mentioned by the troubadours. In fact, we first hear of them in a book by Martial of Auvergne dating from the last half of the fifteenth century, three hundred years after it has been said they flourished. And, further, the very nature of chivalric love—if the love were in earnest—required that lovers should not be known as such ; how, then, could they argue their claims in open court ?

Still there was a custom resembling the fanciful institution; something far more graceful and appropriate. When all were thinking of love and its complications, it was natural to speak of them. Great ladies of the " world " undoubtedly discussed all phases of the subject, and these informal discussions of real or imaginary cases became a favorite amusement of polite society. Difficult questions were certainly referred to recognized leaders of fashion, and their opinions helped, of course, to establish the principles and the usages of courtly love.

In all this formalizing and regulating of the " grand passion," Ermengarda was a Moses, and Rogier her Aaron Her castle was an *avant-courier* of the Hôtel de Rambouillet. She and the famous Maria de Ventadorn in the Midi, and in the north Maria, the countess of Champagne,° a daughter of Queen Eleanor, endeavored to create a system that should bind man to the service of woman somewhat as the priestly ordinances of chivalry bound him to the service of the church.' In this case the instinct of love, as in that the instinct of war and adventure, was to be the means ; and Rogier's dialogue may be called a " Shorter Catechism " of the new creed

A " Longer Catechism " was the poet's other songs to Ermengarda and his life at her court. His lady was always represented as flawless. Whatever was good in him came from her. "Long desires" for her were worth more than all the joy that any other woman could bestow. " Of nothing else but her " did he think or meditate. His only longing was to serve her. Though far away, he was " truly near her, for no one can separate lovers if their hearts desire to feel together." Even the wind that blew from where she was gave more satisfaction than the nearness of any one else. She gave him smiles and laughter, and he would be foolish to " ask more of her." Merely from seeing her face,· he was " happy and joyous " Never had he told her of his love nor had she discovered it, but still he loved her as much as if she had already accepted him. He did not even ask of her " gentle act or gracious look." " All covertly and secretly and quietly" he paid her an unceasing court in his heart. She did not know the good she did him, but none the less he gained, "through her, joy and reward "; and it did not even matter that he was only one of six that adored her. Such were the orthodox attitudes of this professional lover ; and as Daniel became a new point of departure in style by sacrificing poetry and song to artistic workmanship, Rogier became a new point of departure in love by sacrificing, more than any one before him, the substance of passion to the forms of boundless devotion.

But the troubadour was human after all and so was the viscountess. It appears that his acting ended seriously; and it even looks as if the prudent Ermengarda took fire.[10] Arnaut Daniel once declared, "There is no lady who does not wish to yield, and none who will not if rightly wooed." The unknown author of *Flamenca* went farther : "She is no longer woman who resists the impulses of her heart. . . . There is not even a dragon or a viper that cannot be tamed with gentleness." One of Rogier's pieces has been supposed to indicate that his prayer for love was granted.[11] Anyhow, says the biography, people began to talk, and Ermengarda felt compelled to send the troubadour away.

It must have been hard to leave the place of honor in the castle of Narbonne and resume the poet's wandering life, and the biography tells us that Rogier felt the blow most keenly. But he was by no means a weakling. "One must not be exultant over great success," he once declared in his didactic way, "and in misfortune a strong man does not despair." At the court of Raimbaut d'Aurenga he found a second home, and he lived a long time at Courthézon, perhaps until his patron died (1173). Then he made a tour in Spain, visiting King Amfos, the fortunate rival of Arnaut de Maruelh, and perhaps also the king of Castile. After that the "good count," Raimon V. of Toulouse, the father of the countess of Burlatz, received him; and no doubt he made the acquaintance there —if not before—of Bernart de Ventadorn, the most passionate as Rogier was the primmest of the troubadours. Life was pleasant still, for his fame was great; all were glad to entertain him, and even his fellow poets admired his art.

But finally he grew old and weary. Thoughts of his priestly youth, not unmixed with remorse, haunted him ; and in the end, like most of the famous troubadours, he sought the peace of Mother Church. Among the sightly mountains of Lodève, north from Béziers, the abbey of Grammont had recently been founded. It was then most flourishing, and the abbot even had the walls of the cloister and infirmary covered with paintings.[1] In this retreat Peire Rogier took leave of the world, and passed an enviable old age in cloister and garden.

But for us there is no occasion to be envious. Never was a cloister walled in as we are,—the towers of the palace, crowned with low roofs of tiles; bouquets of foliage against their grey walls ; and the multiform basilique looking, through the tall trees, like an assembly of castles worshipping in conclave. And never was a garden so fascinating as this one ; a garden not made with spades ; of a shape geometry could not describe; of a value algebra could not formulate ; a cool corner in a dusty world ; a garden richer in thoughts than any other is rich in flowers.

Narbonne is now only a dull provincial town. It no longer has a commerce, for centuries ago the port silted up ; it no longer has its castle, no longer its once proverbial fortresses, no longer its walls, no longer a name save for honey. But one thing it always will have,—a history.

This is Narbo, founded probably by Phœnicia, adopted certainly by Rome, the capital city of Gallia Narbonensis, a province so dear to Rome that afterwards when she had many such it was still and always *the province*. Here the stern proconsuls and the legions marched. Around us are piles of Roman blocks covered with warlike faces, inscriptions, pompous ornament, and scraps of triumphal emblems.   Not a stone's throw distant is the spot where the Roman galleys were moored ; and yonder in the marsh are piles of masonry worn by their grappling irons.[18]   Here lived Varro, the first man beyond the Alps to achieve distinction in Roman letters.   Here came Augustus from looking on the dead face of Cleopatra, to summon a council of all the Gauls.   Here were born three emperors of Rome, and here played the boy Sebastian, destined to wear the crown of a double martyrdom.

Then the Vandals poured over the city, and the tides of Goths flowed and ebbed ; and after them the Saracens came, entrenching themselves so deeply that even the Hammer of the North, Charles Martel, could not break their wall ; but the traitor undid them, and they also disappeared.   And now we are here.   Perhaps our civilization, too, is to pass away ; but we are here now, the plane trees and the evergreens above, and the palms around us.

Stretched out at full length on a bench, fanned by gently swaying shadows, one lets the mind float idly at anchor.   The future does not exist ; the present is far away.   There is no approach for troublers but the one small entrance in the wall ; at the worst only a little bore could find room to pass, and besides, the iron door is closed.   Now the imagination dares open all its windows ; the Civilizations march past ; the centuries glide one upon another.   Long slender thoughts unroll themselves delicately in the mind like ferns in the depths of a forest. Pictures of Ermengarda, of Alazais, of all things beautiful, of all things ancient, brighten and fade, fade and brighten, like the palpitating auroras.   And the music of the fountain is so low ; and the touches of the air, now and then, are so gentle,—so caressing ; and the murmur

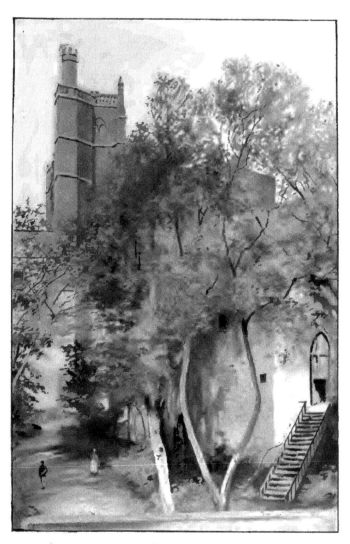

A BIT OF THE OLD GARDEN, NARBONNE.

of the old city grows so mellow,—so faint,—so far distant,
—so dreamlike,——

Ah, it is not Then but Now, and the train goes in half
an hour.

But what spot on earth can be worth leaving this one
for ?

PERPIGNAN, CASTELL-ROSSELLO, AND CABESTANY

Guilhem de Cabestaing

FEARFUL tragedies were common in those days : we expect them ; but Roussillon, famous for its black sheep and red wine, is yet more famous for a story so romantic and so terrible that—well, you shall be the judge of it.

Perpignan, the capital of the district, seems a fit introduction to such a tale. Though for two hundred and fifty years a part of France, it still wears a foreign and mediæval air. Red caps, crimson sashes, and sandals no longer find their way from the mountains into the town as they used to do; but the people, mainly Catalans in Stendhal's time, seem more Spanish than French even today, and the buildings—here Romanesque, there Moorish, there Gothic, and yonder all of them at once—appear capable of harboring the darkest secrets,—an impression deepened by romantic balconies, mysterious awnings, and shadowy courtyards.

In Perpignan the kings of Majorca lived, and their warlike spirit still survives in castle and fort. Not long ago the town ranked as a fortress of the first order, and it is important today. The city is encompassed with earthworks and forts, old but apparently formidable. One of the gates is provided with a genuine drawbridge. Beside peaceable dwellings rises the Castillet crowned with towers, and all these features reach a climax in the citadel, which Charles V., Vauban, and many others have labored to make impregnable.

Still in keeping with our story, everything comes upon you at Perpignan as a surprise.   If you go for a drive into

AT PERPIGNAN.

the country, the town suddenly vanishes as you leave it, and suddenly envelops you as you return.   If you take a walk, it ends abruptly and you find the point of a bastion glaring out upon you from the trees.   A little stream loiters along through what was once a moat, and precisely when it grows idyllic you come upon a massive bridge with a screen against bullets.   Surrender to the warmth of the day and the luxuriance of southern vegetation, and presently you discover through the foliage a sharp summit of the Pyrenees riven by volcanic energies.

To gain any view of the scene of our drama, we must go up to the citadel, and then climb to its highest point At our feet lies the mystery of Perpignan, and for a wonder we find ourselves able to see more than one thing at a time Beyond the city spreads the fair green plain of Roussillon. Like a bird in flight the eye travels to and fro across its fields and gardens, its flashing channels of water, and its three meandering streams. And in the distance we gaze alternately upon the shimmering Mediterranean on the one side, and on the other upon the vast pyramid of Canigou draped with glistening snow.[1] But after all, this is only a general view and we must go nearer.

Five o'clock in the morning, then. The air, whether it comes from sea or mountain, clear and crisp. Perpignan looking very pleasant among the abounding green. The enormous plane trees of the promenade standing at ease, but with bowed backs ready for the strong north wind. Roses blooming on the gate-posts. Palms fluttering and rustling as a breeze touches them. Vineyards fresh and verdant beside the road And ourselves with barouche and pair, and a driver who calls himself a postilion,—this is—for us—the first setting of the drama

Perpignan was not always the chief city of this region.[2] Long before it was important, long before it existed, probably, Ruscino, some three miles to the east and near the sea, guarded the passage from south to north. To Ruscino the Roman senate despatched ambassadors, praying that Hannibal and his army should not be allowed transit, but the city, Phœnician by descent or at least by affiliations, permitted the Carthaginian to pass and even to tarry. As Rome triumphed, it was perhaps natural for this contumacious town to decay. So it did, at all events; and finally in the eighth century the Normans wiped it from the earth so completely that only slight vestiges of walls and foundations are discoverable.

But the position was important, and as early as the twelfth century the castle of Roussillon (R o s s i l l o n) was erected on the spot as a border fortress. More fortunate than the city, the castle is still something besides a name. Perched on the edge of the bluff there stands today a lofty tower, bare and almost solitary, called the Castell-Rossello,[2] its round wall confronting equally the snowy top of Mount Canigou, the wide valley of the boisterous Tet, and the crested waves of the Mediterranean. Behind the tower is a chapel, old though not ancient; and below it have gathered some half-a-dozen cottages to escape the loneliness of the fields.

CASTELL-ROSSELLO.

Two or three miles to the south of Castell-Rossello lies the quiet village of Cabestany,[4] a trim, bright, thrifty hamlet among the vineyards, with houses of large brown cobbles provided by the Pyrenees and rounded by the torrents that brought them. The stones are kept in place and sometimes entirely covered with mortar generously applied; while the corners, the doorways, and the windows are edged with brick. Lines of brick are often laid horizontally among the stones of a wall to add a look of regularity ; and sometimes bits of dark pottery, broken brick, or stone are set into the mortar in rough circles around the larger cobbles. A little brook runs through the village Carts are tipped up here and there against a wall Huge piles of twigs cut from the vines are tied in bundles ready for burning. The children are going to school, the men are in the fields, and the sturdy, brown-faced women in white caps—always trimmed with a frill —are sewing, knitting, or gossiping in their doorways, or busying themselves within.

The fields around Cabestany are not infertile and the whole region thrives. But in the days of the troubadours Cabestaing, as the name went then, was only a small castle surrounded by marshes, and the sea pushed a lagoon almost up to its moat. There was little scope for ambition in a place like that , and so very naturally Guilhem, the son of a poor knight of Cabestaing, presented himself when twelve years old at the rich castle of Rossillon, and asked Raimon, its lord, who was also his father's lord, to receive him. Poor though he was he did not come without good training of its kind, for his father and mother had impressed upon his mind the first principles of , knightly living,—to be fearless and true, to reverence God, to be generous, and to shun the low-born ; and Raimon, seeing that he was a handsome and agreeable boy and promised well, told him that he was welcome and should abide in his court.

This opened a future to the boy. Without delay he was taken to the church and given a belt and a sword by the priest , and as he was then an esquire, a novice in the order of chivalry, his education began forthwith. Every hour was a lesson in courtly manners and the usages of society. From the chaplain he gained some elements, more or less, of book knowledge,—very possibly learned to write. The chief joglar taught him to sing a song prettily, and play an accompaniment for himself or others. Somebody—one of the ladies, perhaps—instructed him in dancing. And some knight or older esquire trained him in riding and in wielding arms.

Occupations of a different sort fell to him, for with two other esquires he performed the duties of a body-servant about the person of his lord. In the early morning he groomed Raimon's horse and his own ; and then, hastening to the donjon, assisted his master to dress and begin the day. If guests arrived, it was his duty to receive them, take off their armor, and conduct them to his lord. At dinner he brought his master's courses from the kitchen, handed him this and that, cut his meat and filled his glass, and had no thought of eating or drinking himself until the baron rose. If Raimon went hunting, Guilhem attended and assisted him ; and if he travelled, Guilhem convoyed the money-chest. In the tourney he aided him to arm, held the charger till he was ready to mount, bore the shield until it was needed, brought his lord fresh weapons, and if he fell dragged him from the mêlée. When, as the custom was in Rossillon, fires on the heights announced the approach of war, he became his master's aide in marshalling and his lieutenant in commanding the troop In battle he bore himself as in the tourney, perhaps rushing in to the rescue, perhaps remaining aloof to guard the prisoners. Occasionally he was called upon to make a robe or a mantle for Lord Raimon. At all times there were armor and weapons to clean and polish. And yet between whiles he found opportunities to perfect himself in horsemanship, arms, and music ; and he passed so many of his hours in hunting with dogs or with hawk, that he became a centaur in spirit if not in fact.'

Such duties—the regular school of young nobles—appear to us menial So much the worse for us. The middle ages held that one destined to rule should first learn the art by obeying ; and the feudal system, though it finally took root as a hierarchy of landed estates, was founded on the principle of personal service. To serve was the beginning of authority; and the chevalier Bayard, *sans peur et sans reproche*, earned his first praise among

A BIT OF CABESTANY.

men by gracefully and modestly handing the wine-cup to his lord.

But Guilhem's esquireship was interrupted. So well had he borne himself that all, "both great and small, loved him," and something—or somebody—put it into Lord Raimon's head to transfer him to the service of his wife. Now the Lady Margarida, for so she was named, was accounted by all who knew her the most beautiful woman of the time, and the most excellent, and the most courtly. But we need not infer that she was tall, stately, and grand,—not at all. Though married she was hardly more than a girl ; a dear, dainty woman, a sweet little golden-face with sapphire eyes, not very prudent or intellectual, but still with ideas of her own in her small head, and more thoughts behind her tongue than upon it.[6]

Guilhem had adored her from the moment he could adore any one. Now, permitted to approach and even to serve her, he exerted himself more than ever "to excel in both words and deeds." Day by day his lady observed

him. Fearless and accomplished on the hunt and in the
tilt-yard, he became instantly as gentle as a girl when he
drew near to her. With bowed head and eyes humbly
cast down he welcomed her command, and, no matter what
she willed, it was done instantly and gracefully, even at
the risk of life or limb. And what a contrast there was
to set him off! For the baron, though courtly in the
manner of the time, was at heart a man of wild and tyran-
nical passions. In his best mood he was cold and haughty;
in his worst, fierce, bloody, and implacable.

So it came to pass that Margarida, as the story goes,
" could not refrain from saying one day . ' Tell me, Guilhem ; if a lady were to show you looks of love would you
dare to love her ? ' " The words were lightly spoken as if
in banter, but they had long been meditated, for the lady
saw that her esquire adored her, but saw also that he stood
too much in awe to dare speak of love. He was not afraid
to reply, however, and his answer was ready . " Indeed,
yes, lady ; if only I were sure that her looks truly showed
her heart "

" By St. John ! " cried Margarida, " you have answered
like a man. But now I would also prove you, and find out
whether you can distinguish between true looks and false."

And when Guilhem heard this he only said · " My
lady, may all be as pleases you."

A new life opened then within him. For no man of the
world was he, no tried gallant, no learnèd clerk, no finished lord ; but just a simple-minded, unselfish, brave,
young fellow, scarcely man grown, rich only in the fulness of a true heart, and wholly unspoiled by experience.
And yet he was more than that Undeveloped though it
was, there dwelt within him a profound love for beauty.
In the depths of his nature lay a dormant fitness for a
romantic passion. And these powers, unconscious though
they were as yet, had dulled the attractions of ordinary

women, and filled him with vague longings for a poetic
satisfaction which afterward appeared to him like fore-
knowledge.   In a word he was just the Walther of
Wagner's *Meistersinger*, and, if you please, Alvary in the
rôle ; and when the lady's words darted a quick ray of
sunshine into the heart of this esquire just made a knight,
it blossomed into song as naturally as the spring-time
into flowers.

> The very day one glimpse of you I caught,
>   When you were pleased to let me see your face,
> My heart took leave of every other thought,
>   And every wish—except for you—gave place ;
>   For you awoke within my heart such longing
>   With one sweet smile and just a simple look,
>   That all things else my memory forsook.
>
> Your wondrous charms, your words with sweetness fraught,
>   Your courtly speech, your loveliness and grace—
> Demurely shown—within my mind so wrought
>   That judgment fled, and madness came apace ;
>   So, to exalt you, though myself much wronging,
>   My mind I give you,—now my pleadings brook !
>   No love like that is found in song or book.[1]

All took pleasure in the new troubadour, but most of
all the lady whom he celebrated.   And so, when it seemed
good to Love, who rewards the efforts of his servants
when it pleases him, she found herself so moved by the
poet's excellence and worth that she had no rest day nor
night.   And after a time, drawing him aside one day,
she said to him : "Tell me now, Guilhem ; have you discovered yet whether my looks are deceitful or sincere ?"
And Guilhem answered : "So may God help me, lady,—
from the hour I began to serve you no thought has entered
my heart, that you are not the best ever born and the
truest in words and in looks.   This I believe, and this I
shall believe, so long as life lasts."
And Margarida said : " Guilhem, I say to you—so keep

me God !—you shall never be deceived by me, and your thoughts of me shall not be in vain.''

The promise was vague, the pledge '' obscure ''; but as they sat together she threw her arm around him, and he, forgetting many a past caprice of hers, felt as if she had at last been won.

But soon the busybodies of the neighborhood suspected that matters were growing serious. Gossip wagged its many tongues, and one of them dropped a word into Raimon's ear. That was his opportunity to show the depth of his courtliness. His wife had not overstepped the line of decorum according to the rule of society,*—no more had Guilhem ; and the husband's part in such a situation was to be neither simpleton nor madman, but strategist. He was to establish an understanding with his wife, help her keep the affair within bounds, and—after these precautions were taken—look upon the honor paid her as honor added to his own.

But the lord of Rossillon was of another type, and finding by careful inquiries that Guilhem had gone with his hawk in a certain direction he concealed arms under his mantle and went after him.

'' Welcome, lord,'' said Guilhem when they met, '' but how is it you come alone ? ''

'' I have been looking for you, to have a chat by ourselves. And have you taken nothing ? ''

'' Hardly anything, for I have found little game ; and ' who finds little takes little,' you know, as the proverb says.''

'' Enough of this talk. Tell me truly, by the fealty you owe me, all that I shall wish to ask you.''

'' By heaven, lord, if it is a thing that can be said I will say it.''

'' I will have no evasion ; you shall tell me the whole truth of the matter that I shall ask about.''

"Since that is your pleasure, lord, ask me and I will tell you the truth."

"Guilhem, so help you God and your good faith, have you a lady whom you sing and love?"

"And how could I sing, lord, if love constrained me not? Know in truth, my lord, that Love has me entirely in his power."

"That indeed I well believe, else you could not sing so sweetly. But I would know, if you please—tell me, who is your lady?"

"Alas, lord, in God's name, beware what you ask,—think whether it be right for one to reveal his love. Tell me yourself,—is it? for you know what Bernart de Ventadorn said: 'It is a foolish and childish thing to lay bare the heart to one who cannot help.'"

"But I promise to help you to the full of my power."

The troubadour was now caught, for that unlucky citation from Bernart gave his antagonist an opening. What should he do? To tell the truth was impossible; to do otherwise would be disloyal. But he felt he must serve God rather than man; and God was Love. And furthermore had he not just now avowed to Raimon that Love was his real master?

"Know then, lord," he answered, "that I love the sister of my Lady Margarida, your wife, and believe my love returned. Now you know it, and I beseech you to aid or at all events not to hinder me."

"Take my hand and my word," cried Raimon, "for I promise and swear to aid you all I can." And when the pledge had been given he added, "Let us go now to her castle, for it is not far distant."

"By all means let us go," answered Guilhem, for there was nothing else to say.

When they arrived at the castle Lord Raimon took the Lady Agnes by the hand, led her to a chamber, and sit-

ting down on the bed said to her, " Tell me now, kins-
woman, by the loyalty you owe me, have you a lover ? "

But Lady Agnes knew of course her sister's heart ; she
knew equally her brother-in-law's disposition ; and she
saw, too, that Guilhem was deeply troubled. Ladies were
quick-witted, especially in matters of love ; and it was in
vain that Raimon endeavored to conceal his aim.

" Yes, lord," she answered with only what seemed the
hesitation of modesty.

" And who is it ? "

" I will never tell you."

But he pressed and insisted ; and in the end, as if with
great reluctance, Agnes confessed that her lover was Guilhem de Cabestaing. Not only so, but she conducted herself with Guilhem that day and night in a manner to
deceive Lord Raimon still more, and completely to satisfy
him that what had been told of his wife was only an idle
and malicious tale. Then he was glad indeed, and returning home on the morrow he recounted to Lady Margarida
all that had taken place at her sister's.

Upon this Margarida was very sad. All night she
suffered torments ; and on the morrow, summoning Guilhem, she called him a deceiver and a traitor. But he,
imploring her mercy as one innocent of the charge, explained the matter fully; and her sister, speedily sent for,
convinced her that Guilhem was not at fault. The tragedy
was averted

But alas ! woman's indiscretion is more fatal than man's
wrath. Margarida, like the maiden whom Cupid loved,
was not satisfied with satisfaction. Sweet, foolish little
woman that she was, she must needs have a song upon it,
a formal assurance that Guilhem loved none but her, a
peace-offering to her suffering vanity.

It is easy to believe that Guilhem felt desperate. He
saw full well the danger. Once already he had been with-

in the lion's jaws   The teeth had gripped his flesh.   Only
by a miracle of address had he escaped.   And now his
lady bade him return and inform the lion of the deceit
Again he wondered, as he often had wondered before,
whether the bewitching, capricious, blue-eyed lady really
loved him, or was only using him as a plaything after
all.

But—what could he do?   He was pledged to obey his
lady   That was duty.   That was honor.   There was no
other.   Only one path was open,—what matter if it did
lead to the precipice?   Was she not there?   Did not Love
command?   Had not everything been done that could be
done to ward off destruction?   Was it possible to turn?
No, it was not possible.   Besides, he would not.   Perhaps
bliss lay beyond; certainly it lay nowhere else   There
was no chance but that , no other choice.   Forward, forward !   And as he realized that but one path could be
taken and that seemed fatal, his heart was buoyed up with
the merciful exaltation of a strong despair , and opening
his arms he rushed upon fate, not with a cry of anguish
but with a song of love.

> The tender musing
> That Love doth oft awake
> Hath sweetest using
> In songs he bids me make ;
> But now, refusing
> Your beauties to forsake,
> Thought grows confusing,
> And words tell not my ache ,
> Although I seem to stray,
> My heart turns not away,
> And soon to you I pay
> My loving supplication ;
> And, lost in contemplation
> Of all your charms, essay
> But praises and to pray.

Love, ne'er excusing
My crime, shall vengeance take,
    If I, abusing
Your trust, my pledges break ;
    The joys amusing
Light hearts I ne'er partake,—
    Your love infusing
A fire they 've not to slake ;
        For I must not display
        The love I bear you ;—nay,
        " I love her not," must say
            With cold asseveration ;
            But this, my desperation,
            Should not your heart dismay
            Though dubious for a day.

    Your noble station,
Smile, color, form, and grace,
    No separation
Could from my heart efface ,
    Such consecration
To God should I embrace,
    I 'm sure translation
Would soon make heaven my place;
        Myself, I feel secure   .
        That love for you is sure,
        Because no others lure ;
            For none who wears a fillet
            I 'd prize one grain of millet,
            Though for your greeting pure
            Her all I could procure.

    To admiration
My passion I can trace ,
    Without cessation,
Sweet Thing, it grows apace ;
    'T is my vocation .
I served you a long space
    In expectation
Before I saw your face ,

So I could ne'er endure
The loves that oft allure,
For you alone could cure ;
    The rest be theirs who will it ;
    My vow,—I will fulfil it,
And trust your pledge obscure
Whence joys e'en now enure.

My heart will dare abjure—
    So, lady, you can thrill it,
    And then with favor still it—
All fealties, to ensure
Whate'er you would secure.[9]

There was no longer any doubt in Raimon's mind,—the song fitted the case too well, and leaving the castle he sent back an attendant with a summons to the troubadour. Guilhem obeyed.   .   .   .

Was it a stab ? Was it a duel ? Did a mountain brook, sparkling in the sunlight, catch his life and bear it on to dye the blossoms along its brink ? Did a tempest from the abysses of the mountain seize his last breath and whirl it amid the storming elements far out upon the sea ? The manuscript does not say ; we can only feel sure that when the lord of Rossillon rode back, Guilhem was not with him, and his quaking servant bore something wrapped in a mantle to the castle.   .   .   .

" Do you know what you have eaten ? " said Raimon to his wife after dinner.

" No, except that it was good and savory."

Then he told her that she had certainly eaten the heart of Guilhem de Cabestaing.   " And see," he added, calling a servant from the next room, " see, this is his head ! "

Margarida, when she heard that, lost for an instant the power to see and to hear, but recovering herself replied :

" You have given me meat so good, my lord, that I will never taste other."

Raimon was seized with double fury then, and sprang for a sword to strike her with ; but she fled to the balcony, and pausing there an instant for one desperate resolve she threw herself down and so died,—her foolish, capricious heart faithful to the death.

The noise of these doings was spread abroad, says the story, through all that region, and so reached the king of Aragon, the suzerain of both Sir Raimon and Sir Guilhem. And the king hastened to Perpignan, summoned the lord of Rossillon before him, stripped him of his castles and of everything he possessed, and cast him into prison. Guilhem and the lady he brought to Perpignan and buried together in a tomb at the door of the church; and he caused the manner of their death to be inscribed upon the tomb, and ordained that all the knights and ladies of Rossillon should come there each year and hold a festival in their honor.[10]

And Raimon of Castell Rossillon died miserably in the king's prison.[11]

XV

BARCELONA

King Amfos the Second.   Guilhem de Berguedan

SPRING in Provence would make any man long to be a poet, and the shore of Catalonia would make him pine to be a smuggler.   What secretive headlands reach far out their sheltering crooks and corners !   What mysterious bays cut just as far into the coast, with numberless dark inlets and coves among the rocks !

This was our outlook for many miles as we journeyed south.   Then sea and forelands disappeared and rich plains encompassed us, themselves encompassed with distant sierras.   Just under the windows of the car thousands of wild poppies, giddy with excitement, stood flirting their crimson skirts at us as we flew along.   Below in the fields liberty-caps of scarlet wool moved about in the green, and under them bent figures cut the forage already waiting for the scythe, while gardens, rich and moist, bourgeoned luxuriantly in the full sunshine.

After a while we had time to think, and of course we thought of the wonderful processions of men and of peoples that have moved to or fro along the strip of earth where the traveller passes from France to Spain.   This has been the forum of conquerors, and at this point the orbits of Hannibal, Cæsar, Charlemagne, and Napoleon have interlocked ; but it has been far more than that.   Carthaginians, Romans, Goths, Moors, Frenchmen, and Spaniards ;

Christians and Mohammedans , the North and the South ;
the East and the West,—they have all swept up or down
between the Pyrenees and the sea, now with shouts of
exultation, now in the foreboding silence of disaster ; and
the forum of conquerors has been also the forum of nations
and of races.

But our thoughts dwelt more on travellers of a very
different kind and of much less violent pretensions,—the
troubadours.

Northern Spain—especially Catalonia—was a part of
their world.[1] They looked on the French as foreigners,
and on the Italians as cousins, but on the Spanish as
brothers.   For generations the same family governed
Catalonia and Provence, besides other fiefs north of the
Pyrenees.   Lang tells us that as early as the end of the
eleventh century the minstrels of southern France followed
the knights and barons beyond the Pyrenees, and sang
at the brilliant festivals and tournaments of Christian
Spain.   This movement never ceased.   The troubadours
were constantly on the route we have taken, and many of
them gained fame and fortune in the south.[2]   Eventually
Catalonia became more Provençal than Languedoc itself ;
and it was a centre of literary activity in the language of
the troubadours and based upon their art, after the sun
had almost set in the home of this literature.

Meanwhile our journey continued and finally came to
an end . " Barcélona ! "

We all understand what is meant by " a fine woman,"—
beauty and brilliancy, with a certain breadth of movement
and an opulence of charms   Barcelona is a fine city.

So it was, for the period, when Ugo de Sain Circ and
Peire Rogier entered its gate.   To be sure it hid behind
walls then ; while now, released from constraint, it has
doubled in area within thirty years.   The busiest avenue,
the Rambla, a double street with trees and a promenade in

the middle, full of sauntering gallants and black-eyed
flower girls all smiles and glances, was then what the
name signifies, a watercourse. The massive quays of the
harbor, screened with a line of palm trees, supported by
the Paseo de Colon and its wall of imposing façades, and
protected by the cannon of Montjuich,[2] was then merely
a roadstead and a beach, sheltered only by the headlands
on either side

None the less the city throve, and above all as a commercial metropolis. The statue of Columbus, looking
seaward from a pedestal almost as high[4] as Bunker Hill
Monument, the first thing and the last thing seen by
every ship, not only testifies that here the intrepid sailor
laid at the feet of his sovereigns the grandest present ever
offered on earth, but reminds us that Barcelona has always
been the home of bold and successful navigators. It was
a mediæval Carthage   It rivalled the ports of Italy in
the rich trade of the Mediterranean. It was the store-
house and market of all Christian Spain. Its coinage was
a standard of value. Its merchants were princes, and
their seals outranked a noble's coat of arms. Ships of
war, too, brought in their harvest. Precisely while Provençal poetry was developing, this tide of prosperity set
in, and Barcelona—proud, rich, and pleasure-loving—was
doubtless, if Toulouse be excepted, the most luxurious
home that welcomed and rewarded the troubadours.

Relics of the past are not wanting. The line between
the new and the old is almost as marked as that between
Paris and Arabia in the city of Algiers. In the Rambla
one eats and sleeps at the close of the nineteenth century,
a square or two away, amid narrow and crooked streets,
quaint and hoary buildings, he walks in the middle ages ,
and if that is not ancient enough he may find antiquity
in a pair of Roman columns and in two Phœnician towers.
In the hall of records we inspect official documents of the

THE FOUNDATIONS OF THE PALACE, BARCELONA.

troubadour age ; and a few steps away we find, still firm
and abiding, some foundation arches of the palace where
the troubadours were entertained.'

A still more thrilling echo of the past is the Cathedral
Begun (1058) ere William of Normandy was hailed as the
Conqueror of England, and before Don Roderigo came to
be known as El Cid, its tardily rising mass was viewed by
generations of troubadours, and the religion of their age
is vocal yet within its walls.

Out of glowing sunshine we passed through double
doors into the Sibyl's cave,—into darkness, gloom, midnight. Little by little, forms and shapes appeared,—some
shadows became less dense than others. After many
minutes we dared grope for seats. After many more we
could follow the chief lines of the building. "Holy,
mysterious, almost terrible!" we thought like Théophile
Gautier. Three vast naves bewildered our eyes. Baffling,
too, was the great choir, filling the midst of the central
nave with dark stalls carved with exquisite and incredible
profusion. And even when the mind had grasped the
main thoughts of the architecture, fathomless glooms continued to hide the depths of the mystery.

A service was proceeding, and worshippers knelt on the
pavement,—nearly all of them women. In her bloom a
Spanish woman is a paper lantern with a flame inside ;
pious and old she is the same lantern scorched and un-
lighted. The gloom of penitence matches the blaze of
impulse, and superstition becomes the measure of passion.
Furrowed cheeks, wrinkled brows, and hollow eyes made
the house of prayer seem rather a house of punishment.
The fierce piety about us recalled memories of savage
cruelty perpetrated in the name of religion. A curtain
seemed rising upon black-robed Inquisitors and the fires
of the auto-de-fe. The scented air grew stifling. The
shadows became terrible.

But we could not go. " Dumb woods, have ye uttered
a bird ? " cried Lanier among the live-oaks of the marshes.
" Cathedral, thou hast uttered an archangel," was the
thought which came to me.   A Voice was chanting.[6]
The singer was invisible, but out of the shadows and re-
cesses of the organ-loft the Voice poured upon us, not
guttural, not nasal, not forced,—but open, deep, rich,
sonorous, and mighty.   The color of it matched the
purple vestments of the priests in the chancel.   It seemed
in plain truth the voice of the Cathedral, for every column
and buttress, arch and vault, every cornice, every sculpture, stained with the incense of centuries, vibrated in all
their, tones of harmony like the wood of a Stradivarius.
The beams of " jewelled light " from the little round windows above the chancel seemed all a-tremble as they fell
upon the pavement.   The flames of the splendid candles
appeared to be quivering.   The crouching forms on the
floor seemed to rise and fall, as if borne up or beaten down
by the massive tones reverberating in tremendous Latin
the terrors of the law or the triumphant glories of the
righteous   And when the organ answered at intervals
with its vast chorus of tones, we seemed to hear the re-
sponse of endless ranks of angels, prophets, martyrs, and
apostles, like the sound of many waters.   The super-
natural began to appear nature ; superstition to appear
reason.   The cloud of incense recalled the awful presence
of the Shekinah.   Even a Protestant could almost feel,
with the trembling worshippers, that before us upon the
altar the Redeemer of mankind, Son of the most high
God, in his true substance, in his own real flesh and
blood, was then and there making atonement as a living
sacrifice for the sins of a lost world   And in that place
and hour I felt nearer than ever before to the mediæval
sense of religion which dominated piety in the age of the
troubadours.

" Barcelona, shrine of courtesy, harbor of the wayfarer, shelter of the poor, cradle of the brave, champion of the outraged, nurse of friendship, unique in position, unique in beauty "; so wrote Cervantes, and so thought many a troubadour who came in want and sojourned in plenty.

For more t h a n a generation, while Provençal poetry was ripening, united Catalonia and Aragon were governed by a king of remarkable i n t e l l i-gence, grace, and liberality. The son of the greatest count of Barcelona (Barsalo-na), who throve by diplomacy, prospered in war, and by a fortunate marriage added a crown to a coronet, Amfos the Second inherited a realm, not of great extent, but rich, prosperous, luxurious, full of gayety and gallantry, and probably after Languedoc the foremost of all Europe in social polish and literary cul-

BEHIND THE CATHEDRAL, BARCELONA.

ture. His father had been sought as an ally by the most powerful monarch of the age ; his sister was betrothed almost in infancy to no less a personage than Richard Cœur-de-Lion ; and he himself, despite his faults, added honor to a family that was to reign after him for nearly two centuries

Still, we approach Amfos with dislike, for did he not wrong Arnaut de Maruelh ? And I, for my part, propose that we take as our guide and escort his bitterest enemy.

Guilhem de Berguedan was a nobleman of Catalonia, viscount, " good knight, and good soldier." He was a poet also, and composed some pleasant and graceful verses as well as many that were neither   It is believed that he wrote stories, too, which have not survived.   Intellect was not lacking in his composition ; and he left this bit of advice worthy of attention : " One should spare oneself the trouble of heeding little things, so as to be able to apply the mind wholly to those of importance." But with all the rest of his qualities he was a finished blackguard.   As Flaubert said of Rodolphe Boulanger, he was at once " brutal and clear-headed "; and in short he embodied the force and intelligence of his age together with all its badness.

One day as he passed along carrying a book, says Francesco da Barberino, some one asked him in the presence of several where he was going.   " To Madam So-and-so," he replied, calling her by name, " and she is going to present me with a garland and make me swear to conceal her name from everybody."

He once declared roundly in a company of nobles that no lord of Provence-beyond-the-Rhone could be named whom he had not unhorsed in the tilt-yard and crowned with horns in his castle   The count of Provence himself was there and exclaimed, " Do you include me ? "   " I will tell you," answered Guilhem, and calling for his horse he leaped into the saddle and cried, " You, my lord, I do not except "

For this insult the ladies resolved upon avenging themselves.   A party of them sent for him one day and when

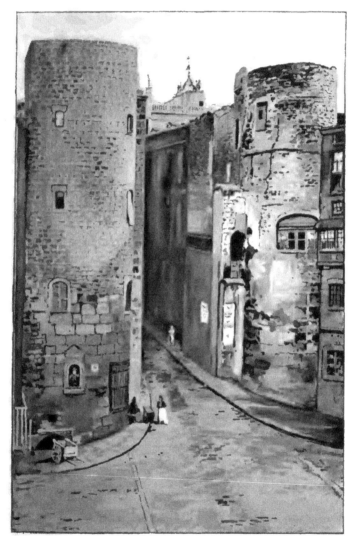

THE OLD GATEWAY, BARCELONA.

he came they surrounded him with drawn daggers, declaring that he must pay for the slander with his life. Guilhem begged to be allowed a last favor, and on the condition that it should not be escape they consented. " Let the worst one strike first," he then demanded.

A young lady to whom he felt greatly attached married, and promised him afterward as a bit of consolation that he might kiss her at every visit. Two years later she recalled the pledge, saying that when she gave it she did not know the difference between right and wrong. The troubadour sought an opinion from the most highly reputed authority in such matters, and the decision was that as love was the supreme right she was bound to restore the poet his kiss. He was not one to be put down.

Such a man was likely to have trouble with his neighbors. Once a bishop crossed his path, and Berguedan at once threatened in a song to cut the prelate's nose off before the frogs should begin to croak. With one of his neighbors he lived on terms of enmity for a long time and finally murdered him. King Amfos would not condone this crime, and the troubadour had to live thereafter as he could on the bounty of relatives. When he repaid their hospitality by wronging their wives, daughters, or sisters, even his relatives abandoned him, and only a robber's life remained. Driven from that he fled to France ; and, after many adventures there and in Spain, was killed by a common soldier in a common brawl.'

No ; on second thought, we shall dispense with Guilhem de Berguedan ; in fact we think the better of King Amfos for making such a man his enemy. And in truth the king was very far from bad, as the fashion was No doubt he flew his falcon wide, and was not tender of his enemies and his rivals ; but has it not always been said that all is fair in love and war ? Now and then a crossbowman rang a bolt upon his shield, or the poet of a hostile camp let fly a sharp sirvente against his fame , but for all that he reigned happily and prosperously, feared and admired in the field, the tilting-ground, and the castle hall. Nearly all the troubadours agreed with Peire Raimon when he sang that the king of Aragon surpassed all other men in worth and fame as the white flowers excel the grass among which they rise , and on his death many were disposed to say like Peire Vidal, " Certainly I should not live, were it not a sin to kill oneself." [8]

But Amfos the troubadour interests us even more than Amfos the king. In poetry as well as in love he was the rival of Arnaut de Maruelh, and no doubt there were many to assure him that he bore away the palm in that as well as in this. We think otherwise , and yet the one poem of his that survives, sung last if not first, perhaps, into the ear of lovely Alazais, is not so very bad—for a king.

> Few the joys to me denied,—
> Pleasures bloom on every side,
> And in groves and meadows wide,
>   'Midst the flowers and the trees,
> Choirs of merry songsters bide,
>   Vocal in the freshening breeze ;
> But nor snow nor summertide
> Can my heart a song provide,—
>   Save as God and Love may please.
>
> Yet, to glad my joy and pride,
> Verdure, sun, and sky—outvied
> By sweet birds that hedges hide—
>   Cheer and set my heart at ease ,
> For delight is now my guide,—
>   So a lady fair decrees ;
> Honor and worth in her reside,
> Joy and beauty,—wit beside ;
>   Naught I grudge, her heart to appease.
>
> Beauty, goodness, worth, o'erride
> All my fears, my course decide :

I would stay and hear her chide,—
    Drink her harshness to the lees,
Though the sweetest lady sighed,
    Fain to cure my heart's disease ;
Hers am I, whate'er betide,
None my fealty shall divide,
    If she 'll deign to heed my pleas.'   ·

So lived and loved and sang the gay and fortunate King Amfos ; and he died and was gathered to his fathers, and Peire, his son, reigned in his place.

How different a fate are we to record for him !

GOITO, SAMBONIFACIO, AND RODEZ

Sordel and the Other Italian Troubadours. Ugo Brunenc, Daude de Pradas, and Blacatz

NORTHERN Italy as well as northern Spain belonged in the troubadour world, and it is natural here to balance Catalonia and Amfos with Lombardy and the poet of Goito

What an extraordinary destiny fell to his lot ! He belied in advance every feature of the portrait known to posterity ; won fortune in his own day by a character the exact opposite of that which gave him glory in after ages ; and finally appeared to the world as an actual trinity,— not three in one, to be sure, but one as three [1]

Sordel, however—or, as Dante and Browning wrote it, Sordello—was by no means the only Italian troubadour, and in orderly processions the lesser dignities go first. There were nearly forty in all—Restori has counted up thirty-seven—and four things are to be said of them in general First, they were Italians who composed in Provençal, for we are not concerned with the next stage of Italian poetry,—songs in the vernacular ; secondly, as was natural, they were later than the troubadours of France who set them the fashion ; thirdly, while the amorous and artistic nature of the Italians led them to admire the songs of Provence from an early period, their society was too full of turbulence for a similar free and luxuriant blossoming of the poetry of love ; and, fourthly, as they were essentially imitators, they need not detain us very long.

First among the troubadours of Italy I shall name St. Francis of Assisi. To be sure we have no troubadour poetry of his nor mention of any, but the evidence apears to me adequate. His father, a merchant, was often in southern France and he changed the boy's name from Giovanni to Francesco in honor of that land. We know that young Bernardone was a gay and convivial fellow. We know that he and his boon companions enjoyed songs of pleasure, and in his youth—he was only some twenty

GATE OF ST. PETER AND ST. PAUL.

years the junior of Raimbaut de Vaqueiras—there scarcely were any save those of Provence. We know that Francesco led in everything, that he was never merely receptive, and that in later years he composed verses. So, for my part, I cannot doubt that when the mountains over against Assisi grew wine-colored at evening, the clouds of the west glowing crimson above them and a haze of purplish-blue mist falling slowly upon the wide valley, the company of richly dressed young fellows clattering gayly down through the gate of St. Peter and St. Paul for a night of jollity at some neighboring castle and rolling the songs of the troubadours from their lusty throats, sang also verses by the future saint of the stigmata.[1]

But this is inference ; let us come back to certainty and the poets whose work is extant.

The line opens with a marquis,—Manfred (II.) Lanza, and from him we have two stanzas of biting satire that we shall find later. These we may place at about the time of the third crusade (1190) [3]

Next we meet the dashing Marquis Albert de Malaspina, and set down in the second place his tenso with Raimbaut de Vaqueiras (probably 1198).

From this time poets multiplied. The literary interchange constantly going on between southern France and Italy was especially active between Provence and Genoa, and that city produced a galaxy of celebrated troubadours. The best poet of them all was Lanfranc Cigala, a man of noble family, a consul of the town, and entrusted by it with diplomacy of the most important kind He was in active life before and after the middle of the thirteenth century. Politics, love, and religion engaged his muse,—especially the duty of the crusade—and he called aloud on kings and barons to help the Almighty for He was " in dire need " Curiously enough, so far as we can determine all the songs we have from him belong to four years (1245–48) in the midst of his political activity [4]

Very different was the life of Bonifaci Calvo. To him poetry was a profession , and his native city showed him about the same appreciation as the Genoese lady showed Raimbaut de Vaqueiras

Spain he found more generous—though not lavish, it would seem—and Amfos (Alfonso) X , who reigned in the third quarter of the century (1252–1284), gave him a home in Castile. Many a lady he wooed in his adopted land, and many a sirvente he sang in the cause of his adopted king , but struggling Genoa was not forgotten, and apparently he returned there after a time. [5]

Still more harshly fared another troubadour in that city. Bertolome Zorgi was a noble Venetian merchant ; and when Venice and Genoa chanced to be at war, the ship he was in fell into the hands of the enemy one night and Zorgi was thrown into prison (1266). There like the starling he sang, not with great originality, but sweetly and skilfully. In one case at least his effect was remarkable. Calvo mocked at the Venetians in a sirvente for letting Genoa outfight them, and Zorgi responded with a song for his fatherland ; the reply was so effective that Calvo felt himself answered, and the two poets became fast friends After about seven years of captivity Zorgi was liberated, and going to Greece as the governor of some Venetian territories in the Morea he married, settled, and there passed the remainder of his life.[*]

Nine or ten miles from Mantua on the right bank of the Mincio is a little town,—tidy, white, and quiet. Around it lie pleasant and fertile meadows crossed with long rows of mulberry trees. At the gate there are just now a few country wagons, for it is early on a Sunday morning and the people are beginning to gather for the holiday fair. Here comes a peasant with the face of a child, the body of a woman, the hands of a man, and the shoes of a stone-breaker ; she carries a picture of the Madonna done in gilt and bright colors on black glass, and is dividing looks of the tenderest and most reverent admiration between the picture and a little girl, just able to walk, that holds her by the hand. They pass within , and out of the gate issues a brass band of eight men A sheepish peasant carries a bass drum on his back, and a girl with faded flowers in her scarlet corsage and her brown cheeks beats the drum with her right hand and clashes the cymbals with her left. This is Goito.[']

Once the city had strong walls and a castle ; and about

the time Raimbaut de Vaqueiras disappeared in the Bulgarian defile with Bonifaz, a bright boy named Sordel, poor but of honorable family, was roaming the fields where young Virgil's feet had trod.[6] Did he also haunt the woods, as he grew up, deep in the reveries of a philosophic

THE ENTRANCE TO GOITO.

poet? Browning would have it so; but one may well doubt it, for he soon appears (1220) unmistakably before us as a brawler in the taverns of Florence. Several makers of rhymes get by the ears there. With scurrilous verses they belabor one another. With cream cheeses they punish each other's heads. One receives an ugly sword-cut in the face. Sordel's part is a wine-flask broken on his crown and a sufficient share in the odium of the fray. Exactly so unphilosophical is his first appearance in history.

His next exploit, about six years later, seems to confirm

our doubts. Mantua was closely associated with Richart, count of Sain Bonifaci, the Sambonifacio of today. The fief was a rich one, for its fertile meadows lay fair and wide around the town, well watered by an affluent of the Adige. Less than three miles from his own donjon rose the towers and sightly castle of Soave,[9] and beyond that were the Alps, lifting high their peaks, white even in midsummer. Wealth, courtliness, and love of beauty were almost products of the soil ; and Richart was not unworthy of his

SAMBONIFACIO.

beautiful and opulent surroundings. His culture was for the times liberal, and his policy generous and progressive. Whether here or at his residence in Verona he maintained a brilliant court ; and it was very natural that our clever Sordel, eager to sell his lance and his lute, should address himself to so appreciative and munificent a lord. He was cordially received and soon became a familiar friend, almost a member of the family.

But there was a greater power than Richart in Verona, —the terrible Aicelin, better known to us as Ezzelino da Romano. The two lords had been intimate and each had married the other's sister ; but now trouble arose, and Aicelin, to dishonor his brother-in-law, wished somebody to run away with Richart's wife, Conissa (Cunizza).[10] It was a reckless and a disgraceful thing to do, but he dared ask Sordel, the liegeman of the count of Sain Bonifaci, to undertake it. We gather from Browning how Sordel must have received this proposal. Shielded by many folds of psychologic abstraction from perceiving how great an insult it implied, he stood a while with bent head, musing deeply :

> The world shall bow to me conceiving all
> Man's life, who see its blisses, great and small,
> Afar—not tasting any ; .   .   .
> Be mine mere consciousness.[11]

But no ! The real Sordel promptly accepted the commission, and carried the scheme through without a tremor or a blush.

He was in love with her, say the biographies. Perhaps the love was conventional and platonic, and he car-

SOAVE.

ried her off purely because Aicelin and his brother Albric requested. So De Vit maintains and others try to believe. But a chronicler of the period states exactly the opposite ; Sordel was not a Peire Rogier, as we know perfectly well ; and Conissa, though Dante placed her in Paradise with a troubadour whom we shall probably send elsewhere, was equal to any deed of wantonness. She became, in fact, notorious, and Sain Circ declared later in a song that she had even forfeited her chance of heaven. A platonic elopement of two such characters would be simply a miracle.

Whatever his conduct in this matter, Sordel concluded it was time to marry.

Then a flash of bitter truth:
So fantasies could break and
  fritter youth
That he had long ago lost ear-
  nestness,
Lost will to work, lost power to
  even express
The need of working.[11]

So much the g r e a t e r need, we may infer he add-ed, of " marrying wealth "; for without more ado than before he carried off a lady of the Strasso house, friends of his, and made her a wife without the knowledge of her family.[12]

Of course he expected no trouble, saying to himself:

A troubadour suppose
Mankind will class him with
  their friends or foes?[11]

But others felt d i f f e r-ently. The Strassos joined the partisans of Count Rich-art in seeking diligently to

VERONA.

do him bodily harm : and the actual Sordel, fleeing to Aicelin at Treviso, took very good care either to stay at home or to go abroad with an excellent horse and a large troop.

This is the turning-point of the troubadour's life and it is worth while to have a square look at this heroic and poetic figure of the ages. Perhaps we may be able to forecast something of his later career

He is now approaching thirty years of age, a man of active and athletic rather than massive build, of somewhat less than medium height, and of a presence not at all imposing. Still you would call him at first sight a handsome and likable fellow His full and well-cut lips appear to smile easily His dark face bears a look of genuine heartiness. Good black eyes and crisp hair—he wears no beard—set off his countenance. A closer examination reveals other phases of the man. The bold though not heavy chin and something in the pose of the head remind us of his recklessness, and we receive in general an impression of daring rather than of courage. There is a strong hint of sensuality in the mouth. The lips would frame themselves to a curse as readily as a song, and the restless eyes suggest cunning and the love of gain. He seems very poorly supplied with genuine character, and we suspect that for him duty consists in getting what he wishes [13]

A man of that kind seems to change as time goes on In youth what he desires is the gratification of his impulses, and he is outspoken, hearty, daring, and even foolhardy As age ripens and passion sobers, intelligence becomes a substitute for principle. He discovers that honesty of a certain sort is the best policy. A good name, as he finds, possesses a money value. Reasonable fidelity proves to be a condition of success. Larger ambitions block the gratification of propensities Wealth and social position become more and more interesting, and the sobriety and thoughtfulness they demand are submitted to. The dishonesty and feebleness of others disturb his plans, and he becomes a preacher of the virtues. The end of life approaches, and the wisdom of laying up treasure in heaven dawns upon his mind. Intelligence and selfishness are enough to make a hero and saint of this description; and as our troubadour has both of these in abundance, we may expect him to follow about this line of development.

Already he begins to weary of the life he has led, and still more of the results it entails His eyes open on wider successes. " Pshaw, what is the good of this ? " he seems to be muttering And so when he gets into trouble with Aicelin he just mounts his horse one day, waves a hand perhaps to the friends he has wronged, and sets off to make his fortune in a land that is unacquainted with him.

Not a journey but a migration was this. Traversing Italy as rapidly and secretly as possible, he entered France. But he found little encouragement there for a poet in the midst of the troublous times ; and, making short sojourns at castles by the way, he crossed the Pyrenees and visited the courts of Spain.'' In Aragon and Castile he was fortunate In Leon, too, he fared not ill, though he felt aggrieved because the king did not give him a mule that pleased him.

It was at this time probably that he visited Portugal. None of his experiments had been more lucky than this ; he seems to have delighted the Portuguese, and his success gained him an honor accorded no other troubadour,— a place in their song books. But Sordel was looking for greater things ; and finally he turned north to try our old friend Savaric de Mauleon, "root of all the courtliness of the world," who treated him very handsomely indeed, it would appear.

Wherever he went he preached the doctrine of pleasure. For him a sober existence was misery :

> It is not life, but rather death, indeed ;
> For one is dead when gladsome life expires,

And whoso lacks the things his heart desires
Is worse than dead,—he lives in woe and need.[15]

The value of money was very appreciable to such a
character. " A poor man, however noble, can find no
pleasure in living," he once exclaimed, and the duty of
the rich was generosity.

At the court one should not live
Save to get or else to give ;
And niggard hearts if courtly fashions cloak
'T is not a court, but crowds of worthless folk.[15]

At the same time he was bright enough to save his own
dignity, for he never thought of descending to the level
of the mendicant joglars. Wealth is after all an accident,
he maintained, it lasts but a time, and the poor may be
just as good as the rich.

Of worth are all who excellence do cherish,—
Both poor and rich, if but the heart be right,
For poor indeed each infant sees the light,
And, food for worms, in poverty we perish.[15]

In consequence perhaps of Savaric's death (1233), Sordel
drifted toward Provence again, and on the way stopped at
Rodez (Rodes).[16]

Few places had more honorable traditions in troubadour
literature than this Several generations of the lords of
Rodez, past and to come, are counted as poets themselves
or protectors of the craft. Ugo de Sain Circ resided with
one of them, as you remember, and he was able to answer
the troubadour's verses in lines quite as good Earlier
still, Rodez produced a poet of its own, Ugo Brunenc,[17]
who made himself agreeable in Aragon, Toulouse, Anduze,
and Vodable, as well as at home, during the last quarter
of the twelfth century. Another poet, born in the neigh-

borhood, had but recently died.   This was Daude de
Pradas,[18] a churchman who sang of love too sensually to
be liked, and wrote a poem of three thousand six hundred
lines on the care and ed-
ucation of hunting-birds.

AT RODEZ.

The fame of the place
and the liberality of its
lords were e n o u g h to
draw Sordel to Rodez,
but there existed another
attraction.   Lady Guida
lived with her brother,
the count, and like many
another Sordel found her
charming enough to fall
in love with.

Six or eight years at
least this fancy seems to have lasted " off and on," though
in the meantime (1235) she married; and eight of his
poems appear to celebrate the charms of his " sweet
enemy."   They were doubtless pleasant music to her
ear ; and one especially, for " Guida " meant " guiding,"
and the poet made an ingenious play upon the name.

> As much—no more—one lives as one enjoys,—
> To other living be the name denied !
> And so I place in lordly joy my pride,
>   That fitting service, free from poor alloys,
>   May prove my love ; for who on sorrow feeds
>   Can have no heart for brave and brilliant deeds ;
>   So mercy bids my lady cease resistance
>   And grant me joy to bind me to existence.
>
> And as the star its changeless ray employs
> To guide the ships on threatening seas that ride,
> Herself a star, she ought my bark to guide,
>   Since for her sake I left the shoreward buoys ;

So tossed am I, so swift the billow speeds,
That I shall perish if my lady heeds
    And helps me not ; for what be my persistence,
    No port I find, no safety, no assistance [19]

To Sordel himself this kind of thing was no longer
serious   During this very period, if we may believe Bertran de Lamanon, he pursued a hundred other flames.
In his eyes love as a passion had long seemed a childish
affair . it was only a game and that for an ignoble stake ;
and his love-songs display merely the commonplaces of
gallantry. To be sure, as the style was at that day, he
professed an ethereal and sublimated passion , but the
sense of another purpose always oozes through his lines,
and the people of his own time seem to have understood
his platonic protestations.   In short, amusement and
pleasure were to be found among the ladies, and a few
songs were not ill spent upon them ; but for a man like
him politics and fortune were the serious affairs of life,
and satirical attacks upon his enemies were the chief use
of his art.

Provence-beyond-the-Rhone was to offer him the opportunity he long had sought.   The love of poetry still flourished there, and while the sad misfortunes of Languedoc
had left but little will to sing and little wealth to reward
the poets, Blacatz [20]—a rich baron of Aups, thirty miles or
so to the north of Toulon—was reviving the best traditions
of the cultured noblemen

In him we see one of those high lords—brave. gallant,
and splendid—who maintained imposing courts, entertained magnificently, made rich presents to deserving
poets, and—to seem not inferior to their guests—composed verses of their own   With him love had the dignity
of the old school, and the essence of it was not pleasure
but honor.   To be sure he sang in a tenso with Peire
Vidal. " I desire that she give me a recompense, and I

leave to you the 'long waiting,'" that Vidal had extolled   None the less it was chiefly glory that attracted him.   " I esteem little a secret honor," he declared, " a gem (carbuncle) that does not shine, a blow I cannot hear, a blind eye, or a dumb tongue"; and he avowed once that the bare name of love from a lady of rank was better than full surrender from one of low degree.

Sordel and he were rivals for the smiles of Lady Guida, but that made no difference to his generous temper, and Sordel was received at his castle as a guest and a friend. Then Blacatz died, and the troubadour no doubt recommended himself to his heir Blacasset [21] by an imposing though not affectionate Lament, the climax of his poetry.

> I fain would mourn Blacatz—let all the world attend !
> For sorrow, grief, and pain my bosom justly rend ;
> In him am I despoiled of master and of friend,
> And every noble trait hath met in him its end ;
> So mortal is the blow, such fatal ills impend,
> We can but vainly hope the grievous loss to mend
> Unless his heart we take and through the nations send
> That coward lords may eat, for that will courage lend.
>
> The first of all to eat, since greatest is his need,
> Shall be the Roman emperor if he would succeed
> Against the Milanese who count themselves as freed,
> For he, despite his Germans, hath the worst indeed ;
> The witless king of France shall next upon it feed
> And then regain Castile, lost ere he gave it heed ;
> But he will never taste it if his mother plead,
> For he would grieve her not—he well deserves this meed
>
> Then let the king of England, timid as a hart,
> Eat bountifully thereof, and quickly will he start
> To win him back the lands which France with lance and dart—
> Because she knows him well—hath taken for her part ;
> And let the Spanish king eat doubly of the heart,—
> Too weak for one good realm while two are on his chart ;

But if he wish to eat it let him go apart,
For should his mother know, her stick would make him smart.[22]

The death of Blacatz did not interrupt Sordel's career,
however, for the count of Provence was himself a patron
of the poets, and the author of that poem to his charger
which we found at Aix.   He, too, died before long (1245),
but the result was only a still greater success for the troubadour.   Six months later Charles d'Anjou, a young
man of twenty, married the heiress of Provence and came
down from the north to govern a restless and unknown
people   Sordel welcomed him with a poem and attached
himself to his party ; and Charles on the other side found
the Italian's political shrewdness, his knowledge of men
and affairs, and his freedom from embarrassing attachments a valuable aid

From this time Sordel played no insignificant part in
public affairs[23] , but it was always evident whose interest
he studied.   When Charles set out for the crusade of St.
Louis, he urged the troubadour to go with him   It was
an enterprise, however, that offered no hope of pleasure
or gain, and Sordel, willing that others should win the
empty glories, explained in a clever poem that he was too
much afraid of rough water.   '' Take Bertran de Lamanon[24]—I know it is agreeable to him,'' he added, for Bertran had promised once before to go but changed his mind
on the point of embarking, and Sordel had a score to
settle with him.

This was not the only time Sordel declined to follow his
lord on an expedition that did not please him, and indeed
relations were sometimes rather strained between them.
The troubadour was always asking for something,—
among other gifts for one of the heiresses that great lords
had frequently the right of bestowing, and Charles wearied
of his importunities   Once when Sordel was ill he sang

out: " Everybody goes about saying that it would do me
good to be cheerful ; they are right, I know, but how can
a man be cheerful who is poor, sick all the time, and unfortunate in lord, love, and lady ? " And then Charles
replied in the same rhymes· " I have always cherished
and honored him. I have given him substantial property
and a wife of the kind he wished ; but he is a fool and a
nuisance, and he would not be grateful if one gave him a
county "

Still mutual interest kept them together ; and when
Charles invaded Italy to seize the crown of Naples and
Sicily, Sordel assisted him with his counsel and apparently
with his arm. By this time the poet was in pleasant relations with the Church, and when he lay sick at Novara
the pope severely censured Charles for neglecting him.
He was not forgotten, however. The expedition, famous
—and infamous—in history, was completely successful.
Manfred, the usurper, was beaten; Conradin, the rightful
heir, was judicially murdered in the public square of
Naples (1268) ; Charles, count of Provence, became
Charles I , king of the Two Sicilies ; and when the spoils
were divided (1269), the conqueror assigned five castles
to his " intimate and faithful friend," Sordel."

That same year the castles passed into other hands, and
the troubadour disappeared.

One corner of our forecast seems unfilled, but in fact
that also was rounded out   Not only did the poet come
to be on good terms with the pope, but he was a preacher
as we expected ; and in a long poem he instructed young
nobles how to win both God and the world, as he defined
success. Polonius was narrower, but not more practical.

> As treasures buried in the earth
> Possess no longer any worth,
> I likewise count good sense quite vain

If one conceal it in his brain   ⸳   .
Whoe'er considers life with care
Will always find,—so I declare,
One thing enjoined by wisdom's rod ⸳
To please at once the world and God.   .   .   .
Excess of praise but harms ; and blame—
Too great—excuses him 't would shame   .   .   .
Let every one be glad to pay
The borrowed money on the day,
For honest men can wear no load
Upon the heart like money owed   .   .   .
Without fidelity exist
No merits that so much assist
A man to prosper as that one
Fidelity in all that 's done.   .   .
No one has learned to see aright
Who sees not farther than his sight   .
To go in safety night or day
Keep e'er the middle of the way.   .   .
If one but study he can make
An evil disposition take
A look less bad, and merits wear—
However good—a better air.   .   .
One is not wise, as wise I deem,
Unless he oft can make it seem
That he is pleased with what annoys
And bored by what he most enjoys ;
And who this maxim e'er applies,—
I' faith I count him truly wise.   .   .   .
A life of baseness and ill-fame
Destroys the body, soils the name,
And sends the rebel soul to dwell
Forever in the fires of hell   .   .
No man of worth, it seems to me,
Should wish to live except it be
For joy and fame, since only these
Give life a flavor that can please.   .   .   .[96]

A notable career none the less was that of Sordel, and
notable was the period in which he lived   He was born
in the full middle ages , he was buried in the dawn of a

modern world. His eyes opened upon the golden age of troubadour poetry ; when they closed no troubadour of power still sang, and the voice of Dante (born in 1265) had been heard.

During his life Albertus Magnus (1193–1280), the Universal Doctor, and his pupil Thomas Aquinas (1225 ?–1274), the Angelic Doctor, brought scholasticism to its culmination ; and as he passed off the stage there came upon it the Subtle Doctor, Duns Scotus (1265 ?–1308), bringing seeds of the modern scepticism that was to destroy the whole edifice of mediæval philosophy. His youth saw a middle-age papacy triumphing in the mighty Innocent III. (1198–1216) over all the temporal powers, but when he died the House of Commons had been established in England (1265), and the grand movement of Europe toward national politics was well in motion.

At his birth the university of Paris came into being as an organized institution ; during his middle life Cimabue was born (1240) and with him the art of painting ; at precisely the same point of his middle life (1240) was written the earliest piece of music for several voices that has been found in any land,—the English Six-Men's Song; and before he passed away Roger Bacon had not only obtained, as Hallam says, " almost prophetic glimpses of the future course of science," but, in his " practical method " for teaching Hebrew in three days and Greek in three more, had already outdone the boldest achievements of modern education.

Still, nothing in the life or the times of Sordel was so extraordinary as the trail of glory that perpetuated his fame, and we must end as we began by exclaiming : What an extraordinary destiny !

Sordel failed perhaps to gain both earth and heaven, but he won both his own age and the ages to come.

Opening a career by abandoning his native land, attaining to fame by singing in a foreign tongue on a foreign soil, and enriched by fighting against Italy for a Gallic oppressor, he became in Dante's poem the ideal patriot, the embodiment of Italian aspirations.   At Palena, northeastward from Naples across the Apennines, one may find still among the vineyards of the lower slopes the vine-clad tower and the gateway of a castle given him by the alien conqueror ; yet we see Dante and Virgil overawed by the " lofty and scornful " air of that " Lombard soul," and the grave, slow moving of his eyes in the manner of a crouching lion ; and it is recorded with joy how they found " that gentle soul . . . so ready, only at the sweet sound of his native land, to give glad welcome . . . unto his fellow citizen." [27]

The error so thoroughly planted throve on the ignorance of Dante's commentators, and still more on the inventive ability of Aliprandi ; and eventually Eméric-David thought that he found three distinct men in the inflated volumes of his legend.

Finally in our own day Browning, instead of seeing this bold, unprincipled, licentious, and unflinchingly practical adventurer as he was, has evolved and immortalized under his name a mystical poet entangled in personal metaphysics, tormenting himself with spiritual searchings, and wasting his actual powers in infinite longings

> To be complete for—satisfy—the whole
> Series of spheres.[11]

XVII

MARSEILLE, SAISSAC, AND ST. GILLES

Peire Vidal

POOR Peire Vidal !
    Despite his wonderful succcess, this is the thought
we find at the bottom of our hearts, and I fancy it was
also at the bottom of his.   For at moments he was intensely sane.   He knew that he was a good poet, for did
not everybody concede it ?   He knew still better that he
was a good singer, for did not people say, like the biography, that " he sang better than any man in the world " ?
And finally he thought he knew that he was also a wit,
for did not everybody repeat his *bons mots ?*

And yet,—Vidal was exceedingly puzzled, I am sure,
in those very sane and serious moments to know whether
people laughed at the things he said, or at the man who
said them; and he was not only puzzled but troubled.
This query was a shadow that clung to him even when
the castle hall was brightest.   Every now and then he
would catch sight of it, and slipping out of the gay throng
would fall to talking moralities with some dowager by the
wall, or politics with some grey-beard at the hearth.
When alone with himself he twisted and writhed, turned
somersaults, and looked between his legs as the joglars
did,—anything and everything to find out whether there
positively was a shadow, and if there were to seize it and
wrench it away.   But finally he gave up.   It came to look

very clear to him that sometimes he was inspired, and that sometimes he acted unquestionably like a fool ; as for the rest of the time, if anybody could tell he would be glad to know, but for his own part he could only take his chances, act out nature, and hope for the best.

Indeed Vidal could not afford to keep even so important a matter as this very long in mind Things crowded upon him, or more precisely he crowded upon them A head so restless and feet so untiring no other troubadour possessed. Many were active but Peire was feverish ; many were nomads but Peire left the roads in smoke.

Doubtless he felt that he must, for his ambitions were high and his antecedents lowly. Toulouse was his birthplace, and not only did his father pursue the humble calling of a furrier there, but—if we can believe the Monk of Montaudon—his own hands worked the peltries. But he was born with a genuine gift of song ; so that, as the biography says, " verse-making came more easily to him than to any other man living ", and in addition to that he possessed an active mind and an aspiring will that nothing could subdue

It was love that set his powers in motion, for though he understood perfectly his obscure position, and confessed, " My lands are not worth a pair of gloves," he dared pay his addresses to a noble lady of the neighborhood. His attitude was humble enough. Comparing himself to a serving-man who died of hunger before a loaded table, he tried to arouse her pity, and then endeavored to alarm her with a picture of Dives punished for disdaining Lazarus. But it was all in vain. The songs were good enough , but the singer was undistinguished, and therefore had no claim to consideration.

Vidal understood the difficulty, no doubt, and realized that he must go forth and win a position in the world. So, while Raimbaut de Vaqueiras was betaking himself to Orange—for the two seem to have begun life at about the same time—Peire Vidal set out with all his intensity aglow in pursuit of fame.' Marseille (Marseilla) was his first halting-place, and there he formed the deepest and most abiding attachments of his life.

What were Marseilla and the people he met there like ?

Today the city throbs and beats with an exuberant sense of the present and has no feeling of the past. Only a few slight indications of antiquity—the base of a column or a hidden fragment of a wall—can be found. All is new , and the city is proud—not without reason—of its modern look. For though it is a checker-board, as Méry says, its air is pompous, grandiose, almost supercilious. It is the façade of France toward the sea and worthy of its place, for no city in the land is more sumptuous ; and under the blue sky and the glowing foliage, gay crowds jostle and laugh. For crown it has the palace of Long-champs, erected when architecture could at least remember, and for training robe it has the sea, now shivering— as Victor Hugo saw it—into short, brusque, and furious waves, and now smoothing its lustrous blue till there is not a wrinkle in it except the white islands among which Monte Cristo passed his years of durance.

None the less Marseille is above all historic. The city-hall bore formerly this inscription. " Marseille was the daughter of the Phoceans ; she was the sister of Rome ; she was the rival of Carthage ; she opened her gates to Julius Cæsar ; and she triumphantly resisted Charles the Fifth." It was here that Milo ate the bearded fish after Cicero's timidity doomed him to exile, and it was here that many a noble youth came to study, drawn by the fame of the Greek schools But we need not stop with Greek and Roman antiquities : Marseille was the cousin of Tyre and Sidon : her groves were perfumed with the smoke of offer-ings to Baal, and a black stone in the museum, covered with Phœnician characters, rècords a price-list of the sarifices.

In Vidal's time the city had neither the pompous grandeur of today nor the symmetry of its Grecian civilization   Roman dignity, too, had vanished almost as completely as the Druid oaks that Cæsar found on the hill of Notre Dame de la Garde   In a word, the city was busy still but no longer attractive.

In the upper town, ruled by the bishop, lay the citadel, but the ancient fortress that Romans, Goths, Burgundians, and Franks occupied in turn had been demolished by the soldiers of the Prophet, and on the plateau where it had braved·Cæsar's veterans for a year had risen the Château Babon, a sort of manor, vast and formidable, defended by wide moats, enormous ramparts, and massive towers, and flanked with humble dwellings.

A second group of houses clung about the abbey of St. Victor, whose dark and massive walls maintain even yet their sombre watch ²

But the real Marseilla, the city of the viscounts, lay below about the port and behind its two guardian towers, divided from the upper town by a wall.³ The oppressions of barbaric invaders had brought the proud city low " A labyrinth of streets, narrow, sombre, and dirty, a mass of wooden houses blackened by time and weather, their steep roofs covered with slates,"—this was the town as Boudin paints it ; and a vision of this cramped and crooked Marseilla still comes back when we hear the people say on holidays, " Today the stairways will turn toward the street."

The viscount's palace was near what is now called the Poissonnière Vieille ; and it seems to have been far from grand, probably a low and somewhat rambling affair Not far away the ships were moored and the merchandise piled. We know what Dickens found on the quays of

THE OLD PORT, MARSEILLE.

277

Marseille · " foreign sailors of all nations ; . . . with red shirts, blue shirts, buff shirts, tawny shirts, and shirts of orange color ; with red caps, blue caps, green caps, great beards, and no beards "; and we may feel sure that a throng quite as heterogeneous and picturesque was to be seen there in Vidal's time, for the quay was already the porch of the Mediterranean, the threshold of the Levant. The spirit, also, was the same ; for Marseille is and was a city of commerce The palace was invaded by this influence, and what the mood of its inmates was we may judge somewhat from the mood of to-day.

Easy *laissez-faire* is a good part of it. Nobody wishes to be bothered or held in. Handsome women, voluptuous and bold, sweep the streets with splendid silks, and gaze about them with the freedom of *lorettes*. The city has always been a little barbaric, and it still thinks more of jewels than of neatness. Hawthorne called it handsome, interesting, and entertaining, but dirty beyond comparison , and Mérimée said that nothing could be prettier or less cleanly.' Prudence and care are not worth while, and the repertory of the theatres almost always winds up with bankruptcy. Everything is broad and lavish ; no ordinary aqueduct would suit, and they have brought the river there and turned it into their pipes in a cataract. Self-confidence like theirs mocks at calculation, and a merchant of Marseille once declared war on England : " Georges Roux to George I."

To enjoy life, to gain and to spend,—here is the first duty of the Marseillais. " Health without money is half-sickness," they say ; and the beginning of their creed is this . " Whoever loses his teeth loses his best friends."

The second duty is much the same,—sociability. Everybody loves to be familiar, to clap his neighbor on the back, laugh, and cry, " My good fellow ! " Everybody is a *viveur*. Everybody hunts, though Tarascon itself is quite

as well off for game.   Here we find again the mocking
but good-hearted pleasantries of Aix, the *galejado ;* and
here we find again that Sunday Eden, the *bastide*.

Do you remember the tournament described by Raimbaut de Vaqueiras (page 41), and how good-naturedly
Lord Barral chased his fleeing horse ?   Barral was viscount of Marseille.

When we have caught the spirit of his town we understand him, and if we know him we can understand some
of the most important events of Peire Vidal's career.   He
liked entertainment ;   Vidal sang to him.   He loved
sociability ;   Vidal was loquacious and witty.   He liked
amusement ;   Vidal's antics made him laugh.   He
abounded in jollity ;   Vidal tried but could not exhaust
his good nature.   He felt strong and sure ,   Vidal's gal-
lantries could not alarm him.   In a word the two were
admirably suited to each other, they soon called each
other by the same name, " Rainier," and the viscount
became the troubadour's generous and unfailing friend.

But this was not the deepest attachment that Vidal
formed at Marseille.   Alazais de Roca Martina, Barral's
wife, was a great beauty, and apparently she as well as
her lord represented the spirit of the town.   Several of
the troubadours were her passionate adorers.   Her charms
were evidently of the sort that intoxicate ; and behind a
superb physical beauty lay an emotional power, a mag-
netism, a luxurious will that swept all resistance away
Vidal could not withstand it ; and before long " Vierna,"
as he called the viscountess, excited a passion in his breast
that was destined to bear surprising fruit.

But Vierna was not his only theme nor Marseille his
only place of sojourn.   From Provence he journeyed to
Spain, and a Castilian lady set off his inflammable heart.[6]
Next he flashed out near Toulouse, and soon after in the
region of Carcassonne   Bartsch thinks he made a sea-trip

to Italy during this time, and returned by ship to Narbonne.   Next he cantered toward the Alps and sang at
Beuil, some twenty-five miles northwest of Nice.[6]   And
then he found his way toward Albi, and coruscated in the
castle of the Orme at Gaillac.[7]

PENAUTIER.

Saissac and St. Gilles saw him at about the same time ;
and these are places that we, too, should visit.

The high-road to Saissac leaves Carcassonne for the
northwest and passes close to Penautier (Puegnautier),
the early home of a famous beauty whom we are soon to
meet[8] ; then it strikes for the uplands.   The hawthorn
keeps us company in running hedges by the roadside.
The apple trees are in bloom, sweet as our New England
orchards.   A few olive groves, dark rather than ashen as
they were in Provence, decorate the slopes.   Here and
there a windmill stands upon a hilltop against the sky,

raising its gaunt arms in a prayer for wind, a prayer not
likely to remain long unanswered.   Tufted poplars line
up beside the roads like the king of Prussia's grenadiers.
Club-headed willows and a tangle of greenery mark out
the watercourses   Then we roll through the picturesque
village of Montolieu, balanced riskily on the brink of a
chasm, and beyond that find cozy brown farm-houses
dotting the fields, each with its cloak of dark cypresses
wrapped about it.

Saissac lies curled up about a doubled and twisted gorge,
looking from the first slopes of Black Mountain toward
the south and the east; and the valley of the Aude is before it   At night the lamps of Carcassonne glimmer
faintly some twelve miles away ; and, if the air is very
clear, the sheeted summits of the Pyrenees may stand
forth in the moonlight.   Now, by day, the country seems
to spread out like a vast plain ending on the shores of an
ocean, which mingles in its turn with the sky.   But the
billows of the sea are motionless   it is only the rolling
country disguised with a soft veil of bluish haze.

The little village was all astir as we arrived, but not for
us.   One of its enterprising citizens, after months of discussion and weeks of bargaining, had bought that useful
contrivance, a pump, and the mechanism was just in advance of us   Following the crowd we saw the affair
taken to the peasant's house, and waited till the new
owner appeared to welcome it, his face very brown and
his blouse extremely cerulean.

" Now," said the wagoner, " show me the water, and
I will set the pump for you."

" Water ? " cried Jacques.

" Yes, where is it ? "

" *Mais, mon Dieu!* if I had water what should I buy a
pump for ? "

A precipitous tongue of land reaches out from the village between two gorges, and at the tip where the gorges unite stand the impressive ruins of the castle. Tradition tells us how its destruction was accomplished. In the time of the religious wars a Protestant family held the fief. Below the castle on the slopes lay an industrial town of the same creed, and above it an older town of Catholics; and its Red Gate, looking in the picture like a dark

SAISSAC.

spot at the foot of the wall,' was recognized as the point of division. When the war of sects arrived, a Catholic army stormed the castle, but its meagre garrison fired it and escaped, and only one person was found there alive, —a lady. Her mouth was stuffed with paper, she was given to the soldiery, and after that she was hanged. The fire burned on; and in the light of it, the Protestants below were exterminated, and the blaze of their houses added to the flames of their castle.

But in Peire's time this was far distant in the shadows
of futurity Saissac was then an important and flourishing fief, and the name appears often in documents of the
period   Its lord held the dignity of provost, and when
Raimon Rogier, the son of our countess of Burlatz, lost
his father, Bertran de Saissac was chosen first among the
guardians of his estates.   Gay company thronged the old
castle then.   Poetry and music made those blackened
walls thrill, and Vidal's high B—for we feel sure he was
a tenor—still haunts their crannies.

Twelve miles west from Arles he sang a different note
at about the same time.

Very unlike Saissac is this region, for St. Gilles—where
Daudet might have married an innkeeper's daughter—
stands in the edge of the Camargue.

" La Camargue ! " we exclaim now, as we cried " La
Crau ! " a little while since ; nature has put the two together, and so must we.

But there is no resemblance.   Only the Rhone divides
them, yet they are absolute contrasts.   While one of them
has more cobbles than arithmetic has figures, a hunter
searches the other in vain for a stone to throw at his dog ;
and while the skill of engineers has made the one fertile,
the blunder of engineers has ruined the other.[19]   For what
was once a granary like the meadows of old Nile, is today
a waste and a desolation

And yet it is something far more interesting than a
granary now, for what symphonic poem surpasses the
Camargue ?

Like an ocean it stretches on and away to the horizon
or the fantastic boundaries of the mirage   Here the dead
soil blossoms in shining crystalline flowers of salt, fatal to
all other blooms , there wide marshes gleam with shallow
ponds, set about with tufts of rushes and thinly screened
with lines of tamarisks.   Indefinable odors, breathing of

the sea or breathing of the swamps, drift listlessly to and fro, and above us the cloudless blue is marked with triangles of cormorants, long files of rosy flamingoes, and circling flights of white sea-gulls. Little by little the stillness becomes conscious of invasion. Distant bellowings and neighings make themselves heard. Louder and nearer they grow, mingled with shouts. A vast, dark mass approaches, the *manade* of some rich farmer. The ground quivers beneath the march of scores of glossy black bulls, followed by hundreds—perhaps thousands—of cows and heifers. Around them hover the mounted guards armed with tridents ; and in the midst of the great migration the swarthy proprietor, calm but alert, rides his powerful white horse with his pretty wife on the crupper. Another moment and the trampling host has passed. The shouts diminish ; the bellowings die away. Stillness resumes her throne ; and presently the ducks and herons, the partridges and bustards, recovering their courage, issue forth again, and—lonely as the bitterns amid the ruins of Nineveh—fill the desert places with mournful cries, answered only by the far low plaint of the sea.

St. Gilles should be called the capital of the Camargue, for though a town it seems equally desolate, and hardly less poetic than the marshes before it. There are people within its gate, but they do not appear to live. Outside the old city, like the ring of wood around the hollow of an ancient willow, is a new and busy place , but beyond the wall reigns the spirit of antiquity, and the people—even the children—move about like shadows. Centuries ago St. Gilles ceased to be ; successive waves of human fury have ruined even its ruins ; and while the façade of its unfinished church—the " ne plus ultra of Byzantine art," as Mérimée pronounced it—is there yet, for its exquisite grace overawed the Reformers of the sixteenth century who wrecked the interior, its loveliness shines upon us

through grime and squalor with all the pathos of beauty
in distress

In the days of the troubadours, just as the floods of the
Rhone fertilized the Camargue, power and commerce enriched the city of St. Gilles. Few places could boast so
proud a name. It was a Greek town at the beginning,
and in the seventh century Hellenic influence again pervaded it, for St. Ægidius, an Athenian hermit, fixed his
residence there. The lords of the city, able and ambitious
princes, extended their sway until finally they possessed
themselves of the rich earldom of Toulouse and its many
dependent fiefs. Its abbey-church was intended to be the
most splendid of the whole world. Though we call it
Byzantine the architects labored to compound from the
art of east and of west and even from the triumphs of
Arabic skill a style of unequalled magnificence , and the
result was a transport of religious æstheticism, an ecstasy of pious dreaming, a passion of luxurious devotion,
wrought into stone beyond the power of time or the ruth-
lessness of man to destroy.

This was the St Gilles that Vidal knew, and when he
rode briskly through the gateway this work was probably
going on " The marble was fresh and white, and he could
see growing hour by hour under the chisels of the stone-
cutters the gleaming forms of lions, dragons, and griffins,
of nameless wingèd creatures in earth or heaven, of saints,
of apostles, and of angels.

Doubtless he gave all this a glance, but a very different
purpose brought him to St. Gilles One of his countless
inamoratas resided here and he came to visit her, chuck-
ling to himself, as he often sang, that husbands dreaded
him,—yes, " more than fire and sharpened iron." But
alas !—as the proverb ran—" The jar kept going to the
spring till it was broken," and he came one too many
times. Discretion though possible was not easy for him,

THE GATEWAY OF ST. GILLES.

—certainly not habitual ; and in one of his foolish moments he boasted of the lady's favor. Well for him had he turned back after that look at the church ! But he did not; and the lady's husband, a knight of St. Gilles, caught him and without compunction bored his tongue."

Poor Peire Vidal ! It was a terrible ordeal for both mind and body, but somehow Peire never lacked a friend. Ugo del Bauz, a nephew of Raimbaut d'Aurenga and afterwards the son-in-law of Barral," took pity upon him ; and, carrying him, I suppose, to the fortress above La Crau, comforted and nursed him, until in due time the offending member was able to boast again.

Probably the troubadour perceived the danger of indiscretion and the unhealthiness of St. Gilles, but he was not cured of love. As yet the passion for Alazais was only pushing its root in the dark, and just then if people inquired for his lady he answered : " Would you know her as she is, seek her near Carcassonne."

CARCASSONNE AND CABARET

Peire Vidal (*Concluded*)

I 'm getting old,—threescore today,
And all my life in dust and mire
I 've labored hard, yet found no way
To satisfy my great desire ;
I see 't is folly here below
Full happiness to count upon ;
My prayer unanswered is to go,—
I have not seen fair Carcassonne

THE grief of Nadaud's peasant is not ours: Carcassonne, the wonderful city, is before us. Once in a while the imaginative traveller has a complete satisfaction the drive from Salerno to Amalfi is one day of rounded felicity; Mont St. Michel is another, and here is a third Fifteen minutes from the railroad, the telephone, and the electric lights we step bodily into the middle ages. " There can be nothing better than this," we say to ourselves , a vignette by Dürer magnified to heroic proportions and wrought out in stone.

A double line of earthy-brown walls ; three barbicans ; forty-eight strong towers, each bearing a name of its own ; a moat without, a mighty castle within ' ;—this was the Carcassona of the middle ages, and this with little change is the Carcassonne of today. Resting at ease on its hill-top like royal Windsor in the fulness of strength, bulwark after bulwark, battlement upon battlement, it puts the stamp of reality at the first look upon a hundred tales of chivalric deeds.

No mere fragment of the knightly age is this, but a whole,—complete, unbroken ; no dusty archæology pain-fully extracted from worm-eaten folios, but the embodied past, erect and real,—the perfect fossil of a social order that never ceases to puzzle and fascinate.

CARCASSONNE IN THE DISTANCE, NIGHT.

We rub our eyes, but the wonder does not vanish. Motionless it reposes before us, the sleeping beauty of mediæval civilization, seemingly conquered by the spell of slumber only a moment since. Whenever we choose we may experience the romance of the long approach, the towers multiplying as we advance, girding up their loins, and marching to outflank us. As often as we please we may compass the circuit of a mile around the outer en-closure. As long as we desire we may gaze at the far higher walls of the inner line.

Nothing melts ; nothing fades.

Here are foundations laid by Roman architects ; here

is a tower built by the Visigoths in the fifth century. Guided by Viollet-le-Duc we study out the skill of mediæval engineers, the loopholes for the crossbowmen to let fly, the chinks for melted lead and boiling oil, the blind stairways intended only to confuse. As amateurs in martial history we fancy an enemy striving to force an entrance through fortifications like the wards of a lock. As lovers of poetry and romance we climb to the ramparts and picture the siege and the battle.

There is nothing to disturb the imagination, no hum of industry, no roar of traffic, no rush of feet. The past is alive, the present dead. Modernity is absent, and the olden time unrolls its pictures.

The foe are swarming about the barbican; they thunder at the postern ; they fill the moat ; they mine the wall. A bridge is let down from their wooden tower upon the parapet. Their bravest make the rush   Yonder on the narrow walk behind the battlements rages the deadly combat   We hear the fierce cries, the stern clash , we see the red vintage ; we see the headlong falls.

Just such a drama was enacted at Carcassonne in August, 1209   From the smoking ruins of Béziers the host of crusaders, led by Simon de Montfort and the legate of the pope, came here. The viscount—Raimon Rogier, the only son of the countess of Burlatz whom we know so well—resolved upon defending the place to the very last. When offered permission to leave the town he muttered, " That will happen when an ass flies to heaven "; and replying to the crusaders he declared, " Rather than desert my people I will be skinned alive."

Valiantly he fought and well , but the sky withheld its rains, and the city began to perish of thirst   Under the straitest pledges of safe conduct the viscount entered the camp of the besiegers for a parley. There he was basely seized by the champions of the truth, immured in his own

castle after the town yielded, and in the gloom of the
dungeon or the torture-room was barbarously done to
death.[2]

But in the days when Peire Vidal journeyed to Carcassona for a call upon the barons of the neighborhood, all

THE CASTLE OF CARCASSONNE.

this was happily undreamed of. The countess of Burlatz
herself was alive then, and as it happened was presiding
in all her beauty at the castle,—for this, too, formed a part
of her husband's fief. Arnaut de Maruelh was there by
her side, and the two poets vied the evening through to
please her ladyship's taste.[3]

But Arnaut was the one to remain, and in the morning
Peire set out for Cabaret. Over the castle drawbridge he
rode, and on through a scene like that we found at Carpentras, barely glancing at the saddlers, the shoemakers,
and the weavers of fine cloth who made the city rich, then
over the Old Bridge, as we call it,—at that day just com-

pleted,—across the plain at a round canter, and so on out of sight among the hills

As for ourselves we set out in pursuit of him with the inevitable barouche and pair, gladdened by the prospect of a fair day,—for it was raining torrents. Soon the fickle sky, true to its capriciousness, cleared, and the drive became delightful.

Nature has not forgotten to beautify even the mountain road we had to take. A clear and lively stream sang along beside the highway. Wild flowers abounded Here were broad fields of the low *brière*, its fine close leafage so full of the little white bells that the green seemed frosted over, and here generous patches of wild broom, *plantagenet*, the royal shrub that decorates an English throne, its yellow blossoms firing the hillside. Here were the *ajoncs*, their flowers of brilliant orange discarding the formality of leaves, and clinging tightly to the thorns that guarded their beauty. And here and everywhere stood lines of hawthorn, adorned with its modest white bloom ; while now and then purple clusters of the odorous thyme added a viola tone to the roadside harmonies.

At Mas Cabardès we lunched at the Franco-Russe café, wondering to find in this mountain hamlet an echo of statecraft, and listening meanwhile to the music of the Orbiel as it foamed through the arches of the bridge and mingled its voice with the chimes of the grey tower. If ever I asked for bread and received a stone it was here Indeed, the loaf was not merely a stone,—it was a complete fortress of rock with bastions *à la Vauban*. As we eyed the strategic engineering and rang our knives upon the masonry, we felt as helpless as the children of Israel blowing horns around the walls of Jericho, and when the bastions yielded we devoutly cried, " Not unto us ! "

There was a certain propriety in all this ; for, despite the lively Orbiel and the blithe wildflowers, the way to

A BIT OF CARCASSONNE.

Lastours is a gorge,—a stern and unwilling concession from the mountains In places there are little meadows where apple-trees and chestnuts yield a tardy harvest. A few poplars have found space to root. A few olives cling to the slopes. Here and there a crumb of a garden has been wrested from the ledges · it is so small you could almost cover it with your cloak, yet walls eight feet high have been constructed above and below to save it from the river and the falling rocks. Earth is precious and humanity cheap; and the peasants on the road—both men and women—go laden with those long conical baskets which were made for donkeys but are capable of fitting the human species just as well.

Cabaret was a proper monarch for such a region. Out of the valley rises a bristling and shivered mass of black Plutonian rock, a thousand feet high, I should say,—not only steep but sheer, not only barren but bare. Scarcely a shrub has found a lodging there. At the foot of it the white houses of Lastours cling like barnacles to the crag, while two broken towers stand far asunder on the summit, corners of the castle that once existed there , for Cabaret was a very extensive fortress, and in fact was justly accounted one of the strongest in the region.'

Its defenders, too, were strong in the time of Peire Vidal, and when the crusaders assaulted it they were driven away and mightily discouraged. But Simon de Montfort was not easily beaten. One day, soon after the massacre at Béziers, a slow procession wound up the valley, climbed the mountain, and craved admission at the gate it consisted of a hundred men taken prisoners at a neighboring castle. Montfort had cut off every nose and put out every eye save one ; and then had sent the victims off behind their one-eyed leader to frighten Cabaret. When the castle was again summoned, it parleyed and finally surrendered.

But love, not war, is our theme.

Peire Vidal presented himself at the gate with both his eyes and looking out of them with all his might   Indeed he could fairly claim the privilege of gazing about him boldly, for his position in the world was an assured one. By this time he possessed not only fame but fortune, and he journeyed in triumph, like a popular tenor hastening from Paris to St Petersburg, and from London to New York   His own accompanist went with him ; he travelled with his own horses, his own servants attended him; and the little company were richly equipped at his own expense.   But he was always in need of love, and it was for that he came.   Loba de Puegnautier lived at Cabaret, the wife of a distinguished knight.   Her beauty was famous the country through , lovers came in troops,—from Foix in the edge of the Pyrenees, from Saissac, and from many another castle far and near , and Peire Vidal felt that he must come too, with songs of praise and of pleading.[5]

But Peire was always a flutterer, and scarcely were the songs off his lips, when he discovered how deeply he loved another.   The image of Alazais de Roca Martina revived in his dreams, and off he set for a thorough siege of Marseille (1186).

Without a doubt this passion was sincere, but unhappily it was not impressive.   In vain he chanted his Vierna's truth and beauty :

> Her friend will ever find her true,
>   Nor would she paint for anything ;
> She need not, for her natural hue
>   Is fresher than the rose in spring.[6]

Though he asserted roundly, " I know the whole business of love and everything that pertains to gallantry," Venus had not blessed his horoscope.   As one could see from the very turn of his head, affection was a vital part of his nature ; but the shelving forehead, the little grey-blue eyes incessantly in motion, and the sudden capricious movements that he could not restrain,' betrayed a waywardness of thought and inconstancy of purpose not likely to win a lady's confidence. Alazais was very willing to be extolled by the famous poet in return for a ring and a vague promise, but his insistent pleadings only wearied her. So she quarrelled often with her troublesome adorer; and then Barral, easy and confident, would bring the two together again, and bid her promise whatever Peire desired.

After a long term of such ups and downs, Vidal began to fear that his quest would prove in vain, and—to quote an expression of his own—the feeling came over him that he was " a sillier thing to love her so much, than the mad shepherd who plays his pipe to a beautiful mountain " ; but then, as he said again, " Beauty makes the sanest man go wild," and what could he do but love and hope ?

What could he *do ?* Yes, that was the thing,—to do, to act, in one way or another to achieve and conquer. Was it not possible ? Was there not always a way ?

How ran the proverb that we meet with in *Flamenca ?*— " Who does not when he could, shall not when he would." This dangerous wisdom got possession of Peire's ear, and quite eclipsed the idea that he once enjoined upon others : " The gallant that is in a hurry has neither sense nor memory." Keyed up to desperation and fully bent on doing and achieving, he stole into the palace one morning —for he lodged elsewhere—and, watching till Barral went out, entered the hall and kissed the sleeping viscountess.

The lady awoke with a smile, and thinking Barral was there began to rise ; but lo ! it was " the fool, Peire Vidal," as the biography puts it, and she screamed instead. The servants rushed in, crying, " What is it ? "

and the hapless troubadour, his calculations dashed again, got away as best he could in the confusion, though not, it would appear, without some pretty hard usage.

On reflection Peire had to admit that the charm had not wrought as he wished, but then, ah! a woman,—her scruples once vindicated, who knew—? So he lingered hopefully for a time in the vicinity, and even wrote a new song in expectation of pardon.

> Like one who gapes, beholding in amaze
> A rich, fair window lighted by the sun,
> By tender thoughts my heart is so undone
> I lose myself when on her face I gaze ;
>   Love beats me well with twigs that I have brought,
>   Because I once—how dear and sweet the thought—
>   In her own palace robbed her of a kiss ;—
>   What joy have they who their belovèd miss? [8]

Not only adoration but humility was amply offered, and that in a most ingenious fashion ·

> Like some poor wight, in mansion rich a guest,
>   That holds his peace when grievously in pain
>   For fear 't would vex his lord should he complain,
> Though wrung with grief I still dare not protest. [8]

Barral did his best again, laughing at Alazais and even scolding her for making such a clamor about the doings of " the lunatic," but all was in vain. She still raged, demanded vengeance for the insult, and threatened the direst punishment ; it was her chance to be rid forever of Peire's unwelcome importunities. Vidal saw then that his case was hopeless, and crestfallen indeed he took ship for Genoa, chanting in doleful measures :

> She hath now my happy heart
> Who can make the wretched merry. [9]

The troubadour's position was in fact rather serious, for besides losing the woman he loved best he could not fail to see that his prestige was menaced. Something out of the ordinary had to be done,—so he made a trip to the Orient.

Tax your fancy to the utmost, you never will imagine what he did there. In Cyprus a young Greek was represented to him as the rightful heiress to the crown of the Eastern Empire, and—presto !—he married her. Dreams of more than royal power turned his brain completely then. He assumed the imperial arms, had a throne carried before him, required the public to address him as emperor and his wife as empress, and expended all the money he could obtain in preparing a fleet for the assertion of his rights. Poor Peire Vidal ! One shudders to think of his undeceiving !

Happily the ground was made soft for his fall. Barral could not enjoy life without him, and would give his wife no peace, we may believe, till she relented. A hint of this appears to have reached Vidal in the east and hastened his return. Barral met him—at Les Baux, it has been thought—and escorted him in triumph to Marseille (probably about 1189). Alazais made him a formal present of the stolen kiss, and the happy poet commemorated what he called the triumph of his submissiveness with a song found worthy of imitation by a minnesinger, Count Rudolf de Neuenburg.

> Now to fair Provence returning
> In my lady's favor strong,
> I must sing a blithesome song,—
> Thankfully this mercy earning ;
> One who does his lord's behest
> Serving with respect sincere,
> Wins a rich reward and dear,
> Prized as grateful thanks attest ;
> Wherefore I must do my best.

Sinless yet repentance learning,
Begging grace though clear of wrong,—
Thus the gift for which I long
I extract from nothing,—turning
    Wrath to kindness, grief to zest,
        Bitter love to sweet ; through fear
        But the bolder I appear ;
    Win by losing, and can wrest
    Victory from defeat confessed.[10]

This was the climax of Vidal's career as man and as
poet. Everything was bright and beautiful in his eyes ;
and his wits, nerved by joy and hope, sparkled as never
before or after.

Oh, 't is good and fair
When the trees all wear
Fresh green leaves,—the air
    Sweet with flowers new,
Song-birds, here and there,
    Chanting full in view,
    While gay lovers sue,
    Amorous and true ,
Loved and lover I would be,
Yet such answers to my plea
    It hath been my lot to find
    That I 've nearly lost my mind.

Strength and heart and mind,
Lovingly inclined,
I have all resigned
    To my lady fair ;
Glad new life I find
    Like the boughs that wear
    Fruit again,—birds air
    All their music there ;
Springing leaves and blossoms new
In my heart I ever view,
    And this joy will ever be
    Mine, for she hath heard my plea

> Though she scorned my plea
> Now she favors me,—
> None so fair as she,
>   Or so clear in mind,
> For she sees I 'll be
>   E'er as now inclined ;
> To her I 've resigned
>   All my life, she 'll find ;
> Thus I 'll serve my lady, —fair,
> Gay, and witty, and will wear
>   Bonds that suit the lovers true
>   Who with real affection sue.[11]

But Peire was ere long saying to himself, as he said in one of his poems, " Whoever in the world would live must oft endure chagrin and pain." For Vierna had no more intention than before of loving him, and soon wearied again of his attentions.[12]

Disheartened at last, the poet sought and found a new distraction and a fresh theme : he became a zealot. " Since all must surely die, he is indeed a fool who lives basely and badly ", this became his conviction. The third crusade was gathering its forces, and King Richard's fleet lay in the roadstead of Marseille. Peire took the cross, exchanged his lute for a clarion, and exhorted like another Peter the Hermit

> Had I but the power, too,
> As I have the zeal to do,
>   And could carry out my thought,
>   Alexander would be naught,—
>   Such my reputation ;
>   For, could supplication
> Move the Lord to help me through,
>   O'er the tomb where He was brought,
>   A debased and slavish nation
>   Should not long have domination.[13]

" My reputation ! " Do not imagine he was jesting ;

not the least in the world.   Besides the delusion that no
woman could resist his charms, whereas the biography
tells us that every one cajoled him, he was fully possessed
with a belief in his terrible prowess, and in comparison
with his martial braggadocio the sonorous fanfaronnades
of Captain Fracasse become as nothing

> When I have donned my double hauberk white,
> And girded on my sword so keen and bright,
>   The trembling ground announces where I go,
> And all my foes, however proud their might,
> Give up to me both road and path in fright,
>   If they but hear the tread that well they know.[14]

Vidal distinguished himself in war about as in love, we
have reason to believe, but he could resist a title no better
than Thackeray , and when Richard invited him, as apparently he did, to join the expedition, he scaled the gang-
plank and sailed for gory triumphs   Adieu to amorous
ditties !   Adieu to love !

Just how long the poet remained with Richard we do
not know ; still less what he did there ; but a year or two
later we find him paying serious court at Cabaret.

How should he prove his devotion to the fair Loba ;
how surpass at one stroke the many lovers casting bold
vows at her feet ?   " Ah, I have it ! " he cried, slapping
his thigh.   The name " Loba " meant " she-wolf"; so
Peire desired people to call him a wolf, too, and made the
wolf his emblem   Of course this Quixotic parade was
laughed at, and very likely the sincerity of it challenged.
Probably he was driven to make good his words,—at any
rate according to several manuscripts he did ; and assuming the skin as well as the name of a wolf, he turned himself loose on Black Mountain, and soon fell a prey to the
shepherds and their dogs.

The jest went farther than he planned, and he was

CABARET.

brought home to Loba savagely beaten and almost dead.
" And when she knew that it was Peire Vidal, she began
to make great sport of the folly that Peire Vidal had committed, and to laugh much, and her husband likewise ;
and they received him with great merriment. And her
husband had him taken and put in a privy place, the best
he knew and could ; and he caused the physician to be
sent for, and had him attended until he was healed.'"' So
ended the second of his grand affairs.

From this time the tender passion seemed less attractive
to Vidal, and public matters, engrossing his interest, invaded still more his love-songs. Indeed he resolved not
long after to abandon poetry and music altogether. " The
good count," Raimon V. of Toulouse, his natural sovereign, died (1194) ; and though Vidal had long since left
his natal city and even had sided with Raimon's enemies,
his erratic nature, or perhaps his unwillingness to be forgotten, plunged him into a frenzy of grief. Turning his
back on all that pleased him before, he shaved his head
and compelled his servants to do the same, let his nails
and beard go uncut, docked his horses' tails and ears,
dressed wholly in black, and went about like one dis-
tracted. But as it happened—or *was* it only by chance ?
—King Amfos of Aragon was then visiting Provence; and
when he and his nobles begged Vidal for a new song to
carry back to Spain, Vidal consented to rouse and be
himself again.

To be himself,—that was to be in motion. Monferrat
was now his goal (1194–95), and a year or so later he
found himself in Hungary, where a daughter of Amfos
was the queen.'" Then after a long journey to Spain he
appeared again in Monferrat, and ventured to dream of
outvying Raimbaut de Vaqueiras in the affections of the
Fair Knight. The departure of the marquis at the head
of the fourth crusade probably severed this acquaintance ;

a few years later (1205) he was heard in Malta, and after that he dropped anchor for his last days at the munificent court of Lord Blacatz, broken by ceaseless toils—and probably an over-fondness for good wine—on the younger side of sixty."

Poor Peire Vidal! What shall we say of him?

On the one hand he could talk like Poor Richard: " Knowledge is the greatest of treasures for one who knows how to use it "; " One must adapt his song to the time, the place, and the audience "; " Be always well dressed but never dandified "; " Whatever be your intelligence, knowledge, and talents, do not boast ; be modest, and others will discover your worth "; " A heart that is full of wrath often causes the mouth to err "; " I do not wish for riches to make all men hate me "; " From good root grows good tree " ;

> Who well begins but leaves the thing half done,
> 'T were well for him he never had begun.[18]

He possessed no little sagacity in political matters, and gave some excellent advice to the great lords of his day. Noble character won his praise, and baseness received his vigorous condemnation. His poetical work was judicious and graceful, artistic, melodious, and highly finished. Though the obscure style was rampant he escaped its influence: " I will compose a song that shall be easy to learn, with courtly words and with a sensible tune "; so he once proposed, and that was the sound method of his art. His love-songs were tender, thoughtful, and insinuating ; his elegies sincere and strong ; his sirventes penetrating and bold. In the expression of his emotion he seemed unaffected, and his pictures were often original and graceful.

On the other hand what delusions in his love affairs, what vaunting of his prowess, what insane fondness for kings and princes, what crazy schemes, and what mad pranks !

The contrast was as much a puzzle in his day as in ours.

The Monk of Montaudon declared . '' Never since he made himself a knight has he possessed either his wits or his memory ''; and even his friend the noble Blacatz exclaimed : '' Explain to me how it is that in many things you display so little judgment, and yet in poetry so great knowledge and skill.''

The Marquis Lanza concluded that he was only a sot and a lunatic, and when Vidal was bearing about the insignia of empire cried : '' We have an emperor without sense, understanding, or memory   Such a drunkard never sat on a throne, such a coward never bore lance and shield, such a poltroon never buckled on spurs, such a rogue never made verses and songs. . . . Would that a sword might strike him on the head, an arrow of steel pierce his body, and hooks tear out his eyes.   Then we will give him some wine and put on his crown an old scarlet hat without ribbons, and for a lance he shall have a long stick · so might he wend safely from here to France.'' [19]   But he found the laugh against him when Peire answered : '' Marquis Lanza, poverty and ignorance are playing the mischief with you.   . . You are like a blind beggar   . . in the street, who has lost all shame and recollection ''; and Zorgi doubtless expressed the general conclusion when he observed : '' Whoever takes Peire Vidal for a fool commits the greatest folly of all, for without real intelligence nobody could write his verses '' [20]

Nor was he merely an intelligent and skilful poet. Though not a soldier in the day of chivalry, nor a handsome gallant in the day of love, he kept himself in the eye of the public and forced the world to remember him While only the son of a petty tradesman he became the companion of princes, reckoned five kings among his friends, won fame in as many countries, and after seven centuries have passed away still lives in fifty songs.

Even his follies helped no doubt,—as I suspect he well understood : he was a court-poet and a court-jester rolled into one, Wamba added to Arnaut de Maruelh ; and then, superadded, he was also a court-singer. Goldsmith who " wrote like an angel but talked like poor Poll " was a little of his kind both as man and as poet ; but Goldsmith was the victim and Vidal the master of his destiny.

In short, he was a genius, unbalanced yet unmistakable; and the best comment on his frailties was his success.

And yet,—poor Peire Vidal !

XIX

FOIX

Peire d'Alvernhe. Rogier Bernart III., Count of Foix

CARCASSONNE to Foix,—a journey from star to
star past the wall of heaven.

Down from the Pyrenees comes the swift Aude, carrying jauntily a load of earth twice as heavy as the Rhone's,[1]
and our course—turning south from Carcassonne—climbed
its valley, until the railway ended at the ruined castle and
rambling town of Quillan.

According to Humboldt the Basque name of the Pyrenees is *Murua*, a wall, and it was literally a wall that
soon confronted us ; for about three miles above Quillan,
still ascending an easy slope, we found ourselves face to
face with a colossal barrier of grey rock supporting a
titanic staircase to the sky, every step a mountain, and
every mountain topped off with pointed crags.   No hills
concealed the magnificent buttresses of the range ; not
even a foot-path dared to scale the precipices ; and, while
water always ends by having its way, we discovered the
Aude issuing from beyond through a cleft so very narrow
that the little river was grievously vexed and troubled
to get through at all.

That was well enough—at a pinch—for the river, but
what were we to do?   At last we espied a door in the
mountain.   There was no Arabic inscription above or
near it, but it seemed an affair of magic none the less.

We passed within ; and while a moment before there had not even been hills, we could now see nothing but gorge, chasm, rock, cliff, precipice, crag, and peak. For a mile and a half the Pierre-Lis defile exhibits these marvels. The road is now on a shelf overhanging the foamy Aude, now is overhung in turn by a bulging precipice, and now pierces a solid buttress that endeavors to bar the way completely. Then one passes a few miles of green valley with farmhouses and villages, leaves picturesque Axat behind, and enters the defile of St. Georges.

THE WALL OF THE PYRENEES (*From Memory*).

What shall I say of this ? My vocabulary of nouns is already exhausted and adjectives are unworthy. Here the volcanic forces of our planet have bowed themselves like Samson in the temple of the Philistines. In a bit of stone I counted eleven alternate layers of black and white —calcite and chlorite—in half an inch of thickness. The mountain has been seized and broken squarely in two, and the ends rise vertically about a quarter of a mile above the pinched river and the narrowed highway. When the drifting clouds gathered about the summits and hid them, it seemed as if we had actually found the pillars of the firmament   We almost dreaded to enter the passage,—what would it be for either peak to shake down a few tons of rock upon us ?   Once there, we recalled the famous Hoellenthal—the Valley of Hell—in the Black Forest, and it seemed a mere plaything in comparison. The wildest gorges of the Grimsel pass are far less towering and infinitely less accented.   The roadway has perhaps thirty minutes of clear daylight in the twenty-four hours ; at other times one walks softly as in the dusk of the gods; and the mind, wearied by vain efforts to surmount the grandeur of the view, falls back upon itself, and can only repeat that sentence of the great French poet,

L'impossible est ici debout.*

Returning to Quillan we took the stage for a cross-country ride of some thirty miles to Foix through scenes familiar to many a troubadour.

If we Americans are ever guilty of " brutal directness," it is in our road-building.   Nature meant the high places of the earth for delight ; but in our eyes the hill is an enemy and the mountain a foe.   Our one thought is to attack, conquer, subdue, trample upon.   The route from Quillan was very different from this.   First it led us across a great offshoot of the Pyrenees, ascending mildly and winding to right and to left past fields, pastures, and woodlands owned by the villages (*communes*), and assigned by lot each year.   Now it encircled a valley, now it skirted a height, and at all times it spread before us views ever wider and ever softer of Quillan, the valley of the Aude, the defile of Pierre-Lis, and the snowy summits of the Pyrenees.

Not a few old castles, all of them in ruins, were perched along the way.

* " Here stands the impossible, erect on its feet "

One of the ruins was Puivert,—an earth-brown group huddled about a broken donjon. Simon de Montfort thought it worth his while to march into the shadow of the Pyrenees to besiege Puivert, but for our minds the ruin told of a different story, for it recalled the famous troubadour, Peire d'Alvernhe the Old, as Petrarch styled him, who was born in the diocese of Clermont-Ferrand, but like Peire Rogier sought a warmer and richer latitude.

As Petrarch intimated and as Dante said, Peire d'Alvernhe was a father among the troubadours. He came earlier than any one we have yet known, unless Raimbaut d'Aurenga was as old, and he was chanting his own music while many of them were only wailing in their cradles Yet he outlasted several of his juniors, and sang (1150–1200) while three generations occupied the throne of Barcelona,—Amfos, his father, and his son.

We know almost nothing of Peire's life, but can be sure that he was at Puivert on one evening at least A roistering crowd of good fellows were drinking, jesting, and laughing in the hall ; wine flowed and torches flared , and Peire, it would appear, was called upon for a new song. He was as jolly as anybody, and with rough and ready wit—for his mind was always full and his invention prompt—he dashed off a series of caricatures of the popular poets of the day,—a piece that prompted the Monk of Montaudon to do the same

Peire was not a little conceited, for had he not made good verse before others got the seed ? and, as the Master of Poets, he dressed down his contemporaries with no gentle hand. Their real vocation was keeping sheep, he said, for they had no true knowledge of the art One chanted like a sick pilgrim, another had eyes like silver, another received so many presents of good clothes for such poor singing that everybody had gone into the business.

Peire Rogier, he declared, was singing of love while he ought to be carrying a psalter and a lighted candle in church,—perhaps he was not so far from the mark just there. As for himself he admitted, or rather boasted, that his verses were hard to understand, but his voice reached from low to high and his tones were sweet and pleasing. Alas for his vanity ! The stanza as it now appears in his poem bears the impress of another hand . the reproach or compliment of obscurity is left, but as for his vocal gifts we are informed that he sang like " a frog in a swamp." [2]

I take a little personal pleasure in this fling at the troubadour of Clermont, and I will explain why. After the satire of Puivert his most famous poem is a long piece about a nightingale. He sends the bird to his mistress with a courteous greeting and an affectionate message, and the bird brings him back the same.

> Now unto my lady's dwelling
> Hie thee, nightingale, away,
> Tidings of her lover telling,
> Waiting what herself will say ;
> Make thee 'ware
> How she doth fare ;
> Then, her shelter spurning,
> Do not be
> On any plea
> Let from thy returning.[3]

So the piece begins, as another hand than mine has transcribed the stanza in English.

Now the idea is pretty but certainly not wonderful, and when beaten out into one hundred and twenty lines it seems passionless, wearisome, and even childish. It reminds one of Peire de Valeria, another early poet, whom the biographer crushes with scant ceremony : " He made verses of little value on leaves, on flowers, and on the songs of birds ; his singing was of no great worth, nor

was he "; and I am conscious of a definite grudge against
Peire d'Alvernhe because this tame and merely pretty
piece has long been quoted as the best of troubadour
poetry.

But a grudge—even if well founded—cannot excuse injustice, and there is more to be said about him.   He was
really a pioneer, and we must not judge him simply by
those who came after.   If crude, his mind was also rich
and independent ; and if affected, it was also fertile and
original.   Fauriel remarked long ago upon the " oriental "
boldness of his comparisons   When the inspiration was
upon him he could be lively, varied, and picturesque,
though when it failed he could be—the opposite.   " As
the sky closes in the sea," was excellent for that age
He declared that a man who did not care for courtly love
was worth no more than an ear of corn with no corn upon
it.   Some of his remarks are worthy to be proverbs ·
" The more one has, the more one fears ", " It is not
easy to quench a hidden fire "; " He that is very hungry
eats bread which does not please him "; " One cannot
well obtain great good without suffering, but joy quickly
makes an end of pain."

Peire was quite capable of simple thinking and straight-
forward expression.

> How fair appears the eglantine,
>   When all the birds again outpour
> Sweet songs of joy as true as mine,
>   Because the world is green once more ;
>   Because fair blossoms hide the boughs
>   With red and yellow, green and blue ![4]

But this was not his characteristic style.   Well educated
and perhaps a canon '—though only of burgher stock—he
saw the faults and the possibilities of the popular songs,
and undertook the improvement of their style.   Nor was

he unsuccessful ; but unfortunately his bold fancy and
thirst for originality often overpowered his taste and
good sense. As a pioneer he felt the pioneer's love of
bright finery, and there is a deal of buckskin fringe and
crimson tassel in his verse. Compared with all who preceded him, he must be termed a master of technique, a
real artist in verse, an example in the study of effect; but
he was also the precursor of Raimbaut d'Aurenga and
Arnaut Daniel in that artificiality and over-elaborateness

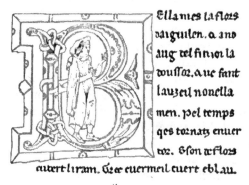

THE ORIGINAL OF " HOW FAIR APPEARS ! "

of diction which tended to petrify Provençal verse. Like
a novelist of the local-color school he thought it fine to
load his poems with hard and peculiar words, and he
wished it made obvious that no technical difficulties could
appall him. Equally anxious was he to show that he
followed no master. It was customary to open a song
with a little picture from nature, and then go on to express feelings in harmony with it. Of course one could
easily change the scheme, as many did, and have a contrast instead of a harmony between the picture and the
feelings ; but the fact is notable that, as Pätzold says,
Peire d'Alvernhe employed the contrast always, the harmony never. A strong imagination, and sincere, simple

feeling cannot be looked for in company with qualities
like these, and from this lack sprang of course his fundamental defects.

' In spite of those defects—and largely because of them,
no doubt—the poet of Clermont enjoyed a vast reputation.
His biographer, who was very likely Sain Circ, informs
us that he " was considered the best troubadour in the
world until Guiraut de Borneil came," and he "was greatly
honored and favored by all the excellent barons and excellent ladies." Nostradamus records a tradition that
after each song he was permitted to kiss the fairest of his
audience ; and this conveys a suggestion that ladies were
not unmindful of his " fair and agreeable person," set off
by the pleasant music that he composed and the pleasant
manner in which—as we are told—he rendered it ; for his
love-songs without these accompaniments are lacking in
warmth and individuality.

But even such popularity as this could not last for ever,
and Peire himself once exclaimed, " How quickly the joy
of this light world turns to bitterness ! " In his later
years he was compelled to see younger poets and younger
lovers preferred, and it was probably in this period that
he composed his pieces against love.

In one of his songs the poet threatened a cruel mistress
that he would forsake the world ; and whether or no her
want of sympathy was the cause, he finally entered a
monastery and there closed his eyes upon a long career.

A little beyond Puivert we came to a wide bowl of a
valley with a castle on a high rock near the brim, and
saw before us at a glance the feudal system in its best
estate : an isolated valley, laborers to work the fields, a
fortress to protect the laborers, and a lord to keep the
fortress. In times of peace the lord watched and the people worked,—the advantage lay with him ; but when the

signal fires blazed out, the work-folk hurried to the castle and the lord provided for them, led them, and fought for them, and the brunt of the care and the danger fell upon him, for he had more than they to do and more than they to risk.

This was the original noblesse, and it involved a principle that we should not forget. The age of the troubadours is called aristocratic, and we are now rid of aristocrats. But who sees the president of a railroad holding the throttle-valve of an engine in a time of danger? What millionaire would stand on guard at the door of his bank, musket in hand? Yet that was the rule in the age of King Amfos II. and Marquis Bonifaz. Titles then stood for duty and responsibility, just as they do now in our armies. The duke was originally the guardian of a province, the marquis kept the border, the count was in charge of a diocese, the viscount (vice-count) represented an absent count,—particularly in cities, and so on to the lowest of the dignities. Wealth meant lands, and lands imposed a military obligation. Even kings had to leave their palaces at the call of duty, and risk life and property in the defence of their subjects. In short, the feudal system not only ennobled service, but it vastly tempered the power and pride of riches by linking them with public responsibility.'

It was only in the decay of the system that names and titles came to be given for social distinction as the insignia of pomp and pride.' The swarms of dukes, marquises, counts, viscounts, and barons multiplied only as their value disappeared. In time the world found out the sham, and unrelenting nature calmly decreed that the race must die. Titles are now an anachronism, and the anachronism is rapidly proving fatal. Today young fellows bearing the proudest names in Europe stand about at receptions perfumed like young ladies, or gather lan-

guidly in groups to discuss actresses or flick the grains of
dust from each other's coat collars,--blasé at eighteen.
For all that, wisdom was not born with us ; and we have
still to learn two fundamental ideas of the troubadour
age : the nobleness of high-minded service and the responsibility of wealth.

All day we reviewed a procession of beautiful valleys,
each worthy to be called, as one of them is, the " Vale of
Love." All day the mighty range of the Pyrenees
marched with us,—fields of snow idealizing the peaks,
and forests of evergreens clinging like black moss to the
bold scarps. All day we met and parted with pleasant
villages, lively in the easy and restful manner of the region. And—what gave our enjoyment of these scenes a
particular zest—everything was natural, unaffected, un-
adorned ; the trail of the tourist was not over it all

As evening approached we descended toward the wild
valley of the Ariège The sky was dark with heavy
clouds , but suddenly just out of sight behind the point a
rift occurred, and across the slope at our left poured a
flood of yellow sunset light. The level beams struck the
poplars, birches, and aspens from the farther side, so that
we saw their radiance through the tender color of the
young foliage. Against the deep shadows of the valley
beyond, the hillside glowed and almost blazed , and
when the light breeze set quivering every leaf in the
myriad sprays of greenish gold it seemed as if we had
quite left the world of reality, and the garden of the Hes-
perides had been found at last.

A few miles farther on but still among the spurs of the
Pyrenees, where the snows cling almost until the summer
solstice, we saw two swift rivers—grey with foam—come
together between two sharp mountains and a high vertical
crag. One of the rivers is the Arget, hurrying down its
valley from the west ; and the other is the Ariège, rush-

ing upon it from the highest peaks of the Spanish frontier.
The steep wall of Mt. Pech, black with fir-trees, closes
upon them on the one side, and St. Sauveur plants on the
other a precipice of tremendous height and almost sheer.
In the angle between the two mountains and the rivers
is the vertical crag.   Below this and around it lies a town,
and upon it are reared three beautiful towers.

" The world cannot show two such spots," we thought :
" this must be Foix.   It is."

FROM THE PROMENADE, FOIX.

Who talks of castles on the Rhine after seeing Foix ?
Penetrate the town, and wherever you go you are startled
every now and then, as your eye follows up the quaint
old fronts of a narrow street, to find one or another of the
towers gazing straight down upon you.   The houses that
frown so darkly with projecting upper stories like scowl-
ing brows appear scarcely nearer, and the mountains that
block the other outlooks appear hardly more powerful.

Try to escape and you will probably find yourself in the
promenade.   The castle is now less threatening but not

less impressive. Walking up and down under the elms and plane trees you study the bold profile of the rock, the precipice dressed out a little with daring trees that grow up or down as best they can, and upon its crown the three towers keeping their watch and ward over the town and you.

But there is another and still better point of view at the foot of Mt. Pech on the other side of the Ariège At the very point of the triangle where the rivers unite, a great weeping willow stands dipping its yellow leaves at the same time into the Arget and the Ariège. To the right, one's eye is led along by an ancient wall covered with vines to a lofty bridge across the Arget ; and to the left, by ivy-clad trees, the sombre choir of St. Volusien ' and a line of picturesque houses to the old bridge across the Ariège, begun (1188) while Peire Vidal was carrying about his imperial emblems. Straight above the willow, above the roofs, above the tree-tops, rises the great crag ; and from that spring the three towers, rearing their battlements four hundred feet, I should think, above the rivers

Now for the castle itself. The ascent is a fitting climax to our succession of views.

One mounts by the mediæval road, pitched as sharply as a flight of stairs, twisting here, turning abruptly there, and flanked at the strategic points with intricate fortifications The grass grows luxuriantly where soil has gathered in the crevices, and the bright heads of dandelions begem it. Blooming lilacs hang down over the ledges. Ferns occupy the niches A sort of broom—the *rataplan*, as it is called in the patois—flaunts gay blossoms of yellow on the face of the cliff, and in sheltered spots roses load the air with fragrance.

On the top of the rock we stop short, but not so much from lack of breath as from excess of admiration.

THE CASTLE OF FOIX.

The loud song of the rivers comes up as a slumberous murmur that must have been very restful to " my lady's " tired ear. Straight below us are the red roofs of the city, tilted and cornered in at every angle. Southward the valley of the Ariège widens into a little plain, walled up at no great distance by the snowy Pyrenees. And on the other side, the bare precipice of St. Sauveur beyond the Arget seems almost near enough to touch, and one can almost fancy a reckless horseman trying to leap the chasm.

The counts of Foix were for centuries a redoubtable succession, and their castle was another Les Baux. The low square tower is said to date from the time of " good King Dagobert." Within these walls a great conference between the Catholics and the Albigensians was held, and a pope was imprisoned. A king of France found an army unequal to the task of storming the fastness. The terrible Simon de Montfort was driven away with arrows and stones ; and though he vowed to return and make the rock " melt like tallow," he never thought it wise to come back. Through good fortune and bad the family battled and schemed, and eventually the lord of Foix came to be recognized as one of the great vassals of the crown, one of the " peers of France."

Music and poetry were no less welcome here than at Les Baux. The bold count who drove Montfort away, Raimon Rogier, was not only one of the greatest captains of his day and a valiant leader in the third crusade, but— so we are assured—a patron of the troubadours and a troubadour himself.[10] The taste both for arms and for poetry continued in his children. Four years before Sordel acquired his castles in Italy, his great-grandson, Rogier Bernart III , began to reign (1265)[11] Peire III., a great-grandson of King Amfos, came in like manner to the throne of Aragon, and both were poets like their ancestors. They agreed none the better for that, however ;

and the count of Foix, after having a taste of Spanish prison fare, paid a dear price to regain his liberty.   In the course of time King Peire, known in Spanish history as Pedro the Great, sounded the note for the Sicilian Vespers, and after the Frenchmen had been massacred received from Sicily a crown and from Rome a bull of excommunication

In those days when a king was put under the ban his estates were no longer considered his, and the pope gave Aragon to a son of Philip the Bold, King of France. Philip set out for Catalonia with an army to take possession, and the count of Foix—believing the day of his revenge had come—hailed the approaching contest with ecstasy.

> The men of Burgundy will soon rush on
> Crying, "Montjoi!" while these cry, "Aragon!" [12]

The lilies of France were already famous and he warned the Spaniards :

> Whoe'er would pluck that flower, know well,
>   Must grip the spear-shaft like the best;
> For how to strike the French can tell,
>   And how to set the lance in rest [12]

Hatred long pent up gloated on the prospect, and the count threatened his enemies with the fearlessness of Agrippa d'Aubigné.   Patarins and Tartarins he called them, names branded on the hated Albigensians. Already he saw King Peire bound with cords and dragged off like a robber, while his family and partisans were starving in dungeons.

> The French—unequalled in the world for heart,
>   Knowledge, and strength—and they of Burgundy
> Toward Rome shall make the Patarins depart;
>   And all who cry out "Aragon!" shall be—

And right it is, too—thrown upon a pyre
Of seething fire ;
 Till all be burned at last,
 And to the winds their ashes cast.[12]

The count's expectations were not realized, for a fever
put the invading army to flight and the king died at Perpignan   But the passions of the day had impressed themselves in literature ; and with these fragments of poetry
in mind,[13] we not only stand here gazing at a wonderful
panorama, and musing upon the remains of a historic
fortress, but we have a glimpse into the fiery furnace of a
great baron's heart.   We realize what sort of men they
were who ruled these castles.   And we begin to measure
the fierce hates, and the loves almost as fierce, of an age
that we often find it hard to understand.

XX

TOULOUSE AND PAMIERS

Peire Raimon. Aimeric de Peguilha

NO city in the world, it seems to me, has been so identified with the cult of poetry as Toulouse, and one feels the spirit of it somehow in the air.

The town, all of brick, is not beautiful, though Coppée's ingenuity has found it a beautiful name, the "Rosy City"; and the pavements can hardly be thought well of unless they were intended to keep the traveller too busy with his own martyrdom to think of the blood shed upon them by more pious ages. Yet, though her vestments are only those of a provincial beauty, Toulouse has not lost the heart of a proud capital, and she possesses a striking individuality. What we find is not a gay levity as in Gascony, nor a headlong petulance as in Provence, but the strong, intense genius of Languedoc. It is the city of Pallas, the wise have said, and something Florentine certainly meets one here

The spirit of a people is always revealed, for example, in the history of religion among them, and the deep religious intensity of Toulouse has been only too brilliantly exhibited. In the lofty pyramidal group of St. Sernin, the finest brick building in the world, there is carved in the choir a pig in a pulpit with this legend . " Calvin the hog preaching." In " the Rosy City " was tested (1229) the first plan of the terrible Inquisition formally organized in 1233.[1] That very year (1229) a papal bull authorized a university here—the first university that can say just when it was founded (1231), and the power of the Inquisition was re-quired to secure their salaries for the Dominican professors. The same he-retical Toulouse prompt-ed the slap in the face given by Philip the Fair to Boniface VIII. But the Inquisition changed all this ; and the convert-ed city, to make amends, burned four hundred schismatics in less than a century. Out of such in-tensity comes a sweetness that is not insipid.

ST. SERNIN.

Even the stranger has glimpses of piquant and fascinat-ing life in Toulouse. The animation of the south quivers in the air. The men are smartly but formally dressed in tightly buttoned frock-coats,—their black beards trimly cut still *en brosse*, as Taine observed. The ladies—nerv-ous figures, bewitching profiles, bright eyes, and smiles quick to bud and blossom—thrill even a Saxon with their vibrant loveliness. Long after dark the sidewalks are still thronged. Eager accents and exuberant gestures attest the southern latitude. Now and then one hears a snatch of dialogue in the patois, rhythmic and musical, intoned from resonant throats. Voices rise quickly to the passion of a quarrel,—sharp, thunderous, and menacing ; but the storm breaks in a burst of harmless violence and an explosion of laughter. On the one side we find Gallic

wit; on the other, Latin elegance. Through this window
we see tables covered with green cloth ready for dominoes
or cards ; through that one comes an air from the opera,
sung correctly and with effect, undulating past us like a
perfume on the soft, caressing breeze.

Among such a people the passion for lyric poetry could
not fail to burn ; but it existed long before the composite
race of today appeared. While the groves of oak were
still sacred, and before the blonde faces of the Gauls began
to be darkened with the blood of the conquered race, bards
and Druid prophets chanted for many generations in the
capital of the Tectosages. Then the Roman came. The
poet Ausonius, as we know, received his education at
Tolosa, and this is a hint that the tradition and the practice of poesy were alive. Raimon, a Tolosan monk, addressed a Latin poem to Peter the Venerable, the protector
and comforter of the stricken Abelard, which the great
abbot of Cluny deemed worthy of a poem in reply   Guilhem, the ninth of that name, the powerful duke of Aquitaine, conquered Toulouse while Abelard was living, and
spent considerable time here. He was the first of the
troubadours, as we shall see. His viol can not have been
silent in the palace where his wife was born, and with him
was ushered in the long line of poets who took up in
Romance the tradition of Celtic and Latin verse.

During the reign of the " good count," Raimon V., so
extravagantly mourned by Peire Vidal, the line of poets
in Toulouse became a throng. Six-and-forty years (1148-
1194) he reigned, while the sun of Provençal verse was
climbing boldly to the meridian. The richest prince of
Christendom, he doubtless had the most luxurious court.
Art was not neglected, and it has been discovered that in
his day Toulouse possessed a school of sculptors not unworthy of admiration [2] ; but music and especially poetry
were the ruling passion   Almost all the troubadours of the

day shared his bounty , probably he made verses himself ;
and besides Vidal two other famous poets went out from
the gates of his capital,—Peire Raimon and Aimeric de
Peguilha.

Peire Raimon was a troubadour of Vidal's time, and
like him the son of a burgher ; but here the likeness ends,
for Peire Raimon had nothing extravagant in his character, nor any such craving for distinction as the other Peire
felt. Though talented he seems to have been retiring,
and while affectionate was not bold enough nor hard
enough to play very successfully the part of a gallant.[3]

The ladies of Toulouse were famous for beauty then as
they are to-day, and Peire soon lost his heart. As a poet
he was bound to be up and away, gaining fame and riches
in a world that knew nothing of his lowly origin ; but he
lingered on still at home in affectionate wooing while he
might have gained more by caring less.

"Sweetly she wounded my heart with a loving glance,"
he sang, and the gentle sentiment of this line seems to reveal his character. Instead of dominating his lady he
was disposed to lean upon her. When she made him conscious of his humble rank, he only endeavored to win her
by still greater devotion ·

> For I love her so
> That the less she deigns bestow
> All the more I love her.[4]

She was the first who stirred his powers, and he felt that
all his talents belonged to the one who gave them life

> The flower, the grove, the field
> Gave me no song afore,
> But you whom I adore
> The joy of love unsealed [4]

Finally, however, his own good sense, the advice of his
friends, and the taunts of his lady prevailed, and he betook

himself to the Mecca of poets, the court of King Amfos of
Aragon. There he won great success. The royal troubadour was particularly delighted with him, and there is
reason to believe that his verses and his presence were no
less enjoyed among the ladies.

THE CASTLE, MONTAUBAN.

Still there was all the while that old love within him.
"What one greatly longs for, one cannot forget," he
sang, and after a long absence he set out for home to pay
his addresses again to the lady of Toulouse.

How glad he was to come in sight of his natal town!
Toulouse was already a rosy city, but it was also a striped
city; for the bricks dear to Ausonius were laid with binding courses of grey stone. Fourteen bastions or barbicans
re-enforced the walls (1219), and numberless towers rose
above them. Against the river on the north was the castle
of Bargarde, and on the south was the still greater castle

of Narbonne, the citadel of Toulouse, flanked by the Eagle Tower, a hint of whose appearance we may perhaps obtain from the castle of Montauban, founded (1144) by the count of Toulouse.[5] A fortified suburb, the *bourg*, lay above the castle of Bargarde, and four bridges of wood led across the Garonne to another dependency.

THE GATEWAY OF THE OLD CAPITOL.

Peire hastened on, we may be sure, without a glance at St. Sernin,[6] then outside the walls, or a thought of the bishop, dragged to his death by wild bulls, whose name it bears. The Jewish quarter, with its many peculiar sights, had no interest for him. On the right, where the Palais de Justice now stands, he passed the count's palace, and on the left the Capitol, where the magistrates of the townfolk held their chapter, and where their archives were sacredly preserved in an iron chest. Nothing was able to detain him. On he flew to the house of the woman he loved, and there he cast himself at her feet with a song of entreaty.

> As when a boy, grown up where he was placed
> In some great court with guardian true and kind,
> Deserts his lord, a better home to find,

But finds it not, and feels that he 's disgraced,
And would return yet lacks the hardihood ;
So 't is with me that stayed not as I should
　With one whom I will thank if she but deign
　To punish me, and let me then remain.[1]

With all his art he contrived a wreath for her fair head,
—a wreath of poetry instead of laurel, with rhymes for
leaves, deftly overlying one another, and brought around
until the circle was complete.

Like the candle, which is burning
　To provide the house with light
　Doth consume itself outright,
　　I, to please one far from tender,
Sing when I would most refrain ;
And my folly is so plain,
　So beyond all palliation,
　When I die with resignation
That another may obtain
Pleasure, that whate'er my pain
　None should mind my tribulation.

For I know through realization
That where love secures domain
Folly, not good sense, will reign ;
　So, as I 've made full surrender
　　To the fairest ever seen,
　　Drawing back were base and mean
　　　Whatsoever ill befall me ,
　　　For the more desire enthrall me
　　All the more I 'll thank her, e'en
　　Though I die , naught else, I ween,
　　　Could in Love's fair court install me.

　　Such a foe may well appall me,
　　But submissiveness will screen
　　From attack ; a humble mien,
　　Praise, and patience can't offend her ;
And her vassal, if she deign
To accept me, I 'll remain,—

True, without dissimulation ,
　For, though fit for reprobation,
　　If I can her presence gain,
　　I would rather be insane
　Than the wisest of creation

　Could I find in any nation
　Richer charms than hers I 'd fain
　Leave her and escape disdain ;
　　　But there is not one pretender—
　Though her wealth and rank invite—
　That is half so fair and bright,
As my thoughtful heart is learning ;
So I stay to save returning
　And give up the useless fight,
　Since there is no better right
That I have a hope of earning.

I am yours,—myself but spurning
　Since I 'm not with you to-night ;
　For I need you e'er in sight,—
Sail for speeding, helm for turning. [8]

　Still the lady smiled at praise but frowned at love, and
gradually the troubadour's passion cooled into artistic
sentiment.

　　And so I choose
　To love her, since 't is she
　That worth and reputation gives to me. [9]

　The love that had cooled, finally grew cold.　As one of
his poems indicates, Peire's wooing came to appear
Quixotic even to himself.　He went again from Toulouse,
lived for a time with Count Guilhem and very likely with
Arnaut de Maruelh at Montpellier ; and then, fixing his
residence at Pamiers, thirty or forty miles from Toulouse,
he married, abandoned poetry, and settled down for the
rest of his days. [10]

" At Pamiers,—dull, dingy, dirty, disconsolate Pamiers," I repeated to myself over and over as I roamed
about the streets there, searching for something to interest
me.

One such thing I found. Raimon Rogier, who defied
Simon de Montfort at Foix, had a castle in Pamiers ; and
the site of it, still known as the *Castellat*, is a delightful
spot. As I sat there under the blooming horse-chestnut
trees the whole town lay spread out before me. Yonder
were battlemented towers,—the church of Notre Dame du
Camp. Close at hand rose the lofty nave of the cathedral, rebuilt by one whose name is proclaimed from the
housetops,—Mansard. Behind me lay the broad sweep of
the Ariège, coming down from the mountains and flowing
slowly on across the wide meadows toward Toulouse ;
while far to the south yet still grand stood the hazy summits of the Pyrenees. But the rest of the place—I said
to myself—if it looked in the days of Peire Raimon as it
looks now, I can understand why he came here to forswear letters, marry, and prepare for death,—in dull,
dingy, dirty, disconsolate Pamiers.

The other famous troubadour of Toulouse, Aimeric de
Peguilha,[1] illustrates once more the natural aristocracy
of talent and its recognition in that age ; for though only
the son of a draper, he was received at the palace and permitted to address poems to the countess, a daughter of
Amfos, the king of Aragon. It was not she, however,
that awoke his love and his talent, but a lady of his own
burgher class, who resided near him in Toulouse.

Aimeric was no sentimentalist like Peire Raimon, and
the energy of his love brought him both success and misfortune. " Too much talking causes many troubles," he
once remarked, and perhaps in his youth he was indiscreet himself. Anyhow the lady's husband, learning of
the affair, personally chastised the poet, and then Aimeric

avenged himself by wounding his enemy in the head.
The blow was dangerous,—possibly fatal, and the young
gallant found himself compelled to flee.[12]

PAMIERS, FROM THE CASTELLAT.

Spain was the refuge to which he naturally turned, for
though Aimeric was perhaps ten or fifteen years later than
Peire Raimon, Amfos the poet-king was reigning still in
Aragon and Catalonia. On the way, however, he fell in
with Guilhem de Berguedan, and apparently won that
ruffian's heart by an account of his exploit. Guil-

hem entertained him royally, and in return for a song
of praise gave him clothes and even his own horse.
Then the two crossed swords amicably in a tenso, and we
begin to have a better opinion of our hero; for while
Guilhem avowed it his purpose to win success through
play and the favor of women, his guest maintained that
sincere love was better than scheming gallantry. For
" no man who does not love has joy and honor ; and, as
culture is preferable to barbarism, so is the man that loves
better than he that never gives but only gets."

By Guilhem's advice Aimeric presented himself at the
court of Castile [13] instead of Aragon, and through his influence was kindly received. In a little while his talents
made him a favorite. Many a lady seems to have smiled
upon him, and that alone was enough to make the
stranger feel rich, for he once declared, " I lack for nothing since I lack not for love " ; but this was by no
means the whole of his good fortune. The old king delighted so much in the poet's company that he armed and
enriched him, and conferred upon him a kind of nobility
by giving him a place in his retinue. Advanced in rank,
famous as a troubadour, admired, loved, and enriched, the
outcast draper found the southern slope of the Pyrenees
as sunny as the northern had been cold.

For one reason or another he transferred himself, however, to Italy. [14] Bonifaz had left Monferrat and perhaps
had already met his fate among the Bulgarian mountains
(1207), but his successor, Guilhem IV., continued the
liberal traditions of the family Another patron was
found in a nephew of our dashing Albert de Malaspina,
who, as the poet comprehensively observed, " maintained
liberality, gallantry, courtesy, and me " [15] Nor were these
his only or his greatest friends A comfortable walk
from Petrarch's house at Arqua brings one to a spacious
piazza, surrounded with broken arcades and guarded by a

tower. This is Este, perhaps the most famous of names
among the aristocracy of Europe. Queen Victoria bears
it ; and in fact Alberto Azzo, marquis of Este, figures as
an ancestor in most of the royal
houses. No less distinguished
is the family among men of talent, and almost every famous
Italian down to Ariosto sat at
their table. Azzo VI. gained a
share in the sovereignty of Verona ; and, at about the time of
Peguilha's advent, a street-fight
in Ferrara (1208) delivered that
city into the control of his family
for substantially four hundred
years. In both of these towns,
and no doubt at Este itself, the
troubadour had a distinguished
place in the ruler's esteem ; and
finally, still hostile to the
Church that had ravaged his native city, he died on foreign soil.

AT ESTE.

   Aimeric's beginning in life
was a stormy one ; but his character was serious, and his
thoughtful mind had perhaps a
tinge of melancholy. "It is
better 'to gain in silver than
to lose in gold," expressed the lesson of his experience ; but not the only lesson, for at another time he
sang : "He does but little that helps the exalted, but he
that lifts up and supports the humble gains friends, God,
and fame." Though he won success in love his natural
attractions appear to have been slender, and a poor voice
marred the effect when he sang. Doubtless in youth his

figure was elegant, but with time he grew thin and lame ;
and his face, always of a serious cast, became so mournful
—if we believe his enemy Sordel [16]—that the mere sight
of it made one think of death. Worse yet he was prudent, and in that age prudence was a vice of such abhor-
rent mien that Aimeric was often called avaricious ; and
it was a bitter squib upon this trait of his which set the
poets to belaboring one another with rhymes in that
famous quarrel at Florence. Even love was not always
gentle with him, for he sang :

> No man can tell what joy is or what pain,
> Till o'er his life hath Love begun to reign ;

and finally, overcome by all the sadness of human existence, he exclaimed : " O false and evil world, oft is he
betrayed that leans upon you ! "

This quality of thoughtfulness marks his poetry, and
gives it an intellectual grace that charms us. " Never
did I find one who could bind so fast with so slight a
bond ! "—how different is that from the cry of naïve and
almost brutal passion ! Such a poet was fitted to write
elegies, and we have several fine poems of this kind from
Peguilha. [17] Felicitous and well-wrought comparisons
please the taste of minds like his, and these we find in
plenty yet not in superabundance. The same intellectual
bias controlled the form of his verse ; and while he could
match any one in the technical mastery of his art, he evidently preferred simplicity. Yet it was not the unconscious simplicity of the fathers, but the finish of a true
literary artist ; and in a word we feel ourselves listening,
when he sings, to one far nearer to our own day than we
expected to find.

> As when a tree too rich a harvest bears
> It only breaks and loses fruit and all,

Excess of love has brought about my fall
　　I lose my heart and her for whom it cares ;
　　　　Yet though 't is I who compass my defeat,
　　　　　　I did not mean to cause myself this ill ;
　　　　　　I thought I worked with shrewdness and with skill,
　　　　But now I see that madness guides my feet.

　　It is not well to be o'ermuch discreet,
　　　　And now and then one should obey his will ,
　　　　Judgment and liking, both, their places fill,—
　　Without the other each is incomplete ;
For too much prudence often makes a man
Against all rules of common sense rebel ,
And so it follows, all should temper well
　　Judgment with folly, who in measure can.

　　But woe is me, for 't is in vain I plan
To rule myself; my thoughts forever dwell
On ways to fail ; nor, lady, can I tell
　　How much I 'd rather fall beneath your ban
　　　　Than win elsewhere ; a joy I count this woe,
　　　　　　This madness wisdom, and this ruin gain ;
　　　　　　For I am e'er, like fond and foolish swain,
　　　　The more your slave, the more you prove my foe.

　　　　There is no "Yes " for which I 'd give your " No,"
　　　　　　Though joy oft fails and only tears remain ;
　　　　　　And I find pleasure, like a fool, in pain,
　　　　And e'en in death, such loveliness you show ;
　　Against the mirror basilisks will fly,
And kill themselves in blissful ecstasy ;
Just such a mirror you know how to be,
　　And so I perish when I meet your eye.

　　You do not care although you see me die ;
And nurses treat a babe as you treat me ;
A golden coin is given the child in fee
　　To check its weeping and to still its cry,
　　　　But when delight has made it laugh once more,
　　　　　　The precious gift is taken away again ;
　　　　　　Again it weeps, and makes an outcry then
　　　　With twice the anguish that it felt before.[18]

Vidal, Raimon, and Peguilha were all subjects by birth
of Raimon the Fifth,[19] and after " the good count " was
succeeded (1194) by his son, the sixth Raimon, brother to
the countess of Burlatz, no more poets like them went out
from the capital of Languedoc.   Wealth and culture did
not decline there, however, and in fact the next few years
were the culmination of their city

Though we speak of Toulouse as a county or earldom,
it was at that period almost a kingdom.   Its count was
also called the duke of Narbonne and the marquis of Provence, and his vassalage to the French crown seemed only
nominal.   To the west his territories embraced Agen and
projected a corner almost up to Castillion.   Northerly
they included Rodez and approached the viscounty of
Turenne.   By the way of Nismes and Alais they reached
the swift Rhone, and on the farther side they included
the region above the earldom of Provence, beginning at
Avignon and Cavaillon and extending beyond Valence
and Die [20]

In this period culminated also the poetry of the troubadours.   Raimon VI. was a poet himself, and showed his
love for the art with no less generosity and with still more
sympathy than his father   For half a generation (1194–
1209) his palace was thronged with poets,[21] and for one of
them, as we shall find, he entertained an almost brotherly
affection.   So deep was the hold of poetry that it served
the turn of hate as well as love.   Men struck with a poem
instead of a poniard.   " I will make a song about you,"
was the direst threat, and so accomplished was almost
everybody in the art that the execution tarried not long
on the menace.

Then came the bad years, the time of the Albigensian
wars and massacres, and still a troubadour was heard in
Toulouse.   How strange a song was in his mouth, and
how marvellous a destiny turned the gay boon companion

of the father into a fanatical bishop, the persecutor of the
son ! But Folquet has not received his cue yet ; he only
crosses our little stage now, beckoning us on,—we shall
follow soon.

During the remainder of the thirteenth century, the art
of the troubadours retained a smouldering vitality in Toulouse, bursting out now and then into bright but feeble

TOULOUSE.

jets, and early in the fourteenth it assumed a new phase.
As the minnesingers were succeeded by the meistersingers
in Germany, the burghers of Toulouse took up the cult no
longer maintained by her nobles. In 1323, while a boy
whom his mother called Giovanni and the world calls
Boccaccio was kicking up his lively heels, a group of versi-
fiers formed the Very-Gay Company of the Seven Poets of
Toulouse, and gathered to talk of poetry in a garden just
outside the city walls. On the 23d of November in that
year, nine years after Bruce routed the English at Ban-

nockburn, these poets issued a call " to the nobles, lords, friends, and comrades, familiar with the science that gives birth to joy, pleasure, good sense, worth, and courtesy," and invited all the poets to meet the following May under the shady trees of their garden—" marvellous and beautiful "

So was founded the *Collège du Gay Sçavoir*" . and this institution, with occasional suspensions and changes of name, has now lived nearly six hundred years, while the seven poets have grown to an élite body of forty patrons (*Mainteneurs*)—the French Academy of the Midi—and the funds of the society from a poet's hope to a substantial endowment. Every May a poetic tournament is held in Toulouse under its auspices—the famous *Jeux Floraux*— and flowers of silver and gold are awarded as prizes for the best verse. It is the great event of the year in the Rosy City; and poetry, music, and eloquence, lovely faces and captivating smiles, keep alive and in honor still the art of the troubadours

An account of my arrest at Pamiers and of a celebration of the *Jeux Floraux* may be found at the end of the Notes on this Chapter.

XXI

MIRAVAL, BOISSEZON, CASTRES, AND MURET

Raimon de Miraval

YOU have not forgotten Loba de Puegnautier, I trust, and the towers of Cabaret, where she lived.

Pursue the gorge some three miles farther, and you will find it widening for a space. The road crosses a little stream and passes a ruinous church. Below the bridge— a single arch of stone—there is a bit of New England meadow. The fresh, cool sward exhibits the same free mingling of native grasses that we find at home. The homely "butter-and-eggs" of our own brooksides welcomes us. Dandelions and buttercups are there, too, with clover in the sunny spots, and forget-me-nots in the dimples ; while one of our own red squirrels, skirmishing behind a tree, challenges us to a game of hide-and-seek.

Above the bridge the clear and tuneful stream ripples against the foundations of the church.

What a touching picture are these broken walls in the midst of the vale ! No English church at Yuletide begins to be so luxuriantly dressed. Sheets of ivy envelop the masonry , thick volumes of shrubbery fill the interior ; evergreens throng the windows ; light bushes crown the ledges and top the walls.

The ministration still goes on. Birds now sing the matins and the vespers. Young fir-trees, the comeliest of acolytes, now swing perfumed censers in the wind. The flower that fadeth preaches from chancel and from porch. A myriad leaves raise prayerful faces to the sky. The stars of night bestow a benediction of unbroken peace ; and all the while, beneath her vesture of leafy green, the earth is reaching up and silently drawing back to herself the stones once given for the use and good of mankind, as an arm clothed in white samite rose above the lake and received Excalibur

Such a spot is an excellent introduction—*lucus a non lucendo*—to the famous troubadour whose birthplace and home it was, for nothing could be more unlike him

There was little to approve in Raimon de Miraval, a good deal to be amused by, and something to admire. He was not really handsome, but somehow he got that reputation, and nobody cared to throw doubt on his own good taste by asserting the contrary. He was not actually witty ; but everybody was ready-primed with a laugh at his sallies, and whoever crossed swords with him was pretty sure of an audacious pinking in the ribs, with a plenty of salt from the bystanders rubbed into the hurt. There was always a suggestion of gun-cotton about his love—much flare and little heat—as the woman he most cared to please was very likely to reflect on the morrow ; but when the hall was filled and the lamps were all alight, when the throng was gay and the wit lively, when the tinkle of music was heard and the dance began, then brave knights and serious troubadours found themselves distinctly outshone, and the lithe and slender Miraval—trim, clever, graceful, and piquantly devil-may-care—was for an hour the lord of the realm.' Light of head, light of heart, light of foot, a sweet singer, a skilful poet, an artist in flattery and courtly banter, he could capture a lady's fancy without half trying—to half try was, in fact, his ablest rôle—and many more hearts were offered him than he could possibly provide for.

AT MIRAVALS.

In truth gallantry was his instinct. Serious he could
be and " blue " he was,—not seldom ; but no matter how
desperate his affairs or how dry the ashes in his latest
intrigue, a pretty woman—whether he cared a farthing
about her or not—would set his mind cavorting in a flash.
Sober thoughts fled ; his chin went up in the air, his
elbows took on a lively angle, and off he would step on
the last points of his dainty toes, as merry and impudent
as a bobolink on a sweet-briar in mating time

He was not rich, for he inherited only a quarter-interest
in the modest fief of Miraval and its population of less
than forty men, and the terrible Monk of Montaudon
twitted him with always being away from home on the
first of the month, when it was the custom for lords to
entertain their people. But he cared little that his patrimony was small, for the great world pleased him and he
studied to please the world. " Have an equal share of wisdom and folly," he sang ; " too much wisdom stands in
the way of getting on." None of your blunt honest fools
was he, and he made no pretence of being. " I would
rather utter a bit of courtly bluster than a stupid truth,"
he admitted. Nor was this his only reason for taking care
to be agreeable, as we learn from himself ·

> For men of worth who cannot please
> Must bear unsolaced love's disease.[2]

So he discovered very early in his career , and—merry,
light-hearted, easy man of the world that he delighted to
be—he found misery of any kind not at all to his liking

Still he was at bottom a good fellow, thoroughly club-
bable—cordial, good-natured, witty, and of " good immoral character "—and that was the sort he liked :

> I would ever meet at court
> Him that wears a genial heart. [3]

What he possessed he gave willingly,—verses and instruction in composing and singing them When winter,
which the painters figured as a butcher, had killed the joy
of nature, it was the custom of the troubadours to repose
from the season past and prepare for the season to come
Amanieu de Sescas has given us a picture of this interlude
in their existence · " When hail and frost cover the earth
and cause man and beast to shelter themselves from the
cold, I am sitting in the house with my pages, singing of
love, of joy, of arms The warm fire burns brightly, the
floors are well covered with rugs, and wines—white and red
—are on the table " So we may picture Miraval between
the hearth and the tankard in his quiet castle, not only
composing new pieces, but teaching Bayonna and other
joglars a repertory of unpublished songs And we may
be sure, too, that his instruction was excellent, for Vidal
once advised a joglar to heed " the lessons of Sir Miraval." ·

In like manner he was not unwilling to receive, and
never suffered for lack of recognition Raimon VI of
Toulouse, the brother-in-law of Richard the Lion-hearted,
befriended the young poet, equipped him handsomely,
and even became his intimate friend They called each
other by a pet name, · and it was Damon and Pythias over
again. The poet gave lessons in making verses, and the
count gave lessons in playing chess, for he was extremely
fond of the game ; and then they went hunting and visiting together, and advised each other, no doubt, in their
love affairs. Neither was the poet a mere protégé of the
prince , he was apparently the shrewder of the two, and
according to the biography had a great influence over the
count as well as over other lords of the time.

His works—we have more than forty pieces—do not stir
us. He believed that he sang most feelingly, and once
boasted ·

> In my heart is born the flame
> That issues through my lips in singing. [6]

But we form an opinion of our own on this point when we
find him singing like this :

> Fair summer gives me stores of pleasure,
> I 'm pleased with every bird that sings,
> The leafy boughs are pleasant things,
>   By verdant fields I 'm pleased past measure ;
> Far greater pleasure from your beauty springs ;
> To do your will another pleasure brings ;
> But you are pleased all favor to disdain ;
> It gives you pleasure that by love I 'm slain [7]

Still he was no doubt a clever versifier. One of his fellow troubadours went so far as to prefer his love-songs to
any others. Were he alive to-day he would turn off excellent vers-de-société, and the magazines would be glad
to take a moderate quantity of his lines at current rates.
Certainly credit is due him for opposing Arnaut Daniel's
theory that verse ought to be caviare to the vulgar, and
one of his stanzas well deserves to be remembered :

> Obscure, harsh verses ought
> To fail and count for naught
>   (They 're only made for selling)
> Against sweet music fraught
> With grace, like this I 've wrought,—
>   The memory compelling
> With fine, clear words, drawn taut ;
>   For what is hard in telling
>   But sets the mind rebelling [8]

But the poet Miraval is less interesting than the man ;
let us return to him.

As I suggested a while ago, hearts were offered him in
plenty. They were,—they must have been ; ask any of
our popular tenors who is on pleasure bent, or even but

slightly inclined ; and therefore it is not surprising to find
the poet extremely vain of his accomplishments in gallantry.   None the less, like all troubadours, the dispensers of
fame, he was liable to be offered a semblance of affection by
ladies who cherished no idea of caring for him.   In fact,
says the biography, " no lady thought herself in good
social standing unless Raimon de Miraval was her friend,"
and there was no one " who did not desire and scheme to
have him fall in love with her,"—not for the sake of his
love, but because no one else could so " honor and grace "
a lady

His first experience of the sort was near home,—in fact
at Cabaret , and the lady was that very Loba⁹ for whom
our eccentric Peire donned the wolf-skin.

Nobody understood better than she the advantages of
having a troubadour in leash.   With many a smile she
accepted all Raimon's compliments, as she did Vidal's,
sighed and blushed at the proper intervals, and finally
gave him a kiss.   But there she drew the line   For two
years and five months she held him where she wished
In songs, in stories now lost, and no doubt in conversation, he spread her fame abroad, and as she herself confessed did more than her own charms to win her " honor
and reputation, friends of both sexes, fame, and praise,"
and not only these but " courtliness and accomplishments "   Naturally he looked for his reward

Suddenly the world was astonished one day to hear that
she was involved in a great scandal with the count of
Foix, a worthy gentleman who had been crusading in the
Holy Land and piously carried home a boxful of sainted
bones,—in fact the very Raimon Rogier who so bravely
drove Simon de Montfort and his army away from Foix.

It was very unfortunate for Loba.   By the ethics of the
time a lady could go pretty far at a pinch with a simple
baron or even with a poet ¹⁰   As Montagnagout expressed

it, " A lady may without the least discredit choose a single
true lover, her equal in rank or a little above her, yet she
does no wrong if she choose one beneath her if she find
merit in him,—provided only there be no insincerity ";
but the rule of society barred explicitly any intrigue with
a great lord. Precisely why is nowhere explained, but
we can imagine a reason. It was perhaps assumed that
great lords were seriously occupied with affairs of state,
and cared for gallantry only as an amusement ; so, as
courtly love required true sincerity and faithfulness and
they were not likely to exist on the part of such a nobleman, the lady who accepted his attentions was looked
upon as only the instrument of his pleasure.

Whatever the explanation, the fact is certain; and when
Raimon Rogier was discovered to be her successful lover,
the fair Loba fell instantly into disgrace. All the neighboring ladies raised their hands to heaven. Her suitors
and admirers fell away, for honor was so essential an
element of courtly love that if a lady were careless of it
her lover was expected to sever the bond. Vidal's malicious tongue shot against her a biting song ; and, so far
as polite society was concerned, she was in fact, as the
biography says, " dead."

The situation of Miraval was little better than her own.
For years he had been going up and down the land celebrating her beauty and her virtues, her partiality for him
and his devotion to her ; and now he found himself ridi-
culed no less than she was blamed

I am sorry to tell what the poet did. Bartsch has called
him the knightliest of the troubadours, but this one incident refutes the praise if more than courtly manners are
implied. " A villain must be beaten with a villainy," he
sang once ; and now, resolving to apply the principle, he
checked his impulse to say hard things like the rest, and
set himself to fighting the tale with all his wit and energy.

Melted to tears by the devotion of her one champion, Loba
confessed that she had been ungrateful, and hastened to
reward him with the love he had craved.   This was what
the poet anticipated ; and merely lingering to pluck the
fruit of his triumph he dropped the poor lady without
ceremony to resume another quest, remarking that he
had only paid her back in her own coin.[11]

Next we find our hero singing the wife of Bernart de
Boissezon

There is always a compensation if we look for it, says
the philosopher   Too often, perhaps, the compensation is
merely the occupation of looking, but Boissezon supports
the principle.   It is only a ragged village on the eaves of
the mountain, about twice as far to the southeast of
Castres as Burlatz lies to the northeast.   It is rough and
ledgy ; its hours of sunshine are too few ; and it has to
cling with all its might and main to the great rocks of a
shivering ravine.   But the compensation exists, and its
name is Bridges   Little bridges, big bridges (pretty big,
I mean), high bridges, low bridges, old bridges, new
bridges, foot-bridges, *tout-le-monde* bridges,—they are all
here, they all delight, and some of them astonish.   On
the farther side of them is another compensation, a fascinating church that has added many cubits to its stature
by climbing to the crest of the hill.   A singular church it
seems, for it possesses a little tower more appropriate for
a castle ; and yet there is no singularity after all, for the
tower did belong to a castle once.   Just where the slender
congregation worships of a Sunday now, there stood in
the days of Miraval one bastion of an impregnable fortress,
and the lord of the fortress was Bernart de Boissezon.[12]

But it does not matter so very much about Boissezon
after all, for Bernart preferred to live elsewhere.   Midway
between Castres and Albi was Lombers and the castle of
Lombers must have been a very cool and pleasant home,

BOISSEZON.

built as it was on the top of a lofty *pic* with a river winding around below, and the cool breezes coming over from
the hills.   The site is there still, but the castle has utterly vanished.   When Plymouth colony was two years
old (1622) the flames made an end of it, and even the
foundation walls have disappeared.   And yet there is a
remnant   not a little tower as at Boissezon, but exactly
the reverse ; for as I tramped about in the grass on the
very top of the *pic*, I nearly fell through the mouth of a
cavity.   Donjon and battlements have crumbled and
melted, but the cistern still exists.   Verily " the meek
shall inherit the earth."

Just about (1193) the time when the long reign of Ermengarda and the long courtship of Arnaut de Maruelh
came to an end, the first baron of Lombers ceded his title
and his castle to Bernart de Boissezon, and hither came
Bernart and the beautiful Alazais his wife.   Hither came
Raimon de Miraval, too.   Hither he came, and here he
lingered, for after a long search he had found the lady
of his dreams, as true as she was lovely and as lovely as
she was true.

Alazais for her part was no less pleased with the troubadour, for what is beauty unless it be praised ?   Besides
that, she could see a horizon still beyond him.   King
Amfos of Aragon, the great connoisseur of beauty, was
no more, but his son Peire II. sat upon his throne and
was said to inherit his good taste as well.   Should he declare her beautiful, then were she beautiful indeed, and
all the other ladies must concede it.   And then, too, if
love were in question,—would not he be a lover worth
while, if—if only—; well, who knew ?

" Only bring him here, Raimon ; do but so much more
to please me——"

The poet meditated.   " Yes, that is the thing to do.
She will be grateful and satisfied, and he will help me

in return for winning him the friendship of so agreeable
a lady."

So, as the biography informs us, he praised the baroness
to the king, until Peire sent her a costly present. Then
he extolled her more, and Peire burned for a visit at her
castle. Miraval secured the invitation, wrote him a poem
of good wishes, and went along with him as guide.

LOMBERS.

As he rode into the courtyard at Lombers behind the
king, he said, " I trust, Lord Peire, that you will not forget about speaking a good word for me."

" Have no fear, my Raimon," answered Peire, rolling
his big fine head, and throwing a glance over his shoulder.
" Count on me."

The next morning our troubadour crept out at the gate
and galloped furiously down the hill,—never to return ;
while Peire and Alazais, their friends, their followers, and
even their servants laughed loud and long at the poor
simpleton of a poet.[13]

We may well believe that Miraval had several quarters of an hour with himself after this mishap, and we know that he complained bitterly ; but in the end he began to reflect. The question was what to do, and from sayings of his own we can imagine how the case was argued. Should he keep on storming ? Folly ; "We never pay heed to the choleric man." Should he forswear the ladies altogether ? Ah, no ; "One who has nothing to do with love can hardly be bold and valiant." Should he turn cynic? "Because a little lady has deceived me shall I become a common grumbler ? No." What then ? "Take the gold and leave the brass." Nothing could be more sensible, and now we shall hope that Miraval has found the path to felicity.

THE OLD TOWER, CASTRES.

Midway between the one bridge of Burlatz and the many bridges of Boissezon lies Castres," and after dashing through the place right and left as we have done we are now to sojourn there a while. We shall not be sorry.

The Roman camp near which the place grew up around an abbey before the middle of the seventh century survives only in the name of the city ; but there are two things to connect the present with the times of Miraval.

One is a large square tower which has done service with equally stolid good nature for an abbey, a bishop's palace,

and a city hall, and now displays above a disreputable tin
tricolor the cross of ancient days, like a sceptical old age
going to church from force of early habit   Like this
same old fellow, stiff of spine and stiff of collar, the tower
could rehearse many strange tales of its earlier days, and
among others, if local tradition may be trusted, could tell
how a Spanish prince was brought here as a captive, fettered to rings that we see in the wall, and finally burned
alive after the prescription of the count of Foix.

Very different are the suggestions of the river that flows
not far away through the midst of the town,—very different and very delightful; for is it not the beautiful Agout,
just come from singing under the windows of Alazais, the
lovely countess of Burlatz ?   It is, indeed ; and it seems
to have brought with it countless reminiscences of romance
and fancy, converted them into visible poetry, and piled
them high on both its banks.   Delightful old houses,
elbowing to get nearer, line it on either side.   The roofs
against the sky would instruct an artist in the power of
the line, if they did not make him forget his trade entirely.
Tiles, windows, arches, brackets, doors, and boats, they
all chime well with each other, well with the bridges, well
with the ivy clambering along the mellowed walls, and
well with the brown gossips beating and rinsing their
clothes at the washing-place, or dreamily hanging them
up beneath tall willows that bend far out above the
stream.

" Who does not hunt is slow to find the game," ran the
proverb, but sometimes the game undertakes to hunt,—a
suspicious procedure !   In Castres lived Ermengarda,
" the fair Albigensian."   She was a particular friend of
Lady Alazais of Boissezon, and on learning what had
occurred at Lombers, invited Miraval to come and see her
A right good visit, no doubt, the poet had   Good-by to
brass ; hurrah for gold !   With sympathy and good cheer

Ermengarda brushed away the clouds from the poet's firmament, and once more he found himself gay and happy. Many a time the old tower saw them passing by with merry company for the hunt, falcon at wrist and endless pleasantries on the tongue. And when the pair were back again in the castle hall—we know how it was then from the poet's lines :

> It is song and lively talk .
> That make love spring up and flourish.[8]

Love grew indeed, and when the troubadour spoke out, Ermengarda answered, " Divorce your wife, and I will gladly marry you," for her husband, a man advanced in years, had gone to a better land, leaving a great deal of wealth behind. " Whate'er one does for love is comely," sang Miraval, and upon that he set out for home.[1a]

Now his wife made verses, too ; and she, too, was in love, though her husband was not aware of it. " Gaudairenca," said he, " one poet is enough in a family; send for your friends, and let them take you to your father " For while Canon Law insisted upon regarding marriage as a sacrament, Roman usage had looked upon it as a contract which either husband or wife could annul at pleasure, and I suppose that we see here another bit of paganism lingering on in spite of Christianity.

The wife appeared very sad, but privately she sent word to her lover to come and take her home if he desired to marry her, and he came with a retinue. Then Gaudairenca said, " My friends have come, and I will go home with them." But when she was out of the castle she asked Miraval to give her away to Guilhem Bremon as his wife. And Miraval did it with right good cheer, and galloped back forthwith to Castres

" You have done well," said Ermengarda " Now re-

turn and prepare for a grand wedding, and then come
for me.''

You remember Saissac and the story of the castle, I
hope. Ermengarda was in love with Olivier de Saissac,

THE AGOUT AT CASTRES.

and when the troubadour left her she sent for Olivier,
went that very night to his castle, and married him the
next day.

This blow nearly finished our hero ; and for two years
he was in a desperate state, a lonely, wretched man, and
the laughing-stock of the world. Nor was this the whole

of it. In repudiating his wife on the ground that she made verses, Miraval had struck at the foundation of literary culture and polite society. His course was reprobated on all sides, and several of his fellow poets denounced him in vigorous measures.[16]

Finally another lady desirous of praise and fame addressed herself to the stricken poet, and curiously enough she was Loba's partner in the ladyship of castle Cabaret, for their two husbands, as we suppose, were brothers and shared the fief.[17] With urgent words of cheer and affection Brunessen sent notice that she would go to Miraval if he would not come to her. Her warmth kindled his heart once more, and he began to sing again.

But his days of love and song were over, for the storm of the Albigensian crusade burst upon the gay Midi, and the tempest invaded even the rugged valley of the Orbiel. Simon de Montfort and his cruel soldiers appeared at Castres. Two heretics had been found, but one was repentant. "Burn them both," cried Simon; "if this fellow is deceiving us, he deserves it more than the other, if not, his present sufferings will shorten his stay in purgatory." They appeared at Cabaret, and though once repulsed they dismayed the garrison, as we saw, with a deputation of eyeless men, and soon were masters of the place. They appeared at Miraval, and the poet's castle fell into the maw of the crusade.

The poor troubadour was inconsolable for his loss His interest in the castle would not have brought much at a sale, but after all the place was a home. Besides, it was dear for other reasons. Even today a singer can conjure mightily with small but distant estates, and Miraval's little patrimony stood him in good stead. As the wicked Monk informs us, Raimon was accustomed to go through the form of bestowing the castle upon each new mistress of his heart, and it is easy to believe that his grand air on

such occasions was not without effect.   Perhaps he succeeded, too, in making the property look as big to himself
as to others ; but anyhow it was all he had, and now it
was gone.

One resource remained   " The soul of the Midi fled for
refuge to Toulouse," as Mistral sings.   There was the
skilful Frotart Peire " of courtly bearing "; good Rogier
Bernart, " who gave heart again to the fallen ", Arnaut
de Vilamur, " a powerful and valiant man, one who knew
well how to promise and how to give ", good Amalvis, who
" knew how to give and to fight "; Chatbert, " well able to
defend himself", Arnaut de Cumenge, " the good and
handsome, the genial, valiant and sage, generous and vic-
torious," and many others hardly less distinguished."
With special reason Miraval betook himself there, for the
count was his friend still and promised the recovery of his
castle.   But the count himself was in the direst of straits
Not merely a castle but a vast earldom was his to lose,
and Simon was rapidly tearing it from his grasp   So
everything was dark and gloomy both for count and for
poet.

At last the day broke.   King Peire of Aragon was
greatly distressed by the course of the crusade.   He had
passed much of his time among the people now so wretched,
portions of the ravaged territory paid homage to him ;
the countess of Toulouse was his sister, and his wife was
the daughter of Guilhem VIII. of Montpellier and the
widow of jolly Barral of Marseille   All his associations
and sympathies drew him to the cause of the Midi, and
policy as well, no doubt.

Peire, though a gallant, was not a carpet knight.   His
triumph at Lombers was not more signal than his victories
over the Moor, and when he decided—though an ardent
son of the Church—to march against the crusaders, the
result seemed beyond all doubt.   Raimon de Miraval had

resolved never to sing again until his castle should be his once more ; but the king's promise to recover it for him was considered equal to a certainty, and he broke forth at once into a song of joy and exultation.

Twenty-two miles to the southwest of Toulouse is the little village of Muret. The ancient castle has disappeared, but the wide plain is there as of old. A scene more peaceful, more undistinguished, more unconscious,

LOOKING TOWARD THE BATTLEFIELD, MURET.

it would be hard to find. Humble crops engross the fields. A vineyard is here, a line of poplars there. Now and then you pass a farmhouse with lilacs by the window, and a clump of chilly cypresses at the well. Beside the road are poppies and buttercups, cornflowers and marguerites. An old cottager is mowing. As you accost him he rests upon his scythe a moment, ponders, and replies indifferently: " A great battle, monsieur ? Then it

must have been before my time and my father's, for I
never heard of it, monsieur." [19]

But history is better informed than our peasant, and we
know that two hostile armies met on this plain on the 12th
of September, 1213. One was led by Peire, the king of
Aragon, a man of heroic stature and striking beauty, an
accomplished knight,—powerful, bold, and fearless, a just
ruler, a rich and famous monarch, an adept in all the culture of the day, generous, brilliant, and magnificent, the
dream of ladies, the text of poetry, and the beau ideal of
romance.[20] The other was commanded by Simon de
Montfort, dark and terrible. On the one side were husbands, fathers, and lovers, on the other—few but desperate
—were adventurers, mercenaries, and fanatics These
were to fight for their property and their lives, for their
homes and their freedom, for their wives and children,
their friendships and their loves, for their poetry, for
their civilization, for their language, for their race ; those
for the love of adventure, for the hope of plunder, for delight in riot, for a Church of statecraft, for a gospel of
cruelty, for hate, for destruction, for the Inquisition, the
dungeon, and the stake

Such were the armies and such was the cause. Bravery
did not fail on either side, but the heart of the king was
too light, and his courage too confident. The stern discipline of the North broke through his host and bore it
down. The battle was soon lost, the bravest fell, the king
was left dead and naked on the sod, the army scattered,
and the cause was doomed. The North triumphed, and
the Midi became a conquered province [21]

Raimon de Miraval was doubtless at Muret among the
knights of Toulouse. It is written that the tide of fugi-
tives swept him beyond the Pyrenees and that he died in
Lerida, far from his quiet vale. Perhaps he returned to
France instead, or possibly he never went to Spain. We

cannot know, and really it does not matter. Whatever became of the man, the gay, careless troubadour was no more. His life was broken and shattered in the roar and tumult of that frightful overthrow, like a shallop of Neapolitan merrymakers caught up in a whirlwind and crushed upon the cliffs of Ischia.

XXII

ALBI AND GAILLAC

The Albigensians

THE city that gave its name to one of the most awful religious crimes of history—how could the traveller enter it without emotion?

The swift river Tarn flows here through a valley—almost a gorge—and Albi confronts it boldly on the southern side.

Three bridges cross the stream. In spite of the grand impressiveness of the scene I could not help thinking of the three bears in the story ; and I called them the big bridge, the little bridge, and the middle-sized bridge

It would be better to say the new bridge, the old bridge, and the very old bridge. The very old bridge dates from about the year (1035) when great King Canute of England died, and to Americans this appears a very dignified antiquity; but the bridge is not proud, for above it in the city rises the fascinating Byzantine tower of St. Salvi, where the sentinel used to stand all night looking out for storms, fires, and the enemy , and this, we are told, was erected early in the days of the Venerable Bede, if not entirely before his time.

And it is not only that we find ancient things at Albi, —the Spirit of the Past is there. And the Spirit does not slumber,—how could it sleep in forgetfulness at Albi ? It walks abroad. It does not avoid but comes to meet us.

As the dusk of evening creeps from the mysterious arch-
ways it marches by our side.   Through the crooked streets
and past the mouldering portals it guides us ; and when,
traversing the wide and vacant square, we stand within
the shadow of the cathedral—it speaks.

Where can one go to find a cathedral so impressive ?

Among those who aided to complete it was the Cardinal
de Lorraine, a man so noted for generosity that one day
in Rome, when he gave a blind man alms, the beggar exclaimed, "You are the Christ or the Cardinal de Lorraine."

The edifice bears the impress of such a liberality.   The
silver shrine is rich beyond price.   The single nave is
covered with one immense vault of blue and gold, the
widest in Christendom except the one at Gerona,[1] where
long processions of kings and emperors, queens and ladies,
march slowly onward to the throne of judgment, conducted by angels and awaited by cherubim and seraphim.
In the choir a glorious company of apostles and saints
look down from above a hundred and twenty seats of
carved oak.   In the middle of the rood-loft hangs a silver
lamp ; and so perfect is the orientation of the edifice that
it catches a beam of sunlight at the summer and the winter
solstice, and flashes resplendently in the midst of the dark
chancel.   The rood-screen, pronounced by Viollet-le-Duc
" certainly the most vast, the most complete, the most
precious," seems to repeat the miracle of Sinai, when the
finger of God wrote the tables of the Law, for a peculiarly
unwilling stone has been made to take on the guise of
spontaneous life, its forms countless, its variety and capriciousness infinite, its intricacy past finding out, its delight and its harmony inexhaustible.

But these things and even the magnificence of the porch
are only details.   What we think of chiefly is the cathedral as a leonine unit, a unit of power, rising out of the
quaint mass of buildings grouped on the headland above

the river, parting the flood of sunlight by day, burning as red as blood in the flames of sunset,[2] or gathering about itself the mystery of night, always filling the city and seeming to dominate the country near and far

In a distant view there is a certain resemblance to English Ely, but the likeness is wholly superficial. Albi is unique; it stands for the Church Militant. Originally there were fortified outworks; these have been removed, and the old battlements frowning from a height of one hundred and twenty-five feet have been replaced with less menacing forms. But the tower stands unchanged. From the spring of its tremendous bulwarks, it is martial in every instinct and every fibre to the highest of its three hundred and thirty-six steps, and the lightest of its many turrets Supported by the archbishop's palace—a castle in look and meaning, with dungeons and keep in the midst and walls and towers for a circuit—it is a fortress, a Bastille.

It is more than that. Other churches, like the Three Marys, have been fortresses; this is a fortress not satisfied to defend. Bold, threatening, and aggressive, rooted on the very spot where the lords of Albi—the viscounts of massacred Béziers—had their castle, it seems to attack, to drive, to pursue, to trample. It seems and it is the embodiment of the Christianity that proclaimed a holy war upon the Albigensians, destroyed their cities, burned their bodies, and so far as it was able condemned their souls to the torments of eternal wrath.

What, then, were the Albigensians? Why were they sinners above all other men that they suffered such things? And how is it that in thinking of the troubadours we must also think of them ?

The last question is easy to answer. We must know something of the Albigensians to understand events we have already witnessed, still more, events just before us;

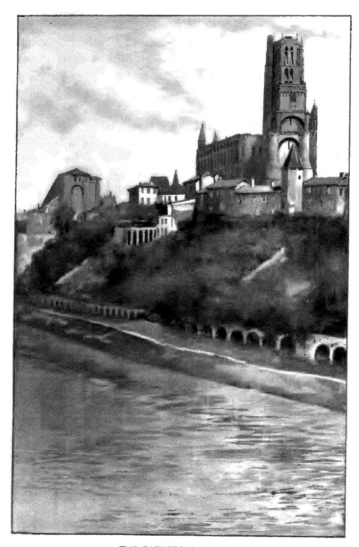

THE CATHEDRAL OF ALBI.

371

and, as we shall see, the bonds of society are so strict and the decress of fate so inscrutable, that the cultured troubadours and the austere reformers, caring little or nothing for one another, were in fact wings of the same army, and were overthrown by the same disaster.

What the Albigensians were, or—more exactly—what they believed, cannot positively be determined For reasons that will appear, their theories were doubtless considerably vague and considerably variant, and nearly all that we know of them comes to us from their inveterate enemies. They were accused of grotesque beliefs and outrageous immorality. Ridicule alternated with denunciation. The pale complexion resulting from their austerities was made a taunt, and the brutes themselves were extolled as more pious and more reasonable.

Even Etienne de Bourbon,[1] the Inquisitor, took delight in such hits. " One day," as he enjoyed telling, " a joglar of the true faith meeting a heretic said to him : ' Hark ye, fellow ; my nag is a better Christian than you are, and I will prove it. You drink no wine : neither does he You eat no meat : no more does he,—*he* does n't even eat bread. You are badly lodged · he is worse And these sufferings must count more in his favor than in yours, for you do not believe and even you deny the articles of faith. Now, since without faith nothing is pleasing to God, nothing that you do can please him. My nag, on the contrary, though he does not believe, does not oppose the faith nor deny the truth. So you see, he has the advantage of you, both as to faith and as to works.' "

So far as the charges of immorality are concerned, they seem not only untrue, but the opposite of true ; for the heretics erred by an excess of austerity, of self-abnegation, of all the virtues of suffering On this point we have a plenty of evidence and one testimony that is actually

startling. Just at the time when the heretics were most
active, only six years before the slaughter began, one
Dominic Guzman went among them   He met the three
papal legates returning discomfited from their discussions
with the " good men "—for so the sect were called—but
in spite of that wearing the pomp of a proud triumph.
He rebuked the legates, and told them it was not by
splendid retinues and costly garb that the heretics won
their converts, but " by zealous preaching, by humility,
by austerity, and by at least seeming holiness." Now
this Guzman was no other than the founder of the great
Dominican Order, St. Dominic himself, the inventor of
the Inquisition.

The charge of doctrinal errors had more to stand upon
The creed of the " good men " seems to have emanated
from the Græco-Slav convents of the Danube valley, and
there to have taken on a color from those Manichæan
ideas which found such ready acceptance in the Byzantine
Empire.   Spreading westward it appeared in several
quarters under several names.   The essential feature was
an absolute distinction between the world of spirit and the
world of matter, and a belief that while God created the
spiritual and good beings, the material and bad were
created by his eternal enemy, Satan   Man, they held, was
originally pure spirit, a creature of God , but Satan seduced him, transported him to his present abode, gave
him a material body, and fettered him to the earth by the
bonds of sex and of property. Jesus Christ, who was the
Holy Spirit, apparently made man, taught the way in
which men could free themselves from slavery to Satan
and rise again to heaven   viz , to renounce all material
things and be wholly consecrated to the spiritual   The
Old Testament was looked upon as entirely superseded
by the New.   Marriage was regarded as at best an inferior
state, no way permissible to the " good men."   Some at

least believed in a form of metempsychosis, and it was held that all souls created by God would sooner or later find their way to him. In certain particulars the " good men " were clearly forerunners of Luther.'

As I have already said, we cannot speak positively of doctrinal details The original ideas were modified by contact with western Christianity, as we see in Italy, and no doubt were modified still more in France. As the right of individual interpretation of Scripture was admitted, many diversities of opinion were certain to arise. Again, there were two orders in their society, the adepts, or " good men," and the " believers "; only the former were expected to practise the severer austerities, and they of course carried their speculations farther than the mere " believers." And finally the Catholic misrepresentations add to our embarrassment.

At all events their doctrinal errors were not so terrible as to arouse the horror of the Church, for the Patarins of Milan were a branch of the same tree, and Gregory VII., the great Hildebrand, found the Patarins orthodox enough to be the allies of Rome.

Neither did the metaphysics of their creed count for so very much with the heretics. The plain Gospel was what they chiefly cared for, and the " good men " were as anxious to bring the Gospel within reach of the people as the Church was anxious to keep it away.* Thanks to their zeal the first translation of Scripture into any tongue of the modern world was made in the language of the troubadours,' and the rendering has no color of doctrinal bias More significant still, the Albigensian ritual has recently been published by Clédat, and what we find there is the simplest and most literal devotion to the Christian ideal of life. Not theory but conduct is emphasized. Those who desired to join the sect were addressed in these words : " Know that Christ has com-

manded men to commit no adultery, nor to steal nor to
lie, to take no oath, nor to do anything to another that
he would not have done to himself; that one pardon those
who injure him, and love his enemies, and that he pray
for his slanderers and bless them ; that if he be struck on
one cheek he offer the other , that if one take away his
tunic he give also his mantle ; that he judge not nor condemn ; and many other commandments enjoined upon
his Church by the Lord.''

How, then, were the '' good men '' so very bad ?   How
did the sheep of Hildebrand become the goats of Innocent ?

Come down with me to Gaillac, a few miles to the west
of Albi.   It is a town worth seeing for its own sake, once
a halting-place on the Roman road , but at present we are
studying religious questions.   Well, Peire Vidal came
here to sing and pay court, but the crusaders destroyed
the castle, and a few years ago the last relic, a well, was
filled up   Here is the old church, and beside it large remains of the abbey, founded as a monastery almost or
quite in the days of Charlemagne   Note the curious
doors and windows opening far above the river, but far
below the foundations !   Do you see that tower on the
water side, ending so abruptly ?   It was once much loftier.
Three hundred heretics, as the tradition of Gaillac runs,
were penned in the top, and then the top was pried off and
fell that horrible distance to the stream , the few wretches
not killed by the fall or engulfed in the stream were finished with spears and axes.   The city gate is no longer
to be seen, but an odor of sanctity clings to the site   In
the sixteenth century De Clairac, a Catholic soldier,
arrived at the gate with eleven Huguenot prisoners, and
called for the public executioner.   There was none, so he
ordered ropes to be brought, and strangled the heretics
with his own hands   Then, says the Canon Blouyn, '' he
rode off with his troop,'' as if nothing had happened.'

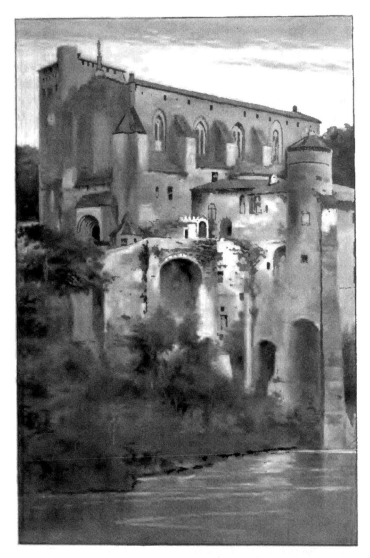

AT GAILLAC.

But we came here for a more specific purpose.   In the
archives of the *mairie* is the ancient charter of the town,
signed by the king, and sealed with half a pound or so of
still fragrant beeswax.   Beside it lies a manuscript history
of Gaillac, prepared by a worthy Catholic citizen while the
American colonies were fighting for independence, and we
can do no better than read.

"About the middle of the twelfth century the laxness
of the clergy in morals, their arrogance, and above all
their luxury made the people indignant.   They saw the
bishops and monks, in spite of their wealth, free from all
taxes.   They murmured against the luxury of the priesthood.   They loudly complained of its corruption.   The
enemies of the clergy set themselves especially against the
simony that made all the dignities of the Roman church
articles of traffic.   With gold even a layman could buy
episcopal functions.   Even the chair of Saint Peter was
put up at auction, and sold to the highest bidder."   ·

In short, the Church, which had established a monopoly
of salvation, had come to be administered largely by
ignorant, dishonest, and degraded priests, who, in the
modern phrase, sold the forgiveness of sins for "all the
traffic would bear," and the people, driven to desperation,
groaned for some other way to reach God.   The dissatis-
faction was general.   Out of it grew the two new orders
of St. Francis and St. Dominic, both of them discounte-
nanced by the pope till he dared resist no longer.'   In
southern France the popular discontent seized upon the
oriental ideas we have just explained, and crystallizing
its forces in this way began a movement for reform.   It
was not the theory that produced the practical results, but
the practical need that utilized the theory.

We read again : "In 1147 the apostles of reform
travelled barefoot through the province, clothed in sack-
cloth, cross in hand, preaching more than gospel austerities

everywhere. They were the first to obey the precepts they taught. The coarsest food sufficed them. They seduced the people by the strictness of their lives. They were always zealous preachers and willing martyrs." [1]

What made the situation still more dangerous for the Church, southern France was peculiarly tolerant, free, and even careless in religious matters. For some reason theology had never taken deep root in that region. We find there almost no relics of the Druids; and so great appeared the religious indifference of the people that the pious Romans were amazed, and Cicero spoke of the Gauls as the enemies of all religion. We all know, too, the liberalizing effect of travel , but Languedoc did not need to travel,—it was on the highway of races, and the world passed by. In the time of the troubadours its people believed, but were willing that others should believe differently. The monasteries were comparatively few and notably unenlightened. The Jews were innumerable and prosperous. According to Michelet the rabbins had opened public schools in the principal cities. Despite the Church, Jews were chosen by the nobles as their financial agents. An active commerce linked the Midi with the Mohammedans, both of Spain and of the Levant. The Provençal merchants who frequented Saracen marts could not fail to return with favorable impressions, and public feeling toward the Infidel became so mild that a bishop of Maguelonne added to the profits of his mint by stamping coins with the emblems of the Prophet. In short, while the nobles of northern France were pious and ignorant, farther south the freedom as well as the culture of our own day was anticipated.

With such tolerance in matters of doctrine, with such a thorough disgust for the priesthood, with so notable an illustration of primitive Christianity in the " good men," no one could fail to see the tendency. Already the churches were becoming deserted. Already the revenues of the pope were falling off. Not only among the common people, but still more—as some think—among the upper classes, the new doctrines were taking firm root. When Peire de Breus, the lord of Gaillac, was lying on his death-bed, he told the bishop to bury him with the heretics, and when the bishop refused he answered, "If I should find no heretics by me I should crawl to reach them." The doctrines of the "good men" compelled them to antago-nize a sensual and property loving organization ; and the time seemed near at hand when Rome, losing completely and for ever the richest of its provinces, should lose with it the dream of uniting Christendom under the supreme lordship of the Roman pontiff.

Something had to be done, and something was done. Preaching was tried ; but, as Dominic has explained, the gaunt heretics were more effective than the fat priests. Discussion was tried, but that left each party only the more convinced. Next came formal condemnation. The first judgment upon the "good men" was decreed (1165) at the very castle of Lombers, where King Peire put Rai-mon de Miraval to rout, and after this act the new party had a name, the "Albigensians." [10] Another condemna-tion was decreed (1166) at the little place where Guilhem de Cabestaing was born. But anathemas, too, proved in vain, and the pope determined then to crush the enemies of Rome by whatever means he could,—believing, I doubt not, that the will of Heaven and the good of the world required him to do so.

From this point events moved rapidly. Most of the heretics were in fiefs belonging to the count of Toulouse, and the pope called upon Raimon VI. to aid in extirpating them. Raimon was orthodox, but he was determined to protect his people, and though not a strong man, was tenacious at least. [11] For ten years he withstood the pressure. Repeatedly in the course of the negotiations he submitted to great personal humiliations. He was ex-communicated four times. Once, in the porch of that beautiful church of St. Gilles, he bared his flesh and sub-mitted to the scourge   More trying still, perhaps, were the harsh words of the pope. One of his letters began thus   " If with the prophet I could break through the wall of thy heart, I would show thee all its abominations "; and it went on with equal scorn and violence, threatening him with every temporal calamity, with immediate punish-ment from God, and with everlasting fire.

Whatever the pope's mind, his policy seems admirably adapted to excite a revolt as if for the purpose of crushing it, and though Raimon's patience proved extremely em-barrassing, chance finally came to his aid. The papal legate, Pierre de Castelnau, was pierced with a lance by some undiscovered enemy near St Gilles, after an almost incredible display of pride and arrogance. Raimon was furious when the news reached him ; for, as any one could see, the crime could not help, and could not fail to injure his cause. But the pope at once pronounced him guilty, ordered that the excommunication of " Raimon the mur-derer " and his accomplices be read every Sunday in the churches, and commanded that no faith be kept with those who had " kept no faith "   " Up ! " he cried to the king of France and his nobles   " Up, soldiers of Christ ! Up, most Christian king ! Hear the cry of blood. Aid us in wreaking vengeance on these malefactors "   Then he summoned every man of war to the crusade, and an-nounced in his call that all the estates and property of the heretics were to be divided up among the sharers in this holy enterprise   The host gathered, and the massacre of Béziers was the first-fruits of the papal harvest

Two more steps complete our journey. At Béziers the need of a military head was recognized and the head was

found. Simon de Montfort " was a champion worthy of
the cause,—a man of great stature and fearful strength, a
brave soldier and able captain, but also a wily courtier,
a cunning diplomat, a pitiless conqueror, and ambitious
beyond all reason or scruple to found a dynasty.

It was no ordinary brain under that mighty shock of
hair. His mind was like his battle-axe : it drove straight
through things and laid the core of them to right and
left,—at least so I read him. You recall, perhaps, how
his experience with crusading pilgrims disillusionized
Raimbaut de Vaqueiras ; Montfort also had been a crusader, and he, too, as I believe, had learned. He came
back realizing, as others did, that a Saracen was about as
good as a Christian; but he turned the proposition around,
I suspect, and in his heart of hearts a Christian was no
better than an infidel. As for the Church, he had discovered its usefulness. When his interests were at stake
the archbishop of Narbonne found that excommunication
had no terrors for him, but before the battle of Muret his
army was edified and fortified by his display of piety.

Languedoc, though apparently strong, was not in a condition to resist the attack successfully. Its very freedom
was a source of weakness when confronted with the stern
military spirit of the North The iron hand of feudalism
was not felt there until Simon de Montfort established his
four hundred and thirty-four fiefs, most of them as short-
lived as they were iniquitous The rule of military service
was laxly enforced. The great principle, " No land without its lord," was not adhered to While peace was not
unbroken, industry and commerce—not war—engrossed
attention. The nobles, perceiving that a profit lay in
promoting free cities, had favored their development.
The lords had prestige rather than power, and owed that
mainly to their riches On all sides the central power
and even the principle of authority were undermined ;

and the pope, knowing well how to avail himself of all divisions, enjoined upon the crusaders to conceal the extent of their designs and conquer one at a time.

The massacre and burning of Béziers set the fashion of the crusade, and after this pattern it continued. Other slaughters differed in extent more than in thoroughness. A little place near Gaillac was captured and every human being in it slain forthwith. No town was quiet enough and no castle remote enough to be exempt from bloodshed. Away off to the northwest of Albi is Cordes, pretty Cordes, shining peacefully on its hilltop in the evening sunlight, with its little river below eddying along beneath crumpled willows ; even here the Inquisitors came and worked, until their fiendishness excited a general revolt and three of them were killed. In Lavaur—between Toulouse and Castres—the noble and beautiful Girauda was brave enough to close her gates. The castle was taken by storm. The knights found there were slaughtered, four hundred Albigensians were burned " with an extreme joy," as Pierre de Vaux-Cernay exclaimed, and the lady of the castle, thrown into a well, was stoned until the well was filled up.

All this was set going because the dignity, revenues, power, and aims of the Church were threatened by the revolt against its faithless ministers It continued because the wealth of the Midi offered tempting prizes to northern adventurers. It ended (1229) after twenty years of desolation, because fire and sword had substantially exterminated religious independence, and the coveted provinces now belonged to the crown of France To compass an end so glorious, hypocrisy, treason, hate, perjury, outrage, robbery and arson by the wholesale, murder unmindful of age or sex, every known crime, and every conceivable sin were pious means.[13]

And so it came to pass that yonder cathedral, dedicated

to the Lord of light and love, has no window within forty feet of the ground, and the name of Albi, reposing before us now in peace under the scintillant sky of a May night, is a bar of death and horror across the ages, like the shadow of the cathedral tower on the moonlit river."

25

XXIII

LE THORONET AND GRANDSELVE

Folquet de Marseilla. Guilhem Fígueira

IT amazes us to find at the heart of all this Albigensian cruelty and horror an ex-troubadour.

Most of the troubadours of that period, while they felt no interest in the questions of doctrine, were intensely hostile to the crusade ; and this was very natural. In the first place, as the way Miraval divorced his wife suggests, classical paganism still maintained some hold upon them probably Apparently, too, there were certain instincts— or possibly traditions—of the craft that carried them back unconsciously to the mystic brotherhood of the Druids.' As poets they were of necessity favorable to free thought and free speech. As bards it was a part of their office to chastise the base and faithless, and the priests fell often under their lash. As men devoted to the joys of life they were a natural antithesis to those who collected toll from the fear of death The Church had always frowned upon the joglar folk, and the troubadours, as near of kin, inherited the quarrel. And above and beyond all these reasons, the nobles menaced with ruin and with death were their patrons, friends, and protectors

A few illustrations will show how deeply the troubadours were stirred Bertran de Lamanon charged the archbishop of Arles with the seven mortal sins, and affirmed that money would induce him to do anything whatever.

Guilhem Rainol,[2] a monk who turned minstrel, exclaimed: " A weak and base rabble clad in the surplice is
robbing the nobles of their towers and their palaces. . . .
I see wickedness mount on high, while excellence and
honor go to ruin." Peire Cardinal[3] sang of Raimon
VI.: " As water in the fountain, so chivalry has its source
in him. Against the basest of men,—nay, against the
whole world, he stands firm." Vidal declared without
reserve that heresy was due to the corruptions of the
Church. Carbonel,[4] though later, may give his testimony
also, for probably the character of the priests did not
greatly change " O false clergy ! "[5] he cried ; " liars,
traitors, perjurers, robbers, lechers, infidels,—you work
so much evil each day that you have thrown the whole
world into disorder."

Still more distinguished as a foe of the crusaders was
Guilhem Figueira,[6] whose remarks upon the " closeness "
of Peguilha stirred up that famous battle of the wits in
Florence.

Figueira was not of noble birth, and had so deep a dislike for polite society that the mere sight of a gentleman
put him out of tune. Like Peguilha he was a native of
Toulouse, and following his father's trade he became a
tailor ; but when the invaders captured the city he fled,
and after that earned his living as a joglar in the cities
of northern Italy, consorting with people of the lowest
morals. Yet, though a man of the populace, he was not
lacking in wit, and besides a pleasant pastoral and some
love-songs that Petrarch found inspiring, has left us the
most furious invective of the middle ages. The Church
was his theme ; and while orthodox himself, as orthodoxy
went, he drew a picture that is first appalling and then
wearisome from its abundance of wrath. Out of twenty-
three stanzas this is one : " Cunningly dost thou spread
thy net, Rome, and many a shrewd morsel eatest thou

despite the hungry   Thou hast the air of the lamb, so
innocent is thy look, but within thou art a ravening
wolf, a crowned serpent engendered of a viper, wherefore
the devil welcomes thee as his bosom friend.'' *

Still there were voices on the other side.   Germonda,'
a poetess of Montpellier, answered Figueira with twenty
stanzas, rhyme for rhyme and blow for blow.   Ugo de
Sain Circ in his far Italian home ranged himself against
the heretics.   Izarn,* a Dominican or at least an Inquisitor, wrote a poem of eight hundred lines which re-
futed to his entire satisfaction a " good man " of straw
already satisfied that his interest lay in orthodoxy.   Perdigo, a fisher lad whose talents won him the golden spurs
of knighthood, allied himself with the same side, and even
crossed the Alps as an ambassador to the pope against the
Albigensians.

This brings before us our capital figure, the spectre that
beckoned us on at Toulouse   Besides Perdigo, the embassy to Rome included two remarkable men and a third
more remarkable still.   The two were the papal legate
who directed the massacre at Béziers and Guilhem del
Bauz, prince of Orange, the unfortunate patron of Raimbaut de Vaqueiras , and the third—was Folquet de Marseilla.

Folquet de Marseilla ; what a strange, what a terrible
fascination there is in the name !   In an age of antitheses
he was an embodiment of antithesis keener than his age.
A nightingale turned hawk, a shepherd allying himself
with the wolves, he made his early sins look white by the
blackness of his later virtues, and made religion odious
by faithfully serving the Church.   It was natural that
Simon de Montfort, a soldier by trade, should represent
the violence of the Albigensian crusade , but it was mon-
strous that Folquet de Marseilla, a poet and a priest,
should represent its fury and sin.

Folquet began life without a hint of his destiny As
the son of a wealthy merchant who came from Genoa and
settled in Marseille, he seemed intended for a business
career   But the pleasures of youth proved more attractive, and he sang :

> I count it better to be poor and gay
> Than rich but joyless, careworn all the day. [9]

He was not compelled, however, to be poor in order to
be gay.   His father died and left him " very rich."
Young, wealthy, well educated, a poet, and a composer
after the manner of the time he seemed to have before him
all that heart could wish.   He was fond of travel,[10] and
soon counted among his friends—besides the merry Barral,
his lord—Richard Cœur-de-Lion, Raimon the " good
count " of Toulouse, and the kings of Aragon and Castile.
The favor of ladies was no less ready, as Folquet intimates,
than the favor of princes.   At Nismes he seems to have
worshipped at more than one shrine ; at Montpellier he
found a friend in Eudoxia, a daughter of the emperor of
the East and the wife of Guilhem VIII., and at Marseille
he paid sincere and passionate court for many years to
Alazais of Roca Martina, the wife of Barral and the scornful mistress of Peire Vidal.

Certainly there was no lack of cleverness in his wooing.

> Such sweet delight I find in loving thought,
>   Which makes my heart its loyal habitation,
> That nothing else can gain a lodging there,
>   Nor count I dear the pleasures once I sought ;
>   'T is life to me—this fatal meditation,
>   And suffering love finds love its consolation,
>   Though Love be slow his promise to fulfil,
>   And cheat me long with looks that feign good-will.
>
> Accept, good lady—if you 'll grant me aught—
>   The bliss of love as I its tribulation,

And then its ills I will serenely bear,
  For we shall seem with equal burdens fraught ;
    But if you choose a final separation,
    Turn not my wits with sparkling conversation ;
      Put off your beauty and your laughter still ,
      Then bid me leave you, and i' faith I will !

Each day more fair, you make me more distraught ;
    I curse the eyes that gaze in admiration ;
No good they 'll do me, I am well aware,
    For subtle gazing all my woe hath wrought ;
      Yet woe 't is not, else had I obligation
      To hate myself ; but now I feel elation,
        Because your hurt would follow on my ill,
        And you must suffer, if my life you kill.

I trick myself, in shrewdness all untaught,
    While true to you with no dissimulation ;
I plan your mischief, but my own prepare,
    I plan to catch you, but am only caught,
      And so my heart dares risk no revelation ;
      But in my looks you 'll find the declaration :
        I vow to speak,—my fears the purpose chill,
        And so my eyes both shame and boldness fill.

My love outstrips my power of demonstration ;
      But if poor wit prove not I keenly thrill,
      Divine the truth with sympathetic skill. [11]

Neither did Folquet lack passion

      If she but speak in passing, lo !
      I feel the splendor of her eyes
    Leap at my heart, her breath o'erflow
      With mingled sweetness as it flies ;
      Upon my tongue a flavor lies ;
    And I know,
    Just because 't is so,
    The words that would her beauty show
      Are not my own, but really start
      From Love, who lodges in my heart. [12]

But there *was* a lack in Folquet, and that a great one,
—a lack of heart, a lack of real human sympathy.

He must rank, no doubt, as the most intellectual of the
troubadours. With him intelligence was far more than
the mere scribe of the feelings, and his poetry reveals a
subtle and penetrating thought, alert and rapid. One of
the chief traits of Provençal verse was a great want of
logical order and systematic development ; in Folquet we
discover attempts to reform this. As he himself said, he
endeavored to bring a song around at the end to the starting-point, instead of simply adding one idea to another
until it was time to stop. Comparison is the basis of
science, and we find comparisons abounding in his poetry:
a single piece contains five in as many stanzas Contrasts
give relief to ideas, and Folquet understood antithesis
His thoughtful character betrayed itself, too, in many
didactic and reflective sayings : Cnyrim has found twenty-
two such expressions in twenty-four songs ; and his ruling
taste for the world of intellect was emphasized by his slight
regard for that of nature. The ordinary was foreign to
his taste ; originality and a personal mark were his constant study.

Unfortunately his qualities were not those of a troubadour. Instead of loving to submerge himself in sentiment, he preferred the intricacies of scholasticism. His
originality studied form, not substance ; and, leaning upon
other troubadours for ideas, it soon became conceit and
mannerism, while feeling was lost in displays of wit.

> Since Love exalts my humble part
> And lets me bear you in my heart,
> I ask and beg you : keep the fire away !
> And this I say
> For your sake more than mine,—beware !
> For since you dwell within my heart, prepare
> To feel and bear

What ills befall, for you are there!
But use the body as you wish or need,
And keep the heart as if 't were yours indeed ![18]

How far is all that from troubadour naïveté, and how
far on the way towards *bel esprit*, towards what Fauriel
called " *la finesse précieuse et maniérée !* " Folquet cares
too much for antithesis also.   When he expresses an idea,
he is morbidly anxious to give it all possible value by con-
trasting it with its opposite, and so he keeps one tossing
between inconsistencies.   He demonstrates, for example,
that Love and Pity should be in harmony, and then adds ·
" Neither Love nor lady permit this.   But what—why
dare I affirm anything about it, since I have never ventured to open my thoughts to the lady ? "   His elaborate
expositions make the simplest things complex.   An excess of personification peoples his verse with graven
images : Worth, Excellence, Fear, Pity, Valor, Hate, and
the like   His literary devices are a step toward art, but
they take him away from nature and bring him nowhere.
Poetry is in his eyes a courtly fashion by which a man
cleverer than the rest can win fame and honor, and, carrying much farther the conventionalism of Peire Rogier, he
stands among the troubadours as the most artificial, formal,
and affected type.[14]

Such a man could not be a good lover, for his feeling
was so intense, narrow, sophisticated, and selfish as to
lose the quality of human sympathy.   Even when he
really tried to feel for something outside himself he made
poor work of it.   He wrote a crusading song, but it had
no clang.   We have a poetical prayer of his, and perhaps
another ; but they only remind us of Eloisa's epistle to
Abelard according to Alexander Pope.[15]   When Barral
died, Folquet felt surprised himself that instead of being
overwhelmed with grief he was sitting down self-con-
sciously to elaborate a rhetorical elegy.

He was just the same in love   It was not instinct that
made him choose this path.   While the real troubadours
were possessed with the spirit of true human desire, of
unquenchable vitality, of spring defying winter, of love
delighting even in its griefs, Folquet was a lover because
his commercial mind calculated that love would be the
most profitable investment of his life.   " I sing as a debt
to folly," he once admitted.   Sentiment did not banish
trade : " One should always exchange good for better,"
was his principle.   Of the annoyances of his pursuit he
spoke in a way that argued a shallowness of conviction :
" I am almost ready to give up love,—so weary am I of
tale-bearers."   His intellect analyzed the lover's absorp-
tion and his judgment condemned it · " The man who
commits himself to one stronger than he is, is a fool."
He was so much an egotist in his love that unlike most
of the other troubadours he had little to say of his lady's
charms, and sang instead : " Who will be faithful to me,
if I am untrue to myself? "

Whether Alazais reasoned on the character of her suitor
we do not know, but certainly his wooing was in vain.
" Waiting makes the flower a fruit," he sang ; but his
flower only hung and faded.   Like Peire Vidal, he found
his praise accepted and his love—utilized ; and in due
time the inevitable quarrel arrived.   Two sisters of Barral's were living at the court, and Folquet was atten-
tive to both of them."   Possibly he thought a twinge
of jealousy might bring his lady round , possibly he was
only trying to conceal the real object of his passion ;
possibly—who knows?   Alazais called him before her,
charged him with disloyalty, said many hard things,
prompted her friends to do the same, and so got rid of
him.

Grievously disappointed the troubadour betook himself
—after a period of lamentation—to Montpellier, and sang

for the willing Eudoxia ; but Alazais, as Folquet declared, would not quite let him die, for she wished the pleasure of killing him again. She appeared to relent, and he returned to Marseille. We are surprised at his persistence, but, as he once explained, he was

> Like one who pauses midway in a tree .
> He dares not turn, so great the peril seems,
> Yet farther progress too precarious deems [17]

But now more than ten years of this courtship had passed, and Folquet was no longer a youth. His fading young-heartedness exposed the lines of his real character. Forsaken by his illusions he could see clearly · Alazais was weary of him.

> 'T is ever so ; too often in the lists
> The noblest charger seems at last but common. [18]

Bitterly he reproached himself for disregarding so long his own better judgment : " Good sense unheeded counts no more than folly." Like the gambler who has lost all, as he said, he resolved upon forswearing Love, who gave what was not desired and withheld what was.

> Deceitful Love, sweet only to allure,
> Attracts to him and binds the foolish lover,—
> So like the moths that round the candle hover,
> And in the flame at last find sepulture ;
>   So I depart ; I choose a new direction ;
>   I 'm ill repaid,—that causes my defection ,
>   And I shall be, like all who thus have slaved,
> The angrier now, the humbler my subjection

> And therefore, Love, your service I abjure ,
> I 'll heed you not,—one slave you 'll not recover ;
> As often pictures—bad, as we discover—

When seen afar our vision please and lure,
I prized you dearly while you escaped detection ;
Too much you gave, though scanting my affection,
For I am caught like him who rashly craved
That all he touched should turn of gold's complexion.[19]

" I 'm ill repaid! " that was the key-note, and he sounded it sharply and loudly. Worse thoughts yet were behind, for he said to his lady, " I know the way to hurt you with a song." So ended ignobly Folquet's career in love.

About the same time his powerful friends were taken from him, one after another. One after another the brilliant courts that had made him welcome fell under the sway of new Pharaohs[20] ; and Folquet, destitute of perennial sympathies, lacked the will and the power to form new ties and win fresh éclat.

He began to reflect ; and the more he studied his position, the more he saw that his entire plan of life was a mistake. " A lie cannot conceal itself so that sooner or later it shall not be seen," he once remarked, and the essential falseness of his career was now clear.

Every purpose had come to naught. Life meant for him not simply to be, to live, to act ; but rather to attain, to arrive, and to get. His nature was not broad enough to see, as many of the troubadours found, that the journey itself was worth while. Folquet's intense character valued only the end, and all his ends had failed him. The glad-heartedness which is itself a success had been with him only the effervescence of youth. Friendships, love, and society,—all these were lost. His art—he never had taken it seriously, and therefore it had no strength to lean upon. Even his rare qualities of intellect separated him from his fellows ; and, as he must have seen, marred the worth of his poems. His poems! Now that he realized how essentially false they were, they became almost hateful to him ; the fame

they had given him seemed only irony, and he wished
never to make another. The investment of his life was a
totally bad one In mind and heart, in love and life, in
friendship and ambition, in social and in professional
aims, artistically and personally—judged by his own
standard of achievement—he was a failure. Others might
be deceived, but he could not be. Life's prizes he could
no longer win, and he did not even care to win. Look
where he might—without or within—he saw before him
that one word, more terrible than death to a proud, passionate, ambitious life,—failure, failure, failure !

What should he do? To fail, and fail utterly, and still
walk about and be seen,—Folquet could never live so.

Then, like a chasm revealed by a flash out of midnight,
a new depth opened before him, as we read. " Suppose,"
he suddenly reflected one day, " Suppose that I should be
compelled to lie for ever on the fairest and softest bed, how
terrible it would be ! I could not endure it. But suppose
that instead of lying on a fair, soft bed I must lie for ever
in unquenchable fire ! " Here was a new ideal, a new
ambition, a new investment of his powers,—to save his
soul from hell. How should he do it ? The Church, the
Church ! And casting gladly from him the world he no
longer could bear, he entered the order of Citeaux and
buried his face in a cowl [21]

Spring had gone before me when I set out from Les
Arcs [22] toward Le Thoronet, and her feet had made the
way beautiful

There was the little olive-green river Argens keeping
me company, as it wound gayly along on its way to fortune. There were the trees above the road,—oaks and
olives, little thickets making themselves useful in the
rough spots, and lines of poplars posing in sightly places
like Grecian wood-nymphs, their draperies revealing,

more than hiding, their lines of grace. There, too, were
apple trees, pear trees, cherry trees, peach trees,—how
they bloomed and blossomed in the fields, here whiter
than snow, and there as red as the roses !

But the greens,—what shall I say of them ? Down in
the valley where the Argens is flashing bright glances at
me, the trees press close together, pushing as near the
stream as they can, and spreading their jealous branches
as wide as possible, while over and through them—weaving an endless pattern—clamber the vines. Some of the
leaves are so yellow as hardly to seem green at all ; some
are so green as hardly to seem yellow at all ; some are
brownish and some reddish, a great many olive, and
others ashen; some are deep and humid, and some pearly
or silvern. It is an orchestra of greens ; but the brasses
are silent,—only the strings and the wood-wind play.
The 'cellos are all in flageolet, murmuring together for
the river ; the violins are all in fluttering arpeggios for
the leaves, the little leaves, quivering in the south wind ,
the flutes are trilling together at their highest for the
birds ; while far away one oboe plays softly a woodland
air for the shepherd on the hillside. And it is all so light,
so quick, so shimmering; pianissimo, delicatissimo, dolcis-
simo; music dreamed, not written,—till suddenly the eyes
become aware of the great blue firmament and the drifting
clouds ; and then the orchestra is silent until it please us
to look that way again.

Ten or twelve miles from Les Arcs we dash up a little
knob of a hill, and through the one street of a dust-colored
hamlet. Who could count the dogs that meet us,—black-
and-tans, yellow curs, mongrel pugs, spaniels with the bar
sinister ; and how they bark as my driver snaps percus-
sion caps from the end of his whip to right and left ! We
pay the respect of a glance to the little church with its
bell hanging aloft in the open, and the graveyard with its

four tall cypresses, hard, slender, stiff as icicles, and seemingly as cold ; then down the hill on the other side, and on
through a rough country growing rockier and more bare
at every step, until—about a couple of miles farther on—
we draw up in the courtyard of an ancient Cistercian
abbey,—Le Thoronet.

Le Thoronet was, however, more than an abbey, for as

THE ENTRANCE TO LE THORONET.

the brotherhood grew it asserted a suzerainty over the
neighboring towns and became the head of a fief. The
monarchy itself was not more deeply intrenched. For
about six hundred and fifty years matins and vespers
echoed here every morning and evening, until at the close
of the eighteenth century the Revolution broke up the
establishment. Even after the lapse of another hundred
years the relics of ancient greatness are still impressive.
The church, the chapter-house, the hexagonal lavatory,

and much of the cloisters are still to be seen. Across the
courtyard shaded by lordly chestnuts is the fountain,
sparkling and singing under the arched windows of its
broken canopy. A walled passage leads down to the old
entrance, a heavy archway covered now with shrubbery
and vines ; and on every side we find the crumbling walls
of dormitories, workshops, library, storehouses, and refectory, all draped with the sombre foliage of the ivy."

What spot in the world is so redolent of peace and rest
as a monastery in ruins? The mossy stones of an old
New England churchyard, hidden away on the hill among
the pines and beeches—the grass uncut, the fence broken,
the inscriptions quaint, the names forgotten—these are
tranquillizing ; but the old monastery gives out suggestions of repose attained not in death but in life. At Le
Thoronet the air seems freighted—though not oppressed
—with centuries of peace. The little old gardener, brisk
and important, is bustling about the spacious courtyard,
filling his buckets at the fountain, passing and repassing ;
but somehow the more he bustles in his little way the
deeper seems the quiet. His goings and comings do not
disturb the long procession of monks which you feel is
winding invisibly from yonder archway across the court
and within the doorway of the church. Still goes on—
unbroken though inaudible—their solemn chant, the
hymn attributed to St. Bernard :

> Terram teris, terram gens
> Et in terram reverteris
> Qui de terra sumens.

The sweet but passionless music of the fountain, slipping past the ear, sings its way inward to the heart: The
shadows glide unhurried along the wall. And still you
sit and think—of what, you could not say. Somehow the
world has left you,—perhaps the old walls have barred it

out, and you find yourself listening without regret or sadness to the closing lines of the hymn :

Cerne quid es et quid eris :
Modo flos es et verteris
In favillam cineris.*

Was it so to Folquet de Marseilla, soon chosen (perhaps

AT LE THORONET.

in 1201) abbot of Le Thoronet ? The walls were not
in ruins then, but within
them reigned a stillness no
less profound, — that stillness which impressed Wil-
liam of St. Thierry so
deeply at Clairvaux. The
monks were only shadows
and their bell only intensified the quiet.

Did he find peace in this
great privacy of the hills ?
When he entered the church
—too simple to possess a
portal —and looked around
upon the massive arches, the
narrow windows, and the
severe ornament,—the piety
of Clairvaux worked out in
architecture, and still more
when he bowed at the austere altar, merely a pile of rough
stones, did the meek spirit of Jesus of Nazareth enter into
him ? When he walked in the cloisters, austere like the

* The English of the two Latin stanzas is as follows: "Thou
dost use the earth, thou dost work the earth, and to the earth re-
turnest thou who from the earth art taken." "Perceive what thou
art and what thou shalt be : only a flower art thou, and thou shalt
be turned into a cinder of the ashes."

church, adorned only with a few leaves carved in the
capitals of the pillars but instinct with calm repose, or
when he passed into the garden yonder, with its corner
set apart for " sweet savors," did a benediction from the
universal Father shine abroad in his heart ?   Did it warm
his feeling of human sympathy to hear the hours of
prayer told off by the consecrated bell, and see the
brothers passing to and fro, each with his little atmosphere of fraternal godliness ? Or did the valley seem
only solitude walled up ?   Had he too much quiet for
thoughts that flew while the thoughts of those about him
only crept ?

Others might sleep or drowse, the abbot could not.   Beside the old failure stood forth a new opportunity.   Already
abbot, he might reasonably be ambitious again; and many
a time during the years at Le Thoronet his eyes rested
impatiently on those distant mountains of Nice, heralds of
the Alps, which seemed now to approach and offer him
the stepping-stone of a great career, now to withdraw dis-
dainfully in the haze of languid summer, and leave him
to be forgotten in his rocky tomb.

But this was not his most besetting thought.   Beneath
his feet the ground seemed crackling, and the flames of
eternity seemed already licking up the garden and its
blossoms   Selfish as before, egotist as before, sophistical
as before, unhuman as before, he was mad to save himself.
The Church, the Church !   To labor, to battle for the
Church,—that was the only escape.   It was not love of
God, not love of men, not love at all.   It was fear,—fear
for himself.   His heart was swept and garnished, and the
devils of ecclesiasticism took possession.   In the wan zero
of renunciation his passion changed its face, and the power
to love became a power to hate

His opportunity soon came (1205), for a bishop was
needed in Toulouse.   He must be a rare man, able, un-

26

flinching, unquestioning, with no conscience to judge his purposes, and no sympathies to check his deeds, a perfect instrument, keen, hard, and strong, like a sword from Castile. Where should such a blade be found? It was found at Le Thoronet, cast in the fire of bitterness, and sternly tempered in the furnace of solitary thought.

Toulouse was familiar soil to the new bishop, for Raimon V., the father of the reigning count, had been his friend, and the town was not without reminiscences of his early career. As he returned home toward evening on a winter's day and passed the count's palace, he could not forget how, but a few years before, Folquet de Marseilla had been the life of the company as Raimon de Miraval was then. The lamps and candles were alight, music was gayly tinkling, some were dancing, through a half-open window a song floated out upon the chilly wind, and within he could almost see—laughing and chatting in the hall, still charming and still voluptuous—the very beauties who once danced there with him.

Folquet was sincere, for the flames were always just behind him, but the old passion had only been smothered, not transmuted. Dining one day at the court of France he was entertained unawares with a song of his own, we are told, and calling at once for water he tasted nothing more at the dinner except water and bread. Far more powerfully was the old nature stirred as he paused a moment before the count's palace.

Again something leaped at his heart, again a flavor lay upon his tongue

He laughed bitterly to himself. How would the loves of his youth enjoy him now? The gnawing of hungry passion had eaten his flesh; his piquant chin had become sharp and stubborn: his delicate nose was long and thin, his white brow pallid and seamed, his fair cheeks bloodless, his brilliant eyes dry ; but the old nature burned, and on he went to tread the cold floor all night, fasting and trembling, until his soul filled and overflowed with " righteous hate,"—hate for that fortunate count, hate for that gay court, hate for that prosperous, happy town."

The day for action came.   Four years after he sat down in the episcopal chair of Toulouse Béziers was destroyed. In all the terrible moves against Raimon and his capital that ensued, Folquet co-operated from within with Montfort without, and because of him one goes about still amid the gayety of Toulouse with sense a-quiver, dreading every instant to hear the paving-stones cry out in a terror not calmed by centuries: " Hist, step aside!   Don't you see it ?   Blood !   BLOOD !"

It was Folquet who persuaded Count Raimon, with lying words of good-will and affection, to invite Montfort and the legate of the pope to Toulouse, and give them possession of the citadel   " a great sin," says the Provençal historian, " which cost the lives of many thousands of men "   It was Folquet who urged hardest that the son of his friend and benefactor should be deprived of his estates.   It was Folquet who travelled through northern France enlisting aid against the heretics and especially against the count, " the worst wretch of them all."   It was Folquet who introduced St. Dominic to the pope, and established the Inquisition in Languedoc.   It was Folquet who would not permit the crusaders to spare Toulouse when they felt that the count and his people had suffered enough.   It was Folquet who ordered all the clergy to leave the city and carry with them the Holy Sacrament, inflicting on many thousands of the faithful the terrible dread of dying as heathen.   It was Folquet who appeared at the Lateran Council (1215) as the implacable enemy of the count, and Folquet who was twice charged there with

causing the death of ten thousand persons in his own
episcopal city.

But this was not enough ; the flames were not yet
quenched. Once more he roused Montfort to take vengeance on Toulouse, and bade him strip its inhabitants
of all they had. On the approach of the army he exhorted
the people to go out and make their peace with the enemy,

THE SIEGE OF TOULOUSE.
FROM A RELIEF AT CARCASSONNE.

promising they should be well received, while Montfort,
as had been arranged, put them in irons as fast as they
came. Folquet himself then began the pillage of the
city, and Montfort came up and set it on fire: Béziers was
to be outdone. With the energy of despair the citizens
drove out the crusaders ; but Folquet gave them asylum
in his cathedral and palace. Then, by an understanding
with Montfort, he went out through the streets declaring
that he had persuaded Simon to surrender his prisoners

and pardon the city if the people would go to their homes and give up their arms. No sooner was this done than Simon, by Folquet's advice, exiled his prisoners instead of surrendering them, and announced that the city would be sacked unless it engaged to pay an almost impossible ransom. When the people dared to promise the ransom he declared that if the last penny were not ready at the appointed time he would kill every one of them. And after the money was paid,—the city was pillaged none the less.

And all this was done by a priest, a minister of Jesus Christ, an apostle of righteousness, peace, and love ; and the people he despoiled and slaughtered were his own children in the Lord. The shepherd threw open the fold, called the wild beasts, and helped them tear the flock. No wonder a churchman of Lyons dared say to his face at the Lateran council " Is it right that so many be sacrificed to glut the passion of one man ? " No wonder he is called, in the Annals of Toulouse, " the cruel fury who brandished the torch over a people betrayed by himself alone." No wonder Figueira cried : " Our shepherds have become ravening wolves ! " **

What could be the end of it all ?

The end of Montfort was terrible and sudden. Once more he was besieging Toulouse (1218). A stone was let fly at a venture from a mangonel, worked by desperate wives and mothers. It crushed Simon's head, and he fell " dead, bleeding, and black," and before his body could be moved five arrows pierced it. So perished the man of slaughter, and a song of fierce rejoicing went up from Toulouse and all the Midi."

But such decrees . ideal justice are rare Folquet, his ally and accompli , lived on for thirteen years, and then died (1231) in the peace of the Church."

Twenty-five or thirty miles · ɔ the northwest of Toulouse there is a wide and gently sloping vale. The road is shaded with lindens and plane trees. The daintiest of marguerites fringe the meadows. Magpies beat up the fresh odors of the grass, and the whirring flight of doves fills the calm air with ripples. This is Grandselve ; and beside the brook Nadesse, beneath murmuring poplars, the scanty remains of a monastery have been built into a farmhouse.[28]

Here stood, in the days of the troubadours, a great

GRANDSELVE.

Cistercian abbey in the midst of a wide forest, and at this abbey were celebrated with splendid pomp the obsequies of Folquet. The candles burned resplendently. The incense was fragrant. The chant was clear and sweet. With sonorous eloquence the assembled prelates called their departed brother " The Blessèd." The Church took up the strain. As " The Blessèd " he passed into its traditions ; and about a century later Dante, immortalizing the tradition, placed him in Paradise as " a jewel costly and lustrous."[29]

NOTES ON VOLUME ONE

The notes are numbered to correspond with the "superior figures" placed in the text.

The heavy-faced numbers in the notes refer to the list of Authorities at the front of Part One.

When a Provençal poem is referred to it is by *the page on which it begins.*

"Vid " means "For the original see."

CHAPTER I.

1. Page 1.—"*Les Iles d'Or*" is the title of a volume of poems by Mistral (No. 304). *Le Moine des Iles d'Or* was the apocryphal author after whom Nostradamus pretended to write his lives of the troubadours (No. 324).

2. P. 3.—Pourrières is supposed to derive its name from the corruption of the dead Germans.

3. P. 4 —Vid No. 41, p. 133.

4. P. 4.—Bertran de Lamanon, an influential noble of Provence, was born about 1200, son of Pons de Brugeiras. Lamanon is in the canton of Eyguières (Bouches-du-Rhône), 10½ miles by rail from Cavaillon. The Provençal biography says " he was a courtly knight and graceful in speech, and he made good society verse (*coblas de solatz*) and sirventes." In history he first appears in 1235. July 22, 1242, he was a witness when Raimon Berenguier, count of Provence, swore at Aix to take Genoa under his protection. Under Charles of Anjou he was equally prominent. Probably he went with Sordel on Charles's Italian expedition. His last appearance, so far as we know, was on April 23, 1260. We have fifteen (?) of his songs, some of them containing bold and bitter invectives.

5. P. 5 —The joglar and his relations to the troubadour will be treated in Chap XXXIV. In general he was the Provençal equivalent of the French *jongleur*. Sometimes, besides singing

the verse of the troubadours, he made verse of his own ; the essential difference was that the former was courtly and artistic, the latter popular and rough. The view of René's castle is from the fair-ground of Beaucaire referred to in the next chapter

6. P. 7 —It should be remembered that there is considerable Provençal literature besides the poems of the troubadours. No. 294 and No 273 give a sketch of it   The fullest treatment is No. 363.

7. P. 9.—Savaric or Savary de Mauleon was one of the most powerful barons of Poitou, and his deeds are historic. He was born about 1180. In 1199 his father, Rao (u) l, and in 1213 his uncle died, so that Savaric came into possession of the whole family estate   This he increased by marriage. Besides owning several castles he had maritime fortresses, harbors, and a fleet, and was even more powerful on sea than on land. Indeed he was sometimes called a pirate, which according to the usage of those times meant only a baron-at-sea   He first appears prominently in history in 1202 as a partisan of Prince Arthur against King John. In the changeful politics of a time when every man fought for his own hand he was naturally first on one side and then on the other He is thus characterized by a writer in No 23 (LII., p. 140): "A finished type of the feudal lord at the beginning of the XIII century." "A violent and rapacious man, an unscrupulous adventurer by sea and land, seeking only his own interest and never hesitating to break his word when his interests demanded   . . In a word, he is a man without morality, but a forceful warrior and even a delicate poet." He died July 29, 1233 (Ledain).

The pleasanter side of his character is emphasized in the Provençal biography (No. 110)   "A fair knight was he, and courtly, and accomplished (*enseingnatz*), and generous beyond all the generous. No man in the world took such delight in liberality and gallantry and love and jousts and singing and social conversation (*solatz*) and poetry and courtly life and in spending. And more than any other knight he was the true friend of ladies and lovers, and wishful of seeing good men and of pleasuring them. And he was the best warrior that ever was in the world   Sometimes he prospered in war and sometimes he fared ill. And all the wars he had were with the king of France and his people [an error]. And of his good deeds a great book might be made by him that would write it, for he was one that had within him more condescension and mercy and true-heartedness and that did more good deeds than any man I ever saw or heard of, and was more fixed in his will to do them." We have from him a song, a "stanza," and the two tensos called forth by Guillerma. The little town of Mauléon, called since 1736 Châtillon-sur-Sèvre, possesses still some ruins of its ancient castle, and Ledain thinks that the gateway dates from the time of our poet. See No. **369,** *livraisons* 239 and 240

8. P. 10.—E. Rudel was the lord of Bergerac (Bragairac), Gensac, Castillon-sur-Dordogne, and Clarens in Nov., 1224. J. Rudel was from Blaye (Blaia), not the troubadour of that name, but doubtless of the same family

9. P. 10.—The original of this tenso may be found in No. 63, col 155, and a translation in No. **158,** p. 203.

10 P 10.—Labachellerie is a pleasant little village crowning a fertile slope shaded with poplars and chestnut trees. Ugo de la Bacalairia was a minor troubadour. We have seven songs from him The Provençal biography says he was "of little worth, and he went about little and was little known. Still he made good songs, a good *descort* (see Note 25, Chap. XXXVIII) and good tensos. And he was a courtly man, right skilful and right well taught."

11. P. 12.—Jeanroy (No. 2, II., p. 443) rejects the story of Guillerma and her three lovers because according to it Savaric chose as judge "*mos gardacors que m'a conquis*"; but this (J. says) could not be Guillerma, for she was chosen by Faidit; therefore she was not Savaric's mistress at all, and the tenso was a mere *jeu d'esprit.* But we are told that Guillerma did not grant Savaric her favors, and though he loved her still, it is easy to believe that he had also a more complaisant friend whom (especially when smarting from Guillerma's unkindness) he might think of as his *gardacors.* In view of so easy an explanation it seems to me unnecessary and unwise to reject the testimony of Sain Circ, who was intimately acquainted with both Savaric and Guillerma My own preference is in general for a good deal of conservatism in rejecting what has come down to us. Certainly we should accept nothing that can be proved fabulous, and must doubt whatever is shown to be improbable; but on the other hand the temptation to incredulity—especially in favor of some learned and ingenious theory—is always lying in wait for us

It is interesting to note the sequel to the incident at Benauges.

Though Savaric was too deeply in love to admit his lady's insincerity, friends undertook to cure his infatuation. At their instance he went to see a noble lady (believed to have been Mascarose de la Barthe, countess of Armagnac) and she accepted him as her knight and appointed him a rendezvous for a certain time. News of this was brought Guillerma, and she forthwith summoned him to attend her that day. Savaric was greatly distressed; and as the provost of Limoges, himself a poet, was his guest at the time he discussed with him in verse the claims of the two ladies. The provost argued that Guillerma was moved not by love but by jealousy and pique, and therefore nothing was due her; while, as the other lady had no feeling but kindness, it would be ingratitude to disappoint her. Savaric, however, was true to the old love, and spoke with some contempt of a heart too easily won. We do not know what Savaric did, but (despite Jeanroy's criticisms) we can hardly doubt the substantial correctness of the story, for it was written down by Guillerma's messenger, Ugo de Sain Circ.

Guillerma's husband was Pierre de Gavarret (Peire de Gavaret), himself a troubadour, the author of a sirvente that has survived.

The words "lover" and "mistress" as used in this book are entirely non-committal as to the morality of the relation.

12. P. 12 —Germs of the drama existed. Of course the crusades added vastly to men's knowledge of certain foreign countries, but this was not—properly speaking—discovery.

CHAPTER II.

N.B —The present spelling is Vacqueiras, while the mediæval spelling omitted the c; hence there are apparent inconsistencies in the text.

1 P 14.—Gui de Cavaillon appears frequently in history from 1202 on He sided with the count of Toulouse in the troubles of the Albigensian crusade, and when Raimon VI. left Toulouse for Spain (1216) he named Gui first among the barons to whom he confided the interests of his son. He had an important part in the siege of Beaucaire that year. He went to Rome and to Paris as a diplomatist for Raimon VII., and in 1229 was a hostage in the latter city According to his Provençal biographer he was "a generous, courtly, and agreeable knight, and greatly loved by the ladies and by all the world; and a good knight in arms and a good sol-

dier." He was the reputed lover of Garsenda, wife of Amfos Alphonse) II , count of Provence, and sister of Peire II., king of Aragon, but Schultz thinks his relations with her did not begin until after her husband's death in 1209. We have five or six tensos and one sirvente from him The siege referred to in the text was at a castle of his called Castelnou. (See p. 112.)

2. P. 18.—Ventoux (Ventour) is the weather bureau of the peasant. The 6000 olive trees were uprooted in 1761 (Papon).

3. P 20.—He might almost be termed a scholar, also, for he wrote a poem in which five languages or idioms were used.

4. P. 23 —The quotation is from No. 347.

5. P. 23 —The *Tarasque*, a monster that was said to have ravaged the country in the first century, from which St. Martha was the deliverer. Until recently a fête has been held regularly in commemoration of the deliverance, and a figure representing the monster has formed a part of the procession. The view on p. 5 was taken from the fair-ground of Beaucaire. For the castle of Beaucaire see Chap. XXXI.

6. P. 24.—Mérimée thought the arch was erected to commemorate the victory of Marcus Aurelius in Germany, but in 1889 Baron de Witte seemed to prove that it was built in 121 B.C. to celebrate Roman triumphs over the Arverni and Allobroges, and that it was restored and embellished in A.D. 21 to commemorate the submission of the Gallic chiefs J. Florus and Sacrovir to Tiberius Cæsar.

7. P. 27.—Representations have been held recently in the theatre at Orange, and it was hoped to make this a permanent custom, but Parisian good sense has been inclined to feel that respect for antiquity did not require one to journey to Orange every year and bring back a cold in the head.

8. P 27.—It was Bertran del Bauz (in French, *Des Baux*) who built the proscenium wall into his castle. It was he that first received (1178) the title *Princeps d'Aurenga* (Prince of Orange), Aurenga being the Provençal name (in Latin Aurasio. See No. 31, XVIII , p. 425). His son was Guilhem IV , the patron of R. de Vaqueiras

9. P. 27.—A diver went down seventy feet in the fountain of Vaucluse and sounded twenty-six feet more without reaching an end of the channel. The stream is a substantial river except in

hot weather, the flow varying from 1300 to 26,000 gallons per second.

10. P 28 —The ruined castle at Vaucluse belonged to Petrarch's friend, the Cardinal de Cabassole, bishop of Cavaillon. Petrarch's house was not where the guide-books would have it, but on the ridge midway between the castle and the village (See No. 5, 1895, p. 398) The poet retired to this spot in 1337. The picture of Vaucluse, based upon several photographs, was composed from an imaginary point of view in order to show the scene completely.

11. P. 31.—Petrarch was found dead in the morning of July 19, 1374, with his head resting upon a book The chair in which he died, his desk, his inkstand, and his cat, stuffed and now hairless, may still be seen in the brick cottage at Arqua. He died in a nook (which has one window) opening from the library Though not, as Chabaneau has said, "a constant imitator" of the troubadours he was greatly influenced by them

12. P. 31.—Raimbaut's *Carros*, of which a translation will soon be given.

13. P. 32.--Raimbaut's boyish experiences are imaginary.

CHAPTER III.

1. P 33 —The prince of Orange (Aurenga) owned the castle of Vaqueiras, and so was Raimbaut's natural lord. He began to reign in 1181 (Schultz), not in 1182 (Diez). Schultz and Carducci place Raimbaut's birth between 1155 and 1160. He was certainly in Orange about 1184–85, for we have a song of his evidently composed there at that time (Diez).

2. P. 34 —Mistral's *Trésor du Félibrige* is a large and very valuable dictionary of the dialect of Maillane which was adopted as their literary tongue by the modern school of Provençal poets, the Félibres. Mistral, however, was not the father of the school, but Roumanille, son of a gardener at St Remy, afterwards a proofreader, and finally a bookseller at Avignon. The third founder was Anselme Mathieu, a vine-grower of Châteauneuf-des-Papes. The Félibrige was formally organized by these three at the castle of Fontségune, May 21, 1854. It is a curious fact that while the Félibres are looked upon by many as the successors of the trouba-

dours, they knew the troubadour literature scarcely more than by name (See No. 335, p. 66.)

3. P. 34 —St. Remy makes a business of raising flowers for the seed. Bonifaci de Castellane, an important historical character and ancestor of a great family, is one of the troubadours whom we find there. He came in August, 1257, to pay unwilling homage to his lord, Charles of Anjou. A few years later he revolted, was defeated, and banished We have three sirventes from him.

4. P. 36.—The stones of La Crau were brought from the Alps by spring floods

5. P. 36.—Madame de Sévigné described the mistral as "the whirlwind, the tempest, all the fiends let loose, determined to carry off your castle." The wind is less violent now than formerly.

6 P. 38 —Mistral told Gaston Paris that the sight of Les Baux made him long to speak the magic word that should repeople its palaces and restore its splendors.

7 P. 38.—It has been questioned whether Dante was ever at Arles, but No. 67 (pp. 166 and 197) holds that he was there; if he was, he doubtless visited Les Baux, the most interesting spot in the vicinity.

8. P 38 —The real founder of the house of Les Baux is not however considered to have been Pons but Ugo, who appears in a charter dated October 16, 1059, and probably died the following year (Mas Latrie)

9 P. 40.—The tomb of Raymond des Baux, grand chamberlain of Queen Jeanne of Naples, bears this inscription: "To the illustrious family Des Baux which is held to derive its origin from the ancient kings of Armenia, to whom under the guidance of a star the Saviour of the world manifested himself"

10 P 40 —In French the motto of Les Baux was "*Au hasard, Balthasar!*"

11. P. 41.—Guilhem's mishap is recorded in No. 110, p. 88.

12. P 41.—The allies of Guilhem especially blamed for not standing by him were Guilhem VIII. of Montpellier and Bernart of Anduze, of both of whom we shall hear again It is an unexplained and curious fact that Raimbaut called the prince of Orange "*Engles*," that is, "English."

13 P 42 —Vid No 42, p. 268

14 P 42.—Raimbaut used these five idioms in a single poem as
if to show that many tongues were needed to fitly praise his lady
(See No. 41, p 77) As foreign tongues were usually acquired in
those days by going where they were spoken, it is natural to sus-
pect that about this time Raimbaut visited the regions of the
Pyrenees. It has been thought that he was entertained by Amfos
VIII of Castile, at whose court he would have heard Portuguese
But there is no certainty of this visit

15 P. 43 —The tenso with Guilhem may of course have been
written after the separation, or, on the other hand, some time before it. We have a tenso of Raimbaut and Aimar (Adhémar)

16. P. 43. — Schultz thinks Raimbaut visited various Italian
courts during 1187-88, while Bonifaz of Monferrat was perhaps in
Palestine ; but as Aimar II. did not begin to reign until 1189 he
would seem to have been in Orange till then (Diez). (Carducci
says that he went to Italy not before 1185 and probably not before
1189 See No 16, 2 ser , XLIX , p 5.)

17. P. 44 —The Genoese poem is noteworthy as the first use of
the Italian language in poetry by a poet of distinction   There has
been some difference of opinion as to the order in time of the first
literary monuments in Italian, and neither Morandi nor Monaci
seems to have been quite right. The true order appears to be
1. An inscription of four lines in the cathedral of Ferrara, 1135
These lines were rhymed but cannot be called literature ; 2 A rude
song by a Tuscan joglar , 3 This piece by R. de Vaqueiras , 4
Four lines (called by the Italians the Cantilena Bellunese) probably
composed in 1193 ; 5. Fragments of a poem from Monte Cassino ;
6 The famous hymn of St. Francis of Assisi. R. de Vaqueiras
stands therefore foremost among those who showed (about seventy-
five years before Dante was born) that Italian could be made a
vehicle of literary expression and so was a founder of Italian
literature.

This poem is noteworthy also as the first example of a dialogue
between a man and a woman afterward so common in Italian literature (Carducci) It illustrates the contrast between courtly and
uncourtly manners. Schultz says it was not written before 1182.
For the original see No. 41, p 131. I have given st. 1-4 The
last line of st. 2 is lit , "Go hence, brother, at a better time," *i e* ,
" at a bad time " (the same ironical usage is heard in Spain to-day),

i. e., "Evil take you !" St. 4, l. 3 ; lit., "In an evil hour may you come and may you go !"

18. P. 45.—Tortona is about twenty-five miles to the southwest of Pavia.

19. P 46.—The song is given in substance after No. **142**, p. 224.

20. P 49.—Albert, marquis of Malaspina, from whom we have only this tenso, was the youngest of three brothers. He appears in history almost every year from August, 1187, until 1202 (No. **7**, II., p 395 ; and No. **31**, VII., p. 188). We know he was in Tortona, July 3, 1197. In 1198 he helped Tortona against Genoa. It is probable that he died in 1210, certainly not later than 1218. He was probably brother-in-law of Bonifaz (Schultz), though he has been called the son-in-law. There has been a theory that the lady of Tortona was his wife. All students of Dante will recall the Malaspina family.

21. P. 50.—The tenso is in No 41, p. 127, and a German translation in No. **142**, p. 226.

22. P 50.—Vid. No. **41**, No 27, st 2, line 7 : "*sirventes ab descortz.*"

23. P. 51.—Bonifaz began to reign jointly with his brother in 1183 ; alone in 1187.

24. P. 51.—After the Tortona episode Schultz thinks Vaqueiras went to Provence, returning the next year, and that the tenso with Albert was composed in 1196 or more probably 1198. We cannot be perfectly sure as to all the details of the chronology.

25. P. 51.—Though Guilhem obtained the title of king (1215), no effect was given to it. Three years after his death the marquis of Monferrat (son of Bonifaz) was made the imperial representative for the kingdom of Arles.

CHAPTER IV.

1 P. 52.—For a bibliography on R. de Vaqueiras see an article by Carducci in No. 16, 2 ser., XLIX., p. 23, and for the house of Monferrat, the same, 3 ser , XIX., p. 680. The investigations of O. Schultz and several Italian scholars have corrected Diez at a number of points.

After Guilhem III went to the East (1183) Bonifaz (I., not II.) and Conrat ruled Monferrat jointly until on Conrat's going (1187)

Bonifaz became sole lord.   Guilhem was living in 1188 but probably not later than Jan. 7, 1189 (No. 26, I , p 445 +).   Raimbaut's second connection with Monferrat began about 1190-92 probably, and his relations with Biatritz in 1196.   Biatritz does not seem to have married until after Raimbaut left Monferrat (1202).   Perhaps she never married, but if she did she was the wife of Enric (Henry) of Carreto the Younger , The Provençal account calls her the sister of Bonifaz, but Cerrato has proved her the daughter (see No. 7, IV , p 81)   Bartsch said that she died in July, 1202, but there seems no good reason for this opinion, nor for thinking as others have done that she died in 1205.

At Bonifaz's court, besides Raimbaut de Vaqueiras, were the troubadours Vidal, Peguilha, and Cadeuet, whom we shall meet later   There was also a Folquet de Romans, born about 1170, a figure of no great significance   He was there when Bonifaz was invited to lead the crusade, and Hugo de Berzé (or Bersi), a French troubadour and knight (No. 31, XVI , p 504), urged him vainly to assume the cross.   He afterward became a guest of Azzo VI. of Este   He was living in 1233.   We have some fifteen poems from him   Romans is a town of about 15,000 people on the Isère near Valence

2   P 53.—Alba and Acqui, the chief towns of Monferrat, were not seigneurial residences

3.   P. 57 —Raimbaut's letters (or letter, as they are better considered) are so interesting that I give them in full.   According to Schultz, No. 395, the first letter (in ——ar) was written probably before August, 1194 (certainly not more than two or three years earlier), and recounts events of 1179–1182 ; the second letter (in ——o) was written after July 18, 1203 (probably before April 12, 1204), and recounts events that occurred between September 1, 1194, and July 18, 1203 , and the third letter (in ——at) was written probably before July but not before spring in 1205, and deals with events that occurred between July 17, 1203, and the spring of 1205. Zenker, however (No 31, XVIII , p. 195), holds that the three letters are only one, composed of three tirades, No 3 coming first, and that the whole was composed about the second quarter of 1205. Although Schultz's authority upon the troubadours in Italy is very high, Zenker's view seems correct, and the letters follow in his order though the old numbers are retained   The poem was after the style of the folk-epic.

III

" Valiant marquis, lord of Monferrat, I thank God that he has
honored you so greatly, for you have won, spent, and given away
more than any other uncrowned man in Christendom. And I
praise God that he has advanced me so much, for in you I have
found the best of lords, for you have supported and equipped me,
and conferred great benefits upon me, and raised me to a high position and made me from nothing an honored knight, favored at
court and praised by the ladies. And I have served you in good
faith and with good will and gladly, and have devoted all my
powers to you. Many a clever stroke have I made with you, in
many a fine place wooed lady's love with you, and lost and won in
arms. I have ridden with you through Greece, received many
blows and given them with you, skilfully retreating and overpowering the pursuers, put them to flight and pursued them with
you. And I have fallen and have overthrown In the ford and
on the lofty bridge have I fought with you and spurred with you
over barriers and entered moat and barbican and have mounted on
guard in high places, triumphing over great hardships. And I
have aided you to conquer dominion and kingdom in this land,
and to take the island and the duchy, and kings, princes, and
principality, and to overpower many an armed knight. Before
many a strong castle and many a strong town have I taken my
place with you, and before many a fair palace of emperor, king
and admiral; and I have besieged the sebastos Lascaris and the
protostrator and many other apostates in Petrion. And with you
I chased to Philopation the emperor whom you have dethroned to
crown another [in his place].

" And if I am not through you [placed] in great power it will
seem as if I had not been with you and served you as I have said;
and you know, lord marquis, that I tell the truth in everything.

I.

" Lord marquis, I will not remind you of all the youthful exploits
which we undertook in the beginning, for I am afraid it might
make trouble for us who used to give lessons to others; and yet
the deeds were so brilliant that a young man could not have done
better. For the first thing a young man of rank has to do is to
decide whether he will gain renown or let it go,—as you did, lord,
who resolved at the beginning so to exalt your excellence that you

27

made yourself and me praised above all,—yourself as lord and me as bachelor [*i. e*, young man]

"And since it is a hard thing, my lord, to give up and leave a friend whom one should prize, I would fain recount and refresh the love [you used to bear me] and tell over what we did with Saldina de Mar whom we carried away from a very high abode—from the marquis of Malaspina at Solar, and you gave her to Ponset d'Aguilar who lay dying in bed for love of her

"Remember also the joglar Aimonet, when he came to you at Montalto telling how they proposed to carry off Jacobina to Sardinia and marry her there against her will. For an instant you sighed, and recalled how at parting she allowed you to take a kiss and begged you so fervently to protect her from her uncle who sought to get away her inheritance. Then you bade five esquires to mount, and we rode by night after supper,—you, Guiot, Hugonet d'Alfar, Bertaldon (who knew how to guide us well), and myself, for I am not willing to omit my part And I took her away [from them] at the port as they were on the point of embarking. Then they began to shout on the water and ashore, and horse and foot they pursued us Great was the chase and speed our [only] thought. Already we believed we had escaped them all when the Pisans came and attacked us. And when we saw before us across our way so many knights, so many hauberks, so many fair shining helmets, and so many banners flying against the wind, we concealed ourselves between Alberga and Finar. There we heard on many sides many a horn, many a trumpet, and many a signal-call. Whether we were in fear I need not ask you Two days we had nothing to eat or to drink When on the third day we thought to get away, we came upon twelve robbers in the pass of Belhestar, [lurking] there to plunder [the passers-by], and we knew not what to do, for one could not use his horse there. But I attacked them on foot and was wounded in the neck with a lance, but I wounded three or four, I believe, so that I made them all turn their backs. Bertaldon and Hugonet d'Alfar saw me wounded and came to my help; and when we were three we cleared the pass of the robbers so that you could go on in safety,—and this you ought to recall. Then we dined joyously off a single loaf without drink and without [water] to wash [our hands] At evening we were with Lord Eyssi at Pueg Clar, who received us so cordially and was so desirous to show us honor, that had you permitted he would have given you (*fera ab vos colgar*) his daughter, the bright-faced Aigleta In the morning as lord and rich baron you wished amply to recompense our host, and you married Jacobina to his son, and regained for her the whole earldom of Ventimiglia, which belonged to Jacobina on account of her brother's death, [recovering it] from the uncle who planned to take it from her. Then you wished to see Aigleta married and gave her to Gui de Montelimar.

"Were I to recount and tell over, my lord, all the famous deeds which I have seen you perform it would be wearisome to both of us,—to me the telling and to you the listening. But I have seen you give a hundred maidens in marriage to counts, marquises, and barons of high degree and never did youth cause you to wrong one of them. For a hundred knights have I seen you provide an inheritance, and another hundred bring low and banish, seize their property, and abase the false and wicked ; and no flatterer could ever please you. So many widows and orphans have I seen you counsel and so many unfortunates aid, that they ought to [be able to] conduct you to paradise if any man may enter there for kindness of heart. For you never allowed any man worthy of aid to go away without it if he asked, and with gentleness you ever wished to govern. And if the truth be told, Alexander left you his generosity, Roland and the twelve peers their boldness, and the noble Berart his gallantry and eloquence. In your court rule all things excellent : liberality, lady's love, fine apparel, elegant arms, trumpets, sports, viols, and song, and you wish no gatekeeper there (there is naught for him to do) as do the miserly lords

"And I, my lord, can boast of this much : that I have known how to win good standing at your court, to give, to serve, to endure, and to keep confidence, and never have I given any man cause to be sad Neither can any man say against me that I ever wished to be away from you in war or feared to die for your glory.

"And since I know so many of your experiences you ought to favor me as much as any three others. And that is reasonable, for in me you can find at the same time, lord marquis, a witness, a knight, and a joglar.

II.

"Valiant marquis, you will never deny, what is the truth, that I stood by you as true liegeman when you assaulted Quarto, between Asti and Annone. Four hundred knights pursued you and you had scarcely ten comrades when you turned back and fell upon them with fury. Then they feared you more than crane fears hawk.

And I went to your aid where you were hardest pressed, and you and I gently raised from the ground the Marquis Albert who had fallen from his saddle.

"For your sake I have been in grievous imprisonment, and for your advantage I have made many an assault and burned many a house. At Messina I covered you with my shield. I came to you just at the moment they had bolts and darts, arrows and splintered lances at your breast and chin. And when you took Randazzo and Paternò, Roccella and Termini, Lentini and Aidone, and Piazza, Palermo, and Caltagirone, there was I among the foremost, as many noble barons saw

"When you went to Soissons to take the cross I had no thought of going beyond the sea (God forgive me), but in the cause of your renown I became a crusader and went to confession. Then was I at the castle Babo and the Greeks had as yet done me no harm. Afterward I fought with you furiously at the palace of Blacherne. Beneath your banner I stood in arms like a Brabançon with helmet, hauberk, and thick gambeson I fought at the tower Petrion and was wounded there below my armor Likewise I bore arms at the palace of Hebdomon till we drove out the base emperor who treacherously overthrew his brother. When he saw the smoke and fire and coals and saw the wall pierced in many places without engines, he came out into the open to make a desperate fight, with so many men that without a doubt there were certainly hundreds for every one of us. And you and the count of Flanders bethought you of defence, and all of us, Frenchmen and Bretons and Germans, Lombards and Burgundians and Spaniards, Provençals and Gascons, were drawn up in order, both horse and foot. And the emperor, with his heart at his heel, and his base comrades spurred on more than a mile Then the wretches turned about We were hawks and they herons and we chased them as the wolf chases the sheep. And the emperor stole away and left us the palace of Bukoleon and his bright-faced daughter.

"As to all this I fear not that any one will charge me with falsehood or mistake, for you know and so do all about you that the whole is perfectly true. And further I will add this that by many a poem (*vers*) and many a song (*chanso*) I have so exalted your fame that it will be retold for all time to the end [of the world].

"And when one serves a good and noble lord, repute grows out of it and he wins a rich reward, and therefore, lord marquis, I hope [to receive] from you a recompense and gift "

4 P. 58.—Schultz (No. 3, Vol. 92, p. 227) believes that the story of the poet's seeing Biatritz brandish the sword was invented by some one to explain the name Fair Knight; perhaps, but this seems gratuitous scepticism, the act may so naturally have occurred.

5. P. 58.—It was never allowable to seek the ultimate favor from an unmarried woman. Love-songs were addressed in but very few cases to unmarried women, but in Portugal this was common. (See No. 183a, II., p. 192.) We must never forget, too, that a large part of the troubadour love-songs were simply compliments in return for what was in effect pay.

6. P. 59.—The overlord always had a right to appoint a guardian for any lady in his domains without father or husband, and with this went the right to select her husband. This meant in many cases that her person and property were offered to the highest bidder. A father would be more considerate, but every noble was in need of allies, and daughters were recognized means of securing them As Canello says, such marriages were a legalized usurpation, wholly wanting in the true divine sanction of nature, and therefore it was essentially justice to protest against them.

7. P. 59.—With reference to the fixed idea of matrimony, cf. line 2093+ of the Clef d'Amors (No. 144). "Des mariz ne me parlez mie. . . . Le mari se veut fere creindre."

8. P 60.—Husbands did not enjoy seeing their wives receive the homage of knights and poets, but they were reconciled to it as a necessity. They could take advantage of the custom too and pay court to other wives. Indirectly it was an honor to themselves. It was a safety-valve as I have said, and they intended to see that it should never be more than that. At the worst, if wives wished to be unfaithful they would be, and it was better to have a noble than a *guirbaudo* for the father of one's children. The ideas of courtly love are to a greater or less extent so familiar to us that we are likely to forget how new and original they once were. From the land of the troubadours they spread north and south, crossed Alps and Rhine, and fastened themselves upon courtly life and poetry. Scandinavia, however, was not affected at all and England but slightly All who care to understand chivalric love should read No. 212.

9. P 60 —The stress of feeling involved in such love was often terrible. In particular a lady was often compelled to decide between the danger of losing a lover through extreme strictness and of losing herself and perhaps him also by yielding. Her promise once given, she had either to break a promise or break a vow.

10 P. 62.—The idea that the world of the troubadours was distinctly corrupt is largely due to ignorance of the manners and customs of the day. For example when we find a poet wishing that he might be present at his lady's disrobing we are shocked But the troubadour assumed the position toward his lady of a " servitor," and it was a feudal custom for the esquire to assist his lord in dressing and undressing. Further, as lord and lady always slept together and the lord rose first, the esquire did this service in the presence of the lady. Further still, as people (except monks) wore no nightclothes at all it was natural for the esquire to see the lady's arm or neck A Spanish king of a somewhat later time required his courtiers to attend at the queen's bath as an homage to her beauty. Temperament and habit made people indifferent to things which we Anglo-Saxons of to-day consider indelicate. Race prejudice and custom are not morals. It may not be inappropriate to remind ourselves of our present customs about seashore bathing and ball costumes It should be remembered also that much of the love-poetry was merely conventional, and finally, that only a comparatively small number of the ladies of the Midi had any share in it. Still the age was passionate and crude, and every sort of intemperance was liable to break out

11 P 63.—Camparetti has remarked, No 123, p 325, that woman owes nothing to chivalry, for it *tended* to make every lady an Isolde. This seems to me a mistake An Englishman might as well say that his railroads are bad because they *tend* to throw him into the sea There are very few moral movements, perhaps none, that do not have dangerous tendencies, and sooner or later need to be checked. They are good while they do good, and bad after they begin to do more harm than good.

12. P. 66.—The Provençal account gives the fact of this interview, the substance of what was said, and the words of her " counsel " to him as translated in the text (the omitted part is a reference to famous ladies who had accepted poets in that way), but of course the words put into her mouth must have been invented by some one as I have invented the rest (except the points suggested

by the poem that follows) Schultz goes so far as to consider the whole scene made up from expressions of the poet's. We have no knowledge of Raimbaut's personal appearance. Vidal's description of Biatritz is in No. 66, p. 26, st. 3 and 4. The Provençal biography erroneously attributed this poem to R. de Vaqueiras. It is to be noted that no suggestion of matrimony appears in connection with Raimbaut's devotion, which marks it as " courtly love " even though Biatritz was probably unmarried.

13. P. 68 —Vid. No. 358, III., p. 258. The whole is given here. I have introduced in the fourth stanza the figure of a steersman and in the fifth the figure of the tower in order to get rhymes (fourteen are required), but both were ideas that Raimbaut might have used To enable the reader to " control " the translation I give a literal translation of this piece, as I shall of other important ones. Note the refrain words " counselled me " (*cosselh*) in each stanza.

" Love now requires of me his custom and usage and makes me lament and sigh and lose my sleep ; for I have asked advice of the fairest in the world, and she bids me place my love as high as I can, on the best lady, and put my trust in her ; for this will give me honor, nobility, and worth, not harm ; and since she is the worthiest in the world I have set upon her my heart and my hope.

" None ever loved before so high as I do, nor so noble a lady, and since I find none equal to her I devote myself to her, and love her as she counselled, more than Pyramus loved Thisbe ; for gladheartedness and worth advanced her before all, and to the noble she is pleasant and cordial and to the base of haughty mien. She is generous and of honored welcome

" Percival, when in Arthur's court he took the arms from the red knight, had not such joy as I have in her counsel and it makes me die as Tantalus dies for I am forbidden that which she gives me in abundance by my lady, who is noble, courtly, of fine appearance, rich, and of noble birth, young-hearted, and sweet of speech, and of good sense, and of beautiful presence.

" Good lady, as bold or bolder was I when I asked of you the present of a lock of hair and that you would counsel me in regard to your love than Emenidus was at the assault of Tyre But I am entitled to the more praise and honor as my boldness in the matter of love was the more But your lover must practise so much boldness that if he obtain not happiness from it he will die of it.

" Let not my Engles blame or accuse me if for her sake I absent myself from Orange and Monteil, for may God give me counsel of her fair self as a more worthy than she I do not believe there is, and were I king of England or of France, I would go away from there to do all her bidding, for in her is all my heart and my desire and she is the thing in which I have greatest faith.

"Fair Knight, in you I have my hope, and since you are the worthiest in the world and the noblest, it cannot be an injury to me for you gave me counsel and confirmed me.

"Lady Biatritz of Monferrat advances herself, for all good deeds go ever before her, wherefore I praise my songs with her praises and improve them with her fair appearance "

14 P 69.—For this estampida see No. 41, p 89. So far as Provence is concerned we have no other specimen of this popular verse-form. The first stanza is as follows. *Kalenda maya | ni fuelhs de faya | ni chanz d'auzelh | ni flors de glaya | non es quem playa, | pros domna guaya, | tro qu'un ysnelh | messatgier aya | del vostre belh | cors, quem retraya | plazer novelh | qu'amors m'atraya; | e iaya | em traya | vas vos, | donna veraya , | e chaya | de playa | l gelos | ans quem n'estraya. |*

15. P. 71.—The original of the *Carros* (composed between July 25 and Oct. 1, 1202) may be found in No. 63, col. 128. There are nine stanzas and two tornadas ; of the former I have given Nos. 1, 2, 7, 8, and 9 ; of the latter No. 2. In the omitted stanzas the rivals of Biatritz are called by name,—a long list. Lines 1, 3, 5, and 9 I have changed from the trochaic to iambic on account of the scarcity of satisfactory feminine rhymes in English. To compensate for evading this difficulty I have carried the rhyme of these lines (twenty in all) through the piece, whereas in the original they run thus : st. 1 —err*a*, 2 —ost*a*; 7.—oj*a*; 8.—endr*e*; 9 —ont*a* The repetition of rhymes in the tornada is in imitation of the original. In l. 3, for *towns* we might read *churls*.

Lines 8–10 are lit., "for so high rises her fame that it buries their worth and holds dear her own " ; ll. 18–21 . "from all sides the women go thither without being summoned, so that their fame, their youth, and their beauty are at stake [because they dare rival Biatritz] "

A word on the construction of this poem There are 3×3 full stanzas ending with 3×3 lines rhyming together ; each stanza consists of 3 groups of 4 lines each, followed by a group of 3 lines, so that there are 3×5 lines in all ; ⅔ of the lines consist of 2×3 syllables. In this analysis the figure 3 occurs 3×3 times   Is there not in this the instinct of the waltz movement?

16. P. 72 —According to MS. R. the marquis once found Raimbaut and Biatritz asleep together, and, though enraged, merely exchanged his mantle for Raimbaut's and went away.   When the troubadour awoke he understood what had occurred, and taking the mantle went straightway to his lord, knelt, and asked forgiveness.   And the marquis, bethinking him of the services Raimbaut had done, pardoned him ; only, as people were standing by, he said that he pardoned his " theft," and that he must never " rob" him again.   And so those who heard thought it was because Raimbaut had taken the mantle of Bonifaz.   And so "only they two knew of it."   We may inquire since only they two and Biatritz knew of the occurrence how it became known to the public—certainly no one of the three would have mentioned it.   Schultz may be right in disbelieving the tale.

17. P. 73.—Vid. No. **358,** IV., p. 112.   It consists of 6 st. and 2 torn., of which I have given st. 3, 4, and 5, and torn. 2.   The omitted stanzas have special personal reference.   The refrain word " cross " (*crotz*) at the end of the seventh line is noteworthy.   The following is a literal translation :

" He that made the air and heaven and earth and sea and heat and cold and rain and sky, wishes [wills] that under his guidance all the good cross the sea as he guided Melchior and Gaspar to Bethlehem , for in plain and mountain the Turks capture us, and God wills not to say a word ; but it belongs to us, for whom he was put upon the cross, to go there , and whoever remains here wills to see his base life and his grievous death, for we are in great sins, which one must fear, from which each will be saved if he bathe in the river Jordan.

, " But our sins so confound us that we live dead, and know not how, for there is none so gay or so excellent that if he has a joy he has not other cares, and if he has honor that disgrace does not overpower it, for the most powerful has a thousand chagrins for one joy, but God, for whom one takes the cross, is joy, and who gains him can lose nothing ; wherefore I prefer, if it please God, to die there rather than to remain here alive and take my chance, though Germany were mine

" God allowed himself to be raised on the cross for us, and received death and suffered the passion, and was put to shame by the false, base Jews, and was beaten and bound to the pillar, and was raised on the beam that was in the mud, martyred with knotted thongs, and crowned with thorns upon the cross , wherefore a hard heart has every man who does not lament the harm done us by the Turks who wish to retain the land where God willed to lie alive and dead, whence befall us great war and great mischief.

"Fair Knight, for whom I make airs and words, I know not whether to destroy myself for your sake or to take the cross , I know not how to go and I know not how to stay ; for your fair person makes me grieve so that I die if I see you, and when I cannot see you I think to die, alone with all other company."

As illustrating the people of that time it is interesting to note that of forty-seven troubadour songs bearing directly on the crusades, only eleven are purely religious. Twenty-nine mix devotion with politics, and seven mix devotion with love (No. 389).

18. Pp 73-75 —The original of "King Louis's glory" is in No 358, IV., p. 275, st 6 ; of " These pilgrims" the same, torn. 3; of "Nor spring" the same, st. 1, 4, and 7. The piece contains seven st. and three torn. It is addressed to Guilhem del Bauz The line "The world as tedious as before " is literally " The whole world seems to me only one spot." This piece was probably composed in 1205

19 P 76.—Schultz is inclined to believe that Raimbaut outlived Bonifaz and returned to the west, on the ground that he would not be likely to entrust the poems written in the Levant to any but a troubadour or joglar and we know of none who went on this crusade except Raimbaut. But it was common for songs to be written out and sent to friends, and we cannot pretend in the least to know of all who did or did not go. Guilhem IV., the son and successor of Bonifaz, was also a patron of the troubadours At his court sojourned Peirol and Peguilha whom we shall study later, E Cairel, and Folquet de Romans.

20. P 76.—Raimbaut's service with Bonifaz illustrates the extent to which the troubadours were expected to fight for the lord to whom they were attached. Of course they served chiefly as a rule by celebrating his praise This was done usually in complimentary envois (tornadas) at the end of songs and also in Laments at his death. The universal struggle for honor was peculiarly keen at this time, and this fact explains in large part the success of the troubadours, whose songs were like the newspapers of to-

day as the means of giving fame. When Vidal went to the king of Hungary he sang . " He shall have great honor if he has me for servitor, for I can make his praise resound through all the world and cause his fame to grow more than any one else on earth." The poet had an interest too in praising his lord, for each reflected honor upon the other. Along with praise of his own lord went blame of his lord's rivals and enemies The lord was expected to protect a poet in this work. Granet said "It is my office to praise the noble and blame the base, . .   and if ill befall me for that, it is your duty to demand satisfaction."

Probably the poets frequently aided their patrons by composing verses which the latter sang to their ladies as their own productions.

CHAPTER V.

1. P. 81.—Daudet says (*Trente Ans de Paris*) that the wines of Châteauneuf-des-Papes were long considered the finest of Provence.

2. P. 82 —The Tour de L'Hers is mentioned in at least one troubadour song.

3. P. 84.—It is not my intention to express a positive opinion as to the spot where Hannibal crossed the Rhone A great deal of study has been devoted to the question, but the data given by Polybius are so indefinite that we cannot possibly be sure. (*E. g.* see No. 268) Roquemaure, opposite the Tour de L'Hers, is said by the people to mean *Rocher des Morts* and to signify that many of Hannibal's troops died there of fever. Henri assured me that his uncle had ploughed up many Carthaginian coins.

4. P. 85.—Albertus Magnus, one of the greatest mediæval philosophers, lived 1193–1280. The reader understands, of course, that the garden of Courthézon may or may not have been laid out in just this manner. All I wish to show is that gardens were so arranged at that time. This is the guiding principle in many similar cases.

5. P. 86.—Raimbaut's brother was Guilhem II , and they divided the earldom in 1150. Raimbaut's sister married Bertran del Bauz, and under their son, Guilhem IV., the patron of R. de Vaqueiras, Courthézon was again a part of the principality, having reverted to Bertran's wife when Count Raimbaut died about 1173 without an heir.

6. P. 89.—The literal meaning of "trobador" is "finder."

7. P. 89 —Vid. No. 358, III., p 15, st 1

8. P. 89.—We have no data as to the personal appearance of Raimbaut.

9 P. 90.—Words put into the mouths of troubadours may be understood to be quotations from their poems unless the text intimates or the notes state the contrary. There are many such quotations and it did not seem necessary to give references for them. Wherever there seemed any doubt as to the meaning I have had some confirmation of my rendering

10. P. 91.—Raimbaut's favorite oath, "By my father's soul," does not appear in the passage where I have introduced it. The extent of his learning is given according to his extant poems.

11. P. 92.—This particular form of song was never employed by other troubadours The original is in No 41, p 77. The second stanza is omitted for lack of satisfactory rhymes, for it will be seen that the five stanzas of the translation require fifteen It is as follows : "Though you charge it against me as folly, I could not for that refrain from saying my mind. Neither could any one blame me for it. I care not a farthing for anything save what I see and look upon And I will tell you why : [it is] because, had I begun and not brought it to a conclusion for you, you would consider me a fool for [attempting] it, for I would rather have [i e., it is better to have] six deniers in my fist than a thousand sous in the sky " The end of the last stanza but one is, I suppose, a covert allusion to something understood by those at Raimbaut's court I take it to mean, "threw herself into whosoever arms she pleased "

12. P. 93.—Among the ladies said to have loved Raimbaut were Maria de Vertfuoil (perhaps Verfeuil near Uzès), the countess of Urgel (supposed to have been the wife of Ermengaud VII who died in 1183, a Lombard lady related to the marquises of Monferrat), and the countess of Dia He seems also to have loved a lady who lived at or near Rodez. Raimbaut called one lady his "devil," and another (possibly the countess of Dia) his "joglar "

13. P. 93 —The original of "So sweet the smile" is No. 358, III., p. 15, st. 5 and 6; "Of all bad women," etc , No. 358, V , p. 401, st. 2.

14. P. 94.—Few as are the facts given about this troubadour they

are all of any importance that we possess. (His grandfather, Raimbaut II., went to Palestine on the first crusade with Raimon of St. Gilles, count of Toulouse.) We have about forty pieces of his verse—many of them hard to interpret. As the text indicates, his personal hopes, his triumphs, his joy, his fierce hatred of busy-bodies, his grief in disappointment, his resentment of disfavor—these were his themes, and the note of triumph was his best. His fancy and vitality led him to personify a good deal. Most of his figures of speech were drawn from common life. He was fond of using precise numbers to enforce his boasts, particularly 20, 100, 400, 500, and 1000. He never became didactic except in jest, nor even reflective. Sometimes he professed an intention to forswear the obscure style since it was criticised, but in one song he expressly declared his purpose to adhere to it. (See Chapter XXXVII.) He valued love simply as a means of enjoyment. Suchier has classified songs according to the nature-scene at the beginning into the four seasons · Raimbaut gives us three spring-, two summer-, and five winter-songs He stood close to Peire d'Alvernhe, and was a forerunner of A. Daniel in the pursuit of "originality." While other troubadours held that rank should not count in love, Raimbaut believed that the lover of rank should be preferred.

CHAPTER VI.

1. P. 97 —Die is said to have had 12,000 inhabitants under the Cæsars, now it has less than 4000. The Roman triumphal arch is the eastern gate. The porch of the cathedral is supported by four granite columns that once belonged, it is thought, to a temple of Cybele, the patron goddess of Dia. The Romans called the place in the time of the Cæsars, Dea Augusta Vocontiorum. It is worth while perhaps to remark that this part of the Midi was linguistically distinguishable from the regions chiefly associated with troubadour literature.

2. P. 98.—These and other tales of Philippa are in No. 430.

3. P. 99.—The father of Biatritz is supposed to have been Guigues VI., dauphin of Vienne, who died in 1142. Her husband was Guilhem I. de Peitieus (William of Poitiers), who was count of the Valentinois from 1158 to 1189. Her son Aimar (Adhémar) II became count of the Diois also in 1199, and died in 1230. She was

an ancestress of the famous Diane de Poitiers. The bust of Biatritz was set up at Die in 1888 with no little ceremony.

4. P. 101.—Some reader may be indiscreet enough to remind me
that Biatritz was probably blonde, though we know nothing of her
personal appearance or her mother's. But it is likely that there
were some brunettes and why not she ? Her poetry seems to suggest that she was dark ↘ As Raimbaut was no doubt blonde there
is the same suggestion from that source. Finally I am positive
that a daughter of the poet Roumanille, whom I had the pleasure
of meeting at Avignon, resembled her , so she *must* have been
dark.

5. P. 102.—We of course cannot be sure just how far the intimacy went or how the poems are related to its successive stages,
but the text seems justified by the poems. In the tenso Raimbaut
used the words: "*pus que me detz joi entier*." Biatritz was
certainly not afraid to express her feelings

> *Bels amics avinens e bos*
> *cora vos tenrai en mon poder ?*
> *e que jagues ab vos un ser*
> *e qu'ieus des un bais amoros ,*
> *sapchatz, gran talan n'auria*
> *qu'ieus tengues en luoc del marit,*
> *ab so que m'aguessetz plevit*
> *de far tot so qu'ieu valria.*   (No 396.)

6. P. 102.—This piece illustrates a peculiar style of rhyme, as I
have indicated in the translation .

> *E pois ieu li sui veraia*
> *beis taing qu'el me sia verais*
> *qu'anc de lui amar non m'estrais*
> *ni ai cor que m'en estraia*   (No. 396)

7. P. 103.—The original (with a French version) is in No. 358,
II , p 188   I have translated it freely in order to give it the tone
of conversation, but without adding anything—not even the pun
on "change." Schultz has expressed doubts whether the countess
of Dia really had a hand in the tenso, but Jeanroy has satisfactorily
answered his objections

8. P. 104 —I do not know that the count's residence commanded

a view of the Rhone, but this seems a fair assumption. On one of the crags opposite Valence are the ruins of Crussol, the finest castle on the Rhone.

9 P. 105 —The words of her meditation are imaginary, based upon the song that follows ; all others attributed to her are from her poems.

10. P. 106.—Vid No. 396 (or No. 63, col. 71, if the last word of the fourth stanza be changed to *covinens*, and we read in l. 4, st 3, *qu'ieus*). I give it complete. The rhymes of lines 1-4 and 6 of each stanza have been changed from double to single because so many of the former would have a comic suggestiveness in many ears—mine, for example—especially as English is so poor in double rhymes that the sense would sometimes have to be forced. It will be observed that the rhymes of lines 5 and 7 run through the piece. Line 7, "dull and plain"; literally "unpleasing" (*dezavinens*). As wit and beauty were the pleasing traits, dulness and plainness were of course the unpleasing ones. Line 10 is literally " But I love you more than Seguis did Valensa " (Nothing is known of the story in which these two figured.) Line 4 of stanza 3 would best be rendered thus, "For words and manner with which I receive you." The word "plain" occurs twice as a rhyme, but in different senses ; this accords with the troubadour usage. The music of this piece is sad like the words.

CHAPTER VII.

1. P. 108.—The father's name was Arman. The location of Sain Circ is unknown. From there the family moved to Tegra, now Thegra, canton de Gramat, not far from Gourdon (Lot) where Ugo was born, probably. According to Casini, No. 8, XVIII., 1, p. 158, the dates of Ugo's life probably were: birth about 1170 ; abandonment of clerical studies, about 1190 ; relations with the count of Rodez, viscount of Turenne, and dalfin of Auvergne, 1190-1200, travels in Spain, about 1196 ; beginning of his relations with Savaric, a little after 1200 ; after that, visits to various courts of Provence [in this period the affair with Clara] ; removal to Italy, about 1220 ; a stay in Lombardy of several years ; removal to the region of Treviso, before 1225 ; death 1240 or soon after. The biography of B. de Ventadorn makes it almost certain that Ugo visited Limousin. His last sirvente (placed by Diez in 1217)

has been fixed by Zingarelli in 1240   (See the volume in memory of N Caix, p. 243.)   He was mixed up with the Da Romanos, and took the part of Alberico against his brother Ezzelino.

2. P 109 —The count of Rodez was Enric I (Chabaneau), and the viscount of Turenne probably Raimon III., brother of Maria de Ventadorn and two other famous ladies whom we shall meet. The Spanish kings who befriended him were Amfos (Alfonso) VIII of Castile and Amfos IX. of Leon.   He was also in Catalonia and Aragon.   The tenso with the count is in No. 63, col. 160 ; that with the viscount in No. 142, p 336, note 3.

3 P. 112.—Lady Castelloza was the wife of Truc or Turc of Mairona, a town now called Merdogne (canton of Veyre, not far from Clermont-Ferrand).   Her lover was Arman of Breon, a place not far away.   We have three songs of hers.

4. P. 112.—This countess of Provence is thought to have been Garsenda de Forcalquier, married in 1191, widowed in 1209, and in a convent in 1222   Her relations with Gui probably did not begin until after the death of her husband   We have only a stanza from her.   For Gui see Chap. II.

5. P 112.—"Fifty knights " ; Clara actually said " a hundred," but fifty are enough, and all the rhythm has room for.   For the poem, see below.   The single MS. from which we learn of Clara's connection with Ugo de Sain Circ is of the XIV. century.

6. P 113.—At the highest point of Anduze is a bit of the old wall founded on the solid rock of the mountain, and higher still reminders of a fortress planted there by the famous engineer, Vauban.   The inn is not unworthy of the town.   The Grand Hôtel du Midi occupies apartments over a stable and a wagon-house. Between these two a flight of stairs, partly stone, partly wood, and partly brick, gives access to a little hall on the next floor   Dark on three sides, open to the world on the fourth, the hall is furnished with a pump, a sink, and a heavy table.   Here, if you please, you may superintend the washing of your radishes and the plucking of your fowl   Or if you prefer you may climb a few more steps, all of brick this time, and enter the tile-paved parlor-sitting-room-dining-room, lighted with a single window-door, beyond which Madame sits upon the iron balcony sewing up a calico dress.   Anduze has one good feature, however   Along the river front is an elevated promenade, narrow but long and pleasantly shaded.   It commands fine views, but is detestably dirty.

7. Pp. 114 and 115.—Vid. No. 63, col. 157. The first stanza reads thus · " Three foes and two bad lords have I ; each labors day and night to kill me. The enemies are my eyes and my heart which make me wish for her who will not belong to me. One lord is Love who holds in his dominion my true heart and my true thought. The other is you, lady, whom I love, to whom I dare not show my heart, nor tell how you kill me with longing and desire "

The second stanza is that of the text. The words " What shall I do ? " of stanza 2, are replaced in st. 3 with " How shall I endure ? ", in st. 4 with " How shall I live ? " and in st. 5 with " What shall I say ? " but the place of these refrains in the stanza is not always the same. The third and fourth lines are literally : " What shall I do, to whom all other joys would be grief if I had them not from you ? " The scheme of the piece is : st. 1 and 2 : a b a b b c c d d ; 3 and 4 : d e d e e f f g g ; 5 : g e g e e h h i i ; tornada : e h h 1 i.

8 P 115.—As this is the only piece we have of Clara's and is only a " half " song I will give the rest of it :

" [Even] He that reproaches me for your love and forbids it me cannot make my love a whit stronger nor increase the longing for you that I feel—the desire, the longing, the yearning ; and there is no one, no matter how much my enemy, whom I do not hold dear if I hear him speak well of our love ; and if he speak ill he can never again say aught or do aught to please me.

" Give yourself no fear, fair friend, lest I bear a heart unfaithful toward you, nor that I shall accept another lover in your stead though a hundred men should beseech me ; for Love, who through you holds me in his power, wills that I reserve and keep my heart for you ; and I will do it ; and if I could remove my person—one has it who should never have it more.

" Friend, such grief and sadness are mine because I do not see you, that when I think to sing, I sigh and lament, and so I cannot add to my song the stanzas that my heart would fain complete." Vid. No. 396.

9. P. 117 —The peacemaker was Alazais d'Altier (a place in the canton of Villefort, near Anduze). Not one but many times was she obliged to reconcile the lovers. We have a letter (*salut*) from her to Clara, written at an early stage of the quarrelling It rhymes like other *saluts* in couplets. (No. 31, XIV., p. 128.)

28

10 P 117 —His Italian inamorata was named Stazailla.

11. P. 118.—We know nothing of Sain Circ's personal appearance, or of the precise time when he wrote the lives of the troubadours. The biographies that we owe to him are certainly those of S. de Mauleon and B. de Ventadorn, almost certainly his own, and "perhaps the greater part of those which exist" (Chabaneau) Diez was of the opinion that he returned from Italy to France, but it seems easier to believe that he retained enough interest in the great events of Languedoc to write a poem on them, than that in his old age, without visible means of support, he moved wife and children so far from their native land. We have forty-two of his songs, besides seven others attributed to him by single MSS. (Bartsch).

12. P. 118 —This seems an appropriate place for a few words on the sources of our knowledge of the troubadours.

1. The biographies. These are as a rule very brief and dry. The best, that is to say the earliest, editions of them are two MSS. of the XIII. century (I. & K.) in the Bibl Nationale of Paris, which include eighty-seven lives, and two other MSS. of the same century, one (A.) in the Vatican library, the other (B) in the Bibl. Nat. of Paris. The former contains fifty-two lives and the latter, a mere extract from the other, only twenty-six.

2. The *Razos*. These are explanations of particular poems, and are frequently long and very much in detail, particularly about the love affairs. There are only about seventy of these, relating to some thirty poets Many of the *razos* probably come from the same period as the biographies and from the same authors. Others were later. Some are from good, and others (like some of the biographies, probably) from irresponsible sources. After a famous troubadour died and even while he lived the joglar who rendered one of his songs prefaced it with a statement more or less correct of the circumstances that called it forth. An oral tradition was thus formed, and in the course of time it came to be written down Some of the *razos* are from Sain Circ. It has been thought by Rajna that these *razos* gave Dante the plan of the *Vita Nuova*, i. e., a series of poems with explanatory introductions.

3. Various later writings the authors of which had before them earlier documents that have since been lost, and either based their statements upon these documents or quoted from them, or both

4 The poems themselves Some poets, Daniel for example,

gave few historical indications in their songs ; others gave a great many. All these hints have been most carefully studied.

5. Chronicles, historical writings of all kinds, deeds, charters, inscriptions, in short every sort of record throwing light on the many difficult questions involved, have now been scrutinized with wonderful patience, ingenuity, and scholarship This scientific study has within a comparatively recent period revolutionized our knowledge of the subject, so that one needs to beware of the older authors and of works based upon them to any extent.

Critical opinion places rather a low estimate—too low, possibly— on the historical value of the biographies and *razos*. (See especially No 3, XCII., p. 218.) Certainly they are not scientific history, but rather like the newspaper gossip of today. We have to be on our guard against their errors incessantly, but it is better to hold them with misgivings than to discard them altogether. Truth mixed with error is better than blank ignorance. For this reason I am disposed to accept some stories that critical history is disposed to reject.' Such cases will be treated in the notes. (For a translation of the biographies and *razos*—not, however, from the best text—see No. 158 ; for the best original text see No. 110)

When the text cites the "biography" or "biographer" or "manuscript" the reference may be to either No. 1 or No. 2 above.

CHAPTER VIII.

1. P 119 —In its Roman period Arles had 100,000 inhabitants, while now it has about 27,000 It was practically a seaport then and long after The amphitheatre was made a fortress, packed with houses, in the eighth century on account of Saracen incursions. How much Greek blood there is now in the veins of Arlésiennes may be questioned, but they claim it Their picturesque costume is not the ancient one. It seems at first rather surprising that Arles and Avignon do not appear more prominently in the lives of the troubadours, but we should remember that the troubadours were a part of the feudal system, and these cities became republics : the former in 1150, the latter in 1154.

2. P. 119. Folquet de Marseilla was at Nismes Folquet de Lunel was born in 1244, probably in Lunel, and there he made his home until his death (about 1300). He may have been an ecclesiastic He particularly admired Enric II., count of Rodez (and

very likely visited his court), and after him Amfos X. of Castile.
We have from him seven lyrics and a moral poem (*Romans de
Mundana Vida*) composed in 1284 ; probably also two tensos with
G. Riquier. It is not true, as was long believed, that he was in
love with the Holy Virgin.

3. P. 120 —For books and study see Chapter XXXVII.

4. P. 125 —The distresses and perils of monastic life were vividly
painted—for instance—by Ethelred, abbot at Rievaulx in York-
shire in the twelfth century in his directions to a recluse. Of
course corrupt monasteries did still less for intellectual life.

5. P. 125.—Plantin or Placentinus, who had taught law at
Mantua and Bologna, began to teach at Montpellier about 1180–
1190 (A. Thomas), though some have placed his advent at about
1160. The medical school (perhaps an offshoot from Salerno, perhaps due to the Jewish and Arabic schools of Spain) is first mentioned in 1137. It is curious to note that in these early days a
sort of protective tariff made trouble. the students of Monpesher
wished to import their wine, while the citizens wished local vineyards to have all the business. Of course in saying that "people
wished to know" I speak broadly. By no means all were athirst
for knowledge, but such a thirst existed.

6. P 126.—Ermengaud studied law, but became a monk at
Béziers and there began to compile in 1288. The Breviary was
well posted on things celestial : "The archangels are far the best
messengers," it remarks in the most matter-of-fact style. The
work contains 34,597 rhymed octosyllabic lines. On Bartholomew's encyclopædia was based *L'Elucidari de las Proprietatz de
Totas Res Naturals*, prepared (in prose) early in the fourteenth
century.

7. P. 129.—Marbodus died in 1123 .

8. P. 131.—Arnaud de Villeneuve was born in 1240.

9. P. 131.—Boucherie gives in No 20 (Jan.-July, 1875, p. 67),
two formulas of incantation over serpent bites and fevers, such as
were used all through the Middle Ages, with many medical recipes
and rules that are very curious. Some of the prayers said in collecting plants for medical use are beautiful and touching. What I
quote in the text is only the beginning of one   It is from a MS.
preserved in the Medical School of Montpellier   An aching tooth
was cured by touching it with a dead man's tooth.   A cough was

cured by spitting into the throat of a live frog. The turquoise was believed to keep horses from going mad, etc.

10. P. 131.—This manual is a translation of the so-called *Epistola Aristotelis ad Alexandrum*, based on Arab sources, though the author attributes the letter to Galian and claims to have drawn from Hippocrates also. It was as early at least as Matfre Ermengaud, for it was cited by him.

11. P 132 —Corbiac is a village near Bordeaux. Peire studied at Orléans and was probably a priest (No. 379) Besides the *Tesaur* we have a religious poem from him

12. P. 137.—Guilhem VIII. married Eudoxia, the daughter of Manuel, Emperor of the East She was betrothed to Amfos (Alfonso) II., King of Aragon, but when she arrived at Montpellier on her way to him she found that he had married another woman. It would have been embarrassing to return and so she finally accepted the hand of a count. Her consciousness of superior birth seems to have proved a cause of trouble. Raimbaut de Vaqueiras blamed Guilhem VIII. for abandoning Guilhem del Bauz. It has been stated that every European sovereign of the year 1630 was descended from Guilhem VI. of Montpellier.

13. P. 138.—The Lez.

14. P. 138.—The lower part of the *Tour des Pins* was probably built soon after 1206, the upper part between 1387 and 1407.

15. P. 138.—While at Montpellier I should mention two minor troubadours of this region, Guilhem de Baulaun (probably Balaruc in the arrond. of Montpellier), and Peire de Barjac (probably Barjac in the arrond. of Alais). The first was a noble castellan, the second a worthy knight, and both of them were finished gentlemen and good poets. Together they courted the muse and the ladies. Balaun loved Guillelma, the lady of Jaujac (Gaujac, commune of Vigon, Gard), and won her heart. Barjac was devoted to Viernenca, a lady of the castle, and his love was returned.

After a time, however, V. quarrelled with her lover. [According to No. 196, XV., p. 448, they decided to break their mutual vows, but felt it would be sin to do so. "Let us go to a priest," said the troubadour then ; "before him we will release each other and then we shall be free to form new ties."] Balaun interfered, however, and brought the two together again ; and Barjac then found, as he confessed, that a reconciliation was sweeter than love unbroken

Balaun concluded that he would like this greater happiness himself. So for no other reason he broke with his lady, refused to answer her letters and messages, or even to listen when she came to him by night to seek an explanation. She became at last deeply angry ; and when he in turn supplicated, it was in vain. For a good year she would have none of him. Then Bernart d'Anduza took up the case and finally on two conditions the lady promised to pardon the offender he was to have the nail torn from the middle finger of his right hand, and bring it to her with a song composed for the occasion. The terms were eagerly complied with, the lady forgave all, and from that time the two loved each other more than ever. The song is still extant, as is one song of Barjac's These events took place about 1200 (?).

CHAPTER IX.

1. P. 139.—The Madeleine, not St. Nazaire, is the cathedral Parts of St Nazaire are comparatively recent, and the Madeleine has been modernized out of all interest. The castle (*Place de la Citadelle*) was destroyed by Louis XIII , and on the site of it there is no war but that of bocks and clashing glasses.

2. P. 140.—It belonged to the lords of Limoges. The place is mentioned by B. de Born.

3. P. 143 —The description of Maruelh is based, of course, upon what I saw there ; but it seemed to me it might have looked about the same in Arnaut's time. The castle of which a picture is shown is two or three miles away, near New Mareuil. Parts, at least, of it are comparatively modern

4. P. 149 —We know nothing of Arnaut's boyhood, or of his personal appearance except that it was agreeable. His biography says that he was " *clergues* " and that he was unable to make a living "*per las suas letras*," and we know exactly what his accomplishments were Comparatively few lords and by no means all of the troubadours were able to write

5. P. 149.—Though the lord of Béziers was only a viscount his wife retained, as was customary, the higher title that she inherited.

6. P. 151.—The neglect of the principles and practices of *cortesia* made one a boor, *vilan*. The words " excellence " and " worth " must be understood in the sense which they bore in that society.

7. P. 151.—On the ages of marriageable girls see *Flamenca*, ll. 2624 and 5598 +.

8. P. 153.—Men sometimes purchased noble rank in southern France by the payment of money (Luchaire)

9 P. 154.—The details of his reception are imaginary.

CHAPTER X.

1. P 155.—Vid. No. 358, III , p 210, st. 1 and 2.

2. P. 156.—Vid. No. 358, III., p. 207, st. 1 and 3 Note the idea of *joi* ("aspiring zeal ") in the last line but one, and of *mesura* in the last line of st. 1. The first line of st. 3 is literally, "Fair lady, whom *joi* and *joven* guide."

3. P. 157.—Vid. No. 358, III , p 218, st. 2.

4 P. 157.—The biography states that Arnaut attributed his songs to others, but Diez objected that he could not have done so for he was bound to display his own skill as poet. To meet the objection I have assumed that, as seems very natural, he concealed the authorship of only the most personal songs.

5. P. 157.—Vid No. 370, p. 16, st. 1. The second stanza begins as follows : "Without deceit or falseness or fickle heart I love you the best man can think " Nothing could be freer from artificiality.

6. P 158.—Vid. No. 358, III., p. 212, st. 5 and 6.

7. P. 159.—This road is known locally as "the old route," and must always have followed the Agout as it does now

8. P. 160.—Burlatz (or Burlas) is a little village, sundered by the Agout but held together by a ponderous bridge whose massive arches have been lifted high to clear the spring floods.
The church (the façade can be seen in the picture) burned by the Calvinists in 1569 is a picturesque ruin completely embowered in vines. The interior is kept as a flower garden, its trim beds marked off with box and hawthorn. For priest there is a schoolmaster , for one of the aisles has been walled up and roofed and there young ideas are instructed in archery. It was a "collegiate" church and the building was altered in the Gothic period.
The description of Burlatz is of course taken from the present. I do not know that a bridge existed there at that day but it is easy to believe that one did.

9. P. 163.—Her eyes were called *vair*, which may mean "change-ful," or more probably "variegated" (in the iris) with spots and lines of different colors. (See note 13 on Chap. XXVIII.) In the text I used the former meaning because the latter requires explanation.

FROM CHARTRES.

10. P. 163.—From the *Salutz*, most of which will be given in the next chapter. Vid. No. **63**, col. 96, ll. 14-25.

11. P. 164.—The word wimple is used for *benda*, a word for which there is no English equivalent. Indeed we are not sure just how it was worn. It was let down when a lady wished to kiss, and she loosened it to hear more distinctly. The dress of ladies is shown, for example, in some sculptured figures of the cathedral of Chartres. In the picture the long ends of the mantle have been knotted,—an extreme of fashion sometimes practised. The girdle as is evident was a very important part of a lady's dress. Sometimes the sleeves of the bliaut were knotted. Besides the simple bliaut of the text (sometimes laced at the back instead of the side) there was a compound bliaut for ladies. It consisted of a corsage with sleeves, an abdominal piece, and skirts. The mantles of ladies might be fastened over the right shoulder but were generally fastened under the chin. They were frequently lined with fur. There was at this period but one style of dressing the hair,—the two heavy braids of the picture, but it was customary for both men and women to keep the hair in place with a fillet, a band of metal, or a garland. After about 1214 ladies often wore a small toque or mortar-like cap held in place with a ribbon passing under the chin, but the hood was still relied upon in bad weather. Ladies' chemises were frequently tinged

with saffron. From about 1140 to about 1230 the bliaut was so long as to conceal the under-garments of a woman entirely.

12. P. 165.—There are three main sources of information about

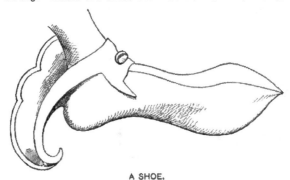

A SHOE.

the costumes of this period : seals, sculptures, and poems. A great deal of most careful study has been expended on these sources, and most valuable results have been obtained. The results do not agree perfectly, however. I have compared the different authorities and endeavored to reach safe conclusions. In cold weather the robe was replaced with a pelisse—necessary on account of the defective heating of castles—which consisted of fur covered on the outside with silk and on the inside with linen. It has been held by some that the robe and pelisse were worn over the bliaut, but this does not seem correct. Fur was often used to trim the neck and wrists of the robe, not for warmth but as an ornament, for people took great delight in furs at this time as a luxury and as a symbol of wealth.

THE HOOD.

The stockings reached above the knee and there met the breeches or drawers, which however in some cases came down to the ankle.

The breeches (made of linen, silk, woollen, or sometimes leather), were held up by a belt and over them hung a long shirt, the edge of which sometimes showed below the robe or pelisse—of men, at least. While the other garments were for service the bliaut was distinctively for dress; it was made as rich and elegant as possible and on ordinary occasions might be dispensed with. The mantle was either semicircular or quadrangular. It was fastened together at the chin or over the right shoulder with a brooch of metal or an *afible* (frog) of silk or hair, or by simply knotting it.

13. P. 167.—Piment contained both honey and spices.

14. P. 168.—Hands were washed both before and after eating, and the usual method was to have a servant pour water on the hands from an ewer and catch it below in a basin. This fête is imaginary but there is good authority for every feature of it.

15. P. 169.—As men and women dressed similarly many of the remarks in Note 12 apply here also, of course. For a bliaut of cendal *cf.* in the *Chanson de Gui de Bourgogne* "*el bliaut de cendal, trés parmi les costès grans bandes d'orfroi.*"

A SHOE.

16. P. 170.—The original (Vid. No. 63, col. 93) contains but four stanzas, a variation from the usual type that enhances the impression of its sincerity. In l. 4 the poet wrote "*rossinhols el jais,*" but I have omitted the jay because that does not represent the sweetest of music to us, and I have felt the more at liberty to do so because *jais* is a rhyme-word. L. 21 is simply "*ab saura cri.*" Arnaut's authorship of this poem has been questioned, but on no strong ground.

17. Pp. 168 and 171.—The conversation is imaginary.

CHAPTER XI

1. P. 172 —Of course ladies had mirrors though not looking-glasses

2 P. 172.—The *Salutz d' Amor* was a popular form of love-poetry and several troubadours have left specimens. When, like this of Arnaut, the Salutz began and ended with the word *Dona* (lady) it was sometimes called a *Donaire*. The method of writing it described in the text was apparently the conventional thing ; Arnaut's may or may not have been so arranged. The original is in No. 63, col 94. It consists of 213 lines In the first cut the poet explained that he pondered long how to convey his thoughts to her but Love commanded him to write a letter. In the second cut the poet describes the beauty of Alazais in detail (see p. 160). He shows how this beauty makes every day a battle for him and every night still worse, for on his bed he turns this way and that, sits up, lies down again, first on one side and then on the other, then throws his arms out and clasps his hands in prayer toward where she is. In the next cut he tells how he falls asleep and for a time has the most blissful dreams, but soon awakes to a full sense of his misery. The proverb is literally " What eyes see not, heart doth not regret."

3 P. 175.—"The rose of June," literally May, but that word occurred just before.

4. P. 175.—"Spirit, grace, and mirth," in the original, *joven*.

5. P. 175.—"Culture " (*ensenhamen*), here education in the usages and accomplishments of polite society.

6. P. 177.—Vid. No. 358, III , p. 221, st. 1. "Gay talk " is *solatz*, the best English word for which is perhaps "conversation " if that be taken in its etymological sense. There is no exact English equivalent except " solace " as used by Chaucer It has been translated by Jeanroy " *humanitas* " and signifies all that goes to make up social intercourse.

7. P 177.—Vid. No. 358, III , p. 219, st. 2 Line 1 : The hope of coming bliss made the troubadours' pains even pleasant.

8. P. 178.—The viscount died in 1194.

9. P 178.—For the stanza in which Arnaut mentioned the " gift " he had received, see No. 142, p. 107, note 1 We do not know that this gift was a kiss, but that is the natural inference.

All the conversations on pp. 178-180 are imaginary. We only know (1) that Alazais wished to get rid of Arnaut because the king was jealous of him, (2) her pretext, and (3) the peremptory way in which she forbade him to visit her or to sing of her.

10. P. 181.—We perhaps do not *know* that Arnaut addressed a song to no other lady, but there is no evidence that he did so.

11. P. 181.—The extant works of this poet are about thirty lyrics, three letters (Salutz), and two didactic poems A. de Maruelh is notable for attaching importance to mental and moral qualities as well as to personal charms. This brings him toward the minne-singers and toward our own day. Another trait that helps us enjoy him is the absence of the conventions and stock allusions often found in troubadour verse. When he refers to nature and the lore of the poets it is with fresh feeling and for a personal rea-son. As a man of sentiment he could not be expected to abound in ideas

12. P. 181 —Amfos died in 1196, Alazais in 1199 or 1200, Arnaut (it is supposed) before Alazais.

13. P. 181.—For his ingratitude see No. 110, p. 13, note 1.

14. P. 182.—The crusaders numbered at Béziers 20,000 knights and over 200,000 villagers and peasants, esquires, clergy, and recruits from neighboring cities. History does not state that the *Veni Creator* was chanted at Béziers, but it was at the assault of Carcassonne.

15. P. 185.—St. Nazaire has been considerably changed and enlarged since 1209.

16 P. 186 —It has been questioned whether the abbé of Citeaux used these words, and the proof is not conclusive that he did. It is immaterial, however. They fitly embody the blasphemous and implacable character of the crusade, and the common sense of mankind has been right in branding him with them. The leaders of the Church and the pope's representative aided and abetted these atrocities, and the Church accepted a share of the plunder. It was therefore an accessory both before and after the fact. At the same time simple justice requires us to bear in mind that the Catholic Church which perpetrated this crime—the Church of the thirteenth not the twentieth century—was a body of men who could not escape the influences of their half-barbarous age, and

also that the pope felt (however mistakenly, as it seems to us) that no cost was too great to preserve the unity of Christendom.

17. P. 187.—The figures I have used, 30,000, are the mean of various estimates from 15,000 to 50,000. Of course many citizens had left the town, but on the other hand many from neighboring places had crowded in there for protection. The massacre is a grewsome topic but it was part of the civilization of the time and I could not omit it. The details of the account are imaginary, so far as this particular event is concerned.

CHAPTER XII.

1 P 188.—While, as Paul Meyer says, it is not correct to speak of Dante and Petrarch as "constant imitators" of the troubadours, it is unquestionable that they studied them with great care. Dante knew Provençal well enough to write it, and we have from him two pieces in this tongue. He said of Daniel, " *Versi d'amore e prose di romanzi—Soverchio tutti.*" This has been variously explained and still is, but as is now agreed does not mean that Daniel wrote prose romances but that he surpassed all other authors of whatever sort.

2. P. 192.—The wording of the scene before King Richard is my own. The story dates in written form from about 1300.

3 P. 192.—Besides the lady of Bouvila mentioned in the biography (her husband's name was Guilhem), it is believed that he paid court among others to Guischarda, Countess of Comborn (who will appear in the story of Bertran de Born), and that he sang to her as his "Better-than-Good" (*Mieills de Ben*). In fact the sestine given later was probably composed in her honor and addressed to Born.

4. P. 192.—Jacques Jasmin was a precursor of the Félibres His first volume appeared (1835) when Mistral was a child of four.

5. P. 192.—Elias was from a spot called Peral, the son of a merchant He was a very good singer, and with Olivier, another joglar, visited the courts of Provence. Amfos II., Count of Provence (1196-1209), *not* Amfos II., King of Aragon, gave them wives and lands at Barjols (near Brignoles in the dep't of Var). Elias loved and sang Garsenda of Forcalquier, Countess of Provence After she died he entered the order of St. Beneit (Bénézet) at

Avignon and died there   He flourished in the first quarter of the thirteenth century   We have twelve or fifteen of his songs

6. P. 193.—In Roman days Agen had temples to Jupiter, Diana, and Bacchus

7. P. 193 —So greatly was the song of the nightingale enjoyed that people of austere principles sometimes put it on the same plane as that of the sirens.

8. P. 194.—The troubadours themselves, as time went on, felt somewhat the narrowness of their circle. Gui d'Uissel said · " More often would I sing, but it wearies me to be forever saying that I sigh and lament for love, for all alike can say that."   There was of course direct imitation among the troubadours but that came for the most part in the later stages which it is not worth our while to consider much.

9. P 194 —It is noteworthy that while the troubadours use more or less frequently a nature-picture as an introduction to a piece, only three—B de Ventadorn, G. de Borneil, and P Vidal—refer to nature in the body of a song , and these references are slight.

10 P. 198 —This piece (particularly admired by Dante) probably was not composed for the lady of Bouvila. Canello thinks that it was probably made for a lady of Aragon. The original is in No. 63, col. 135, st. 1 and 4. The second stanza of the translation does not follow the original very closely, for it did not seem worth while to spend a great deal of time on a labor of doubtful value. All I wish is to show the form and the general style of Daniel's manner. For the same reason I have allowed myself to make l. 1 ◡ — ◡ — instead of — ◡ — ◡, and have rhymed ll 5-11 instead of 2-8, and 4-12-16 instead of 3-12-16.   "Destroy," l. 17, is to be regarded as of three syllables. The repetition of " mates " ll. 9 and 10 of st. 1 follows the original . " *pars e non pars* " The usual plan—to have lines that rhyme together equally indented—was not feasible in this case.

11 P. 201.—Canello found 77 words peculiar to Daniel and about 40 used in a peculiar sense. He tried many kinds of verse, and though his forms were so difficult we find but little mutilation or padding of thought. Besides R d'Aurenga, he was preceded in the use of *trobar clus*, the close and difficult style, particularly by P. d'Alvernhe and Marcabru. The variety of his rhymes is shown by comparison. In 17 pieces he has 98 different rhymes while R.

d'Aurenga has 129 in 34 pieces, and P Vidal only 58 in 54 pieces attributed to him. His rhymes were strict, too Like A. de Maruelh, Daniel was familiar with Ovid's *Ars Amatoria* in the translation of Chrestien de Troyes.

12 P. 203.—The character of the sestine could perhaps have been shown better by composing an imitation, but that would not have been Daniel's The terminal words of the original are *intra*, *ongla*, *arma*, *verga*, *oncle*, *cambra*, and any one who pronounces them aloud will perceive their musical relations and effect. In the original the first line of each stanza contains 8 syllables and the following lines 11 ; for the latter I have substituted 10, as I thought the English ear would not readily understand the change from 8 to 11. The original is trochaic, but that would not be possible in English without a nearly complete change of the essential words ; "uncle" must pass as monosyllabic. For the music of the sestine see No. **25**, III., fasc. 2, p. 243. It was very simple.

The first line of st. 3 is "*Del cors li fos, non de l'arma.*" The change in the meaning of *nails*, st. 6, l. 1, is in imitation of the original. I have used the text of No. **63**, col 138. See also No. **41**, p. 67, and especially No **100**. The sestine concludes with three lines in which the three end-words are introduced:

> "*Arnautz tramet son chantar d'oncl' e d'ongla*
> *ab grat de leis que de sa verga l'arma,*
> *son Desirat qu' a pretz dins cambra intra.*"

It is worth while to consider also, for a moment, the musical significance of Daniel's art Theoretically the stanza was divided as to its music into parts I. and II If I. was divided into A and B, the music of A was repeated for B, and II. (Coda) had a strain of its own. But if I. was not subdivided, then it had no repetition of music, and II was subdivided into C and D, which had corresponding strains. (The sonnet-form is a relic of this system.) There were thus always three parts, two of which balanced each other while the third was independent. So much repetition of music in the rendering of a song did not please Daniel. In fact others—Bernart de Ventadorn and R. d'Aurenga, for example— had found it monotonous to repeat the same strain 14 times in singing 7 stanzas, and for that reason had used the indivisible stanza, called *oda continua*. Daniel carried this improvement still farther, though it is not true, as Dante said, that he used only the oda continua By neglecting the rhyme within the stanza and avoiding the repetition of musical strains he moved in the direction of unity and freedom of ideas, though he left it for others to see the real value of this movement.

We must not, however, lay too much stress upon the supposed relations between verse and music. Restori says: "Whoever should study the stanza of a trouvère or a troubadour   .   .   in the hope of understanding and making understood its nature and musical structure would err and that greatly." See the notes on Chap. XXXIV.

It is noteworthy as an evidence of Daniel's high opinion of his own skill that he usually introduced his name at the end, as in this sestine.

Dante's sestine in imitation of Daniel's begins:

"*Al poco giorno ed al gran cerchio d'ombra.*"

Dante made all the lines of the same length.

13. P. 204.—From Layamon   See No. 314 a, p. 209. The lines mean: "And she shall make my wounds all sound, make me whole with healing draughts."

14 P. 205.—This story is from Benvenuto da Imola, a contemporary of Boccaccio We have no information as to Daniel's personal appearance. Almost nothing remains of the castle at Beauville

15. P. 205.—Daniel's science was recognized in his own day. The author of *Flamenca* wrote, "*Daniel que saup ganren.*" (l. 1717). His fame brightened, faded, and brightened again with that of his admirer, Dante.

CHAPTER XIII.

1 P. 209.—A part of the palace is now the city hall, the façade of which was designed by Viollet-le-Duc in mediæval style.

2. P 210.—St Just was founded in 1272 For a plan and description of the palace see No. 443, VII , p 21.

3. P. 212.—Rogier came from Mirepoix in Auvergne His biography says he was a "*gentils hom,*" but that is not proof that he was of noble family.

4. P. 213.—Vid. No. 43, No. VII., st. 7.

5. P. 214 —Vid. No 63, col. 81, st. 1, 4, 6, and 7. The piece consists of seven st and a tornada. Appel omits l. 8 of st. 4. Ob-

serve the refrain-word "her" at the end of each stanza. The abrupt change from "you" to "her" (st 2), is in the original. The reader may wish a literal translation of st 6 and 7, and although the translation is pretty close I give it: 6. "Alas! What do you bewail?" I fear death. "What is the matter?" I love. "And much?" Yes, so much that I am dying. "You are dying?" Yes "Can you not find a remedy?" No. "And why?" I am so sorrowful "About what?" Her, whence becomes my trouble. "Endure." It avails me not. "Beseech her for pity" So I do. "Do you get no succour?" Little. "Think not of it if you suffer ill from her; never cause her the same" 7. I have a plan "Of what sort?" I will take myself away from her. "Do it not." Yes, I will do it. "You seek your own harm." What else can I do? "Do you wish to have joy of her?" Yes, greatly. "Believe me." Now speak "Be humble, true, generous, and noble." If she treats me ill? "Endure in peace." I am ready. "You are?" Yes. "If you will to love and if you believe me, you shall in this way be able to have joy of her" The word translated "noble" (*pros*) has no exact equivalent in English. It comprehended all the elements of personal merit while "rich" (*rics*) had reference to the nobility of birth and fortune, for feudal wealth was landed property and that went with rank.

Similar debates (*e. g.*, between water and wine) became common, and suggest the possibilities of Provençal literature had it been given an opportunity to develop in the line of the drama. Rogier was one of the first to use dialogue in a poem His artistic judgment is shown by his not carrying the dialogue all through this piece.

6. P. 214.—*Flamenca* is a wonderfully clever story, and as it has been translated into French by the greatest of Provençal scholars, Paul Meyer (No. **291**), all should read it A new edition of this translation is expected. It is a poem of 8087 lines, the longest of the *Novas* (tales, novels), and was composed in 1234. It is of the greatest value for the light it throws on the civilization of the age, and I am indebted to it for many points.

7. P. 216 —While a belief in troubadour Courts of Love has been taught even recently by English writers, the best authorities are agreed in renouncing it; *i. e.*, in renouncing the theory that formally constituted tribunals of ladies existed, which heard actual cases and rendered formal and binding judgments. Martial d'Au-

vergne died in 1508 Apparently he derived his idea of the Courts of Love from the Parliament of Paris. Early in the present century (1817) Raynouard gave the theory a standing by his dissertation on the subject (No. 358, Vol II.), but Diez, the father of Romance philology, soon disproved his view, though his dissertation (*Ueber die Minnehôfe*, 1825) did not have the attention it deserved

The silence of the troubadours is especially convincing against the alleged Courts because we often see them feeling their need of such a tribunal and finding themselves compelled to choose their own arbiters Further, these arbiters were men rather oftener than women whereas the Courts were supposed to have consisted of women only

It is true that the troubadours speak of the Court of Love (*e g*, see the last line of st. 2 of Peire Raimon's song, page 334) but they meant the court of Love the god, and (says Rajna, No. 355, p. 29) "in all that age [*i e.*, the Middle Ages] from the most ancient Provençal and French poets down to Martial d'Auvergne no one —absolutely no one—understood by the expression 'Court of Love' anything but the 'court of the deity.'" There were—at least in northern France—assemblies of ladies who discussed points of love, but these were merely gatherings—not tribunals—their decisions had no binding force, and it is a question whether real cases were *ever* considered by them Rajna, Trojel, and Crescini hold the affirmative, and Gaston Paris the negative See particularly No. 355 ; No. 27, 1883, p 529 ; No. 27, 1890, p 372.

8. P. 217.—Maria de Champagne was the patroness and inspirer of Chrestien de Troyes In the *Flos Amoris* of André le Chapelain, seven opinions on matters of love are referred to her, four to Queen Eleanor, and three to Ermengarda.

9 P. 217.—How far love travelled from the simplicity of natural passion is shown also by Guilhem de Montanhagol or Montagnagout, who said "The true lover cannot desire anything of his lady that could touch her honor, repute, or worth . . . for love is only that which works for the good of the one loved ; and whoever seeks aught else belies the name of love." This poet was a knight of Provence (or Toulouse) of about the middle of the thirteenth century. He sang of Jauseranda of Lunel We have fourteen lyrics from him. (See Coulet's recent edition.)

10. P 218.—The name under which he celebrated her was *Tort*

n'avetz,—"Iu this you are wrong." It is an allusion to her with-
holding her love, selected—I fancy—because as she was a just
ruler a complaint of injustice would touch her more than the usual
one of hard-heartedness

11. P. 218 —The song "*Entr' ir' e joy*" (Appel).

12. P 219 —I am not able to say with certainty that the walls
of Grammont were painted before Rogier went there, but think
they were Lodève is about forty miles north of Béziers, and about
half a mile from the town are the buildings of the abbey, still well
preserved but converted to the uses of a farm The time of
Rogier's birth or death is not known. We can only say that he
flourished in the third quarter of the twelfth century Petrarch
mentioned him iu the *Trionfo d'Amore* as "the other Peter," *i e.*,
not Peire Vidal Only eight or nine pieces have come down from
him,—all of them lyrical. Ermengarda abdicated in 1192.

Another troubadour who entered the abbey of (St. Michel de)
Grammont was Guilhem Azemar, who flourished toward the end
of the twelfth century. He was of Merueis (Meyrueis near Florac,
Lozère) in Gevaudan, the son of a poor knight. His lord knighted
him, but he was not able to maintain his rank and became a joglar.
He composed *novas* (novels, tales), and we have twelve or fifteen
of his lyrics. The following, quoted by F. da Barberino, is worth
preserving. "If you wish to be a finished knight, have a loving
heart and you shall be perfect, for to please the one you love you
will make yourself agreeable and will please all, in the hope that
your repute will reach her ears."

13 P. 220.—Vessels reached Narbonne in Roman days by a
canal 2000 paces long, 100 paces wide, and 30 paces deep. The
ancient basin for ships is now a basin for washerwomen.

CHAPTER XIV.

1. P 226.—Mt. Canigou was long considered the highest peak of
the Pyrenees.

2. P. 226.—Perpignan goes back only to the ninth or the tenth
century.

3. P 227.—The tower called Castell-Rossello dates from the
twelfth century. Rossillon was the mediæval name.

4. P. 227 —The name Cabestany (*Caput Stagni*) is thought to
prove that the *étang*, now more than a mile distant, once reached

the village. In troubadour time the region was doubtless marshy, for the work of reclamation did not begin until the twelfth century.

5 P 229.—What is said of Guilhem's duties and education as a lad is intended as a general picture of that period in the life of a boy of good family. A boy became an esquire at twelve, and usually an esquire became a knight when between fifteen and twenty-one years old. I have assumed that Guilhem had passed the latter point before the tragedy began. Singing and playing were almost as essential to a knight as fencing, and hunting was not only a passion but an art

6. P 230.—No details are given in the story as to the lady's age or personal appearance, but expressions in Guilhem's poems have suggested to me a small person of the winsome, capricious type, and the story as a whole suggests that she was young As previously explained a girl might become a wife as early as thirteen.

7 P. 232.—Vid. 358, III , p 106, st. 1 and 2 The last three lines of st. 2 are literally · " I give it [my sense] to you (to increase your repute and honor) whom my true heart beseeches for pity so sincerely that no man can have a better love."

8. P. 233.—Guilhem's last song is evidence that the proprieties had not been trangressed for it shows that he did not feel sure even then that he possessed Margarida's love

9. P 238 —Vid No. 63, col 73 I have omitted st 5 and 6 and the second tornada. I have used the word " secure " twice but as different parts of speech, which was allowable in Provençal A literal translation is as follows . 1. " The sweet reveries which Love oft gives me, lady, constrain me to say many a pleasant song of you. In thought I gaze upon your dear and comely person, which I desire more than I express. And although I make myself disloyal [to you] for your sake, I do not renounce you, for soon I am praying to you with true affection. Lady, adorned with beauty, many a time I forget myself to praise you and implore your pity. 2. Evermore may I be hated by the Love that keeps you from me, if I ever turn my heart to another understanding [i e , affection]. You have taken from me laughter and given anxious thought. No man experiences a martyrdom more severe than mine. For you, whom I desire more than any other lady in the world, I dis-avow and deny and dis-love in appearance. All that I do for fear you must accept in good faith, even when I do not see you. 3. I

hold in memory the face and the sweet smile, your worth, and your beautiful person, white and lithe. If by faith I were as true to Gŏd, without fail I should enter paradise alive ; for I have given myself to you so from the heart without reserve that no other lady brings me joy, for no one wears a *benda* with whom I should consider it a compensation to lie nor to be her accepted lover in exchange for your greetings. 4. Desire ever stirs me, so greatly attracts me the bearing of you to whom I am devoted. It seems to me well that your love conquer me, for before I saw you I knew that I should love and serve you, for thus have I remained alone by myself without other helps for your sake, and thus have I lost many a boon,—who desires them let him have them, for I am better pleased to wait with no known covenants for you from whom joy has come to me. 5. Ere pain become a flame upon my heart, may pity and love descend into you ; lady, may gladness give you to me and take from me sighing and tears. Let not high descent and rank keep you from me, for every good thing is forgotten by me if mercy avails not for me with you. Oh beautiful, sweet Thing, great nobleness would it be if you loved me at the first when I sought you or not at all, for now I know not which it is 6 No resistance do I find against your excellence,—for this feel pity that shall be an honor to you. May God never hear me among His suppliants if I desire the income of the four greatest kings, so with you avail me not pity and my good faith. For I cannot possibly part from you on whom is my love fixed even were I ruined by it In kissing, were it not pleasing to you, never should I wish to obtain relief 7 Noble, courtly lady, never was a thing so strictly forbidden me, that if it pleased you I would not do it sooner than bethink me of [doing] aught else. 8. Lord Raimon, the beauty and excellence that dwell in my lady have bound me and taken me captive."

Diez and others have been unable to see in this song anything revealing Guilhem's love, but it seems to me that ll. 9–11 of st. 1, and ll. 9–15 of st. 2 in connection with preceding events were clear enough intimations for a jealous man.

On the value attached by Guilhem to his lady's greeting *cf* Dante in the *New Life:* "And when this most gentle lady saluted me not only Love had no power to shade for me the insupportable bliss ; but he, as if through excess of sweetness, became such that my body which was wholly under his rule oftentimes moved like a heavy inanimate thing ; so that it plainly appeareth that in her

salutation abode my bliss, which oftentimes surpassed and overflowed my capacity "

10. P. 239.—As Margarida had killed herself she could not be
buried in consecrated ground, but the king wished both to bury
the lovers together and to bury them in a hallowed spot

11. P 239.—In recounting the story of G. de Cabestaing I have
taken the Laurentian MS (P) as my basis except that at the end
I have fallen back on A. and B. to gain the conversation at dinner
and to avoid bringing King Amfos into a story with which he had
no connection,—for according to P. it was he that avenged the
lovers.

This story stands on a radically different basis from the stories
of the other troubadours. How much of it is to be believed?
Nothing, say some. Certainly not all related in the text. There
was a G. de Cabestaing who fought against the Moors at Las Navas
in 1212. There was a Raimon of Rossillon, who in 1197 married
Seremonda (the name given Guilhem's lady in the oldest accounts).
Seremonda was already a widow and she outlived Raimon, marrying for a third time in 1210 and living at least until 1221. It seems
to me wisest to believe like Beschnidt and Groeber, for example,
that Cabestaing and she were the lovers, and be satisfied to ask no
more about them. Anything like full or positive knowledge we
cannot have As Gaston Paris says, "It is quite useless to search
for history in these tales as some have done, and to use their pretended historical facts to establish the dates of G. de Cabestaing's
life."

Whence, then, the story of their tragic end? There is a considerable body of literature on this subject. See, for example, No.
80, No. 196, XXVIII., p. 352 (G. Paris on Jakemon Sakesep);
and No. 27, VIII, p. 343, and XII, p. 359. The story seems to
have come from a Provençal tale not extant, derived from the old
French *lai* of Guiron, also lost; and is thus ultimately of Celtic
origin. It seems likely that the tale was attached to a man of
southern France in order to make it more popular there, and G.
de Cabestaing was selected (though he was evidently not the first
whose name was used) because of his intensely passionate songs.
Perhaps also a confusion of names helped lead to this, for the first
Provençal to serve as hero for the tale was called Guardastaing,
and still appears in Boccaccio's version as Guardastagno (*Decam.*,
IV., 9). The same story was told in France of the Châtelain de

Couci, and in Germany of the minnesinger Reinmann von Brennenberg.

As an extreme of criticism it may be well to cite Canello, No. 6, II., p. 78, who concludes that G de Cabestaing lived about 1150 on terms of friendship with Raimon Trencavel, viscount of Béziers, and of love with Alazais or Saura his wife. A hundred years later there came to be associated with him a story partly true and partly fabulous told by R. de Miraval of a Provençal knight. The true part was the violent death at the husband's hands, the false part was the eating of the lover's heart by the unfaithful wife. The latter came from the story of the Châtelain de Couci as its direct source, and ultimately from a series of popular tales current all over Europe.

Petrarch knew of the story and spoke of the troubadour as "that Guglielmo" who shortened his life by his singing

We have eight songs from G. de Cabestaing. The absence of sensuality in his poems is worthy of note as also his tribute to his lady's virtue,—"*Uns no la tenc devestida.*" It is in keeping with Guilhem's character that instead of allusions to history and the romances we find references to God and the Bible. Such evidences of innocence and sincerity make the poems especially touching.

The following quotations are striking "Like one who bends down the bough and plucks the fairest of the flowers, I have chosen from the top of the copse (*en un aut bruelh*) the most beautiful flower of womanhood"; "Yet even if I become old and as white as snow I will no way complain of my lady"; "The fire that consumes me is so great that the Nile could no more quench it than a slender thread could hold up a tower"; "Within and without I am covered with love more than the hyssop with blossoms."

CHAPTER XV.

1. P. 241.—Serveri of Gerona, a Catalonian town on the line to Barcelona—very picturesque and very squalid—flourished about 1280 and has left a large number of pieces, most of them unpublished as yet.

2 P. 241.—The Spanish court most frequented by the troubadours was that of Amfos (Alfonso) II., and his son Peire (Pedro) II., kings of Aragon and counts of Barcelona, but this was by no means the only one. Amfos VIII. of Castile (1158–1214) was visited by A. de Peguilha, Gavaudan, G. de Cabestaing, G. de Borneil, G. de

Calanson, P Vidal, P Rogier, R. Vidal, S. de Mauleon, U de S Circ, U de Mataplana, Folquet de Marseilla, and (some have thought) R de Vaqueiras. Amfos VII of Leon (1126-1157) was visited by Marcabru and P d'Alvernhe. Amfos IX. of Leon (1188-1230) was visited by E Cairel, G Azemar, G. de Borneil, P. Vidal, and U. de S. Circ. We shall hear more of Amfos X of Castile (1252-1284) later. He entertained A de Belenoi, B. Carbonel, B. de Lamanon, B. Calvo (F. de Lunel), G. Riquier, A. de Mons, and others. In the reign of his predecessor Castile was visited by Azemar lo Negre, E. Cairel, G Azemar, G. de Borneil, and Sordel

Catalonia is the richest part of Spain and Barcelona its finest city. The walls of Barcelona were demolished in 1868, and the city has doubled in size since then

3 P. 242—Montjuich is a fort, commanding city and harbor, on a hill almost twice as high (750 feet) as Edinburgh Castle.

4 P. 242 —The total height of the Columbus monument is 197 feet.

5 P. 245.—My authority for the identification of the arches of the mediæval palace was the Keeper of the Records He personally pointed them out to me, and while I am aware that some have placed the palace elsewhere, I see no good reason to question his authority

6 P. 246.—The Voice of the cathedral was produced, as I discovered later, by two singers, both of them men of tremendous physique, who alternated as trumpeters do in the army, each with a phrase, so that the chant rolled on without break or diminution. Their voices were almost exactly alike.

7 P 251 —G de Berguedan (see No. 9, VI., p. 231) was of the county of Cerdagne (diocese of Urgel) in northern Catalonia, and he was the lord of Madorna and Riech He was the eldest son in a family of distinction that went back to the time of the Goths, and was born in 1149. His first quarrel seems to have been with Marquis Pons de Mataplana, one of his neighbors,—cause unknown. The man he murdered (in 1174) was Raimon Folc of Cardona, "a richer and a greater man than he " He probably left Spain in 1176. For some years he was with Henry II. of England, and he became the dear friend of Bertran de Born. Returning to Aragon about 1181 he was imprisoned, but after a time was released. Early in 1184 he wrote a sirvente against Amfos, his king, declaring that a man to whom Amfos owed 200 maravedis

killed a Jew in a brawl, that the Jews then offered Amfos 200 maravedis for the culprit and his accomplice, and that getting the men
in this way the Jews killed them at Christmas. From the same
source is the story of the king's treatment of the countess of Burlatz (see Chap. XI.)   Both tales had some basis of fact, perhaps, but
must be taken with much allowance for we know that Berguedan
was capable of lying. He had a love affair with Estefania de
Berga to whom Vidal also probably paid court. (Fancy these two
as rivals!) He was killed about 1195. We have something over
twenty of his lyrics and an epistle   His poems are chiefly interesting in a literary way on account of the influence of the Catalonian
folk-songs that they reveal.

8. P. 252.—Amfos (Alfonso) II. was born in 1152, began to reign
in 1162, and died in 1196 in Portugal while endeavoring to arrange
a general league against the Moors. The capital of Aragon was
Saragossa (Saragosa), but as Barcelona was the home of his fathers,
his pleasantest and richest city, and nearest the centre of his do-
minions, it was natural for him to spend much of his time there.

9. P 253.—Vid. No 63, col. 85. There are five stanzas, all on
the same two rhymes. I give st. 1, 2, and 4. L. 3, "groves,"
literally, *gardens*

CHAPTER XVI.

1. P. 254.—Eméric-David made out three Sordels: 1, the troubadour ; 2, him of Dante's *Inferno ;* 3, him of Dante's *De Vulgari
Eloquentia*

2. P 255 —There has been much dispute about the poetical
work of St. Francis and most of the pieces attributed to him seem
to have been later ; but it appears certain enough that the Hymn
of Brother Sun was composed by him about two years before his
death. Certainly too, as Ambros has said, St. Francis was "deeply
poetical and always inspired."

3. P. 256.—Apparently there were Italian troubadours before
Lanza, for the satire of P d' Alvernhe alludes to a Lombard poet.
In fact the ready recognition of the Provençal troubadours at the
close of the twelfth century and the ability of the Italians to cope
with them in tensos appear to show that their language and literature had been familiar in Italy for a considerable time. Manfred
II. Lanza, Marquis of Busca in Lombardy, first appears as such
June 13, 1190 (see No. 31, VII., p. 187). Peire Vidal answered him,
as we shall see (Chap. XVIII.).

4 P 256.—Cigala represented Genoa in negotiations with the count of Provence in 1241, and doubtless that business brought him into relations with Bertran de Lamanon (see Notes on Chap I.). In 1243 he was a magistrate and in 1248 consul of Genoa He appears constantly in public acts until 1257 He attacked Bonifaz III., marquis of Monferrat, in a sirvente, praised Louis IX. of France, denounced the obscure style of verse, and celebrated two ladies. In 1245 was composed *Estier mon grat mi fan*, etc., and in 1248 *Si mos chans fos de joi*, etc. Schultz thinks it probable that he wrote songs before 1240, however. We know of thirty-odd pieces of his, several of which have been lost

With Guillelma de Rozers, a lady of Provence living (perhaps married) in Genoa, he had a tenso, according to MS. P. (Laurentian, 14th cent.), on the basis of the following story : Two brothers, dearly loved by two ladies, kept a castle jointly and had agreed that as the neighboring barons were hostile they should not both be away at the same time on any account whatever As it chanced, the ladies summoned their lovers for the same time Each asked the other's permission to go but neither would consent to remain, and they set out in company, ordering that the castle gate should be opened to no one during their absence. It was storming violently, and about three leagues away they came upon some knights and heard them comfort themselves by saying that the two brothers would show them bountiful hospitality. But as things stood the strangers would be refused admission The brothers discussed the situation, and finally one of them turned back, on the ground that he would honor his lady more by observing the duty of hospitality than by visiting her. Which of the two deserved the greater praise?

5. P 256.—From Calvo come seventeen poems but we have no biography. Two of his poems are in Portuguese. He appears to have been residing at the court of Castile from the first months after the accession of Amfos X. (1152) through 1153 and 1154. Most of the poems that we have from him were probably written there. We do not know why he went to Spain.

6 P. 257.—Zorgi, probably born between 1230 and 1240 (Levy), was governor of Modon and Coron in the Morea for two years How long after that he lived we do not know. He disappears entirely. We apparently have an account of him from a contemporary, not at all constructed from his poems His sirvente in

answer to Calvo was his best poem; his love-songs are rather weak   His imprisonment (usually placed between 1266 and 1273, but about two years earlier by Levy) seems to have been easy. Levy thinks that he died about 1300 but there are no data   We have eighteen pieces from him, not in the best of Provençal. Restori names five other Genoese troubadours of about this period.

7 P 257.—I was pleased to find at Goito that the name of Sordel is known. To ascertain this I asked some questions of a man I met in the Square and presently found myself the hero of an interested circle. The brass band soon drew my glory from me.

8. P. 258.—One of the biographers makes Sordel the son of a poor knight named El Cort. He was probably born about 1200 (Schultz).

9 P. 259 —The town of Soave was in existence as early as 874, and the castle as early as 934. The castle and the town with its wall and twenty towers, rising about the plain on the foot-hills, present a distinctly mediæval appearance as nothing in Sambonifacio does.

10. P. 259 —Albric joined Aicelin in instigating the carrying off of Conissa.

11. Pp. 260, 261, 272 —From Browning's *Sordello*.

12. P. 261.—As Aicelin was at Treviso from the summer of 1227 to the early months of 1229 the date of Sordel's third exploit can be approximately fixed. His wife's name was Otta.

13. P 262 —The picture of Sordel is entirely imaginary, except that Peire Bremon furnishes a hint when he calls Sordel a manikin or puppet (*bagastel*) among knights   Of course if this taunt had been groundless it would not have been worth making. Several facts tend to cast doubt on the heroic quality of his courage

14. P. 263.—Sordel reached Spain shortly before 1230. (It has been conjectured that the cause of his trouble with Aicelin at Treviso was improper relations with Conissa.) In Spain he visited Jacme (James) I. of Aragon, Ferdinand III of Castile, and Amfos (Alfonso) IX of Leon who died in 1230.

15. P. 264 —The originals of these quotations are in No 258: "It is not life," etc., XV., st. 3 ; "At court," etc, XIII. ; "Of worth," etc, XV., torn.

16. P 264.—Rodez is a high plateau bounded on three sides by steep slopes 150 feet high, the bases of which are washed by the

winding Aveyrou   Its cathedral, begun (1274) about the time of
Sordel's death, makes an imposing effect   Two towers that belonged to the fortifications are still erect.   In the library I found
an old map on which the site of the castle was indicated, but of
the castle itself I found nothing

17 P 264 —Ugo Brunenc was born in or near Rodez and educated for the Church.   His verse was pleasant but of no special
merit   The eulogy of his friend Daude de Pradas shows him as a
lovable person   At Vodable the Dalfin of Auvergne reigned (see
Chap XXIX.)   Brunenc loved a burgheress of Aurillac but she
preferred the count of Rodez, Ugo II., and Brunenc in disgust entered the Certosa.   A remark of Daude's has caused some to question whether he did become a monk ; but it might be taken to
indicate, I should think, that he died shortly after doing so.   We
have seven or eight lyrics from him.

18. P 265 —Daude de Pradas (Prades near Rodez) became canon
of Maguelonne.   He knew Gui d'Uissel well, and probably R. de
Vaqueiras,—at least he knew his patron, the prince of Orange.   His
chief work is entitled *Dels Auzels Cassadors*   (It is interesting to
add that the great emperor Frederic II. thought it worthy of him
not only to compose Provençal verses but to prepare a treatise on
the falcon.)   We have also from him a poem on The Four Cardinal
Virtues and about twenty lyrics.   As for love he seems to have
cared only for its carnal side.   He died about 1228–30.
Several other poets frequented the court of Rodez.   One was
probably F. de Lunel, as already suggested   Another was named
Bernart de Tot lo Mon , and a third was Bernart de Venzac, who
addressed a piece to Count Ugo (1227–1274) proving that he like his
successor Enric II (patron of F. de Lunel) prided himself on his
poetic talent   G. Riquier (Chap XLIII) exchanged tensos with
Enric II., and probably passed considerable time at his court.

19. P. 266 —Vid No. 41, p. 72   The piece contains five st. (of
which I give 1 and 3) and two tornadas, the first of four and the
second of two lines   The rhymes are unchanged.   St. 2, l. 5, lit ,
" So worn out by buffeting, distressed, and dismayed " ; l. 8, lit.,
" (I find) no shore nor port, ford, bridge, nor bulwark "   The poet's
metaphors were rather mixed, for a storm-tossed mariner would
not be much helped by a ford, bridge, or bulwark.   Schultz doubts
whether the " sweet enemy " was Guida

20 P. 266 —Blacatz, probably born about 1160, appears in history from 1176 to 1237. Possibly he lived until 1241 He grew still richer and still more generous as he grew older. Besides his chief residence, Aups, he owned Sarrenom, whence came the poetess Tibors. He entertained Cadenet, Vidal, and many others. The earliest piece we have from him is a tenso with Peirol. He exchanged verses with R. de Vaqueiras, F de Romans, and Pelizier (?) We have from him nine tensos, one sirvente, and one song. For a study of Blacatz see No 31, 1899, p. 201. He seems to have deserved the laudations showered upon him by the poets. Perhaps it is worth while to add that even when this cannot be said of one whom they praised it does not follow that they were insincere, for a baron might be hard and unprincipled in public life and yet personally amiable and cultured. One of the chief duties of the court poet was to sing his patron's funeral oration.

21. P. 267.—Blacasset seems to have been born about 1200, and is mentioned as a hostage in 1288. We have ten or twelve poems from him. It has been queried whether there were not two Blacassets, one of them the son of Blacatz, the other the poet.

22. P. 268.—Sordel used "light music" (*leugier son*) for the Lament because it was really more sirvente than *planh*. For the original see No 258, or No. 63, col. 205, which differs only in the spelling of a few words. The "Roman emperor" was Frederic II., against whom Milan had rebelled The king of France was Louis IX , who, influenced by his mother, did not insist upon his right to the throne of Castile. The English king was Henry III , who allowed France to retain Normandy ; and the Spanish king was Ferdinand III of Castile, also thought to be too much under the influence of his mother. The three remaining stanzas deal with minor potentates, concluding with the counts of Toulouse and Provence. Two tornadas follow, the first of which is "The barons [*i. e* , the princes whom he has reproached] will be offended with me for what I justly say, but let them know well that I esteem them as little as they me." The second is addressed to the poet's lady, " Restaur " Both tornadas are of two lines and rhyme with the last stanza.

Schultz has placed the composition of the Lament between June 4 and Nov. 27, 1237; but De Lollis, objecting to any precise date, places it at about 1240.

Bertran de Lamanon wrote a parody of this Lament, dividing

the heart of Blacatz more fitly, as he asserted, among the ladies of
whom the departed was so fond   A part was assigned to Guida
of Rodez   Peire Bremon Novas Ricas made a poem providing a
still different division. (Another poem that was parodied was
La douss' aura of B. de Ventadorn.)

After this Lament, as De Lollis thinks, came the three poems
against Peire Bremon Novas Ricas, a troubadour who has left us
some twenty lyrics. These pieces are, next his Lament, Sordel's
best poetry,—energetic, original, almost worthy of a Dryden, but
not of sufficient interest to merit translating   On the order of
these poems the last word does not seem to have been said   One
stanza (No. 258, VIII , st 3) is as follows · "Now shall we see the
base hypocrite appear, faithless toward God and false to his lord.
After this, since peace and the gay springtime come, he should
show himself with a garland of flowers , but while there was war,
so frightened was he that his greatest enemies never saw him
under arms   And the lady who gives her love to such a knight is
as good in repute as he in valor "

23   P. 268.—Sordel appears repeatedly—1252, 1257, etc —as a witness to important public acts, and was doubtless of assistance in
helping Charles against his rebellious cities during these years.
For the dispute between Charles and Sordel see No. 258, XI

24   P 268.—Bertran de Lamanon probably accompanied Charles
and Sordel on the expedition to Italy.

25. P. 269 —These five castles were all in the Abruzzi district
Charles added the life use of another. By an exchange Sordel
obtained Palena   His castles changed hands Aug. 30, 1269   He
may have continued to live, but if he had done so we should in
all probability find some record of him.

26. P. 270 —This poem is called *L'Ensenhamen d'Onor.* It
contains 1327 lines, and appears to have been dedicated to Lady
Guida. Vid. No. 258, XL   I have selected lines 1-, 89-, 355-,
365-, 415-, 490-, 719-, 745-, 777-, 901-, and 1261-.

Sordel says of love that a lady may have one lover, but must be
very prudent in selecting him and then leave him no more than if
they were married

27. P. 272.—How Dante came to have so erroneous an idea of
Sordel is difficult fully to explain. Merkel, taking the bull by the
horns, maintains that Dante was justified by the facts, but this view

does not seem likely to be accepted. It seems probable that Dante was ignorant of Sordel's part in Charles's invasion, and, impressed in early life by his great reputation as a poet, and later by the grandiose Lament, chose him as the most available figure to express patriotic ideas that he wished to embody in some one In fact, as Mott has said, the Sordel of the *Purgatory* can be drawn from this Lament plus the single fact that Sordel was Mantuan. (See *Purg.*, Canto VI.) Schultz, however, does not believe that Dante could have been ignorant of Sordel's doings after he left Italy, and Appel thinks it clear from the *De Vulg. Eloq* that Dante had information about him which we do not possess. There has been recently an interesting discussion upon Sordel between Torraca (see *Giornale Dantesco*, IV. and V.) and De Lollis (see No. 7, XXX, p 125).

From Sordel we have thirty-nine lyrics and one didactic poem.

CHAPTER XVII

1. P. 275.—There are three systems of Vidal's life. The first one was planned out by Diez. Bartsch (No. 66) making a more special study doubtless improved upon this Finally Schopf (No. 393) has undertaken to improve upon Bartsch at several points

According to Bartsch, Vidal's peregrinations were as follows: Love affair near Toulouse ; Castile ; Montesquieu, near Toulouse ; Montalin near Carcassonne ; Italy (probably by sea); Narbonne (probably by sea); Marseille ; Beuil (Biolh); St. Gilles ; Cyprus (marriage); Fanjau (near Mirepoix), Saissac ; Gaillac (Galhac); Cabaret, Monrial ; Marseille (1186), Sault ; Marseille (banishment), Genoa (by boat); the crusade, Les Baux, Marseille (reconciliation); Cabaret (prob. before 1192, wolf episode), mourning for Raimon V. (1194); Monferrat (1194); Aragon (before 1196); Monferrat ; Hungary (after the beginning of 1196); region of Carcassonne (Loba's scandal); Monferrat (attempt to rival R. de V.), Monferrat (left at the time of the crusade, 1202); Malta (1205); Toulouse ; with Blacatz in Provence.

Schopf seems to be right in arranging certain events in a different order, thus: Marseille, Aragon (Castilian lady); Montesquieu, Beuil (Biolh), Cabaret ; Marseille (a long visit, banished); Genoa; Cyprus (marriage); Provence (about 1187–88); Beuil ; Marseille about 1189 (reconciliation); Sault ; crusade ; return after Barral's death (1192); Cabaret (wolf episode, 1192); Loba's scandal ; Monferrat (1194–95); Hungary (after the death of Amfos, 1196); Spain;

Monferrat (and probably the fourth crusade) ; Malta , Blacatz.
(I do not believe that Vidal took part in the fourth crusade).

Needless to say   1 The arguments for this or that sequence of
events are often so slight as not to be convincing , 2. The precise
order is in many cases of really no importance , 3. Vidal doubtless
visited many places not in the list—certainly some—so that in no
case do we feel sure of having his complete itinerary.   In the text
I have not mentioned all the places which we know he visited
One is tempted to believe that Vidal's marriage occurred when he
went to the East on the crusade, and Restori does so ; but this view
meets with serious difficulties

2 P 276.—The abbey of St. Victor was founded in the fourth
century.

3 P 276 —The Greek city lay on the north side of the Old
Port. Above it rose the Acropolis with a temple of Apollo and a
temple of Diana.

4. P. 279.—Marseille is by no means as dirty now as formerly
and I cite testimonies to that feature of it merely as illustrations
of the easy, careless temper of the people.

5 P. 280 —She was of a Narbonne family, and her name was
Guilhalmona.

6. P 281.—At Beuil (Biolh) Vidal paid court to the wife of
Guilhem Rostanh   Another of his ladies was Estefania, wife of
Bernart d'Alion, lord of Son (now Usson) near Foix. Another
castle that he frequented was Fanjau near Mirepoix, and he visited
Lord Agout at Sault, a fief belonging to the viscount of Béziers

7 P. 281 —I do not know that the castle of Gaillac in Vidal's
day was the Château de L'Orme but assume that it was

8. P 281.—Penautier (Puegnautier) is only about two miles
from Carcassone. There is and long has been a château at the
right of the round tower. From the appearance of things it seems
reasonable to suppose that the baron's residence was always there.

9. P 283 —The ancient road to Saissac went up the ravine,
through the lower town, and by the Red Gate to the upper town.

10. P. 284.—La Camargue was ruined by erecting dykes against
the fertilizing inundations of the Rhone.

11. P. 286.—The church of St. Gilles was begun in 1116   Archæ-
ologists differ as to the date of the west front, the part particu-

larly referred to. Vöge assigned it to 1150, Marignan places it about a century later. I have taken a mean of the two dates.

12. P. 289 —Precisely how Vidal's tongue was treated we do not know. The Monk of Montaudon said he needed a tongue of silver after that, but of course this was a jest. Boring seems the most probable form of the punishment, though the biography says that the knight " caused his tongue to be cut."

13 P. 289 —Ugo married Barrale, daughter of Barral. (This gave the viscountship of Marseille to the house of Les Baux.) They had a son named Barral del Bauz (des Baux) who became podestat of Arles and Avignon (1250). His court was gay and liberal and the joglars were well received there A troubadour named Paulet de Marseilla, from whom we have six—perhaps eight—pieces and possibly a tenso with G. Riquier and two others seems to have frequented this court and he composed a Lament when Barral died (1270).

CHAPTER XVIII.

1 P. 290.—The castle is a double cube with ten towers, one side of it forming a part of the wall. The prison and torture-room may still be seen in the basement. The chief barbican no longer exists. In the time of Simon de Montfort the outer wall had not yet been built. Carcassonne, that is, the old *cité*, has very few inhabitants It has been restored by the government and is maintained as a " Historical Monument."

Arnaut de Carcasses was the author of a tale in verse in which a parrot plays the part of messenger and confederate in a love affair with great cleverness but no regard for morality. (See No 24, I., p. 36, and No. 27, VII., p. 327.) The parrot plays a part in Provençal somewhat as in Hindu literature.

2 P 293.—The crusaders gave out that Raimon Rogier died a natural death ; but they did not convince the world then, and it still holds them guilty of this foul crime.

3. P. 293.—This meeting may or may not have occurred.

4. P. 297.—Cabaret was mentioned by Gregory of Tours as early as 585. Tradition has it that an underground passage nine miles long connected it with Carcassonne. The lord of Cabaret, Peire Rogier, was in Carcassonne at the time of its siege. Afterward he made a bold attack on Montfort in the same town but accomplished

nothing   When he surrendered Cabaret he was given estates of
equal value elsewhere.   His wife Brunessen befriended the troubadour R. de Miraval.   His brother Jordan, who was part-owner of
the castle, is supposed to have been Loba's husband

5 P. 298.—We may place Vidal's first acquaintance with Loba
at about 1185, some nine or ten years before the countess of Burlatz dismissed Arnaut   .The Vieux Pont was built in 1184

6. P 298.—Vid. No. **66**, p. 43, st. 7.

7. P. 299 —We have no knowledge of Vidal's personal appearance.   A piece in No **115** seems to indicate that Alazais gave
him a *cordon* as a love-token.

8. P. 300.—" Like some poor wight," etc   Vid. No. **66**, p. 70,
first half of first stanza ; "Like one who gapes," etc. , same, st. 2.

9. P. 300.—Vid No **358**, III , p. 318, st. 2

10. P. 302.—Vid No. **63**, col 107. I have taken sts 1 and 2.
St. 2 is literally · " Without sin have I assumed penitence, without
wrongdoing have I sought pardon, and from nothing I have
derived a fair gift ; and from sorrow have I favor , and from weeping [I have] full joy, and from loving [I have] a sweet savor ; and
through fear I am bold ; and I know how, losing, to gain, and to
conquer when I am overcome." In the next stanza he says "All
other lovers will be able to find encouragement in me, for with
extra-ordinary labor I draw bright fire from cold snow, and sweet
water from the sea " The sixth stanza reads : " And he that blames
long waiting makes a great mistake, for they of Brittany now
have Arthur, in whom they placed their confidence , and I by long
hoping have obtained with great sweetness the kiss that force of
love made me steal from my lady, who now deigns to make me a
present of it " (The allusion is to the ill-fated Prince Arthur of
Brittany, born in 1187; who, Vidal suggests, is the King Arthur
of the Round Table for whose return Brittany had long been
hoping) The next and last stanza is devoted to the praise of
Barral, whom the poet will serve and praise.

11. P. 303 —Vid No **66**, p 5, or for these sts. only No. **142**, p
138, note. These are the first three stanzas of the piece. The
arrangement is peculiarly interesting for not only the rhymes but
the rhyme words are repeated in the original as in the translation.
A literal rendering is : " It is very good and fair to me when I see
anew the foliage on the bough and the fresh flower, and the birds

sing above the verdure and the true lovers are gay with love ; lover and accepted lover am I, but so grievous are the sufferings that I have long endured that I have a little lost my mind in consequence. 2. Yet with good reason I love with good-will love, and *joven* and everything that is fair to me, for in joy I long live and renew [myself] with the fruit on the bough when the birds sing , for I have in my heart leaf and flower which keep me all the year in verdure and in full joy, wherefore I feel nothing to make me sorrowful   3. For, whereas she was harsh to me, now I am counted as her own by the fairest and most sensible lady under God, for she discerns well that I love her with good-will so that in my youth and long after that I will serve her fair, gay, supple, and lively person according to the law of the true lover whose entire heart is in love."

In l. 10 of st. 3 as given in No. 142, a new word is introduced— *isnelh* instead of *novelh*,—but I have followed the text of No. 66; the former text is the better however for line 5

12. P. 303 —Not long before his death Barral repudiated Alazais and married Maria, daughter of Guilhem VIII. of Montpellier

13. P. 303.—Vid. No 66, p 38, st. 2.   Peire became acquainted with Richard considerably before this.   This song ends with two formal lines to Vierna

14 P. 304.—Vid No. 63, col. III.   I give st. 3.   The hauberk was in general a jacket or coat, usually of leather, covered with rings or plates of iron or steel, though later it was a coat of mail without leather   "White" has reference probably to the shining of the metal.   "Double" signifies that it had a twofold protection of metal or an extra thickness of leather. Line 2 is literally : "and gird on the sword that Guido gave me the other day."   The rest of the piece, which is really a request for the gift of a horse (the only begging poem that we have from Vidal), is as follows : "1 Lord Drogoman [a person unknown or perhaps a fictitious name like Rainier for Barral.   See another mention of him in No 42, p 329], if I had a good war horse my enemies would find themselves in a bad fix, for barely to hear my name they fear me more than quail [fears] hawk, and they value not their lives at a penny, so haughty, fierce, and savage they know me to be. 2. And if I had a steed that was a good courser, the king [Amfos II. of Aragon] would live in peace on the side toward Balaguer and would sleep sweetly and peacefully, for I would maintain order in Proensa [Provence]

and Monpeslier so that brigands and freebooters should not ravage Venaissi [Autaves, according to Paul Meyer] or the Crau. 4 In boldness I am as good as Roland and Olivier, and in gallantry as Berart de Mondeslier (Montdidier) [a hero of the *chansons de geste*] ; and my prowess is such that I have great praise Messengers come often to me with a ring of gold, a black and white girdle [embroidered *cordons* were often given by ladies as pledges of favor], and such love-letters (*salutz*) that my heart rejoices   5 And if I get at the mockers and tale-bearers who treacherously attack the pleasure of others [attack their betters, P.M] and both openly and privily destroy gladness, they shall know in truth what sort of blows I strike, for though they had bodies of iron or of steel it would not avail them a peacock's feather. 6. In all things I show myself a knight. That I am indeed, and I know the whole business of love and all that pertains to gallantry, for you never saw one so charming in a lady's chamber nor one so proud and so mighty in arms , for which reason [even] such as do not see or hear me are afraid of me. 7. And if the king turn on sandy Toulouse, and if the count [his own lord, the beloved Raimon V., for whom he mourned so deeply] come forth with his miserable dart-throwers [or archers] who all cry, 'Aspa! Assau!' [P M.], I boast this much, that I will give the first blow and I will do [it] in such fashion that they shall re-enter [the town] twice [as fast] and I with them if the gate be not closed against me." This piece is addressed to Vierna For a special study of it by Paul Meyer, who terms it a "*chef d'œuvre de la gasconnade*" see No. **27**, II., p. 423. Also the same, I., p. 104. The composition of it was assigned to 1181 by Bartsch, who called it Vidal's first sirvente.

Paul Meyer speaks of Vidal's having gone to Palestine with Richard, which implies that he thinks his courage held out so far.

15. P. 307 —This wolf incident is no more astonishing than other performances of Vidal's, and is quite in accord with the opinion that he won among his contemporaries Still some recent critics have found it too improbable to believe. The only argument against it, so far as I know, is that of Novati in No **27**, who (1892, p. 78) shows that the story might have grown from a poem in which Vidal, to honor his lady, declared that he thought it no disgrace to be called a wolf and the shepherds might hunt him. But it is one thing to show that the story might have come from the poem and quite another to show that it did. It seems to me that

Vidal's bragging may easily have brought him into a place from which a challenge to make it good left him no escape except by doing as the story recounts There is a natural feeling that so good a poet and so famous a man ought not to appear in situations so discreditable as this and others related of him, and hence there is a temptation to extricate him by special pleading. But to argue that he was not at times a fool is to argue that all the rest of the world were fools, for it is perfectly clear that those who knew him thought that he often acted like a madman. Before trying to explain away the tales told of him we must explain away the prevailing opinion of him and this appears impossible. Besides, Vidal was only one of many who teach us that artistic talent may be only a trick of the brain quite apart from general intellectual soundness. Indeed in a morbidly boiling brain like his the difference between the subjective impression called memory and the other subjective impression called imagination might easily be lost sight of.

16 P 307.—The king was that Aimeric or Emmerich, who dared to enter an army of rebels, quelled it by his sublime courage and the splendor of his royal bearing, and with his own hands led their commander away captive.

17. P. 308 —Vidal died between 1208 and 1210 (Bartsch). He has left us 47 poems (Bartsch); many others have been attributed to him His qualities as a poet have been alluded to in the text. The mingling of love and politics was his fundamental fault (though the fashion became popular), and not only was it artistically bad but it made his expressions of love seem insincere, for a man truly in love does not talk politics and love together As Vidal himself said : " No man can escape from Love, once in his power   . and know well that a man in love can give himself to nothing else ; he runs where Love wills and no longer takes account of discretion and folly." Spontaneity, ease, variety, absence of conventionality, abundance of metaphors and comparisons are his great merits. His poems show few formal introductions He was particularly fond of figures drawn from the sun and fire and made a notable use of allusions to the Old Testament. Probably his restless life marred his artistic development

Francesco da Barberino quotes a tale of Vidal's that is worth repeating. " Peire Vidal said that a prudent knight must not give his love to a lady who enjoys hearing her beauty praised, for if it

be easy to win her heart it is no less easy to lose it ; and in proof
he cites an example A young lady, neither beautiful nor ugly,
was travelling by the way of Orange Some young knights there
who had nothing better to do, began to follow her, and to pass in
front of her, saying in such a way that she could hear · 'Heaven
protect her from every mishap ! How charming she is, how graceful, how winsome, how beautifully moulded ! What adorable hair,
what melting eyes, what a correct bearing ! How well she walks,
how gracefully she salutes, how well her garland is placed, how
fairly her girdle is adjusted ! What delicate little feet, what a fine
manner, what a hand to kiss ! Have you ever seen a young lady
so perfect?' And they continued in this tone, asking everybody
' Who is this young lady?' They followed her home, and with
such effect that the moment she was within doors she began to gaze
at herself and adorn herself, with the idea that she was as beautiful
as they had said,—if not more so. From that time she was forever
to be seen at the window, at church, in the street. Our young
fellows perceiving her folly devoted themselves to following her
and talked about her to their friends and these to still others In
a little while she was more followed for the fun of the thing than
the handsomest lady in Orange was for her beauty , and whereas
formerly she had been considered a reserved and proper young
lady, she came to be called only The Silly. Some worthy people
informed her father, and he spoke to her, but without effect. Her
husband saw what was going on and remonstrated, but she took
no notice of that either, telling him that it was only jealousy which
made him speak in that way, and that it was he that had persuaded
her father to speak. At last the thing went on so far that one day
when she was passing the palace of Guilhem d'Aurenga the children began to stone her for a crazy woman ; she ran to a place near
by, and there she was stoned to death.''

18 P. 308 —Vid No 66, p 70, torn. 2.

19. P. 309 —For Lanza's verses and Peire's reply, Vid No. 66,
p. 65. Of course Lanza exaggerated Peire's drinking habits, but
there must have been a basis for the charge

20 P. 309.—As a specimen of Vidal's vigorous style I will quote
the following apropos of King Richard's imprisonment (No. 66,
p 43) "Into such distress have the pope and the false doctors
brought the holy Church that they provoke God's wrath ; they
have excited heresy by their folly and their sinful living, for sin is

so disseminated by them that it is hard to resist it; yet will I not accuse. The whole mischief comes from France, from the very ones who formerly were the best; for the king [Philippe Auguste] is not true and sincere toward God and honor; he has abandoned, bought, sold, and bartered the [Holy] Sepulchre like a servant or a shopkeeper—whereby his Frenchmen are dishonored. The world goes so awry that bad as it was yesterday, today it is yet worse. Since he forsook the guidance of God we have not heard that the emperor grows in fame and dignity, and yet if he like a fool allows Richard to escape now that he has him imprisoned the English will laugh at him. Also I must complain of the kings of Spain, for they make war on each other and out of fear send grey and brown horses to the Moors. They have doubled the pride of their enemies and are themselves vanquished Better were it to keep peace, truth, and faith among themselves." It is at the end of this piece that Vidal speaks of his lady as near Carcassonne.

CHAPTER XIX.

1. P. 311.—The Aude carries down 1,800,000 cubic metres of earth each year; the Rhone ten times as much. But in proportion to its volume the Aude is twice as heavily charged as the Rhone.

2. P 315.—The date of Peire's satire is of importance, but cannot be fixed positively. Suchier assigned it to 1180, but Appel believes it was composed before R. d'Aurenga died (1173). I prefer to think of it as a bit of caustic but not malicious wit, and it seems to me that the circumstances amid which it appears to have been produced, as well as the poem itself, justify this view. Vid. No. 41, p. 117 The three texts have been printed together by Appel in No. 31, XIV., p. 160.

3 P. 315.—This extract is from No 347. Vid. No. 63, col. 77. The following saying of Peire's is worth quoting · " Good love has one quality in common with good gold when it is true, for whoever serves nobly becomes purified in goodness."

4. P 316.—The text of the stanza of which a facsimile and a translation are given is as follows . *Bella m'es la flors d'aiguilen | Quant aug del fin joi la doussor | Que fan l'auzelh novelhamen | Pel temps qu'es tornat en verdor, | E son de flors cubert li reynh | Gruec e vermelh e vert e blau.*

5. P. 316.—Bernart Marti, a troubadour of the school of Marca-bru and P. d'Alvernhe, said that Peire d'Alvernhe was a canon and became joglar, but it has been suggested that perhaps he confounded him with P Rogier Of Marti we know only that, as he tells us, he was a painter He has left us eight lyrics

6 P. 319.—In southern France there were many exceptions to the feudal régime, and in fact the feudal system was not strictly in force there. In Provence, besides the great barons and a lower order of nobles with fiefs, there was a third class of nobles without fiefs. As already stated, in some at least of the towns men of noble birth became partially merged in the burgher class, just as some of the latter became through wealth and culture nobles in effect

7. P. 319.—In the troubadour period the word baron was a general term for any one of feudal standing Jesus Christ and the Apostles were sometimes called barons. Titles were little different from the grades in an army, convenient means to indicate a man's place in the system of government. A simple *de* was a sufficient social distinction, and we often find a titled noble designated in that way.

8. P 320.—The forest of Bélesta is called the finest in the Pyrenees.

9 P 322 —St. Volusien was built in troubadour days. The castle was probably erected to protect the abbey. The palace of the later counts of Foix is now the *Palais de Justice* but has been greatly changed.

10. P 325.—See No. 139, *old ed.* III., p. 328 ; but this is very possibly an error.

11 P. 325.—Raimon Rogier died in 1223 ; Rogier Bernart II. in May, 1241, Rogier IV., Feb. 14, 1265 ; Rogier Bernart III , less than twenty-five years old, succeeded him.

12. Pp 326 and 327.—"Whoe'er would pluck," etc., Vid. No 358, V., p. 114. Line 4, for "lance" Diez uses *Pilgerstaben* "The men of Burgundy," etc., are the last two lines of the same fragment. The other extract begins on the same page.

13. P. 327.—For still another fragment Vid. No. 358, V., p. 291 (wrongly attributed to Peire II of Aragon.)

CHAPTER XX

1. P. 329.—The Inquisition was active in Toulouse for about a century, ceasing only when there were no longer any "suspects"

2. P. 330.—Even in the early part of the twelfth century a vigorous school of sculpture existed at Toulouse.

3. P. 331.—Nothing is known of Peire Raimon beyond what is given in the text and it is not at all certain that the relations and order of the songs were as given there. According to Diez he flourished from 1170 to 1200, but it is now thought that he lived a little later   Three of the five MSS. of his life call him Peire Raimon the Old ; and, although we know of no younger poet of the name, Chabaneau has suggested that the poems bearing his name—some twenty in number—do not all seem to come from the same hand.   Two of the MSS. give "St Leidier" instead of "Monpeslier" as the place of his later sojourn.

4. P. 331 —"For I love," etc., Vid. No. 358, III., p. 120, st. 4. "The flower," etc , Vid. No 358, V., p. 328.

5. P. 333.—Nothing remains of old Toulouse except a small bit of wall.   The description of the city is based upon a chart of 1219, a few years later than Peire Raimon's return.

6 P. 333.—The sanctuary of St. Sernin was consecrated by the pope in 1096.

7. P 334 —Vid. No. 42, p. 248, st. 1 , or No. 358, V., p. 326

8 P. 335 —Vid. No. 63, col 87   The piece consists of six stanzas and a tornada.   I have taken st. 1, 2, 3, 5, and the tornada, but have arranged the rhymes so as to make the pattern complete. The scheme of the translation is as follows, the italicized rhymes being double · st. 1 : a b b c d d e e d d e ; 2   e d d c f f g g f f g ; 3 : g f f c d d e e d d e ; 4 : e d d c b b a a b b a, 5 (torn) : a b b a.

9. P. 335.—Vid No. 358, V., p. 330.

10. P. 335.—The name of Pamiers is supposed to be a corruption of Apamia, a place in Syria, which Rogier II. of Foix helped to capture and from which he brought some holy bones to the abbey at this place   The castle was built for the protection of the abbey ; but count and abbot did not always agree, and Raimon Rogier was said by a contemporary to have shut up the latter and his ecclesiastics for three days without food or water, and to have

lodged a company of dissolute women in the refectory. Any one whom the priests did not like, however, was likely to be slandered, and some of the count's family were Albigensians. The abbot invited Montfort to take possession of the place after the fall of Carcassonne, and Pamiers became a head-centre of the crusaders' authority. Any one who cares for an illustration of the extraordinary complications sometimes resulting from the feudal system may find it at Pamiers; see No. 76, XXXII., p. 1.

11. P. 336 —It is well to bear in mind that, as one of the nobles told Simon de Montfort, most of the inhabitants of Toulouse were considered "gentlemen." Diez places Aimeric's activity from 1205 to 1270, and Chabaneau from 1205 to 1266; but as G de Berguedan was not alive, according to Bartsch, after about 1195, these dates seem too late. I follow Bartsch in supposing that he was born about 1170 and probably lived until 1245 at least. See No. 9, VI , p. 267. Like Jeanroy we may place the tenso with G de Berguedan between 1185 and 1190.

12. P. 337.—Bartsch says that Aimeric killed the man in Toulouse while MS R. (XIV. cent) states that the wound was not fatal

13. P. 338.—The king was Amfos VIII., who began to reign in 1158.

14. P. 338.—According to MS. R. the husband of Aimeric's Toulouse love went on a pilgrimage to the shrine of St. James of Compostella after his recovery. Aimeric hearing of this at once asked permission of the king to visit Italy. The king soon discovered that he was going by way of Toulouse and perceived the reason , so he provided him an escort to Monpeslier, wished him luck, and sent him on his way. Proscribed as he was he could not be seen in Toulouse, but his wit discovered a loophole. The lady he wished to see was of the tradesman class ; so he sent one of his escort to obtain a lodging for a relative of the king of Castile, taken ill on a pilgrimage The lady consented very cordially to provide for the sick man, and Aimeric was taken to her house by night. In the morning she was brought to the room to see her suffering guest and at once recognized him, and soon learned what it all meant Pretending to arrange the bedclothes she gave him a kiss. After ten days Aimeric went on to Monferrat.

15. P. 338 —His Italian patrons were Guilhem IV. of Monferrat, Guilhem de Malaspina, Azzo VI. (of Este), and Bonifaz (of Sain

Bonifaci), lords of Verona, and Azzo VII. (of Este, 1215-1264), lord of Ferrara.

16. P. 340.—For Sordel's words, which the text follows, see No. 258, p. 149

17 P 340 —Aimeric wrote elegies or Laments over Guilhem de Malaspina, Azzo VI. (two poems), Raimon Berenguier IV. of Provence (the poet-count), and a Countess Biatritz (Aldobrandini), but not the Lament for Manfred His piece on the death of Biatritz (between 1234 and 1245) is the latest that we can date. We have about fifty pieces from him. One illustrates again the capacity of the Provençals for the dramatic style , it is a dialogue in alternating lines between a lover and his lady and then between the lover and Love. Vid. No 63, col 159.

18. P 341.—Vid. No. 63, col. 161. I give the whole of the piece except a tornada of two lines containing a compliment to Teriaca.

19. P. 342.—The other troubadours especially associated with Raimon V. were B de Ventadorn, P. Rogier, Folquet de Marseilla, Ugo Brunenc, and Bernart de Durfort, a special friend of the count, from whom we have only a sirvente of doubtful authenticity. During the reign of Amfos (Alphonse Jourdain), who preceded Raimon V., Toulouse was visited by the poet Marcabru.

Another Tolosan poet was Giraudo lo Ros (the Red) who has been placed by P. Meyer in the time of Alphonse Jourdain but by Suchier and Chabaneau a little later. He devoted himself to the daughter of the count of Toulouse and in her honor wrote poems of elegant form and sincere feeling though of no great originality or power. We have seven pieces from him,—all love-songs.

20 P. 342.—The boundaries of Toulouse are from a map representing the state of things about 1200 ; see No 259. The southern part of the region east of the Rhone, (i. e., that next the sea) was governed by the *count* of Provence ; to the north of this lay the *marquisate* of Provence belonging to the house of Toulouse.

21 P. 342.—The troubadours specially associated with Raimon VI (1194-1222) were R. de Miraval, A. de Peguilha, and Aimeric de Belenoi. The last was a Gascon from a castle named Lesparra near Bordeaux, nephew of the Peire de Corbiac whose *Tesaur* we examined at Montpellier. He loved Gentils of Gentilis of Rius (Rieux, near Muret, Haute-Garonne) but went finally to Catalonia

and died there. His dates are 1210–1241 (Chabaneau), and he has
left us twenty-two pieces His only special claim to remark is the
singular fact that he was among the comparatively few troubadours mentioned by Petrarch

22. P 344 —The Provençal name of the organization of 1323
was "*Sobregaya Companhia dels VII Troubadours de Tholoza.*"

SUPPLEMENT TO CHAPTER XX

I. My Arrest at Pamiers

Before I left America it occurred to me that my camera might
some time give me the look of a German spy, and as I was trudg-
ing about at Pamiers disconsolately, thinking what a laughable
town it would be if there were only something to excuse a laugh,
I said to myself, "If I am ever to be arrested I wish to be arrested
now." What magic lamp I brushed against without knowing it I
cannot say, but the very next instant an "Oh, monsieur!" was
thrown directly at my head, and turning around I saw an officer
hurrying after me,—a short, bow-legged, toothless policeman
dressed in a rusty uniform, and bristling with importance. Words
got badly tangled in the grizzly mustache that nearly hid his chin,
but he soon made it clear that Monsieur le Commissaire desired to
see me, and I followed him at once to the office.

The stage was worthy of the drama   Except the weedy church
that adjoined it, the police office proved to be the most disreputable building in the disreputable old town. Too poor to own a
flag, the edifice flaunted on a stick a dingy sheet of tin, once
painted to represent the national emblem, I suppose. On three
sides, the tired walls were compelled to stand erect by huge wooden
props Some of the absinthe placards had crept over from the
church to escape all odor of sanctity. Windows lacking glass,
great blotches where the stucco had wearied of clinging, a door or
two nailed up, shutters holding on by a single hinge,—these were
some of its other beauties.

In a little room off the dirty hall, an elderly man dried with
snuff and malaria was curled up—I nearly said coiled—behind a
table. Under the frown of this functionary a fire smouldered
timidly in the grate as if it were longing to go out but dared not.
Proclamations of " We, the mayor of Pamiers," adorned the walls.

A respectably dressed woman whom the Commissaire had evidently been threatening left the room in tears, and it was my turn.

The policeman had tracked me well and he related how I had taken photographs, how I had traversed every highway and byway of the town, scrutinized buildings, questioned people, skirted the fringes of the place, paused, pondered, and scribbled. The Commissaire shook his head. He was even more perspicacious than the gendarmes who arrested Mr. Hamerton on the Saône, and he read my plot like an open book.

"Who are you?"

"An American."

"Grossly improbable, monsieur   What are you here for?"

"To find the picturesque and the historic."

"What do you find of that sort here?"

"Exceedingly little."

"Ah, you are looking for the picturesque and the historic and you come to a place where there is neither. You refute yourself. It is very grave, monsieur"

He shook his head and nodded solemnly to himself a long time, and I began to feel rather guilty.

"Very singular, monsieur, very singular. It may be, it may be; but very singular, very singular. Have you no papers, nothing?"

"Oh, yes." I handed him a letter from our embassy in Paris recommending me to the authorities of southern France.

"It is a forgery," he exclaimed after reading it. "Anybody could get up such a letter. How do I know whose signature that is? It is not authentic   It is a forgery. If it were genuine why did n't you produce it sooner?"

I was clearly convicted not only by his logic but by my own papers.

"How long did you propose to remain here?"

"I shall leave by the first train, I assure you."

"Ah,—perhaps"

A deeper gloom overspread his features. He seemed to be putting on the black cap in imagination, or perhaps he was gloating over the figure I should cut in front of the firing squad   Matters were getting desperate. Something must be done

"Is there any harm in photographing an old house?"

"Ah, monsieur, if you photograph an old house, you may photograph other things for aught I know."

"What is there in Pamiers that it could do any harm to photograph?"

A shrug of the shoulders. "How can I tell the extent of your designs?"

"But is it contrary to law to take photographs here?"

"Ah, what did you say? H'm, no, not contrary to law. But it is our office to watch over the Public Safety. You should have asked us for permission. It would have been granted you at once. Without that you are suspicious, dangerous."

"I have photographed in more than twenty places already and have had no trouble before."

"What is that to us? Others may answer as they can to their consciences and to the country. We, we know our responsibility. We know our duty. We know that we are charged with the Public Safety, and we do not sleep at our post. I do not understand why you have not been stopped before."

Now that I had forced him to admit that only his petty pride of authority had been violated, I was quite indifferent.

"I have always met with sensible men up to the present——"

"Do you insult me?" roared Public Safety "Do you insult me at my own tribunal? Do you dare, monsieur? Do you dare?"

"——and I always expect to," I continued calmly

The poor Commissaire was in distress Had I meant disrespect? Doubtless; but my words had been perfectly proper. It looked as if he had thrown away his temper and his dignity and yet could not punish me for it. And besides, how should he get the lion-skin over his ears again?

The scanty hair seemed to rise and fall on the top of his head as if the cranium were electrified His brows bent, his eyes reddened, and he gripped the edge of his worm-eaten table till the woodwork squeaked for mercy. I began to be alarmed for him; but happily it all ended in a terrific fit of coughing, and Public Safety was Itself again

"Have you no other papers? Is this document, this non-authentic document, all you have? Have you nothing else? Nothing?"

It was becoming a little tiresome after all, for I have omitted long colloquies, so I replied cheerfully

"Oh, yes, I have a passport."

"A passport! Why have n't you produced it?"

"We have only just finished discussing the letter Voilà, monsieur."

He spread it open and muttered incautiously, "It's in English!'"

In English it certainly was, and evidently he could not understand a word ; but two square feet of parchment had great illuminating power for his bureaucratic mind

"It is entirely regular, monsieur "

He tore up his copious report of the interview, gave me back the non-authentic document, and said with a bow :

"I salute you, monsieur "

Just outside the door on a bench sat the ragged officer. My pocket was full of copper coins. I drew out a handful and said . "I am indebted to you   The hour has passed very pleasantly. Permit me.''

He was about to put out his hand, but the shadow of the Commissaire darkened the threshold, and he shook his head regretfully instead

2   THE FLORAL GAMES (*Les Jeux Floraux*).

The honest burghers who founded the Collège du Gay Sçavoir did not propose to allow any excess or license on their Parnassus ; in their opinion poetry—even love poetry—was illuminating, but they resolved upon having the flame without the oil   Ideas and emotions were to be obtained not from dangerous experience, but from a wholesale pillage of the real troubadours of the past , and the songs were addressed, not after the old fashion to a woman of flesh and blood, but as a rule to the Holy Virgin under the names " Amors " and particularly "Clemenza, ''—Love and Pity   In the course of time, this Clemenza came to be thought a real person ; the name Isaure was then added from a noble family interested in poetry ; eventually her tomb was conveniently discovered, like the tombs of saints, and finally public honors consecrated the legend of Clémence Isaure as the patroness of the Collège.

At first (up to 1335) only one prize was given each year,—a violet of gold provided by the magistrates of the city ; but in later times the recompenses have multiplied, until now the jury awards —though not all the same year—five different flowers of gold, and five flowers of silver, each for its particular sort of verse, besides a golden jasmine for a discourse in prose, and a silver pink that may be given for a piece of any kind   Meanwhile the seven poets have grown to a body of forty patrons or Mainteneurs, and the funds of the Academy produce now a substantial $2000 a year.

Certainly the traditions and the rewards of poetry in Toulouse are brilliant; and yet, when the muse of Provence chose in these later years to speak again, it was not through the Academy. She preferred to call Jasmin, the barber of Agen, and Roumanille, the gardener of St Remy, and she has left the poets of the Floral Games uninspired, as if to show that genius needs no reward but the joy of expressing itself, and an academy of poetry is no more wanted than a dancing school for the waves.

But we did not think of this, looking down on the brilliant scene of the Flower-Fête. At one end of the long hall of the Musée was a lofty stage ; and along the edge of this behind a reading desk sat the forty Mainteneurs in a row of arm-chairs, with a sort of table, covered with green baize, in front of them   By the courtesy of M Deloume we visitors from abroad had places in the next line.   Behind us were other guests, and beyond them a large military orchestra.   At our left stood Clémence Isaure in marble , and below, crowding the hall to the doors long before the hour, were the fairest and gayest of Toulouse

What shall I say of them ?   It was a flower garden before us ; yet no ordinary one, but a rood or so of Indian orchids under glass. Many of the gowns and bonnets were purple, and the rest were either blue or red of one shade or another.   Lovely faces and sparkling eyes gave life to the colors   A subdued agitation, a hum of expectancy intense though still, the rustle of silks, the murmur of countless quick whisperings,—these were the breezes of the garden , and for sunbeams it had the gleaming helmets of cuirassiers, flashing out every now and then among the flowers

After the regulation Eulogy of Clémence Isaure, Rewards of Merit (*Prix de Vertu*) were distributed with a brief statement of each case.   Eight purses, amounting in all to $800, were given. Petronille Germier had supported for over thirty years the family that was rich when she entered its employ but had long since become destitute, and of late not only them but a paralyzed sister. For forty-four years Jules Lafeuillade had gathered together every Sunday all he could of the needy of Toulouse, as many as a thousand sometimes, and though poor himself provided a lunch for his " children," his " good friends," as he called them   For fifty-one years Mdlle. Sol had freely taught the poor girls of her locality, though herself almost as poor as they   Mme Poignet during eighteen years had induced at least 150 unmarried couples to legalize their union, and had given moral training to their children

As these and the others came forward one by one in their poor clothes, mounted to the stage, received the purse, listened in confusion to the kind words that accompanied it, and heard the warm applause of the brilliant audience, tears rolled down their tanned and furrowed cheeks, and their eyes shone with joyous but humble surprise as if they already heard the glad saying, "Come, ye blessed;—ye did it unto me." Nor were their cheeks the only ones watered with tears. . . .

At this point, before the marquis of Aragon, Perpetual Secretary, began to read a report upon the literary competition, a Deputation of the Mainteneurs was sent to bring the prizes. Close to the bank of the Garonne stands the church of the Daurade,[1] doubly sacred as the successor of a temple to Apollo, and as the traditional burial-place of Clémence Isaure. Here the flowers of gold and of silver, each of them a leafy stalk about five inches high, standing on a round base, and blossoming at the top, had been blessed and placed upon the high altar; and the Deputation, receiving them from a priest, bore them solemnly to the Academy.

Holding the flowers in their hands these gentlemen were just ascending to the stage, when a loud crash was heard above. Some youngsters had found their way into the attic, and instead of going to sleep like Paul's auditor and properly falling down somewhere, they craned so far over to look through a lifted pane of the ceiling that one of them broke the heavy glass in saving himself.

Down from a height of thirty feet falls a shower of jagged and flashing missiles straight upon the heads of the Deputation. A miracle—nothing short of that—can shield them.

O Dame Clémence, if thou carest aught for thy servitors protect them now!

A hoarse low cry of horror wells up from the audience. With rattle and thud the fiendish missiles strike. But the miracle has been wrought: a red stream pours down but one face, and the wounded man, helped quickly from the hall, is reported not dangerously hurt.

By this time we are all on our feet. Distress, anger, sympathy, and rejoicing agitate the assemblage.

Suddenly there is another gleam and another crash. All is confusion. We look up. Fragments of glass are hanging yet in the sash, ready to fall. Amid the excitement a soldier makes his way

---

[1] Shown on the right in the picture of Toulouse, page 343.

to the attic. The hall is instantly as still as the grave The man lays himself across the framework so as to have as much support as possible, and then works at the pieces, one by one Amid, cheers and the clapping of hands, the last bit is finally extracted, the orchestra plays, and the troubled sea of faces gradually calms itself.

After the report had been concluded, each of the successful poets read his piece. His flower was handed him then with a few words by the Préfet of the city, the audience applauded wildly, and the orchestra burst out with a flourish of music. One of the poets carried away two prizes,—a priest slightly deformed, dark, melancholy, and passionate ; but the rest were only bright young fellows, just the sort of men to delight in getting together and saying "we poets," and I grew a little weary, I must confess, of their "infinite," "eternal," "unspeakable," "everlasting," and the like.

But in time the poems were all read, and amid a long crash of music the audience rose. Again the rustle, the murmur, the flash of eyes, congratulations, gayety, enthusiasm The Floral Games were over for another year, and I went away reflecting that even if Toulouse cannot make Clémence Isaure live it will at least never let her die.

CHAPTER XXI.

1. P 346.—We have no information as to his personal appearance.

2. P. 349.—Vid. No. 358, III., p. 357, st 1.

3. P. 349.—Vid. No. 358, III., p. 359, torn. 2.

4. P 350 —In one case, at least, Miraval had the chagrin of finding the skill that he had taught a pupil turned against himself. Miraval understood Portuguese and wrote a little in that tongue. Bayonna was his own joglar

5. P. 350.—The count and the troubadour called each other Audiart.

6. P. 351 —Vid. No. 63, col. 151, st. 2.

7. P 351.—Vid. 63, col. 152, st 1.

8 Pp. 351, 361 —"Obscure, harsh verses," etc. Vid. No 63, col. 149, st 1. In the original the number of syllables varies thus . 6, 7, 6, 6, 7, 6, 7, 6, 6, which would produce in English a jolting effect.

"Drawn taut " : literally, "gracefully closed up."   " It is song,"
etc. ; Vid. No. 63, col 151, st. 1.

9 P. 352.—Loba's husband is supposed to have been Jordan,
brother of Peire Rogier and partner with him in the ownership of
Cabaret

10. P 352.—It has been questioned whether, as a matter of fact,
ladies did to any considerable extent yield special favors in re-
sponse to love-songs, and some have thought that when it came to
serious amours barons were almost always preferred to poets.
This opinion cannot be verified or disproved, but it may have a
certain bearing on our view of the conduct of the troubadours.

11. P. 354 —Chabaneau thinks Loba's successful lover was
Rogier Bernart II., the title being given him by anticipation.
But Loba's disgrace occurred about 1196 (Bartsch) or perhaps a
year or two earlier (Schopf), when Raimon Rogier, who did "ses
premières armes" (No. 139) in 1190-1193, was of the right age,
whereas Rogier Bernart II., his son, was quite young. Raimon
Rogier was, besides, a famous gallant. Further, would a *bachelier*
like Rogier Bernart (he did not become count until 1223) have
ruined Loba's reputation? The woman to whom Miraval paid
court after leaving Loba (he had been in love with her for some
time) was the wife (probably the second wife) of the lord of Menerba
(Minèrve), a castle situated in the fork of two streams in the wild
country above Narbonne. It should be added that Loba excused
herself to the troubadour for her long delay in rewarding him by
quoting some lines of his own in which he said that a lady should
not be in haste in such matters.

12. P. 354.—My experience at Boissezon illustrates some of the
embarrassments of searching for antiquities. I questioned every
likely person in the village for remains of an ancient castle   Most
of them confessed complete ignorance of the matter. Others,
perhaps more anxious to please, gave me various hints, all of
which proved unfruitful. Finally a man was found who appeared
to know. Certainly he was positive enough, and with an esquire
to carry my camera I set out according to his instructions. As
usual his estimate of distance was soon found quite incorrect.
Still, confiding in his knowledge of direction, I followed the road,
and at a distance of about three miles discovered—a huddle of old
stone barns. It was my custom to search the public libraries and
bookstores of the towns I visited, and when I was in Albi I found

a local history which told all there was to tell about the remains of the castle of Boissezon and its original character. I was glad enough to take the next train back. The castle possessed four strong bastions

13. P. 358.—The conversations and soliloquies of the affair at Lombers are imaginary. Schultz has rejected the story on the ground that Peire would never have gone so far out of his way on such a quest. This seems to me another case of excessive scepticism An enthusiastic hunter would have given himself much more trouble for the chance of running down a stag that had made himself famous. But even if we called it improbable we need not reject it. As Gaston Paris has said, " The improbability of a tale when it does not go directly counter to credibility is not a sufficient reason for rejecting it *a priori*."

14. P. 359 —Castres was held at one time by the Saracens, and was besieged by a Christian army. A fragment of a poem on this interesting event is given in No. 29, I , p. 589. According to some of the guide-books there is a fragment of a castle dating from troubadour times inside the inclosure of the collège at Castres. I spent considerable time and money to get permission to photograph this, but found it an ecclesiastical ruin of no particular interest.

15. P. 361.—Only about half a dozen poets made love to marriageable women

16. P. 363.—One of the troubadours who attacked Miraval was Peire Duran, from whom we have only three or four pieces ; another was Ugo (or Uguet) de Mataplana, a nobleman of Catalonia, who died in 1213 of wounds received at Muret. The latter was a personal friend of Miraval's. He has left us the sirvente against Miraval and one or two tensos.

17. P. 363.—Brunessen's husband was Peire Rogier ; see note 4, Chap. XVIII.

18. P. 364.—For the nobles at Toulouse see No. 290, ll. 9457 + They were there in 1219 ; I introduce them here merely to show the manner in which lords were thought and spoken of.

19. P. 366.—All traditions of the event have not perished at Muret, for a tomb in a garden is shown as the resting-place of the king's body.

20. P 366.—King Peire long enjoyed the name of poet, but Kolsen (No. 220, p. 56) seems to have shown recently that the verses

attributed to him belong to his father Amfos.   Very likely he wrote poetry however

21. P. 366.—The battle of Muret was one of the great and decisive combats of history. Simon had about 900 cavalry (he took about 750 with him to Muret), while the combined forces of Aragon and Toulouse numbered about 3000 cavalry (Oman thinks Peire had about 2000 in action) and 40,000 foot.   But of this great force only a small part was actually engaged, for the troops of Toulouse held aloof   The odds against Simon were only about two to one, and this disparity was far more than offset by (1) the superiority and experience of his men, (2) their conviction that defeat meant extermination, (3) their faith, more or less pure, in the holiness of their cause, (4) the wonderful ardor for battle worked up by the religious preparations of Simon and the priests, (5) the military incompetence of Peire when compared with Simon, and (6) his marvelous over-confidence and lack of morale : he passed the night before the battle in licentious carousing, and though perfectly fearless was physically unfit for battle.   Montfort's strategy was masterly and he caught his enemy wholly unprepared to meet him   Why the count of Toulouse and his troops held aloof is not known   It has been suspected that they dreaded the victory of Peire almost as much as that of Simon ; but I venture to suggest that— anticipating no such complete overthrow of Peire—they preferred to hold themselves in reserve, and when the combatants had exhausted themselves decide the battle and possess the fruits of victory.   Besides, Simon's attack was sudden and perhaps they had no time to get into the battle before it was a rout.   As it was they were scattered, pursued, and slaughtered.   The camp of the Toulousans is thought to have been on the low hill Perramon, and the battle to have been fought near the river Louge

Though the Toulousans did not literally share in the battle to any great extent, the picture of the opposing forces as presented in the text is substantially correct, for the fate of the Midi was at stake, and but for the overwhelming results of Simon's attack they would no doubt have taken part.   The cause was theirs and the defeat theirs.

At the same time the cause was Peire's as suggested in the text, for the establishment of a new and aggressive power, under a man like Simon, on the border of his territories was a very serious matter for him.

CHAPTER XXII.

1. P. 369.—The church at Gerona was built in imitation of this at Albi.

2. P. 370.—The sunset effect of the cathedral is enhanced by its being of brick.

3. P. 373 —Etienne de Bourbon was a Dominican and a prominent Inquisitor   He died at Lyons about 1261.

4 P. 375.—There were points of analogy between the "good men" and the Provençal knight.   Neither was to care aught for money.   Each considered his word as good as an oath.   Each loved spiritually with will, sentiment, and thought   Each educated and trained an apprentice—the one to be an adept, the other to be a knight.

5. P. 375.—A list of Inquisitorial questions recently published (No. 2, III , p. 368) shows that no one was allowed to have the gospels, epistles, psalms, or prayers in the popular tongue.   It shows also that complete non-intercourse with heretics was required

6. P. 375.—Five chapters of St. John's Gospel were first translated into Provençal, presumably for liturgical use.   We have a copy of this, probably dating from the middle of the twelfth century.

7 P. 376.—I do not wish to leave the impression that all the cruelties were on one side.   Butchery once begun by the Church, the other side—I do not refer to the "good men" themselves— were sure to retaliate.

8. P 379 —Until the Franciscan and Dominican orders were founded preaching was an exclusive privilege, long confined to bishops.   This custom, and that of keeping the Scriptures in Latin, were of great value to the Church in preserving its monopoly of salvation.   For illustrations of simony in the Midi see No. 19, CLI., p. 361.

9. P. 380.—The heretics' patient endurance of suffering embarrassed the Catholics, for it was a reminder of the early Christians. It was finally explained as due to the devils   The "good men" ate fish, but not the flesh of birds and mammals.

10. P. 381 —The name "Albigensian" has been variously explained   Some think it was given because the "good men" were

especially numerous in the territory about Albi (in Latin *Albiga*), some that it was given because they were first condemned at Lombers in the Albigensian region. Etienne de Bourbon says the heresy first appeared in the valley of the Tarn. The name does not signify that Albi was particularly heretical. It would seem, indeed, orthodox, for when St. Bernard preached there and called on the faithful to hold up the hand he saw every person before him make this profession. Still this was early (1147), and naturally the heretics would not flock to hear themselves denounced. The sect is often called "The Albigenses."

11. P. 381.—Raimon VI. was of course influenced by his personal interests and feelings ; but it is noteworthy that in a time when the Christian church accounted a heretic worse than a murderer this secular and none too moral prince risked life and property to protect his subjects from torture and death

12. P 383.—Simon was not the first choice. Several great nobles, to whom the leadership of the crusade was offered, declined it. The cruelties of Béziers shocked them ; and, while opposed to heresy and willing to increase their possessions, they were not disposed to depopulate the Midi or completely ruin Count Raimon. Indeed, they could hardly afford to set such an example. Many left the host of the crusaders about this time and returned to their homes. Simon, though a nobleman, was not very prominent. He had everything to gain, and not much to lose. The scanty ruins of his home castle may still be seen at Montfort-l' Amaury, between Paris and Dreux. The castle was evidently small.

Extraordinary as it seems, Simon de Montfort, the crusader, was the father of Simon de Montfort, called with more or less justice the "Father of the English Parliament" and the "Bulwark of Liberty."

13. P. 384.—The pope wished the heretics and their sympathizers destroyed, but of course had no animosity against the orthodox nobles. He tried to protect the latter against the rapacity of the crusaders. The king of France, Louis VIII., intervened directly in 1225, for Amaury, son of Simon de Montfort, was evidently unable to sustain the struggle. In 1226 the last revolt of Toulouse was crushed. The count of Toulouse had been repeatedly driven away, and had as often been able to return. In 1229 Raimon VII. ceded most of his territories to Louis IX. of France and bound himself to marry his only child to Louis' brother.

14. P. 385.—The Albigensian crusade was essentially a crusade against freedom of thought, democratic tendencies in politics, the culture and the pleasures of peace, and in general an easy and luxurious civilization. It accomplished the great result of making the French nation, with its national language, literature, and civilization, but its promoters did not think of this. It is also true that the crusade put a more vigorous and virile society in the place of that prevailing in the Midi. The people of the north were more brutal, and with their glorification of Tristan and Lancelot seem more boldly immoral, but on the other hand the Provençal refinements of passion made it less healthful, and therefore probably more insinuating and more dangerous to robust social life

CHAPTER XXIII.

1. P. 386.—It seems clear enough that Druid traditions and influences were alive in the time of the troubadours, for they live now, and with them there may well have been bardic survivals Recently A. Bertrand has based an account of the Gallic religion upon the "*survivances*" that are still to be found, and G Boissier, reviewing his book in No. 11, says, "*On les y trouve assurément.*"

2. P. 387.—G. Rainol, according to his biography, was a knight, but it appears from a tenso of his with Guilhem Magret that both had been monks He was from Apt, near Vaucluse His special style was the sirvente, and his sharp tongue made him feared He flourished at the close of the twelfth and the beginning of the thirteenth centuries and has left us two sirventes and three tensos He composed his own music Magret was a low-lived fellow, spending his gains in the taverns. He died in Spain.

3. P. 387.—For Peire Cardinal see Chapter XXVI.

4. P 387.—Bertran Carbonel was of Marseille and lived in the second half of the thirteenth century. He was of good family, but poor He studied, but travelled little. We find him citing Ovid and Terence. His love-songs were commonplace, but his satires vigorous and some of his maxims worth preserving We have 17 or 18 poems and 71 little stanzas (*coblas esparsas*) of his. Some of his sayings are . "Good blood cannot lie " , "Necessity has no law " ; "No man can walk so prudently as never to stumble " ; "One does ill to shut up a young lady who is in love " ; "Honesty carries no knife " , "The pitcher goes so many times to the

water that at last the handle remains there "; " The only pleasure
one gets from a mill is the grist it turns out."

5. P. 387.—G. Figueira was born about 1195, went to Italy early
in 1215, wrote his sirvente on Rome between Sept. 29, 1227, and
Jan. 1, 1229, and received a sword-cut across the face in the Florence brawls. He favored the emperor, Frederic II., but did not
visit his court. The date of his death is unknown ; Chabaneau
thinks he lived until 1250. His extant poems according to Chabaneau are eight, according to Bartsch eleven.

6. P. 388.—The invectives quoted are merely a few specimens.

7. P. 388.—We know nothing of Germonda and have no other
piece from her.

8 P. 388.—All that we know positively of Izarn is that he was
an Inquisitor. The heretic was Sicart de Figueiras, an Albigensian
" bishop " from Usson (Son) near Foix. The poem seems to have
been written a little after 1244 Sicart had resolved to surrender
from reasons of policy, and all that really remained was to settle
the reward of his apostasy. He therefore granted the force of
Izarn's arguments (reinforced by the stake in full view) while still
remaining apparently of the same opinion. Izarn was not familiar
even with the Gospels and attributed to the Albigensians views
directly the opposite of theirs. The poem has but slight literary
value. See an extract in No. 63, col. 187, and a complete edition
with a French translation in No. 403

9. P. 389.—Vid. No. 358, III., p. 156, st. 1. His father was
named Amfos. Perhaps he was himself engaged in the business
for a time.

10. P. 389.—We know very little of Folquet's travels It seems
likely that he visited Poitiers, Castile, and Aragon. Pratsch thinks
that when Alazais became jealous he went to Aragon, then returned to Marseille, and then (being dismissed by Alazais) went to
Montpellier. Not long afterward he was again received at Marseille. Very likely Raimon Rogier, count of Foix, was a patron
of Folquet (see 458, p 6). He loved or at least admired three
ladies of Nismes.

11 P. 390.—Vid. No. 358, III., p. 149. The poem contains five
stanzas and three tornadas, of which the translation gives st. 1, 3,
4, and 5, and the first tornada. In the second half of st. 3 the
poet means to say that, as he belongs to his lady, she will suffer

loss if he is killed   The first tornada has three lines, the other two have four.

12. P. 390.—Vid No. 358, III., p. 151, st. 4   The piece has five st. and a torn

13 P. 392.—Vid. No. 63, col. 121, st. 2.   There are five st. and two torn

14. P. 392.—As an illustration of Folquet's style take his proof that he lost nothing by losing love : Today I am truly rich, since I ask nothing of you ; for riches and poverty are only subjective : we count him rich that considers himself satisfied, and him poor that is ever seeking for more , therefore I can be called rich, and I possess the highest joy when I turn my back on love, for a while ago I was sad, but now I rejoice, and so all things considered I am satisfied that I have gained.   Another illustration is the following: "Love committed a great sin when she was pleased to place herself in me, since she did not bring with her Grace with which to alleviate my pain ; for Love loses her name and belies it and is Dis-love plainly, since Grace cannot succor when it would be worthiness and honor to her; since she will conquer everything, let her just once conquer Grace." (Love was feminine in Provençal)

15. P. 392.—Recently it has been suggested that the two religious poems usually attributed to F. de Marseilla were by Folquet de Romans. (*E. g* , see No. 31, XXI., p. 335.)

16. P. 393.—The names of Barral's sisters were Laura de Sain Jolran (St Julien) and Mabilia de Ponteves (a place near Brignoles).   Laura was the one of whom Alazais was particularly jealous.   Zingarelli (No. 458) thinks Folquet really loved her. According to one MS. Folquet's attentions to Eudoxia were the cause of Guilhem's repudiating her, but there seems reason to believe that her pride of superior rank and the title of " empress " which it gave her had much to do with it.   Still she does seem to have overstepped the bounds of propriety.   Eudoxia was repudiated in 1187 ; so that if Folquet's attentions were Guilhem's excuse we have the precise date of this episode.   Anyhow it was not later than 1187

17. P. 394.—Vid No. 358, III , p 156, st 2

18. P. 394.—Vid. No. 358, III , p 153, st. 3.

19. P. 395.—Vid No 63, col 123   The piece is addressed to

Aziman, Tostemps, and Plus-Lejal. It contains five stanzas (of which I give 2 and 5) and two tornadas. The last lines of st. 2 are: "*e segrai l'aip de tot bon sofridor | cum plus s'irais fort s'umilia.*"

It is impossible to say positively to what circumstances all of Folquet's songs attach themselves, and the order of the text is adopted simply to present the quotations in some order. The last piece seems to belong—as it is represented—in the final stage of his relations with Alazais.

20. P. 395. — Folquet lost his principal friends as follows: Eudoxia went into a convent in 1187; Barral died, 1192; Raimon V. died, 1194; Richard did not die till 1199, but his accession to the throne of England naturally severed his intimacy with Folquet; the fate of Alazais is uncertain,—according to Folquet's biography she died before he entered the convent, but Papon says she was alive in 1201. It seems probable that Barral re-

CISTERCIAN MONKS.
FROM A MS.

pudiated her shortly before his death (1192). Zingarelli places Folquet's retirement from the world between 1192 and 1195, very likely in 1194.

21. P. 396.—The anecdote of Folquet's characteristic antithesis of the bed and the fire is related by Etienne de Bourbon. Dante suggests another reason for Folquet's conversion, for he makes him declare that he loved as long as befitted his hair, *i. e.,* his age. When Folquet renounced the world he caused his wife and two children to do the same.

22. P. 396.—Les Arcs is between Nice and Aix, not very far from Toulon.

23. P. 399.—The monastery of Le Thoronet (Torondet) was removed to this spot from a place near by, probably in 1146. The remains of Le Thoronet are one of the most interesting illustrations of the religious architecture pervaded by the spirit of Citeaux and Clairvaux. They show a designed contempt for the richness

and elegance of Cluny The arches of the cloisters have no mouldings at all. The tower of the church was only large enough to serve as a belfry. The windows of the church were hardly more than loopholes. Yet with all the austerity there are grace and originality, and in the church suggestions of the new pointed style seem to manifest themselves in spite of the builder

24. P. 403.—The form of his name under which Folquet appears in French history is Foulques. We know nothing of his personal appearance, and the account of his subjective history is my own interpretation. The incident of his passing the count's palace is imaginary. Robertus de Sorbona tells the story of Folquet at the French court. Pratsch doubted whether the troubadour and the bishop were the same, but as Zingarelli and Zenker say this is really beyond question.

25. P. 405.—In 1217 Folquet commanded a part of the crusading army.

26. P. 405.—The manner of Montfort's death (June 25, 1218, five years after the battle of Muret) seems too just to be true, but while the agency of the women is not absolutely proved, the evidence makes it credible. The song of exultation over his fall as I found it in a MS. at Gaillac was ·

> " *Montfort*
> *es mort!* (thrice)
> *Viva Tolosa*
> *ciutat gloriosa*
> *et poderosa!*
> *Tornan lo paratge e l'honor,*
> *Montfort*
> *es mort!* (thrice) "

27. P. 405.—Folquet died Dec. 25, 1231.

28. P 406 —A religious community was already in existence at Grandselve in 1113, and in 1114 it was connected with the order of Citeaux For two centuries it was very rich and greatly favored by princes. The Black Prince of England destroyed it in 1355. The nearest railroad station to Grandselve (about ten miles distant) is Grisolles.

29. P. 406.—It should be added for the credit of human nature that Folquet was not absolutely inhuman, and a few small acts of common kindness appear among many of awful cruelty. On the

other hand the Monk of Montaudon accused him of repeatedly perjuring himself

Two anecdotes may be cited to illustrate his readiness of wit. Once in a sermon he described the orthodox as sheep and the Albigensians as wolves, whereupon an Albigensian whose nose had been cut off by Montfort rose up in the audience and asked, "Did you ever see sheep who bit a wolf like this?" But Folquet was not at a loss, and at once replied that the Church had sent a good dog, Simon de Montfort, to protect the sheep, and the dog had bitten a wolf who was devouring the sheep (Etienne de Bourbon). At another time he was near the wall of a town of his diocese that the crusaders were attacking, and those within called him "a bishop of devils." "They are right," said he, "for they are devils and I am their bishop" (Guilhaume de Puylaurent). These and some other anecdotes are quoted in No. 110.

We have twenty-four pieces from Folquet, all lyrical (Zenker). His poetry was popular in northern France and he was imitated by Rudolf of Neuenburg (Zingarelli).

Folquet took for himself one fief out of Montfort's plunder, the castle of Urefeuil with its thirty villages. As bishop he was very rigid in exacting the tithes (No 458), and pomp, courtliness, and lavishness reigned in his palace.

In conclusion. of course if one look upon Folquet's zeal for the Church against heretics as a capital virtue one may draw a different picture of his character; but I do not see how any one can exonerate him from egotism, selfishness, and inhumanity. (He was charged also with cruelty, trickiness, and avarice, against which Zingarelli protests, though the only argument he advances is that we cannot judge men of that day by the ideas of our own. No. 458, p. 3.) It was no doubt his zeal for the Church that led Dante to entertain so high an opinion of him ; the scattered classical allusions in his poems would not have impressed Dante.

END OF VOLUME I.